MY L ... ME

My Life and the Beautiful Game:

The Autobiography of Pelé

by Pelé

with Robert L. Fish

Foreword by Shep Messing

Skyhorse Publishing

Originally published by Doubleday & Company, Inc., 1977

First Skyhorse Publishing edition, 2007

www.skyhorsepublishing.com

10 9 8 7 6 5 4 3 2 1

ISBN-13: 978-1-60239-196-3
ISBN-10: 1-60239-196-3

Library of Congress Cataloging-in-Publication data
Pelé, 1940-
My life and the beautiful game : the autobiography of Pele/ by Pele [i.e. E. Arantes do Nascimento] with Robert L. Fish.— 1st Skyhorse pub. ed.
p. cm.
Originally published: Garden City, N.Y. : Doubleday, 1977.
ISBN-13: 978-1-60239-196-3 (alk. paper)
ISBN-10: 1-60239-196-3 (alk. paper)
1. Pelé, 1940- 2. Soccer players—Biography. I. Fish, Robert L. II. Title.

GV942.7.N3A35 2007
796.334092—dc22
[B]

2007032405

Printed in the United States of America

I dedicate this book to all the people who have made this great game the Beautiful Game.

Pelé

I was born, grew,
Because of this I am here,
I pass by,
I walk by,
Not hurrying to arrive,
I go much faster
Than those who run
Without thinking

This is not our life
Everything here is a game
A passing thing,
What matters is what I've done
And what I'll leave behind,
Let it be an example
For those that come

I am leading he who comes
But following he who has already gone by
If he reached the end he has already rested
I also will reach the end
Because I want to rest

There are many people
With the will to fight
Life is not just this
Truth is farther beyond.

Pelé

FOREWORD

One of my former teammates on the Cosmos, Peruvian midfielder Ramon Mifflin said, “I never see anybody sleep like Pelé. Once, when we play for Santos, I see him sleep from Brussels to Tokyo. Twenty-six hours, half a world, Pelé never opens his eyes.”

After traveling with Pelé for many years, I'm not so sure he sleeps so much as simply shuts his eyes to close off the rest of the world that wants to touch him, talk to him or get an autograph on an airline napkin. “It is sometimes the only way to be alone,” he told me. “Very simple to close the eyes.”

The night before Pelé played his final professional game, I stopped by his room in our hotel to hang out and see how he was feeling. I wondered what he could be thinking with just a ninety minute game for the championship standing between twenty-two years of glory and retirement. He was sitting on the edge of the bed, wearing a lime green jacket and a sphinx-like smile.

Sometimes, Pelé can look a thousand years old. He acted as though I had asked him a difficult riddle and he didn't answer right away. While I was waiting for him to speak, I noticed his hands, so black against the cream colored bedspread. For a man who has made his living with his feet, they are abnormally calloused, cool and hard when he grasps yours, as though the millions of handshakes have worn them smooth as stone.

"When I retired from Santos, it was different," he said. "I still play many exhibitions, still busy with the football. Now it is really the finish. I will stop playing and that part of me ..." He paused, smiling again, "That part will die. But it's okay because another life will be born. In my mind, it will be hard. I think someday I will wake up and get my things and go to the stadium because this is what I do all of my life. Now, I must remember to go to the office. I don't know how I will like this, to sign papers, to speak on the telephone, because twenty-two years of my life is professional soccer. I have been very lucky. If I could not have been a footballer, maybe I would be a housepainter. Maybe work in the factory, work in the shop. I would have the same life as everybody else in the town and I would only have tried to do my best job, wherever I am. For me, it has been simple. I never wanted to be anything but the best I could be."

This foreword for my friend and former teammate, Pelé, is not about his technical skill on the ball, his explosive first step or his ability in the air. Better writers than me have documented his legendary prowess on the field, his meteoric rise to international fame and his ability to delight crowds around the world.

No, my finger on the pulse of Pelé is two-fold.

He carries himself with a grace, humility and dignity that is unparalleled. He has a way and a manner of touching all who come in contact with him and leaving them knowing they made a personal connection with greatness. He is selfless and unassuming, proud without any sense of entitlement. As a friend, there is no better one than Pelé.

As a teammate and on the field he was a fearless warrior. Yes, he played with a sense of joy, a mischievous smile and a smiling goal celebration, but on the field, in the game, he was tough as nails. He was the ultimate teammate, always ready to do whatever it took for us to win. Although to the world watching, it was all about Pelé, to Pelé, it was never about him. It was about each of us and the team.

When Pelé played his final game, half for Santos and half for the Cosmos with 77,000 fans selling out Giants Stadium, the game ended with the rain teeming down. I, with the rest of his teammates, lifted Pelé on our shoulders to take him around the stadium for a victory lap one last time. As the crowd roared and we ended our lap around the field, Pelé whispered, "one more time ..."

For Pelé, there will always be one more time ...

Shep Messing

INTRODUCTION

This is a book about a man who excelled and still excels in a game with which few Americans are as yet familiar. It is, however, a game that is growing in popularity in the United States. In America the game is called "soccer" but throughout the rest of the world it is known as "association football" or simply as "football," and it shall be referred to throughout this book as football. It is, in truth, the only game that merits the name of football, since it is the only form of an ancient game where the feet are used predominantly and in which the use of the hands is specifically prohibited by the rules of the game. A brief history of the game and the rules under which it is played is given in Appendix I.

Edson Arantes do Nascimento—Pelé—is the athlete best known throughout the world. He is the only three-time world champion in football; the only man who has played on three world champion teams. To appreciate what this means, one must realize that 140 countries vie for this championship once every four years. Two years before this tournament, elimination rounds are held between these 140 countries, and only the best fourteen, plus the previous winner plus the host country, comprise the sixteen teams that go into the finals. For a team to win in those finals means it is the *world* champion in every sense. If baseball were played in every country in the world, and elimination rounds were played in every country in the world, then we would have a true World Series, not an American series. And for a team to win the world championship three times is truly remarkable. Pelé is the only man in the world who has played on three world championship teams.

He is as famous in the farthest reaches of Asia Minor and the deepest interior of Africa as he is in the capitals of Europe and the Americas. More people have seen him play football than any other athlete in any sport, anywhere, at any time. More people know his name and face than any other person who has ever lived; he has been photographed more than any person in history, including movie stars and statesmen. He has visited eighty-eight countries, has met with ten kings, five emperors, seventy presidents, and forty other chiefs of state, including two popes. He is an honorary citizen of more cities and countries than any person in history.

In Nigeria a two-day truce was declared in the tragic war with Biafra so that both sides could see him play; the Shah of Iran waited three hours at an international airport just to be able to speak with Pelé and be photographed with him. Frontier guards of Red China left their posts and came into Hong Kong to see him and compliment him when they heard he was there. In Colombia when Pelé was sent from the game for arguing a referee's decision, the crowd stormed the field, the referee had to be rescued by the police, a linesman was hastily appointed referee, and Pelé was forced to come back into the game, a definite only-time event in the long history of international association football.

His record number of goals—nearly 1,300, as listed in Appendix III—is more than double the number for his nearest competitor and comes to an average of almost one goal per game, a record that will probably stand for all time.

He has given more interviews in more countries to all forms of the media than any man alive, and of all athletes he is probably the most accessible to newsmen and by far the best liked. He is the highest salaried team athlete in history, as well as probably being the richest. *Sports Illustrated* claims Pelé to have the most perfect physique of any athlete in the world. Over ninety songs have been written in various countries in which Pelé is named; in his own country, Brazil, he is known not only as an athlete but as an actor in movies and television, as well as a fine poet and an excellent musician.

With the barest of educational opportunities as a youth, after reaching the pinnacle of fame he made the effort to study and eventually received a university degree. Through his many travels and through much personal effort, Pelé speaks fluent Spanish, quite passable French and Italian, and is rapidly attaining fluency in English, as well as being remarkably expressive in his native Portuguese.

These are all very interesting facts—impressive facts—but who, really, is Pelé? What winds him up, what makes him tick? What makes him *Pelé?*

How did a quiet, shy, sometimes-introspective boy of fifteen, picked to try out with an excellent but relatively small club in Santos in Brazil, within twenty months become the idol of the international football world? Where did the charisma develop that has brought him the adulation he receives wherever he goes, as well as the admiration and respect of every player he has either played with or against in his career? How has he been able not only to maintain that popularity but to increase it in the twenty years since he first amazed the world with his exceptional skills?

Possibly one cannot explain his unique genius at the game of football any more than one can explain the genius of Mozart in writing the music he wrote at the age he wrote it. Genius is its own explanation. It has been suggested that there is a sort of built-in computer in Pelé's head that instantly corrects itself according to the constantly changing position of the ball on the field and the ever-different location of the other players, bringing him to the right place at the right time to make the most effective play. If so, that would become its own definition of genius. Still, there can be no doubt that if Pelé has that sort of built-in computer, the computer has been programmed with years of hard practice, by much grueling experience, and by a life of total dedication to the constant learning of his craft.

Almost every reporter who has interviewed Pelé has come away to speak of the simplicity of the man. Humble, possibly; modest, certainly—but simple, no. No human being is simple, least of all Pelé. Perhaps by learning of his life as he saw it himself, we can come to understand a bit more of the mystery of this extremely complex person. ...

Robert L. Fish, 1977

MY LIFE AND THE BEAUTIFUL GAME

Chapter 1

Göteborg, Sweden—June 1958

The Nya Ulleví Stadium is jammed to capacity, crowded with people come to see the team of the Soviet Union demolish Brazil in this, the third game of their fight in the Jules Rimet Trophy competition for the football championship of the world. Of the sixteen teams in the competition, fourteen have qualified in matches throughout the world the previous year; the other two, West Germany and Sweden, are present as the former champion and the host country, both automatically qualified. Many think Russia might well win the championship, although they concede that Wales is also strong, and one cannot discount West Germany, the champion, nor Sweden, which, although present without having to qualify, is known to always be dangerous.

Newspapermen are here from all over the globe, waiting for the Russian team to appear, anxious to see in person players like Simonian, the agile Armenian center-forward, Iachine, the magnificent goalkeeper, Igor Netto, the left-half and captain, and Salnikov, the highly intelligent inside-left. Radio and television interviewers are anxious for the game to start and then be done with so they can interview the winners, the Russian stars of such noted teams as Moscow Dynamo or Torpedo Moscow or Dynamo Kiev. Other than the Brazilians present, nobody really expects too much from the South American team. True, they had beaten Austria, 3–1, in their first game, but those who saw—and reported—the game knew it had been far from as one-sided as the score seemed to indicate. And the best the Brazilians had been able to do against a weak English team playing without men like Mathews, their great outside-right now retired, or Lofthouse, the squat, powerful center-forward—bringing to the games, in fact, only twenty players although entitled to twenty-two—had been a scoreless tie, and the Brazilians had had to play their hearts out to gain that.

Russia, however, is a different matter. The players on the Big Red team, as it is called, are large and tough, selected from the thousands of subsidized sports clubs throughout the vast land. This is the first time they have entered World Cup competition and they qualified with ease; had they played in all of the previous World Cup matches, they might well have already retired the trophy with three wins. And Brazil has not only never won a championship, but the only time they reached the finals, in 1950—and playing in their own country, on their own field, before their own fans, and against an admittedly weaker team—they had ignominiously lost. And in 1954—well, the less said about the Brazilian effort in 1954 the better! It had not been anything to brag about. So nobody is expecting any miracles from Brazil.

When the teams come trotting out of the tunnel from the dressing rooms, the crowd looks down to see a skinny little black boy in the uniform of Brazil trotting out onto the field, with the others in the same uniform dwarfing him. That skinny little black boy is me—Pelé. Most of the people in the stands have to assume I'm either the team mascot or the son of a friend of the coach; I can't be the son of the coach because the coach is white. Those who had attended the Austria-Brazil and the England-Brazil matches may have remembered me limping onto the field to take my place on the Brazilian bench, screaming my encouragement to the team together with the reserves, as if our few voices could possibly drown out the huge crowds cheering for our opposition.

But this time when the players leave the bench to take their positions on the field, this skinny little black boy—me—also gets up and goes out onto the grass and the people see I am wearing a shirt with a big number 10 on it. I am sure the newspapermen and the radio announcers and the television broadcasters are all consulting their lists to see who the devil No. 10 is; if they are, they will see I am Edson Arantes do Nascimento, seventeen years old. I am sure that some of those in the stands are faintly amused to see a child on the field in a World Cup match, and some are probably outraged that as important an event as a World Cup match should be reduced to parody by having an infant on the field. The more sentimental, however, probably feel pity for a team so reduced in talent as to face the need to bring children along with them. The entire Brazilian team is young as teams go; everyone knows that—but they undoubtedly feel that this is ridiculous!

When the band strikes up the first chords of the Brazilian national anthem, all of us Brazilians feel a strange force within us. I cannot describe it; I doubt if any of us could describe it. If the people in the stands are amazed to see me down there on the field, I am far more amazed. All of us are living in a dream, but none more so than me. I try not to waste time trying to analyze this strange feeling; I know this is no time to be distracted. Instead I try to concentrate on how I will play; but the thought keeps intruding: How is it possible that you are here, in the Brazilian Selection, in Sweden, about to play for your country in the Jules Rimet matches? It has to be a dream. ...

The Russian team taking their positions on the field is certainly no dream. A nightmare, possibly, but no dream! Each man is larger than his opposite on our team, and their goalkeeper, Iachine, is a giant. He looks as if all he has to do is spread out his arms and he will cover the entire goal. Getting the ball past this monster, I think with sinking heart, is going to be almost impossible.

To my left as we line up for the game's opening kick is Zagalo; to my right I see Vavá, then Didi, then Garrincha. Garrincha in Portuguese means the cambaxirra, a small bird, and like that small bird Garrincha can dart about the field. We have given him the nickname of Mané; it means fool or half-wit, but less a fool or a half-wit on the field than Mané I have yet to meet. As usual Garrincha even appears slightly bored. I look behind me, more to avoid studying the giants in front than to check our defense. There is Nilton Santos, a tower of strength at mid-field with Zito, the other mid-fielder, grinning at me comfortably. Then, beyond, there is Belini, our captain, Orlando, De Sordi, and behind them all, relaxed and sure, Gilmar, our goalkeeper. Zito claps his hands, winks at me, and calls out loudly:

"Okay, gang! Let's surprise them!"

Vavá looks at him, frowning, but there is a twinkle in his eye:

"What do you mean, surprise them? They expect to get beat! Let's *not* surprise them!"

And then the game has started and I forget the kidding, even forget what I know very well—that the kidding was meant to relax us all, but principally me. I forget the crowds and the stadium and everything. This is just another football game, that beautiful game I love so well, the game I live to play, and nothing else is in my mind. We aren't playing the Russians—we're playing an *opponent,* and winning is all that counts!

The Russians have the ball and they are quite good at handling it, make no mistake—until one of them, oddly enough, does make a mistake and the ball is at the feet of Garrincha. Our little bird takes the ball between his feet and starts down the field in a spectacular dribble that has the crowd on its feet.

He evades defenders as if they were not not there. I race over, knowing the Russians will close in on Garrincha in force, but Garrincha is feeling his oats. He dribbles the ball expertly around the nearest man and kicks for the goal with all his force, not even breaking stride to do so. Iachine leaps in the air, extending himself to the fullest, but the ball just clears his fingertips. I have "*Goal!!!*" in my throat when the ball strikes the top crosspiece and bounds back onto the field! I expect Garrincha to swear but he doesn't waste the time. He is a total professional and has judged the ball's trajectory and is prepared to recover it when it returns. Once again he kicks, but this time he is rushed and the ball sails out of bounds.

The game is just beginning but we can already see a great weakness in the Russian defense. The offense is strong, but we are not too worried about that; Nilton Santos and Belini and Orlando and De Sordi and Zito and Gilmar will handle that! Garrincha is inspired; he seems to have been waiting for this game all his life. He goes through the defenders almost at will. The crowd, suddenly aware that the game will not be so easy for the Russians, are screaming at the top of their voices, some of them beginning to root for us. They cheer each dribble we make; each tackle that takes the ball from a bewildered Russian opponent brings increasing yells of appreciation from the fans in the stands. And all we can think of is stuffing the ball past Iachine's gorilla arms into the net!

Didi has the ball and I can read his mind. I dodge between two defenders, prepared for what I know will happen; he kicks the ball toward me as if he had measured the distance with a tape measure. The ball slides past me as I expect and want, and without breaking stride I kick it toward the goal on the dead run. Iachine leaps for it but I know his timing is off; he has not expected the speed of the move. Once again I have the scream of "*Goal!!!*" in my throat—and once again the miserable ball hits the crosspiece and bounds back to the field where Iachine grabs it and hugs it thankfully.

I glare at the goal posts: "*Cagão!*"

Trotting near me, Didi laughs. "Relax, son. It'll go in. Give it time."

My knee is beginning to throb from an injury that had kept me from the first two games and almost from the World Cup games altogether—an injury that is a story in itself that we'll come to in time—but I am in no mood to worry about a mere knee. Didi has the ball again. I get free to let him pass it to me, but a defender is coming over fast to cover me, and Didi, without breaking stride or even indicating his intention by moving his head or his body, passes the ball in a totally different direction to Vavá. Vavá, charging in, has clearly expected the pass, but the Russians have not. Vavá's foot touches the ball lightly to bring it to the proper speed even as he is running, and then in the same motion, he kicks!

Gooooooaaaaaalllll!!!!!! Brazil!!!!!!

We are all over Vavá, screaming, thumping him, pummeling, jumping in the air, waving our fists hysterically. Iachine is stretched out on the ground, looking at us sadly, as if we were bad children who had somehow disappointed a permissive parent.

The game goes on. Now we feel more secure; we feel, in fact, that the game will be easy, and that is always a mistake. As a result we do not score again in that period. I am overanxious. I want to wrap the game up and go back to the hotel where I can hug the memory of it, as a child hugs a favorite toy. My dribbling is good; my evasions, my feints, my tackles, bring shouts of approval from the crowd, now strongly behind us. But I lose two sure goals through not being relaxed enough at the moment of kicking. The others on the Brazilian team are more relaxed but nothing any of us can do results in any more goals and we go back through the tunnel at half time with the score 1–0.

The second half is much the same; the Russians attack strongly, fiercely, but our defense is impregnable. Gilmar has not permitted a goal so far in the tournament, and even getting past Orlando or Nilton Santos or Belini or De Sordi is extremely difficult for the Big Red team, let alone getting a shot at the net with Gilmar guarding it. But the Russian defense has also tightened and—it seems to me—Iachine has grown bigger during half time. There simply does not seem to be any room around him to get into the net. Time is running out, and then I see Didi with the ball again, and from everything he is doing I know he is going to pass the ball to me. He kicks it with that indescribable accuracy of his, as if there were only the two of us on the field, and I stop it momentarily and then start to dribble it in almost the same motion toward the goal. Defenders come in a rush; time is running out for them, as well, and they trail. But we have expected them to do just this, of course, and they have overlooked Vavá, who is totally prepared when, without any indication of purpose, I suddenly pass the ball to him. It slows down as it nears him and Vavá kicks it neatly without losing a step. The defense has attempted to change direction; Iachine swings his large body toward the ball, but even his size cannot compensate for the accuracy of Vavá's kick.

Gooooooaaaaaalllll!!!!!! Brazil!!!!!!

Iachine is sitting up, staring at us with that sad look on his face again. We run for Vavá—he is crying with emotion.

And the game ends: Brazil 2, Russia 0.

That night, after we have celebrated our victory with an incredible meal, and after we have relived the game over and over again, complimenting each other exaggeratedly (our coach, Vicente Feola, lets us do it to get it out of our systems, but we all know that tomorrow he will clamp down relentlessly on such egotism), I go to my room and slowly undress. I climb into bed and lie back, replaying the entire game, move by move, tackle by tackle, dribble by dribble, kick by kick. I realize that I was overanxious. I twinge when I think of the lost opportunities for goals—but I also realize that I hadn't played badly. After all, the World Cup isn't exactly a mere club game against some team from Santo André or Mogí das

Cruzes; the Russians aren't exactly pushovers. And we *did* win! Maybe nobody knew who that skinny little black kid, Pelé, was before today, but they do now. I have nothing to be ashamed of. I wonder what they are thinking this moment in Baurú, what my parents are thinking, my brother and sister, my Uncle Jorge and Dona Ambrosina, my grandmother, my friends. I can picture the elation in the streets, and people all talking about Pelé, the little *moleque* who such a short time ago was being punished for kicking a football into the first street light on our street, breaking the bulb, and plunging the neighborhood back into darkness.

I bring my thoughts back to the game. I promise myself that if I am scheduled to play in the next match, I will be calmer, more relaxed—like Garrincha or Didi or Vavá or Zagalo. I will be more professional, I promise.

I still cannot sleep. My thoughts once more return to Baurú and to all the incredible steps that brought me to this point where I am playing with the Brazilian Selection in the World Cup matches in such a short space of time. It had to be God who did it—but why? Why had He chosen me? What could have been His motive?

I knew it was futile to consider His motives. For whatever reason, though, it had to be a miracle. ...

Chapter 2

I was born on the night of October 23, 1940, in the small town of Três Corações in the state of Minas Gerais in Brazil. I was baptized Edson Arantes do Nascimento, but it was some time before I discovered that was my name; everyone in the family called me Dico. I've been back to see the house where I was born, partly out of natural curiosity and partly out of respect for the town which named the street after me and which also put a plaque on the house, and it isn't very much as houses go. It is part of a shabby row of dwellings built of used brick and held together by cracked plaster and peeling paint—and the plaque probably helps, too. I was too young then to know it wasn't a castle; actually, when I was older and living in Baurú, beginning to become aware of things, I still didn't fully understand the difference. Everyone I knew lived in houses like that.

I've often tried to picture in my mind the scene in that small house the night I was born. I can imagine my young mother, Celeste, eyes shining, proudly holding up this scrawny wriggling tiny black figure, my grandmother Ambrosina beaming with pleasure, my Uncle Jorge saying, "Well, he's certainly black enough!" and my father, almost as young as my mother, leaning over to study me, his first born, lightly squeezing my thighs and saying matter-of-factly, "Well, he should make a good football player. He's got the legs for it."

And if I've pictured the scene correctly, the chances are that that remark wiped the smile from my mother's face. I imagine her dragging me back into her arms protectively and saying sharply, "Not if I can help it! One football player in the family is enough. Enough? It's too many! This one is going to be a doctor; he's going to amount to something. A football player? Don't wish him bad luck!"

If my mother, Celeste, didn't say it at the time, she certainly said it often enough through the years as I grew up. My father, João Ramos do Nascimento, was a professional football player known as Dondinho, and while he was an excellent player and well known in the area, he was certainly neither the luckiest nor the most prosperous. For a man to live on the meager earnings of a professional football player in those days—especially playing for a small club in a town the size of Três Corações—was close to impossible, and trying to raise a family on those minuscule earnings was clearly ridiculous. In addition to the fact that the salary was what we called in Portuguese a *mixaria*—a not-very-nice word meaning less than nothing—there were few victory bonuses that today are so much a part of the professional's earnings. But football was the thing my father knew and the thing he enjoyed doing most, so he stayed with it despite the constant haranguing of my mother, and despite the needs of his growing family. He lived in the hope that one day he would be asked to play for an important club in a major city, and then we'd all be out of the woods and living like kings.

And it actually happened, or at least the first part of the dream. His big opportunity came in 1942 when a scout saw him play and he was invited to play for Atlético Mineiro, an important club in Belo Horizonte, the state's capital. I was too young to remember, but I can imagine the excitement around the house the day he packed a bag with his few belongings, kissed the family, and left home. I know the exaggerated hopes he must have had; I can almost taste the rosy future he saw for all of us. Dondinho was an excellent player, crack quality, and he had no doubt at all that all he needed was a chance to prove himself. From then on everything would be *up*.

Well, as I said, Dondinho was unlucky. In the very first game in which he played, against São Cristovão of Rio de Janeiro, he had a violent collision with Augusto—the same Augusto who later played for Vasco da Gama and was selected for the World Cup team of 1950 and was captain of the team—and when Augusto picked himself off the ground, Dondinho was still down there, writhing in agony. The ligaments had been severely torn in his right knee. It isn't the first time it has happened to a top player, and it won't be the last, but it's tragic in every case. The game ended in a tie, 1–1, and in the second game, Atlético versus América, my Dad was unable to play.

They gave him his ticket back to Três Corações and I give him credit for coming back at all, but I guess he loved us all very much, because it never occurred to him to do anything else. I've known many men since who would have just kept going. But he came back—completely discouraged, and not particularly helped by having to limp around in constant pain, nor by having Dona Celeste constantly nag him.

"Dondinho! It was bad enough before, when you had two good legs, and we couldn't eat on what you made playing football! Forget this insanity! Get a job; earn a living! Jorge, tell him. ..."

But Jorge didn't tell him, because Jorge loved my father and Jorge secretly envied my father his ability to play football and have people cheer him from the stands, and have people cross the street to come over and say hello when he walked through town. My Uncle Jorge, my mother's brother, is younger than she is, and has always been more like an older brother to me than an uncle, almost as if he had been Dondinho's son rather than Celeste's brother.

Dondinho continued to play football. The knee remained swollen, always painful, but Dondinho was afraid to have surgery, and considering the state of our local clinic in Três Corações, he probably was right. Instead, he kept it packed with cold pads between games and continued to play for Três Corações. It was the only way he knew how to make any money at all.

These are things I've either been told or picked up listening as I grew older. My own memories begin in the town of Baurú in the state of São Paulo when I was about four years old. I know that Dondinho's football career took us briefly to the town of Lorena and even more briefly to the town of São Lourenço always trying to make a living and never making it. But Baurú was to become our permanent home. For the first time a football club had not only offered Dondinho a job playing football but also promised to arrange a public-service job for him to supplement his football income. My mother, who had been about to start a small war when she heard we were going to move again—and for another football job, yet!—surrendered instantly when she heard about the public-service job. It was the sort of thing she hoped and prayed for ever since marrying Dondinho—and we were off again, this time for a final move.

My first real memory begins with the train ride to Baurú. I don't remember where we were, but I vaguely recall our being taken to the railroad station in an old wagon drawn by a bony and almost creaking horse. I think the man driving the wagon was my grandfather, my mother's father, and that he made his living cutting wood, splitting it, and selling it for kindling. The wagon was half-filled with split wood, and the rest of the space in back was taken up with our few possessions and my father and myself. My mother sat on the seat beside my grandfather, holding my baby sister in her arms, and with my baby brother under the protection of one elbow. I seem to remember that wagon ride, but I'm not sure it isn't something I was told about later.

I'm sure about the train ride. I had never seen anything of the world before, not that I could remember, and everything I saw was new and fascinating. The trains in the interior of Brazil in those days—and many to this day—kept their windows open as the most feasible, or at least most economical, form of air conditioning, and I kept my chin against the sill, staring wide-eyed at everything that passed. The train went slowly, which helped; it chugged complacently along, as if there were no urgency about the trip, nor any particular destination in mind. The scenery I saw, I suppose, really wasn't much different from where I had come nor from what I came to know in Baurú: rolling hills of brown dirt with stubby trees clinging to the sides fighting for sustenance in the meager soil, an occasional stand of thicker trees bending over the track, inducing momentary darkness, and every now and then a shack leaning drunkenly beside the track with the inevitable naked baby or babies playing in the mud area and staring up at us incuriously as we grandly passed them at our stately fifteen-mile-an-hour pace, the inevitable clothesline before the shack strung with pitifully worn clothes flapping in the wind, and an occasional *bananeira*—banana plant—with half-filled stalks hanging down obscenely, furnishing poor shade for those condemned to live there.

And then the train went around a curve and I clearly remember forgetting all my parents' injunctions and leaning halfway out of the window to see where the engine was taking us. I could see it clearly, the smoke puffing from the stack, staining the cloudless blue sky, the engineer leaning indolently over the side of the cab, puffing on his pipe in rhythm with the engine, the sun glinting from the track ahead—and then the next thing I knew I was being jerked inside none too gently, given a smack on the ear for emphasis, and made to spend the balance of the trip seated rigidly between my parents, with Dondinho's glare keeping me in place, and Dona Celeste ready to back him up with another smack should any idea of revolt enter my mind.

Baurú, unfortunately, did not turn out to be the promised land the family had hoped for. The Lusitana Club, which had contracted my father, had become the Baurú Athletic Club, with new directors, and while they were willing to abide by the football contract, they quite conveniently denied any responsibility for getting Dondinho the public-service job that had been promised. So we were right back again in the same rut, only this time in a strange city without family, and with a household that had expanded to include my grandmother on my father's side, Dona Ambrosina, and my Uncle Jorge. So there were seven in the house: my grandmother, my uncle, my brother Jair, my sister Maria Lúcia, my parents, and me. The arguments in the house increased and Dondinho, in addition to having to play football with a painful knee, also had to split his time between trying to convince Dona Celeste that he honestly *had* been promised that public-service job and trying to convince the directors of the club that it was their responsibility to get him either that job or another in its place. But it was all without success.

Uncle Jorge cut wood for a while and sold it door to door, a trade he had learned working for his father, but there was too much competition in Baurú and it paid very little. Then he found work in a large wholesale house that handled everything from eggs to ax handles, and his salary helped support us to a great extent. In addition, my Aunt Maria, Dondinho's sister, who worked as a maid for a rich family in São Paulo, would come to Baurú on her day off, bringing fruits we had never seen or even heard of, like pears and apples, as well as hand-me-down clothes from her employer. And so we existed. But as I grew up I began to learn what poverty is.

Poverty is a curse that depresses the mind, drains the spirit, and poisons life. When we didn't lack things—simple things, like enough food in the house, or the small sum that was needed to pay our rent—we were very happy. There was a great deal of love in that small house, love that overcame much of the hardship, love that has survived until today. But there were also many bitter arguments, virulent recriminations, painful battles over the lack of necessities, things that Dona Celeste stubbornly maintained were our birthright because Dondinho had been promised that public-service job.

The house we had moved into was made of wood, and the man who laid down the tile roof should have been in another trade. It leaked like a sieve, but unlike a sieve, for some unknown reason it never seemed to leak in the same place twice, so one was never sure where to drag one's mattress and be assured of a relatively dry night's rest during some of the torrential rains that strike Brazil. But that leaky roof was not poverty. Poverty was having my mother worry herself sick, or upbraid Dondinho for not having a job that could earn the money to pay the rent on that leaky roof.

Nor was poverty having to go out in the dark and fumble for the latch on the outhouse, and then sit there, frightened, wondering what all the strange sounds coming from the chilly night might portend. No, even our neighbors who were better off than we were had outhouses. Nor was poverty wearing hand-me-down clothes that seldom fit, or not having shoes, or having all of us sleeping in the tiny kitchen on a cold night, huddled around the wood-burning stove, trying not to sleep on top of one another, and still trying to keep warm. (Why do all Americans think that all of Brazil is constantly hot?)

No; poverty was wondering what would happen if we couldn't raise the money for the firewood. Poverty was begrudging and even hating each stick of kindling that went into the hungry maw of that stove, and being forced to feed it, anyway.

Poverty, in short, is being robbed of self-respect and self-reliance. Poverty is fear. Not fear of death, which, though inevitable, is reasonable; it is fear of life. It is a terrible fear. ...

During those first years in Baurú, however, poverty was a problem for my parents or Dona Ambrosina or Uncle Jorge—

not for me. I was very happy in Baurú. There were a large number of kids around my age living in the neighborhood, black, white—if any Brazilian is completely white (but a good deal whiter than me)—and Japanese. We played from dawn to dusk. At first we set up a circus in my back yard, making a trapeze from a mango tree that grew there, but the best rope we could find was pretty badly worn, and the first time Dona Celeste saw me swinging from the tree was the last time. The rope came down, the other kids were sent home, and I got my usual cuff alongside my head.

So we decided to play grown-up games, like the football we had seen exhibited by my father and the other professionals at the Baurú Athletic Club—or BAC, as it was more familiarly called. We couldn't afford a ball so we did what most other kids did for a ball: We would stuff the largest man's sock we could find with rags or crumpled-up newspaper, roll it into as close a ball shape as we could manage, and tie it around with string. As we became more proficient in the game, and as we grew bigger, we would use more and more stuffing, making a bigger and a heavier ball. Some of the socks we used for our balls or for their stuffing were taken from clotheslines before the owner was aware that he had contributed, but we felt our greater need justified the borrowing. A man could always walk around without socks—we did—but a kid needed something to kick.

Years later, when I was doing my service in the Brazilian Army, I was told by someone, jokingly, that in the American Army they had a saying, "If it moves, salute it. If it doesn't move, pick it up. If it's too big to pick up, paint it." If we had a similar slogan in Brazil, it would have been, "If it moves, kick it. If it doesn't move, kick it and make it move. If it's too big to kick, trade it in on something smaller and kick *that*." Brazilians learn to kick as soon as they learn to stand up; walking comes later.

Our field was the street where I lived, Rua Rubens Arruda, and our goals were the two ends of the street—one where

Rubens Arruda ran into September 7th, the cross street, and the other where it dead-ended into an old practice field of the Noroeste Club, a rival to BAC. Our sidelines were where a curb might have been had the street been paved. As it wasn't, it took a bit of skill just to be able to keep one's balance on the surface. It also took skill to kick our ball, since it varied in weight depending on how lately it had been stuffed, and also on whether it ran through many mud puddles as we kicked it. But it made no difference; the pleasure of kicking that ball, making it move, making it respond to an action of mine, was the greatest feeling of power I had ever had to that time.

My mother wasn't too pleased by my constant attention to football. She put it in the same category as bank robbery and the seven deadly sins, but it did keep me out of more damaging mischief. It kept me more or less in sight, and it was also sort of a trade-off. The price I had to pay for being allowed to play was having to take care of my younger brother, Jair, known by his nickname of Zoca. Besides, I had already announced my firm intention never to be a professional football player. I fully intended to become an aviator when I grew up, an idea that had developed as I watched the planes take off and land at the field of the local Aero Club. Still, taking care of Zoca seemed a high price to pay for being allowed to play football in front of the house; playing any active game and baby-sitting at the same time is never easy. Zoca was small and kept trying to get into the game, and every time someone would fall over him he would go screaming into the house and I'd end up getting an ear slapped. But when my mother said I had to take care of Zoca, there was no use trying to argue.

Dona Celeste was—and is—a small woman who then weighed about ninety pounds with a heavy skillet in each hand. She was slight in build with small, very regular features, and with a beautiful full head of glistening brown hair, of which she was quite proud. When she smiled it was the most beautiful smile in the world, but unfortunately none of us in the house ever did much to make her smile. But anyone who made a judgment of Dona Celeste based either on her lovely smile or on her petite figure was in for a surprise. She ruled the house with an authority that was absolute. Her code was rigid: The Arantes do Nascimento family were poor, but we behaved. We didn't steal, we didn't beg, we didn't lie, we didn't cheat; we didn't use swear words regardless of the provocation; we believed in God and prayed to Him regularly, although we didn't expect Him to solve our problems for us; we treated people older than ourselves with respect; and above all, we obeyed our parents—*or else!*

The "or else" being too terrible to contemplate, in general we followed the rules, although I am now forced to wonder why, if I obeyed them so well, I was always getting my ears slapped or my bottom walloped. One reason, I suppose, was that another of Dona Celeste's rules was that I stay within range of her voice, which, for a small woman, was considerable and should have provided a field of activity more than ample. Unfortunately, the Aero Club was beyond that range. I would sneak off to the field whenever I couldn't get a football game going, and sit there, watching the small planes take off and land, the gliders being towed to take-off and swooping higher and higher, like birds, seeing the flyers in their romantic goggles and leather jackets climbing down from their marvelous contraptions, and I would dream of the day when I, too, goggled, jacketed, and booted, would climb into one of those beautiful planes and take off into the lovely empty sky with all the freedom of a bird. All worries would be forgotten, all poverty past. I would look down and see our tiny house and the rutted road before it, the muddy back yard with its skimpy mango tree, and then I would fly away. In my dream I saw myself always coming back, first for my mother, then for my sister and my father and my grandmother and my Uncle Jorge—but not for Zoca—and then I would fly away again. I swore I would do it as soon as I grew up.

Zoca always wanted to accompany me on these excursions to the Aero Club, but I usually refused him, because he had to be watched constantly, and if he got loose and walked into a plane or wandered onto a runway with disastrous results, I knew who would be held responsible. But if I didn't let him come he'd run into the house, crying:

"Mama! Dico went to the Aero Club again!"

And that meant another pulled ear or slapped bottom, plus the punishment I would get later for teaching—or, rather, trying to teach—Zoca not to go running home with stories.

When I was about seven I started to shine shoes. A friend of mine helped me build a box in the rough semblance of a shoeshine kit, and Uncle Jorge financed the initial supplies. To tell the truth, my first idea was that shining shoes would give me a legitimate excuse for going out to the Aero Club, since obviously the type of men who flew airplanes were the type with enough interest in their natty appearance to keep their shoes gleaming. Dona Celeste was firmly opposed and said—with what I am sure she considered perfect logic—that if I wanted to shine shoes I could stay on our street and shine the shoes of our neighbors. Since most of them were as poor as we were, I couldn't see building an enterprise of any great magnitude in that area, but when Dona Celeste spoke, I obeyed. So for a week I dutifully went from door to door, asking if anyone wanted any shoes shined that day. In the entire week one neighbor finally let me shine his shoes, whether out of pity or because he got tired of my constant knocking on his door, I don't know. I do know that when I finished I didn't know what to charge him, and as I took whatever he offered—which I'm sure was minimal—I promised myself to find out what the service should carry before finding myself bankrupt for my efforts.

The neighbor's shoes, of course, were not the first ones I shined. My Aunt Maria had brought me a pair that her employer's youngest boy had outgrown and which I saved religiously for Sunday and church. They were in good shape; the boy had been more careful than most in their use, and I was quite proud of them. Dona Celeste insisted that if I wanted to shine shoes, I could practice on my own, and under her watchful eye I did. (I remember that pair of shoes particularly; rather than outgrowing them, as my benefactor's son had done, I used them one day to play football and brought them home in ruins. With the usual punishment. But I had wanted to know how it felt to kick a ball with shoes on. ...) I also polished Dondinho's football shoes and a pair of shoes of my grandmother's. It's a wonder I had any polish left when I finally went out to shine the shoes of the world!

After the demonstrated inability of Rua Rubens Arruda to furnish sufficient custom, I finally prevailed on Dondinho to talk Dona Celeste into letting me go to a BAC game the following Saturday and let me go through the crowd in the stadium shining the shoes of anyone wanting to impress his girl, put down a competitor, or whatever reason people had for getting their shoes shined. I never fully understood it in those days, but there was no doubt that for some mysterious reason adults liked to have their shoes shined. To my surprise Dona Celeste gave in, with the condition that Dondinho keep his eye on me throughout the game. Dondinho, of course, could scarcely play football and watch me at the same time, but when the game was over and he came to pick me up, I had earned over two cruzeiros! We went home, arm in arm, two breadwinners!

After that I was allowed more leeway, and I naturally gravitated to a railroad station, which seemed to be where most of the shoeshine boys congregated. Baurú was principally a railroad city; it was the main reason for its existence. The three principal railways of the country all passed through Baurú—the Soracabana, the Paulista, and the Noroeste (the Northwest). The Noroeste also sponsored the Noroeste Club in Baurú, the major competitor and bitter rival of BAC, and the owner of a larger stadium than its rival. I went to the Northwest station for several reasons: Dondinho had played for BAC on their field many times and was known to many people; as his son I might have an edge over the other shoeshine boys around the station. I also had used their abandoned field at the end of our street for practice and felt a sort of kinship with them for this reason. But the main reason, the reason that counted most with my mother, was that it was the closest to home.

I used to enjoy downtown Baurú very much. At that time I thought it had to be a metropolis, on the order of São Paulo or Rio de Janeiro, although I imagine now that its population in those days couldn't have been more than eighty or ninety thousand. But for the interior of Brazil in those days, it was a large city. It had the color of many older cities of Brazil in those days—color which has disappeared under the pressure of growth and the evaluation of land, so that today Baurú has skyscrapers where in those days it had small houses, perched one above the other leading up to the church, all painted in contrasting colors, pastels against wild greens and deep blues. The few large buildings they had were in Colonial architecture, and gave one a feeling of permanence, of being a part of Brazilian history. It was a good feeling, a feeling of belonging.

There were stores crowding the narrow streets, displaying all the things I wished I had but didn't; there were small hotels, one of them directly across the street from the railroad station; there was a movie house with colorful posters to wildly stir the imagination. And there was always the supreme thrill of seeing the huge engines come snorting into the station, puffing and blowing like some boastful dragon, and the people climbing down with their welter of suitcases and boxes and packages held together with hemp, and even, occasionally, a coop of chickens—in the interior of Brazil the best way to keep food fresh is to keep it alive. And I would wonder at the strange and exotic places they had come from and were going to, and wonder if I would ever see them.

Sometimes there would also be ranchers riding down the street on horseback, a dyed sheepskin their only saddle, no cinch straps, no stirrups, their feet poking out like an open clothespin, their accordion boots muddy and scratched from mesquite or thistle, their leather hats tied beneath their chins with cord. On a Saturday afternoon it was not uncommon for one of them to tie his horse near the station and actually have his boots cleaned, although why was a mystery to me, since they would be muddy and scratched again in no time. But at that time I was too young to know that it was considered very bad manners to go into a bordello with muddy boots.

Still I never allowed my shoeshining to interfere with my football. The trains at the Northwest station came in and left on a rigid schedule, and since there was no purpose in remaining there after the last train had departed in the middle of the afternoon, I was off to the field, dropping my shoeshine kit at home with the money I had earned, and dashing off to meet the other kids, my sock-filled ball under my arm. And we would run up and down the field, kicking, trying to dribble past each other, tackling with fury, until the last light had gone and my mother's voice—or Zoca, her messenger—made return inevitable.

It was at that time that I began to dread Saturdays, because I would come back from the railroad station to find the roadway in front of our house filled with kindling, for that was the day it was delivered. Nor could I go out to play until every stick of it had been brought inside and neatly stacked. It was a chore that took most of the afternoon and almost always precluded football. But I found a solution. I would call the team over and say:

"I can't go out until this is all stacked inside. And if I don't go, the ball doesn't go. ..."

At first they grumbled quite a bit, but they ended up helping me carry the wood inside, until after a few weeks it became a habit, and if someone asked one of the gang where he was going on a Saturday afternoon, he would look at his questioner as if he were mad not to know, and he would say:

"Over to Edson's to stack kindling, of course. ..."

It was about that time—I was going on eight, or had just turned eight, I don't recall which—that a public-service job for

Dondinho finally came through, only three or four years after it had been promised, which many people would say is not bad by Brazilian standards. It was a job for the state, as an aide in a health clinic, and involved the sweeping of floors, cleaning bedpans, helping to carry litters from the ambulances to the emergency ward, making coffee, loading and unloading supplies; in short, doing whatever he was told to do at the time. It wasn't the greatest job in the world, but it changed the atmosphere in the house at once. Although the pay he received didn't take us from the poverty level, it raised us to the upper echelons of the poverty level, you might say, and that was a giant step forward. It also removed the major cause of argument in the house and brought us all closer together.

Very often, after the last train had left, I would forgo football and go down to the clinic to help Dondinho in any way I could. I could make coffee and I did. I could empty and scour bedpans and I did. What I sensed, subconsciously, was that I wanted to be with him. And when there was a spare moment in his day, which wasn't very often, we'd sit and he'd tell me of the different teams he had played with, the famous players he had known, and his love of the game came through every word he uttered. He spoke of an uncle I'd never known, his older brother, Francisco.

"If you ever become a professional football player, Dico, I hope you inherit his skill. He died when he was only twenty-five. I was sixteen and I thought I would never get over his death. But he left me something; he left me the tricks I know of the game. They called him Chico do Jonas. Older men still remember him and his football in places like Mococa, Casa Branca, and in the south of Minas."

I think it was those moments that brought us together, not just as father and son, but as friends. Dondinho was, and is, an extremely handsome man, with an excellent physique. Not the build apparently so admired in the United States, that of the weight-lifter, all muscles and shoulders, but a straight supple body, flat belly, sinewy arms and legs, all hidden strength—the perfect build for a football player. But where Dona Celeste was peppery, Dondinho was calm, even-tempered, always thinking carefully before making a pronouncement, and then sticking by whatever he said. He was—and is—a wonderful father. One night when we had a break he sat me down for a man-to-man talk.

I still remember that night; the dim light—light bulbs at state health clinics always seem to run to forty watts, when they're available at all—the tile shining from Dondinho's most recent polishing, the worn linoleum on the floor, the ever-present odor of carbolic, the pregnant silence, waiting for someone to cry out in pain in the night. I also remember the satisfaction at knowing he wanted to talk to me seriously.

"Dico, what do you plan to do when you grow up?" he said.

Somehow I was sure he expected me to say I wanted to be a professional football player like him when I grew up, like my unknown Uncle Francisco had been. I was positive he expected me to have forgotten my earlier resolve. But instead I said, at once:

"I'm going to be an aviator and fly airplanes."

To my surprise, Dondinho seemed completely satisfied.

"Good enough," he said, and he sounded sincere, "but do you know what you have to do to become an aviator?"

"Of course," I said, amazed that Dondinho would think I didn't know. "You have to learn to fly an airplane."

Dondinho smiled at me affectionately.

"That comes later, I'm afraid. Aviators have to know how to read maps, you know; they have to be able to navigate to get from one place to another without getting lost. Don't you think it would help you if you knew how to read and write, and understood arithmetic and science and things like that?"

I hadn't considered it before, but now that Dondinho mentioned it, it made sense. I had no aversion to going to school; as a matter of fact, the more I thought about it, the better the idea struck me. Reading, for example, could prove useful. If you knew how to read, you wouldn't have to depend on the scratchy radio and only follow one football game at a time; if you could read you could follow the accounts in the Baurú *Daily Journal* and keep up to date on all the league games and all your favorite players. I decided, in fact, that there were probably other reasons for knowing how to read and write if one really looked for them. But there were problems.

"But—*Papai*—what about my shoeshining?"

"After school you can still get to the station before the train comes in."

"But—my football?"

Dondinho smiled faintly.

"If I know you—with school, with shoeshining, with helping me here at the clinic, and with you doing your school homework—you'll still manage to find time for football." He winked at me. "You're still my son. ..."

So began my school career. In Baurú, school consisted of four years of what was called primary school followed by four years of secondary—or *ginásio*—which brought one to what would be the second year of high school in the United States. Then, if one wished to go to the university, one had an additional three years of what was called *collegial,* or preparatory school, in preparation for university. Because of the compacted lower and middle years, my age—eight—was not unusual for entering.

When I look back, now, on the excitement and anticipation with which I walked into the Ernesto Monte Primary School that first day, I find it hard to believe I had so much trouble there. My clothes were all newly and neatly patched, I had been scrubbed until I tingled all over, I was wearing my Sunday shoes (polished to a brilliant shine, naturally), I had a real school case in my hand furnished with two blank notebooks and a box of colored pencils, and my heart was pure and my resolve to learn was as the resolve of ten.

The first thing I learned was that the teacher seemed to be less interested in teaching you how to read and write and figure maps and the other things I wanted to know in order to become an aviator as soon as possible, as she was in enforcing discipline. Our teacher, Dona Cida, apparently felt one could never learn to read if one whispered in class, and learning to write if one squirmed in his seat was clearly impossible. The fact that despite my talking and squirming, I was learning everything she was teaching did nothing to change her mind. Still, I must admit that Dona Cida merely scolded. She didn't go to the extremes of punishment I was to know later in my school life.

But an eight-year-old with any kind of imagination learns one way or another, in school or out. One lesson I remember very clearly. One afternoon—it must have been either after school or on a nonschool day, because that was the one year when I didn't cut classes—we were playing near the local hospital when one of the gang went to peek in a window that fronted on an area where we were kicking a ball. It was a basement window and looked down into what seemed to be the morgue. At that particular moment several doctors were in the process of stripping the clothing from an aviator who had died in a glider crash near the Aero Club, preparing to do an autopsy on him. I don't remember exactly which of the kids discovered the gruesome affair, but I can still hear his excited yell:

"Hey, gang! There's a guy on the table down there! I bet he's dead!"

The macabre fascination in his voice brought us all running and I shoved my way through to press my nose against the streaked glass with the others. I got there just in time to see one of the doctors try to pull the shiny leather jacket from one of the flaccid arms. I remember the dinginess of the room, the tile walls much dirtier than Dondinho would have permitted, the linoleum on the floor that had holes in it and should have been replaced, the same standard forty-watt bulbs, barely suitable for the work they were trying to do. The jacket sleeve stuck—from coagulated blood, I was suddenly sure, from all my extensive experience at the clinic—and the doctor pulled harder, raising the arm and twisting it. I don't know how it happened, but the movement brought a sudden gush of blood from the dead man's mouth. It flooded the wall, running down in crimson streaks, staining his mouth obscenely, dripping from the edge of the table to the floor. The doctor hastily dropped the arm and jumped back, startled. I was petrified, and when I turned to get violently sick, the rest of the gang had fled in terror.

For a long time after this experience I would wake at night, screaming, frightened by the nightmare of dreaming the scene over and over again, except that instead of the dead glider pilot on the table it was me, my arm being raised and twisted, my blood pumping out of me to spurt against the already-stained wall, to run down my cheek to soak my nightshirt and clog my throat and choke me. I could see the doctor's face, feel his hands on me, sense the growing weariness as my blood left me, and my screams would become hysterical. Dona Celeste would come hurrying into the room and turn on the light. She would hold my head against her breast until I stopped my shaking, and then she would hold my hand and murmur soothingly to me until I could fall asleep again.

From that moment I never had to be told not to go to the Aero Club again, and from that moment I dropped the idea of ever becoming an aviator. Every time I get into an airplane, which is very often, I try my best not to think about that scene I witnessed through that hospital basement window.

It was about that time everyone began to call me Pelé. I have no idea where the name came from, or who started it, because it has no meaning in Portuguese—or any other language, as far as I know. I've been back to Baurú many times, and have asked all my old friends from those days, but they also have no clue as to its origin or exactly when it started. They say it just began one day and after that it stuck because it seemed to fit, whatever that means. At the time, though, I know that I hated it and it was the cause of many fights at school. I must have lost most of them, because the name stuck.

One friend said it may have been given me inadvertently by one of the many Turks who lived in Baurú. They ran many of the businesses and some lived near us. According to this friend, he thought it possible that whenever I'd accidentally touch the ball with my hands, they would say, "Pé—le," meaning "foot" in Portuguese, and possibly "stupid" in Turkish; or maybe what they considered "stupid" in our language. Another story had it that there was once a famous player in Minas called "Belé" and that when I was a child trying to say his name, it came out "Pelé." The truth is I don't remember ever trying to say "Belé." I have no idea where the name "Pelé" came from. All I know is that from the time I was nine or so, I was Pelé to everyone I know, except to my family, who continue to call me Dico to this day.

Names, of course, are the cheapest things around, so even the most poverty-stricken Brazilian can afford to be generous with them. And he is. He is equally generous with nicknames, possibly for the same reason, and very few of the nicknames have any meaning. "Dico" is a common nickname for Edson, although I would not be surprised to discover ten other nicknames for the same name. Nor do I know why Zoca was the nickname my brother earned when his baptized name was Jair. I sometimes have a strong feeling that nicknames—especially short nicknames—were either invented, or at least encouraged, by radio announcers. A Brazilian radio announcer, describing an important football game, sounds like a hysterical machine gun with the stutters gone mad. It helps him a good deal, of course, to have players called Pelé, Didi, Vavá, or Pepe. I can hardly picture a radio announcer using the full imaginative range of the average Brazilian father in his broadcast:

"... *Edson Arantes do Nascimento receives the ball from Sebastião da Silva Tenorio Texeira Araujo and passes it to*

Valdemar João Mendes de Morais, Filho, who dribbles it past Artur Ribeiro Carvalho José Brito to pass it to Ruy Moreira Acácio Guimarães, who heads it ..."

The game would be half over and the crowds all going out for a beer before he finished describing one play!

Chapter 3

Göteborg, Sweden—June 1958

I still cannot sleep. The excitement of the game with Russia is still within me. I stare at the ceiling and consider my luck.

I was extremely lucky to be in Sweden for the matches, at all. I had been injured in a game before leaving Brazil and never expected to be taken along with the rest of the team when it seemed clear to me I wouldn't be able to play. The final team that goes to the World Cup is reduced to twenty-two players maximum, one player for each position and one reserve. Under those restrictions, deadwood can scarcely be tolerated. But both Dr. Hilton Gosling, the team physician, and Mário Américo, the team masseur, and a most important man on a professional football team, were certain I would get better in time to contribute to the team's effort.

I remember as if it were yesterday the day I was selected for the preliminary tryout for the Brazilian national team; it is scarcely something any football player could ever forget. I had played with a selection of Brazilian players before, in the Copa Roca, a traditional meet between selected players of Argentina and Brazil. The Brazilian team had been selected by their coach, the great Silvio Pirilo; we had lost the first game, 2–1, and won the second, 2–0, and I had scored a goal in each game. It was a great honor to be selected for that group, but it still wasn't the same thing as being asked to try out for the team that would compete against the best in the world for the World Cup.

I had been playing for Santos on a regular basis for almost a year at the time, and playing well. Del Vecchio, the regular center-forward of the team, alternated with me at the position, but although I didn't play in every game I was still the leading scorer of the team. In fact, I led the state of São Paulo in goals that year, with thirty-two. Still, I never really thought I would be picked to play for Brazil in the World Cup. I was, after all, still only sixteen years old, and Brazil was full of top players who were more mature, more experienced, and less likely to crack under the tremendous pressure of playing for the Selection.

Anyway, this fine day I was in Baurú, visiting my family. I was alone in the house at the moment, listening to a sports broadcast on Radio Bandeirantes (by this time we could afford a radio that picked up São Paulo as well as Rio de Janeiro, which hadn't always been true), when I heard the announcer say something about the invitations to the Brazilian Selection. I got up quickly and walked over, bending over the radio, listening intently. I didn't want to miss a word. When he started to rustle his papers before reading the list, I felt myself grow cold. I knew I wouldn't hear my name. I promised myself I wouldn't cry, or kick the furniture, or pound my head against the wall if I wasn't mentioned, but I wasn't sure. Oh, I knew how young I was, and I knew I only had one year of professional football behind me instead of the ten years most of the top players had, but I could always hope, couldn't I?

The announcer began with that deep, pompous, pontifical tone that all Latin American radio announcers have. If a player doesn't have an *r* in his name they can roll for five minutes, they feel cheated:

"... Castilho ... Gilmarrrrrrrrr ... Djalma Santos ... Nilton Santos ... Mazzola ... Pelé ..."

I didn't even hear the rest. I found myself back in my chair, trembling violently, wondering if I had really heard it or had allowed my imagination to tell me what I wanted to hear. But the list was being repeated, and so was my name. And at that moment my mother walked into the room. She took one look at my face and frowned with concern.

"What's the matter with you, Dico? Are you coming down with something?"

I could hardly get the words out. My teeth were chattering.

"Mama! I've been invited to play with the Brazilian Selection!"

I might have been speaking Greek for all the understanding in her look. I said it again.

"Don't you understand, Mama? *I have been invited to play with the Brazilian Selection!*"

I doubt if she even heard me.

"Let me feel your forehead," Dona Celeste said worriedly. "You don't look at all well!"

The 1958 Brazilian Selection was the most completely serviced of any selection to that time. In addition to the coach and his staff, and the man in charge of physical preparation, there was also a full-time doctor, a full-time dentist, masseurs and assistants, and even a psychologist. We also had more players than we were allowed to take into the World Cup matches. One of the tragedies of the selection system as it is usually operated is that many more players are invited than are eventually retained, and a number must be cut from the roster when the final selection is made. All of us who had been invited had trained like demons, we had all followed orders implicitly, we had sacrificed all personal lives for the life of the team, we had worked like horses—harder than most horses—and had come to feel like a family. Now there were going to be some deaths in that family.

Each man who had been invited was a star, a crack player, but the responsibility of determining which of these many stars could best play together as a *team,* and therefore remain, lay with our coach, Vicente Feola. Now the time had finally come, after months of training, when the cut was to be made. Everyone was too nervous to think. Veterans of past championships, veterans of past World Cup matches, were biting their lips, sweating—so one can imagine the fear we newcomers felt. We stood and waited, our knees pressed together as tightly as we could, our kidneys quaking.

Dr. Paulo Machado de Carvalho, the head of the Brazilian delegation, had brought us all together in a large room; at his side stood Feola, with whom and for whom we had worked so hard. Dr. Paulo began with a speech, but I didn't hear a single word of it and I doubt if anyone else did, either. We were waiting for only one thing. Then Feola spoke, probably complimenting everyone on their hard work and thanking them for their co-operation, although again I can't be sure because I wasn't listening. I was only listening to my own fears running around inside my head and stomach like crazy mice, while at the same time trying to compose a proper excuse to give them back home when I went back there, rejected.

Dr. Paulo couldn't avoid the issue any longer, and with a long face he finally began to read the list of those who had been cut. My name was not called, and for a moment I wondered if possibly he had read the names of those who were to remain. When it came to me that I was actually on the final selection, my relief was indescribable. Then an even greater emotion took over as I looked at those who had been on the list. Most of them were crying openly, unable to stop, their fists clenched to keep them from trembling or from pounding something or somebody. Luisinho, the star forward from Corinthians of São Paulo, was there, his face white, his eyes staring in disbelief; Gino, one of the greatest center-forwards Brazil had ever produced, was standing with tears streaming down his cheeks, stunned by the shock of being eliminated. Dr. Paulo and Coach Feola looked as if they, too, were about to cry; then they turned and abruptly left the room. We followed in dead silence. And when those who had been cut got on the bus to go back to São Paulo and wherever they would go from there, nobody knew how to properly tell them good-by.

It is very difficult—in fact, it is impossible—to argue with the decision of a coach in his selection or rejection of a player in the Brazilian system. The coach is picked by the CBD—the Brazilian Commission of Sports—and from then on his word is law. There are few greater authorities on this earth than that of a coach of a Brazilian Selection. He picks the players he wants, trains them as he wants—and the only way an order of his can be challenged is by replacing him. But this does not mean that a lot of newspaper reporters, as well as those indefatigable Monday morning quarterbacks, do not make the charge that the coach was either prejudiced or blind or insane—or venal—in making his final choices.

In São Paulo there were many people who thought that a great injustice had been done to Luisinho, of Corinthians. He had a tremendous reputation in those days, although I must confess that in our training and in the practice games we played before the cut I never attempted to analyze whether Luisinho was better than the others (including me), worse than the others, or about the same as the others. He had to be good to even be there, and I know we all gave our very best during the training period. I know it would never have occurred to me to question a decision of Vicente Feola, and not just because I had remained and not been cut. I would have wanted to crawl into a hole and pull it in after me had I been cut, but I know I would have accepted it, if only because there wasn't a single thing you could do about it.

Apparently the people of São Paulo, all the many millions of them, felt differently. The wave of protest over the rejection of Luisinho—on the radio, on the television, in the newspapers, the magazines, on the street—was tremendous, and to make matters worse, some idiot arranged a training game, almost on the eve of our departure for Europe and the World Cup games with—of all teams—Corinthians! It was a great chance for Luisinho to prove to the world that Vicente Feola and the CBD were insane to leave him out of their calculations.

I remember that game very well; it came close to ending my young career before it got started. The game was being played in Pacaembú Stadium in São Paulo, the largest stadium in the state at the time, and at that time the second largest in the country, and it was loaded to the gutters. When the Brazilian Selection entered the stadium—and we were supposedly the cream of Brazilian football and the heroes who were shortly to fight for our country—we were greeted with the biggest booing I can remember in my life. All of São Paulo must have heard it. I think that everyone in São Paulo, whether normally a fan of Corinthians or not, had by now become convinced by the newspaper and radio propaganda that the honor of the city itself was at stake, that the city of São Paulo itself had been robbed, and that those of us who had managed somehow to make the team were the ones who had personally done this terrible thing to Luisinho and the Bandeirante capital. And when Corinthians came trotting out on the field the place exploded. Everyone was screaming.

"Corinthians! Luisinho! Corinthians! Luisinho!"

One would have thought that Corinthians was the Brazilian Selection and that we were Uruguay or some other deadly enemy in the finals of a World Cup match!

Orlando was the man whose position as a back gave him the assignment to defend against Luisinho, the one who was supposed to contain the great Corinthians star. I know Orlando was nervous before the game, but then we all were. It would look pretty bad for the Selection to lose to any Brazilian club team; we were supposed to be the best. But there was nothing to worry about; Vicente Feola, whether we knew it or not, had molded us into a truly great team. Corinthians never had a chance to get properly started. Our defense made them look like what they were, just another club team among hundreds, while our attack demonstrated the accuracy and wisdom of Feola's choices.

By the time we led them 3–1 some of the crowd began to cheer for us, which took a bit of courage in that partisan crowd; but the fact was we *were* the Brazilian Selection, we *were* going to Sweden to fight for Brazil—for all Brazil, including the city of São Paulo—and we were also slaughtering Corinthians. I made our second goal and Orlando handled Luisinho with ease. The great star of Corinthians accomplished exactly nothing throughout the entire game.

But it might not have been such a great idea to overpower them; it got them irritated. The ball was passed to me and I was just in the mood to jam one right down their throats. I took the ball on a fast dribble through their intermediary and right to their goal area, avoiding the majority of their defense—at which point Ari Clemente, of Corinthians, apparently tired of being ineffective and probably even more tired of this young upstart, Pelé, came down on me like a wagonload of bricks. The next thing I knew I was on the ground in agony; my right knee felt as if some giant hand had twisted it off. Mário Américo, whose job it was to see to our physical well-being, tore out onto the field like a maniac. When he got through screaming at Ari, he bent over me anxiously, massaging the knee carefully.

"What do you think, Pelé? Can you go on?"

I certainly wasn't about to say no. We had been awarded a free kick on Ari's fouling me, and I wanted to be the one to stuff it down their neck. I nodded assent and Mário Américo helped me to my feet. I pressed my foot against the ground, testing the knee. It hurt, but I still didn't want to leave the game, definitely not before I had made the score 4–1. But when I went to kick the point, the knee simply collapsed and I found myself on the ground again. And the score stayed where it was.

Not that my goal attempt was so important, because the rest of the team went on to wipe Corinthians out. The final score was 5–1, but I wasn't there to see it. I was in the dressing room with Dr. Gosling and Mário Américo, looking from one to the other, hoping they'd tell me my knee was fine and that I was just imagining the pain. Dr. Hilton Gosling would make an excellent poker player; his face was totally devoid of expression as he patted my shoulder and spoke to Mário Américo.

"Put some ice on it for now. I'll examine it in detail later."

Mário nodded and started the treatment, talking all the time.

"Don't worry about it, kid. Leave it to Daddy. I'll have you chasing girls again in no time!"

It sounded very nice, but I didn't believe him. I had a cold feeling in my stomach that when the plane took off for Sweden, someone else would be taking the ride instead of me. I knew what a similar accident had done to Dondinho and how it had affected his career, his whole life. Oddly enough, I felt no anger against Ari; in fact I didn't even think about him until later, when the reporters and the radio commentators began a polemic.

From the Rio papers: "Ari did it on purpose ...!"

From the São Paulo papers: "The Rio papers are prejudiced! Ari would never do a thing like that on purpose ...!"

The truth is to this day I have no idea if Ari fouled me on purpose or by accident, and after all these years I doubt if Ari himself knows. All I do know is that I had endless treatments and endless examinations, always facing Dr. Gosling's expressionless face, and it wasn't until I was actually on the plane that I was sure I would be going to Europe with the squad. That didn't mean, of course, that I still couldn't be dropped from the team and another man flown over from Brazil to take my place; until the final six games substitutions were permitted.

On the plane and in Italy, our first stop, I began to forget the knee for a while and start to enjoy myself. The team was like a big family—Mazzola, Garrincha, Didi, Zagalo, Mauro—everyone.

There were never any arguments or disagreements, and Mário Trigo, our dentist, always had a joke to entertain. I never saw Mário Trigo when he was not in a good mood, but as Garrincha said:

"Why shouldn't he be happy? He's behind the chair, not in it!"

In Italy we played friendly games first with Internationale and later with Fiorentina, both exhibition games, and we won them both—but I was on the bench for both and I was getting more discouraged every day. The knee seemed to stay the same despite the treatments, and the picture of Dondinho and the result of his injury loomed larger and larger in my mind. I also began to appreciate, probably for the first time, exactly the full extent of the sacrifice Dondinho had made for his family. I wanted to play, but I wasn't being forced to—in fact I wasn't allowed to—but my father had gone out onto the field and done his best, game after game, with a knee that must have tortured him, just to put bread on the table.

Before we went to Sweden from Italy, I went in to see Dr. Paulo, the head of the Brazilian delegation. I told him the knee didn't seem to be getting any better, and I didn't want to see our team enter the finals a man short, so why not ship me back to Brazil and get a proper replacement? He looked at me coolly:

"Pelé—you don't make those decisions, and neither do I. Dr. Gosling is here just to answer questions like that. Let's hear what he has to say."

So there was another examination. Dr. Gosling frowned.

"Well, the truth is the knee hasn't healed as fast as I'd hoped. That's a fact. But I'm sure you can still play, at least in some of the games, if you have the guts to undergo a really tough treatment. Well? Do you?"

There wasn't much one could say except to be grateful and agree. And when Dr. Gosling said the treatment was tough, he was not exaggerating. Mário Américo and his assistant, Chico de Assis, would boil water until it could warp steel, dip towels into the steaming affair, and then somehow manage to wrap them around my knee without having their fingers fall off. Pepe and Didi, who had also injured their knees in the games against the Italian team, joined me. The three of us would sit there, tears coming from our eyes from the pain of those steaming towels, but not one of us dreaming of opening our mouth to complain.

And every day the doctor would examine my knee again, and every day he would nod in his noncommittal manner and say the knee was coming along fine, but when the roster was posted for the first of our final games, against Austria, I was still on the bench. And the same was true when we went against England. On the other hand, stars like Zito and Garrincha and Djalma Santos were also on the bench as reserves and they hadn't even been injured, so I suppose I really had small cause for complaint. But that didn't stop me from complaining loudly and clearly—but only to myself. I wanted desperately to play, but complaining wasn't the way to get on the field.

And then came that beautiful day when Dr. Gosling looked up from his examination and nodded.

"You can play."

And that's when our team psychologist got into the act!

Our new psychologist was named Prof. João Carvalhaes. He was a pleasant-enough person, who wandered about studying us all idly, as it were, usually dressed in a gray sweater and either forgetting to shave, or unshaven because he preferred it that way. He explained that he was not in favor of addressing the players as a group, as little was ever accomplished in this manner. On the other hand, to talk to the players as individuals often made them nervous, increased their problems, and made any diagnosis unreliable. Instead, his method was to have the players all draw pictures of a man. The players with the most sophistication—if we had any on the Selection—would draw the most complicated and detailed figures; the least sophisticated would be apt to draw skeletal childlike line sketches. His theory was that one of each of these two types should work well in the wing positions. (He never explained his theories, he merely expounded them.) A further theory of his was that forwards should be defensive while defenders should have an aggressive attitude but be able to control it. He claimed he could differentiate between the types by the manner in which they drew his favorite art subject, man.

On the basis of his tests he reported to Feola that it was obvious that putting Garrincha into the game would be a mistake, as Garrincha's lack of sophistication went even beyond the limits imposed by the theory. And as for me:

"Pelé," he said, "is obviously infantile. He lacks the necessary fighting spirit. He is too young to feel the aggressions and respond with the proper force to make a good forward. Besides, he has not gotten the feeling of responsibility so necessary for team play. No, he definitely should not play."

Fortunately for me—and for Garrincha, and for the team as a whole—either Vicente Feola didn't understand what the man was saying or, understanding, treated it as all Brazilians treat most statements from others. Brazilians have a tendency not to believe anybody on any subject, and Coach Feola proved to be no exception. He listened to the psychologist go through his arguments, and then he would nod his head.

"You may be perfectly right. The only thing is, you don't know anything about football. When Pelé's knee is ready, he plays!"

And so, when the third game came up, the game against Russia, I finally found my name on the roster of those who were to play. Still, I must make an addition to the story of Prof. João Carvalhaes. This was his first attempt at the use of psychology in relation to the game of football, and in later years he was the first to admit he made mistakes in the beginning. In time, his theories developed to a point where there is no doubt they contributed much to the game of football, and much to the development of young football players, and I should not like to speak of the good professor without mentioning these facts.

Chapter 4

Göteborg, Sweden—June 1958

After the game with Russia and before we met our next opponent, Wales, life returned to its familiar rhythm: daily training, treatment for players injured in the game with the USSR as well as in earlier games, a daily bout with the steaming towels for me—because while the knee allowed me to play it was still not 100 per cent—strategy meetings, some recreation, and, of course, interviews. Our victory over Russia had brought us to the attention of the sporting world, and reporters swarmed over us, interested in a team as young as we were, and especially one sporting the youngest player in the games.

Pepe remained on the injured list, but even if he had not, I doubt he would have been listed for our game with Wales. Most commentators were of the opinion that Feola would be foolish to change a winning combination, although I am sure their comments made little impression on Feola. He did, however, have to replace Vavá, who had been hurt in the game with the USSR. Mazzola, who had been hurt playing against England, and who had been replaced by Vavá, now came back into the line-up, but otherwise the team was left intact.

I must give a good deal of credit to those who were called upon to remain on the bench, injured or not. Mauro, for example, was the reserve for Belini; he was a top player—many said he was better than our captain—but he remained on the bench without a complaint. The same was true of Castilho, our reserve goalkeeper, as well as Djalma Santos, the reserve for De Sordi. I never heard one word of envy or jealousy or anger because a player wasn't given a chance to show what he could do. It's true we all wanted to win, but I'm not sure I could have sat on the bench once I was in condition, without feeling resentment against *somebody* for not being on the field.

When the day arrived for us to play against Wales in the quarter-finals, we were the favorites. Nobody really believed that Wales could give us much trouble, and with all the praise we received from the newspapers and the other media, I'm afraid we began to believe it ourselves. Confidence is good, even necessary, but overconfidence can be a dangerous thing. We went back to the Nya Ullevi Stadium convinced we had nothing to worry about, and that the game would simply be an easy warm-up for whoever we would be called upon to face in the semifinals.

Possibly because of this overconfidence—or just possibly because the Welsh team had been greatly underrated, despite the newspaper articles—we found ourselves in the toughest struggle of the entire tournament to that point. Jack Kelsey, the Welsh goalkeeper, while not as big as the Russian Iachine, always seemed to be just where our kicks went, catching them, blocking them, tipping them over the crossbar, all with a calmness that was uncanny. In our anxiety we also missed many opportunities, sending the ball into the side posts, or over the top of the net, and when the first period ended we went back to the dressing room with the score tied at 0–0.

There was an air of preoccupation in the dressing room, and it was deserved. It was all very well to consider that throughout the tournament to that point nobody had managed to penetrate our defense, nobody had as yet scored on that great combination of Nilton Santos, Belini, De Sordi, Orlando, and Gilmar—and it didn't look as if Wales could or would—but the sad fact was that we already had one tie with England on our record and we couldn't stand another tie if we wanted to get into the semifinals. We had to win!

Coach Feola gave us new instructions, to which we listened attentively, although we could see nothing in the new instructions that would make Jack Kelsey or the rest of the Welsh defense any less effective. Dr. Paulo Machado de Carvalho, the head of our commission, told us he had complete confidence that we would come through in the second half, as did Paulo Amaral, our trainer, and everyone else on the Technical Commission, down to the massage experts. The only thing they didn't tell us was how to break through that stone wall defense of Wales!

We went back to the field full of determination, but the Welsh must have had a similar pep talk in the locker room during the interval, because their defense seemed equally determined, and the game appeared to be a duplicate of the first period. It seemed that time was running as fast as we were—faster, in fact—and we were getting nowhere. It began to get discouraging. The harder we tried, the more goals we missed. I lost chances, Mazzola lost chances, as did Didi, Garrincha, and Zagalo. None of us felt very happy. We could see the championship slipping away from us by the minute.

And then, suddenly, there was that opportunity we had been waiting for. We had brought the ball down into their penalty area and Didi had the ball. He passed it to me on the run with that incredible accuracy of his when I was only a few feet from the goal area. I was about to kick when I saw a foot swooping down to tackle the ball. I touched the ball lightly, bouncing it toward me as the foot passed beneath; I let the ball fall and kicked it. To my disappointment I saw Kelsey dive to intercept, but just as he seemed sure to block the point, the ball struck the foot of another defender and skidded past Kelsey into the net.

I have no idea how many times I ran and jumped, ran and jumped, all the while screaming *Gooooooaaaaaaallllll!!!!!!!!* like a maniac. I had to get rid of that tremendous pressure of relief, of joy, of I don't know what was inside of me! I was crying like a baby, babbling, while the rest of the team pummeled me, almost suffocating me. That was certainly my most unforgettable goal—my luckiest, as has been said, possibly—but definitely my most unforgettable. It was the goal that was most decisive for our Selection, for it ensured our continuing in the World Cup games.

The more difficult a victory, the greater the happiness in winning. After the game, back at the hotel, we read and heard on the radio that we were fortunate to have won at all, that our attack was weak, that only our defense saved us from being murdered, that I should be ashamed of accepting a goal that was practically given me by the Welsh team(!). When we heard all this we laughed like hyenas, partly in relief because to a certain extent it was true, but mostly because, after all, we were the ones who had sweated out those ninety minutes of almost unbearable tension, and we had won! I doubt if, at that moment, any of us gave a thought to how badly the other team must have felt to lose such a close game; the truth is they had an excellent defense, Kelsey was a wonderful goalkeeper—but they hadn't won. We did. And that's the way football is.

At the hotel we also learned that France had won and would therefore be our opponent in the semifinals a few days later.

So—come on, France!

Before my starting against Russia, only the Brazilian reporters or commentators had known who I was or had come to interview me, and especially to ask how the knee was coming along and if I thought I'd get to play. But after the game with Russia, and even more so after the game with Wales, things changed. I was being interviewed with the same regularity as the older and more famous names on our team. It left me a bit confused, I'll admit—I was still only seventeen years old and away from my home country for the first time—but I must also admit I liked it. I knew that in Brazil, in Baurú, my family and friends were following events here very closely, by way of radio and newspapers, and it was exciting to think of their reading and hearing about me. It was good to know that I hadn't done anything on the field to make them ashamed of me—at least not yet.

Swedish girls, with hair so blond I had only seen the like on dolls in store windows, came to talk to me, to ask for my autograph, and at times to rub their hands on my arms and face. Some seemed surprised, as if they found it odd that my color didn't run. I took a lot of kidding from the others on the team.

"Tell them it doesn't come off, Pelé! You can go out into the rain without worry!" Or: "You'll be safe with him, lady. Nobody will know. He doesn't run. ..."

They would look at whatever girl I was with and say sadly:

"Even a bath doesn't help him, lady."

One girl in particular I remember; her name was Lena. We were both seventeen, a very romantic age. She would come to the hotel and we would go walking, hand in hand, thrilled with each other's different color, and happy to be together. I remember she cried when we left, and I remember what a big man it made me feel to have a girl, a beautiful girl, crying because I wouldn't be there. Seventeen is a marvelous age, but one which unfortunately ends after a mere 365 days!

Garrincha at this time was the superstar of the team because of the way he made the Russian defense look foolish with his extraordinary ball handling in that game. He was married and with four or five children at the time, but at times he acted more childlike than me. But we were all so worked up, so filled with our own importance, that it was impossible to merely act nonchalant.

Still, in our training sessions and in the daily discussions we had with Coach Feola leading the talks, we gave serious thought to the French team. We knew of Fontaine, Kopa,

Piantoni, and Vincent, the formidable forward wall of the French, all men who were extremely dangerous no matter how good one's defense might be; up to that point in the tournament their attack had resulted in more goals than any other team. Feola pointed out to us that everyone had expected France to be weak—but now they were winning, and winning by large scores, they had confidence and would prove difficult. Still, he added, we could beat them and we would. We didn't need to be told. We had come this far and we didn't plan on being stopped by France or anyone else!

We traveled to Stockholm, where the game was to be played in the Solna Stadium. When we trotted onto the field I felt perfectly calm, and looking around, it seemed to me the rest of the team did, as well. Vavá was back in charge of our attack, and somehow I was pleased with this. I seemed to work a little better in harmony with Vavá than Mazzola, which is certainly not to take anything from Mazzola. It's simply that inner recognition a player has as to a feeling of greater accord on the field with one player rather than another, and it usually results in more goals.

The game had barely started when a combination play from Didi to Garrincha to me to Vavá resulted in a goal, catching France by surprise. I was sure at the time that this goal, made only in the second minute of play, would have a demoralizing effect on France, but if anything, the opposite occurred. In the ninth minute of play Fontaine found an unprotected corridor through our defense, made a remarkable dribble down it, and when Gilmar went to meet the attack, Fontaine calmly kicked the ball past him into the net.

This was the first goal that had been made against Gilmar—against the Brazilian defense—in the entire tournament, the first goal permitted in four tough games, and we all felt the impact. We had come to believe that whatever else happened, at least we were safe from being scored upon, and here we had just seen it happen! While the French were congratulating Fontaine, I dashed into the net, retrieved the ball, ran to the center of the field with it, placed it down, and screamed:

"Let's go! Let's get started! Let's quit wasting time!"

The rest of my team stared at me. The action was certainly out of place for the newest and youngest member of the team, but it was completely automatic on my part. I wanted the game to get started so we could go ahead again; the clock in football doesn't stop for a small thing like a goal, and the time was running on.

But for the next ten minutes after play resumed, nothing went right. Our passes to our teammates went to our opponents instead, our kicks never came close to the net, our dribbling was amateurish, when we feinted to draw off an opponent all we fooled was a teammate—in short, it was bad! Twice I had chances to break the tie and twice I missed the net entirely; Vavá was off-target, Garrincha was kicking poorly, and the French, now firmly believing in their superiority, attacked unmercifully.

Then, to make things worse—if possible—Garrincha finally executed a goal but before we would even begin screaming, the referee's whistle called it back, claiming Garrincha was offside at the time! It was absurd, and the cries of protest from the stands clearly indicated that the crowd agreed with us—but no referee in any sport takes back a decision, right or wrong. I felt a cold rage sweep through me, such as I thought I had learned to control, but before I could run for the referee and at least voice my disapproval, or before any of the others could do the same, Belini was there, shouting at us, almost barking, angry.

"Calm down! Take it easy! No complaints, not a word! Don't give this character an excuse to throw somebody out of the game!"

This was in the days when there were *no* substitutions for *any* reason in a World Cup game—there are only two substitutions for any reason today—and being thrown off the field was to give your opponents a tremendous edge. So we swallowed our anger, but we never forgot it. I had heard that

European referees didn't like Brazilians—either our color or our skills—and that their adverse decisions had hurt us in past World Cup games. This offside call against Garrincha seemed to me to bear out these claims. We were seething, but we kept our mouths shut and tried to take out our anger on the ball—with the result, of course, that we played even worse.

Then, as if in compensation for the offside call, we got a break. Bob Jonquet, the French center-half, was injured and had to be carried from the field; two minutes later Didi took advantage of the weakened center and started down the field with me running alongside on the left and Garrincha on the right, and with Vavá within easy passing distance. Everyone expected Didi to pass the ball off, since he had such fantastic ability at moving the ball where he wanted, but he fooled them all by taking it through their defense himself, with everyone spread out to intercept Garrincha, Vavá, or me. Abbes, the French goalkeeper, couldn't take a chance on such a pass, and his indecision was what Didi had been waiting for. A quick feint and then the kick; Abbes tried to twist and throw himself in the direction of the ball but he was out of position and knew it.

Gooooooaaaaaaallllll!!!!!!!! Brazil!!!!!!!!!!!!

We ran over and smothered Didi, with the French team now calling sharply for the game to get started. Now it was they who didn't want to waste time getting back the goal they had just lost. But time in the half was running out and the period ended that way: Brazil 2, France 1.

When we came out for the second half our full confidence had returned; we were tranquil again. With our defense, that one-goal advantage should prove enough, but that didn't mean we didn't want more. Almost immediately after play resumed, Vavá kicked into the goal area; Abbes raced out fast to grab the ball, but not fast enough. I had come in on the run when Vavá kicked, and before Abbes could reach the ball and smother it, I had kicked it past him into the net. It was the third goal for Brazil and my second of the tournament. After that the

French made every effort to regain their drive but they were beaten and they must have realized it. Moments later—almost like a television replay of the previous goal—Vavá started the ball toward the net, Abbes dove to intercept, and I was there before him to kick the ball past him into the net. Four to one! We had no fear of possibly losing after that.

One of the French team, undoubtedly angry at the loss he knew his team was facing, came into me with all his force, raising his shoe, kicking me violently in my recently healed knee. I went down, my knee hurting like the devil, and then rolled over to glare at the player with pure hatred. With our team ahead 4–1 and time running out I was in no fear of being thrown out of the game for knocking him down for luck; our team could win without me. The only problem was that the knee was too weak to support me in a fight. Our team came racing over, cursing the player who had kicked me, calling on the referee to indicate what was clearly a foul. But the referee, who had been able to clearly note an offside on Garrincha where none existed, miraculously managed *not* to see my being fouled!

Didi raised his voice, talking to all of us:

"Look, we've got them beaten. We still have the finals to play. Let's not let anyone else get hurt at this stage of the championship!"

We therefore changed our tactics. We had the game won and there really would be little sense in starting that last game with one or more of our top players on the bench or in the hospital, either because of an attack or because of a brawl on the field. So instead of attacking we merely passed the ball back and forth, from me to Vavá to Garrincha to Didi to Zagalo back to Didi to Vavá to Garrincha to me, with the French team getting a bit irritated at our tactics, frustrated in their efforts to tackle the ball, to get control of it. But they had small chance. In ball passing I honestly believe that Brazilian team of 1958 was the best ever assembled, and that Didi was the best who ever lived. The crowd loved every minute of it, and the cheers as we continued to waste the clock by calmly passing the ball from one to another rose to a crescendo.

But while we were passing the ball one to another we also were not adverse to advancing it at the same time through their intermediary, and suddenly I found myself with the ball and the road to the goal almost open. The same Frenchman who had kicked me ran forward to contest the play with me. I lifted the ball with one foot just over his head—what we in Brazil call the "hat" play—and when he skidded to a halt, trying to recover his equilibrium, it dropped behind him, and before it had struck the ground I kicked it. I don't believe Abbes even saw it going into the net. I felt better about that goal than the other two I had scored that day. Kick *me*, will they!

With the game totally sewed up, we went back to our previous tactic, passing the ball from man to man, taking no chances of having a man tackled viciously or kicked either inadvertently or on purpose, and the French became more and more frustrated as they tried to get the ball from us. And then, when the referee was about to blow the final whistle, Piantoni of France managed to get the ball and kick it past Gilmar. At that point we didn't begrudge him the shot or the goal.

The game ended: Brazil 5, France 2.

That night, in our hotel, our happiness was almost complete. One more game and we would have done it! We would have wiped out all the hurt and shame of the previous championships in which Brazil had lost or hadn't even qualified for the finals. Everyone came around to compliment me on my three goals in the game. My knee still hurt from where the Frenchman had kicked me, but still nobody could have been happier than I was. I wondered if Lena had heard back in Göteborg of what I had done that day; then I knew she must have. The whole world must have heard. It was a strange feeling. ...

But there was still that final game.

"Who's the next victim?"

"Sweden! Our host!"

"We'll prove poor guests!"

"They'll be duck soup!"

But as I went to bed that night I made myself promise that I, at least, would try not to be overconfident at the finals. We had thought Wales would be duck soup, and barely came out of that game ahead. And, of course, no Brazilian would ever forget 1950, the only other time Brazil reached the finals, when Uruguay was also supposed to have been duck soup. ...

Chapter 5

Stockholm, Sweden—June 29, 1958

When we came to the finals against the Swedish team, we were the favorites, which was to be expected after our 5–2 victory over the strong French team. We were the favorites, that is, with those who were not prejudiced in Sweden's favor—which included the Swedish newspapers, their radio, and, of course, their fans. The Swedes had a good deal going for them; the field was theirs, the crowd was solidly behind them, and we also weren't too sure about the sympathy of the referee. We had run into trouble with referees who didn't like Brazilians before.

But we had several things on our side: We had a brand of football that combined great team play with the best of individual talent; and we also had our driving ambition to take the World Cup back to Brazil, which we, at least, were sure was greater than anyone else's ambition.

The Solna Stadium was even more crowded than for the Brazil-France match, and when the national anthem of Brazil was played, I felt even more swept with emotion than the day I heard it standing in my place for the game with

Russia. I trembled as I stood and listened. I suddenly thought of Dondinho, back in Baurú, at this exact moment, sitting before the radio, straining not to miss a sound or a word. What was he feeling? Was he nervous? Of course he was nervous! But was he praying that we on the field in Sweden, at least, were less nervous than he was? And my mother—I knew she would be out of the room, determined not to listen to the game, although I was equally certain that as soon as the game was over she would be deluging Dondinho with questions as to how I was physically and how I had done. She didn't have to listen to the radio to know how the game was going—every goal by Brazil would result in screams of joy from the front room, not to mention the explosion of fireworks all over town, just as every opponent's goal would be greeted by a loud groan heard throughout the house.

The whistle blew, interrupting my tumult of thoughts, bringing me back to the field and the game. Djalma Santos had replaced De Sordi, who had been injured in the game with France; otherwise the team was the same as in our last match. I was happy for Djalma; he had worn the uniform of the Brazilian Selection more times than any other player on the team, but he had had to sit on the bench so far in this tournament, watching but not being asked to participate.

As soon as the game started the Swedes began handling the ball with an expertise we had really not expected, challenging our defense, testing it to the utmost. Somehow, subconsciously, I think we had underestimated the Swedish team, mainly because, being the host country, they had not had to qualify to appear in the final six games. But whether they had qualified automatically or not, they still had to win to get where they were. They had beaten Mexico and Hungary and tied Wales to win their fight, and had then beaten Russia and West Germany, the previous champions, to reach the finals. Somehow I think we had overlooked this. And as their attack developed strongly, our own seemed to falter. Our passes never seemed to go straight, our kicks were erratic, our reactions were slow. The game was only four minutes old when Gren, the Swedish right-forward, passed the ball to Liedholm, the center-forward; Liedholm picked his way past both Djalma Santos and Nilton Santos in the penalty area and beat Gilmar with a low shot into the right-hand corner of the goal. Sweden was ahead, 1–0!

For a moment we were stunned, deaf to the screams of delight from the stands, as if we couldn't believe such a thing could happen to us. It was the first time in the entire tournament that we had been behind. George Raynor, the manager of the Swedish team, had predicted to the news media that if we went down a goal we would, in his words, "panic all over the show," but quite the opposite happened. Didi ran toward the net to retrieve the ball. He picked it up and turned, calling out:

"Let's go!"

Someone else on our team yelled:

"Come on! Let's get started! We're wasting time!"

It was Vavá, but there was no panic in his voice. On the contrary, he was looking excited, as if the Swedish goal was what Brazil had needed all along to pull us out of our slump. We started off again and suddenly I felt a strange calmness I hadn't experienced in any of the other games. It was a type of euphoria; I felt I could run all day without tiring, that I could dribble through any of their team or all of them, that I could almost pass through them physically. I felt I could not be hurt. It was a very strange feeling and one I had never felt before. Perhaps it was merely confidence, but I have felt confident many times without that strange feeling of invincibility. The goal of Sweden, rather than making us "panic all over the show," brought us back to our senses.

Garrincha, on my right, began to do his own particular brand of ball-handling, which is little short of miraculous. He took the ball on a pass from Zito on the right wing, brought it up to Parling, the Swedish back, feinted him out of position, caught Axbom, another back, off-balance with a swerve, and accelerated down the line to pass to Vavá, who was charging in. Vavá disregarded the feet of those attempting to tackle the ball from him and kicked it on the dead run. Svensson, the Swedish goalkeeper, didn't even see the ball go by him.

Gooooooooaaaaaaaaaallllllll!!!!!!!! Brazil!!!!!!!!!!!!!!!

We all ran to smother Vavá but he didn't want to have anything to do with any tactic that might delay the game. After all, we had merely tied; we still had to win. He pushed us all away.

"Let's play ball! We've got them now! Let's move! Let's go!"

But although the score was merely tied, we suddenly knew we really did have them. Our attacks were begun and carried through with complete confidence. Before, Gilmar had been made nervous by the opening goal; now he was his old self, stopping everything in his area, covering all entrances to the goal, shouting encouragement when the play came near him. We knew we were safe with him behind us. It was up to us to make the goals that would ensure the victory.

The game went on tirelessly, the score tied, with nobody gaining any advantage, but we felt sure we would win. We were getting stronger with time, while the steam seemed to be going out of the Swedish effort. But we weren't scoring goals, and getting stronger by itself doesn't win games. Then Garrincha repeated his previous play; once again he left the opponent's left flank standing and once again Vavá was ready when the ball was passed to him on his charge. *Goooaaalll!!!!!* We were ahead. Vavá was crying and laughing insanely at the same time and this time he didn't try to stop us from swarming all over him.

That was the way the half ended: Brazil 2, Sweden 1.

In the dressing room during the interval Coach Feola finally got us to keep quiet and listen to him.

"We're going to win this game and take the championship back to Brazil. If we don't lose."

We stared at him, puzzled. He went on evenly.

"By that I mean the Swedes can't beat us. The only ones who can beat us now are ourselves. Let's try not to do it."

We went back to the field thinking over Feola's words. The Swedish team still had the backing of the fans, who kept screaming without stop, trying by sheer volume to convince us to quit and let Sweden tie the game and go on to win. Actually, if Sweden had managed to tie the game at that point due to a mistake on our part, it might well have changed the complexion of the game, possibly even have brought them victory, although that is hard to visualize. But we were aware of that and determined not to make any mistake.

I'm sure both teams lost goals through overanxiousness, but with Brazil pressing the attack constantly, we had to get results. The ball was being passed back and forth, not, this time, to waste time as in the French match, but rather to keep the ball from Sweden until the proper opportunity came to capitalize upon. Nilton Santos was playing a combination of attack and defense, those strong trunklike legs of his churning up and down the field tirelessly—it was Nilton Santos, in our earlier game against Austria, who decided to attack rather than always defend, and made our second goal, a rare thing for defenders in a World Cup game—and now, when he was in Sweden's intermediary he kicked a long high ball toward those of us in the goal area. I stopped it on my thigh, kicked it in the air, whirled, and kicked it toward the goal as it came down. Svensson made a valiant effort to block the ball but it was to his left and it happened too fast for him to adjust. He was stretched out on the ground, his arms outstretched, as the ball went into the net.

I was screaming *Gooooaaaaalllllll!!!!!!!!* and running and jumping in the air with a release of unbearable tension, and then I was being suffocated by my teammates swarming all over me, seemingly trying to break my back, jumping on me from as far away as they could leap, wrapping their arms around my throat, half-strangling me. But I didn't mind; I didn't even feel it. That extra ensurance goal made victory certain.

Brazil 3, Sweden 1.

From the stands the Brazilian fans were keeping up a growing chant, finally making themselves heard over the partisan Swedes: *Samba! Samba!* On the field we were babbling almost hysterically.

"We've got them! We have them beaten!"

"They're done! Finished!"

"We're going to be the world champions! *We're going to be the world champions!*" And under our yelling was always the surprised undertone: "Can you believe it???? *Us?????*"

We were riding high, but the game still had to go on. Zito and Didi were switching play now, Djalma Santos was coming up from full-back to attack, Vavá and myself were passing the ball back and forth, probing their defense, careful not to permit the Swedes to take control at this stage of the game. Zagalo was playing in front; Vavá passed to him and Zagalo went past Boerjesson, the Swedish mid-fielder, then past Bergmark the fullback, and kicked it neatly into the net. It was a work of art, a thing of beauty!

Brazil 4, Sweden 1!

Sweden made a second goal at a moment when our offensive drive had been slowed by our very success, which was not unusual when we had a three-goal advantage. But that goal of Sweden had absolutely no effect on us. We knew now there was no possibility of our losing. The only effect of their goal was to make us tighten our defense again. We passed back and forth, Didi to Garrincha to me to Zagalo to Vavá to Didi, keeping the ball from the disheartened Swedish players. Then, moments before the final whistle, Zagalo kicked into the area. Both the Swedish back and myself went as high as we could, but I out-jumped him and headed the ball past Svensson for the final goal of the game.

As the whistle blew, ending the game and the tournament, I had a strange feeling that I was going to faint. It was over. It was finally over! And we had won! We were the champions of the world! *We were the champions of the world!* I felt my knees collapsing under me and reached out to prevent myself hitting the ground; and then I was being lifted, raised to the shoulders of my teammates and being carried around the field. Everyone was crying; tears streamed from my eyes as I hung on wildly. Gilmar reached up and squeezed my leg.

"Go ahead and cry, *moleque!* It's good for you!"

He was crying as he spoke. Everyone was crying: Belini, Vavá, Zagalo, Djalma Santos, Didi, Nilton Santos—everyone. Mário Américo, wonderful Mário Américo whose healing hand and scalding towels had made it possible for me to play at all, was diving into the net to retrieve the ball from our final goal. The referee—who usually keeps the winning ball in major games in Europe—blew his whistle furiously, and moved as if to intercept Mário, but Mário was already at the mouth of the tunnel, holding the ball in the air, screaming in Portuguese I'm sure the referee didn't understand, even as I'm sure he understood the gesture.

"*Try* to get the ball from me! Just *try!*"

Everyone was on the field: reporters, photographers, radio and television personnel, fans who had poured from the stands undeterred by the police. The police were doing their best to keep the crowds from crushing us. Our captain, Belini, held up his hand for our attention.

"Let's do an Olympic march around the field!"

A Swedish flag suddenly appeared and Belini caught it up and carried it at our head as we marched around the field with the crowds in the stands on their feet, cheering us, and with a mob of fans beside us and behind us. The Brazilians in the stand and on the field were waving Brazilian flags and chanting *Brazil! Brazil!* Reporters and photographers trailed us and ran ahead of us, trying to get pictures as we marched. Once again we heard the Brazilian anthem and then we could see, above the stadium, the Brazilian flag being raised to wave above all the others. The tears continued to flow, leaving trails in the sweat that still covered our faces.

King Gustave of Sweden came down on the field as we ended our Olympic parade; he shook our hands in turn and complimented us on our game. I'm sure he must have felt the loss Sweden suffered that day keenly, but there was no sign of it as he congratulated us. I might say here that of all the countries where we have played, before and since, there has never been a country where the fans are better sports than in Sweden. They cheer their team, but they also recognize other teams as deserving of esteem, which is more than can be said of many countries, particularly those in Latin America.

In the dressing room, when we finally got there, general bedlam prevailed. Dr. Paulo Machado de Carvalho, the head of the Brazilian delegation, hugged each one of us, the tears pouring down his cheeks. Carlos Nascimento, his assistant, Paulo Amaral, our trainer, Vicente Feola, our coach, Mário Trigo, Mário Américo, Dr. Gosling—everyone was shouting, weeping, laughing, all at the same time. Some Russian reporters fought their way into the dressing room to present me with a cup as being the youngest player in the tournament. The television cameras were there, recording the scene; still photographers blinded us with their constant flash bulbs, even following us into the showers.

And when at long last we were finally showered and dressed and went outside to catch our bus to the hotel, the crowds were still waiting, paper and pencils in hand, asking for autographs, and we literally had to fight our way through to get on the bus.

And when, after our victory dinner and the dance that was put on in our honor, and after the fuss that was made over those of us who were *crioulo*—black, and therefore somewhat of a curiosity to our hosts, to the pretended irritation of our whiter teammates, who claimed we were taking unfair advantage of our color—when I finally got to bed I was far too excited to even think of sleeping.

What were they doing in Baurú at this moment? How were they celebrating our victory there? Would Nicola Avalone Júnior, our mayor, come to our house to congratulate my parents? Or would he possibly invite them to his big house? Certainly this victory would make a great difference in all our lives, once I got back to Brazil.

Were they talking about my six goals in the tournament? I knew they were no record; Fontaine of France was the leader in that department with an incredible twelve or thirteen, but I knew my six goals were an achievement to be proud of, and I was equally sure that Dondinho and Zoca would be reliving each goal over and over again, even as I knew I would relive them over and over again when the thrill of victory was a little less acute and when I had the time and the frame of mind to consider the games more objectively. Because no matter how many goals I had made, or our team had made, we had lost far more opportunities for goals than we had made, and when we came to study the films of the games later, we would learn a great deal. But that was for some future date; enough for today to remember that we won. It seemed impossible, but it was true. We were the champions of the world, and I contributed to that victory! We were bringing the Jules Rimet Cup to Brazil for the first time in history!

And then my thoughts turned to Santos and Vila Belmiro, the site of the Santos Football Club, where I had been given my first chance to show what I could do, thanks to a coach of mine named Valdemar de Brito. What a party they must be having there right this moment! It would be almost morning there at this hour, but that wouldn't make any difference! After all, we had three players from the Santos team on the Selection: Zito, Pepe, and myself, and we had done ourselves and our home team proud. I had a feeling that when we finally got back to Brazil, the party would still be in progress.

I reached up, turned off the light, and lay back, reveling in the darkness and that warm knowledge inside of me that we had won. We had done it! Now, after being in Europe more than two months, I was more than ready to go home to Baurú and then back down to Santos, my new home. What a difference between this trip to Santos and my first trip there—when? Eighteen, twenty months ago. Good Lord! Was it that short a time? Then I had been a skinny kid of fifteen, nervous and frightened at being away from home, and here I was, a world champion, completely sophisticated and totally adult—at seventeen! I grinned to myself at the thought and let myself drift off to sleep.

The return trip from the World Cup games in Sweden in 1958, even now after almost twenty years, still seems like a dream. We were all very tired; we had worked hard in training, had played hard on the field, and we were all a bit emotionally unstable, I suppose. We were keyed up and we couldn't wait to get back to Brazil. For most of us it had been our first trip away from our country, and for us the trip had been a long one.

We came back, as we had gone, on a Panair do Brasil plane. It was before the days of jets, of course, and it was a long flight. On the plane one could constantly hear, usually in a peevish voice:

"When the devil do we get there? *Caramba!*"

"Relax. We'll get there." That was usually an older player, accustomed to trips, demonstrating his insouciance.

"We *are* relaxed, dammit! Only when the devil do we get there?"

Then, after most of us were firmly convinced that the pilot was completely lost and that we'd spend the little time we had left flying over water before crashing into it, suddenly there was land ahead and I knew how Columbus, or Pedro Álvares Cabral, felt—or rather, how their sailors felt. Columbus and Cabral were sure there was land ahead; their sailors were not. The plane started to descend to land and refuel. Recife! Our first stop on Brazilian territory!

The plane taxied to a halt, the door was swung back, and there was a mob waiting for us. A yell went up as we started to climb down the aluminum steps; it grew louder and louder as the crowd grabbed Vavá and hoisted him to their shoulders. Then it was my turn and after that the rest of the team.

There was no way to avoid being raised on high and carried precariously through that packed mob, nor much point in advising them that heights always bothered me. The only thing to do was to go along with it.

Then, later that day, Rio de Janeiro!

There was pure carnival in the streets: traffic diverted, the avenues jammed with people, shouting, singing, dancing, drinking, clogging any artery of traffic and not being particularly bothered by the honking horns nor the edging bumpers. There were regular carnival bands and many irregular ones; there was shouting, screaming, laughing; there were fireworks—it was a madhouse! We were finally brought together with our families in the offices of the magazine *O Cruzeiro*. Tears were general. My father hugged me, barely able to speak for the emotion he felt.

"Dico!"

My mother was also crying, but at least these were happy tears.

"I missed you, Dico!"

"I missed you too, Mama!"

Dona Celeste partially dried her tears and smiled.

"There was such a party in Baurú! You should have seen it! Our house was full, the street in front of the house was full! All the people who used to complain about you making too much noise, or breaking the street lights, or being too fresh, or fighting all the time—even your schoolteachers—they all came to tell us how they always knew you would be a big success, how they were all so proud of you."

I had to laugh; after all, I was now all grown up, an adult. I had decided that in Sweden.

And all around us the scene was being repeated endlessly; fathers, mothers, wives, children, brothers, sisters, in laws—everyone hugging somebody and laughing and crying at the same time. And outside the offices of *O Cruzeiro* the people in the street yelled and screamed, wanting the world champions—*their* world champions—to come to the window, where at least they could be seen even if they couldn't be touched.

I have no idea at which hotel we spent the night in Rio, but I do know that it was all utter confusion, with running back and forth between rooms, hugging total strangers for no reason at all, and then sitting and talking with my parents until almost dawn before getting a few hours' sleep. And then we were being driven to the airport, eyes half-closed, wondering if it all really happened.

In São Paulo the scene was even madder; it had to be: São Paulo had more people. The game with Corinthians was obviously forgotten. As soon as we reached Congonhas Airport we were assaulted by the mob. We were protected by a corps of bombeiros—the Brazilian version of firemen, except in Brazil the bombeiros are armed and form a part of the military. We were put on the parallel benches they carry on their personnel carriers and off we went. It took hours to reach the center of the city from the airport; the crowds filled the streets and refused to budge, even for the big trucks that continually edged forward against them, horns blowing—although with all the other noise it was impossible to hear anything. Balconies on both sides of the streets were jammed with people, throwing confetti, or torn newspaper, or dropping firecrackers, or food wrappers, or cigarette butts, completely disregarding anyone below. Roman candles and rockets were going off everywhere. It was an insane asylum, run by the inmates!

Nor had we time to eat. We were worn out, half-starved, ready to trade our medals for a sandwich and a few minutes' rest, weary of grinning like idiots for hours at a time, our arms tired of being held up high with our fingers split in a victory salute. We envied those of the team who lived in Rio and had managed to stay there. And when we finally got to Pacaembú Stadium, the insanity increased. Everything that happened before was repeated on a concentrated scale. There were fireworks again, screaming, yelling, hugging—plus speeches, which was the last thing we needed. By this time I was so exhausted that the whole scene seemed unreal. Ever since we had arrived at Recife I seemed to have lost track of what was going on. I have no idea of what I said in answer to the questions reporters were throwing at me, or what I said to anyone. Everything seemed to have a dreamlike quality to it.

And when the last three of us—Zito, Pepe, and myself—finally got to Santos, the party was repeated once again. It got to a point where, while we were being paraded through the streets, we demanded something to eat or we would go on strike. We would flatly refuse to continue. Someone disappeared and came back with some sandwiches. They were dry and only made us thirsty, and then we were on the move again. It was only late that night that we finally managed to escape and I made my way to my boardinghouse, Dona Georgina's, ready to sleep for a week. My fellow boarders had stayed up for me; they wanted to take advantage of having me all to themselves and started to deluge me with questions, apparently feeling that their sacrifice of sleep demanded no less of me. Fortunately, Dona Georgina, who always treated me more as a son than a boarder, stepped in.

"Let the boy alone, for heaven's sake! Let him get some rest! Can't you see he's almost asleep on his feet?"

And so, at last, I was able to drag myself to my room, undress, and slide between the covers. And then I dropped off to sleep, tranquilly and dreamlessly, for the first time since we left Sweden.

For the next few days the Selection was held together in order to accept all the honors which it was felt were due us. We were invited to endless dinners, luncheons, cocktail parties, and every kind of gathering imaginable. We visited the President of the Republic, Dr. Juscelino Kubitschek, who presented us with gold medals for our victory. We were constantly being interviewed, usually to find the same meaningless questions being asked time after time. How did it feel to win? Fine ... fine ... How did you enjoy Europe? Fine ... fine ... Who was the toughest team you had to face? Fine ... fine ...

The newspapers published lists of the presents we had received or were about to receive. They spoke of houses, land, washing machines and dryers, refrigerators and stoves, of boats and automobiles, or lifetime passes on railroads, or bus lines, or to the movies; of high-paying public-service jobs on the side, and God knows what else. We were millionaires! The only problem was that it was only newspaper talk, and Brazilian newspaper talk at that. The promises were never kept and the gifts, of course, were never delivered—but only an idiot would ever have expected them to be. And as for me, I was still earning the same six thousand cruzeiros a month, although we had earned a nice bonus from the World Cup games.

But at long last we were free of any obligation to the Brazilian Selection and I was able to travel to Baurú to see my family and my friends. The plane also held quite a few reporters and photographers who wanted to see and report on the reception I would receive in my home town. But they could hardly have been as interested as I was. After all, I had left Baurú less than two years before, an inexperienced and wondering kid, traveling in a second-class seat on a local train with only my family to see me off—and here I was returning by plane to be greeted by the entire town. For a brief moment I wondered if Neuza would be there—she had been a girl I had admired as a young boy—but then I put the thought away. It had been a long time, comparatively, and I had never let her know of my admiration; and anyway, a girl that pretty didn't stay unmarried very long in the interior of Brazil.

As the plane banked to land I could see the crowds jammed against the railings and could see the police standing in front of the terminal building ready to hold the people back from storming the plane. I began to feel the excitement building up in me as I hadn't felt in Recife or Rio or São Paulo or even Santos. This was my home. And then the plane settled to the ground, taxied to a halt, and the photographers were climbing out first so that they could snap me coming down the steps.

There was a big truck waiting for me, all ribbon and bunting, newly painted, it seemed, for the occasion, and standing before it was Sr. Nicola Avalone Júnior, the mayor. He was the first to reach me and give me a strong Brazilian *abraço*, the bear hug so common among friends in our land.

"Baurú has been waiting for you, Pelé!"

I looked for my parents but couldn't see them; then I was being hoisted onto the truck and I looked around. There they were, making no attempt to break through the crowd but content to wait until the parade was over and we could be alone at home. My mother was there, looking proud; Dondinho, looking at me gravely but secretly smiling, my Uncle Jorge, Zoca, and Maria Lúcia waving, both of whom seemed to have grown quite a bit since I had last seen them. I didn't see Neuza but I saw her brother Nilo and many of my old friends. As the truck rolled from the airport and through the streets of the town, many of them would hop up on the running board for a quick handshake, give me a wink of comradeship recalling old times and adventures, and drop off to be replaced by another. And all through the town banners were hung from flagpoles or draped over the railings of balconies.

"*Welcome, Pelé, Son of Baurú, Champion of the World!*"

It was unbelievable! Every place we passed reminded me of some scrape or other I had gotten into: the Ernesto Monte Primary School, naturally; the railroad station where I had shined shoes and stolen peanuts and sold meat pastries, the Noroeste Club where I had played and where I had had that stupid fight. Well, at least Dona Celeste and Dondinho were having the pleasure of seeing a son honored who had only given them grief until a short time before!

When at last the parade was over and they delivered me to my house, my grandmother, Dona Ambrosina, was there, hugging me and crying, but they were quite different tears from those when I left. Uncle Jorge gave a strong *abraço* and grinned at me.

"It's good to see you again, Dico! You've become famous, you know!"

And then Zoca came running in, all excited.

"They're going to give you an automobile, Dico!"

I laughed.

"I've heard that before, in São Paulo and Santos. Don't let it bother you, Zoca. It's just a story. It's just newspaper talk."

"No, no! Senhor Nicola told me, himself! You're getting a car, a real car—it's a gift from the people of Baurú!"

A car? A real car as a present? I couldn't believe it. To an American, I suppose, the gift of a car does not seem so unbelievable, but in those days in Brazil, it was quite different. Cars were all imported, the duty on them being many times the original cost of the car abroad as a means of discouraging their import, and they cost a fortune. They cost, in actual fact, more than the average Brazilian could hope to earn in a lifetime. Let me show you what I mean.

If a man earned thirty dollars a month, which was what the minimum wage was in most parts of the country—and the maximum wage for the huge majority of workers—and if a car cost $20,000, which was about the cost of an automobile like a Ford or Chevrolet, imported with all duties paid, then it would take him about fifty-five years to pay it off. Assuming he started to work at the average age of twelve, and even assuming he could earn the minimum wage at that age—which he could not—he would still be sixty-seven years old when he finished paying for his purchase. Of course, he would have to forgo eating or paying rent during that period and devote his entire wage to the car, but since we're assuming everything else, let's assume that as well. Now, since the life expectancy for the average Brazilian in those days was far less than sixty-seven years—even for people who ate—you can understand what I mean. An automobile was such an impossibility that no average Brazilian would have wasted time in even dreaming of ever owning one. His maximum dream had to be confined to the possibility that one day he might be able to afford a secondhand bicycle purchased on long-term conditions.

Things have changed greatly since then; today Brazil is a leading producer of automobiles, and it is no longer inconceivable for a person to dream of owning a car, or even of owning one—but in the year 1958 it was a wild dream, indeed.

I, personally, had never considered owning a car, not only for the reasons above, but because I could see no great necessity for having one. Everywhere I went with the Santos team I was taken; everywhere else I went in Santos I walked. And enjoyed it. Still, there was no doubt that the thought of owning a car was exciting; on a par, I imagine, with a poor American's thought of owing a sixty-foot seagoing yacht with a full crew and permanently provisioned.

That night after the street party in my honor was completed and I had been given trophies and medals by the various organizations and merchants of the town, Edson Leite—a famous announcer of Radio Bandeirantes of São Paulo and another native son of Baurú—made a short speech and then unveiled the car. All through his talk I had been eying the hooded shape on the platform next to ours, trying to imagine what other object it could be, because I was sure it wasn't a car. It was too small to be a car. A motorcycle with a sidecar, I had about decided, when Edson Leite drew aside the cloth. It was a car, all right—a Romisetta, a three-wheeled contraption which was briefly popular in Brazil because of the ease of parking: It only took a very small space. The front of the car swung back to let the two occupants emerge; there were no doors. For a second I was disappointed; somehow from all the talk I must have been expecting a miniature Cadillac. Still, it *was* a car, and it had cost a lot of money by any standards, and I was truly grateful to the people of Baurú for their gift.

The following morning the car was in front of our house, delivered by some unknown, keys and all. I went out to get a better look at it from close up, swung the front back and climbed in, twisting the steering wheel as if I were driving it down the winding Via Anchieta to Santos, and then got out and called my father. When he came out I waved my hand at the car, possibly a bit grandiloquently for a seventeen-year-old, and got into my first fight since I had come back to Baurú.

I smiled at my father.

"It's yours."

He stared at me as if I had lost my senses.

"Mine, nothing! It's yours!"

"You don't understand, Papa. I'm giving it to you as a present."

"You're the one who doesn't understand! You got it as a present. You can't give it away."

"You still don't understand, Papa! I want you to have it. I can't drive it to Santos. I don't know how to drive. And I don't have a driver's license."

Dondinho looked stubborn.

"You can get a driver's license. Someone will drive it to Santos for you and you can take lessons and learn to drive there."

"But I don't want it in Santos! I don't need it in Santos!" I got an idea. "I know! I'll sell it. We can use the money to pay off the house, or even to buy a better one—"

"Sell a present?" Dondinho began to really get angry. "You would *sell* a *present?* What kind of an upbringing did we give you? Going to Europe didn't make you any smarter, did it?"

We had come full circle.

"All right," I said, as stubborn as Dondinho. "If I can't drive it and I can't sell it, there's only one left to do, and that's to give it away. You'll have to take it as a present."

"No—!"

Dona Celeste had been drawn outside by the argument.

"Dondinho—have you ever thought of the trouble Dico could get into with a car in Santos? A young boy his age? Have you thought of the accidents they have there, with all those other cars? Have you thought of the girls he might try to pick up if he had a car—?"

Anybody who would try to even kiss a girl in a Romisetta would have to be a contortionist, but fortunately Dondinho didn't comment on that. He gave in. Grudgingly, but he did give in.

"All right. I'll keep the car here, but it's still yours. When you're older you can learn to drive and come and get it."

And that was that. Zoca, at least, was overjoyed at the solution. But I have a feeling that Dona Celeste may have regretted her interference, because not long after, Dondinho persuaded her to join him in a spin in the country. The roads around Baurú not being the best, and Dondinho not being an experienced driver, he managed to leave the road and skid down into a gully headfirst. The car was wedged there, and since the only way to get out was by swinging the front back, there they sat, with Dona Celeste staring at the driver coldly, and Dondinho looking sheepish. Finally someone came along and arranged to have them dragged out. After that the car sat in front of the house most of the time.

So the few days at home passed all too quickly, and then it was time to go back to Santos and football again. The first time I had left, everyone saw me go with tears in their eyes; this time nobody cried, not even Dona Ambrosina. Once a person has traveled to Europe across the Atlantic, going to Santos represented little more than going downtown in Baurú, or to the BAC Club. ...

Chapter 6

It was a good thing I developed some skills at the game of football when I was growing up in Baurú, because as a student I was a total failure. I don't believe I was really stupid; it was just that my teachers and I never seemed to see things in the same light.

My third year at school started out poorly and steadily got worse. How our new teacher ever got to be assigned to a mere school for youngsters instead of a penitentiary for hardened criminals, I shall never know. Any warden would have been pleased to have her on his staff, because she was an expert in devising and administering punishment.

For talking in class she would make me stuff my mouth full of balls of paper until my cheeks hurt—until I discovered that by chewing the paper when she wasn't looking I could eventually end up with a small wad that wasn't uncomfortable at all. All I had to do when she looked my way was to puff out my cheeks and appear in pain, and we were both happy. For more serious crimes—throwing spitballs or pinching girls or fighting in class—this teacher had devised a small square in one corner of the classroom which she had filled with uncooked corn beans, which have the hardness of granite pebbles. Here the criminal, usually me, would be made to kneel with his bare knees pressing on the beans. This was far more painful than chewing on paper. But for every plan there is a counter-plan, and by slipping a few beans into my pocket whenever she wasn't frowning in my direction, in a short time I would be kneeling on bare floor boards, which felt soft by this time, although to the casual observer it looked as if I were still on the beans. And when I got up I managed to spread the remainder around so they looked as if they covered the area. I ended up with a pocketful of hard beans, which made excellent ammunition for throwing across the room when the teacher's back was turned.

The teacher—whose name I choose not to remember—had another favorite punishment, making a child stand with his back to the class, his nose touching the wall, his arms outstretched like a crucified Christ. When one's arms got too tired and dropped she would walk over and jerk them upright again, painfully. The answer to this was simply to continue to drop them, tired or not, until she would have to abandon her teaching altogether to stand beside the criminal constantly jerking his arms up as fast as they dropped. She usually tired of the game before I did, especially in view of the embarrassing giggles her performance earned from the rest of the class.

Admittedly I was not a good pupil, and I know from what I've said that this unnamed teacher appears a monster. She wasn't. She was honestly trying to educate us and undoubtedly felt that the punishment she inflicted was for our own good, and to help us concentrate more on her lessons. But I believe her methods were exaggerated. We were ten-year-old children in that class. I do know this, whatever her intent, she turned me from schooling and from learning for many years, because from the first time she inflicted her special skills on me, I concentrated more on how *not* to learn, than on how to learn. I felt that to learn would be to give satisfaction to a demonstrated enemy. The one who suffered from this attitude, obviously, was me, but I didn't see that until, years later,

I made a determined effort to make up for my lack of education. But, to be honest, even in those later years when I finally did see the need for learning, I still blamed this particular teacher for my ignorance.

Other memories come back from that year when I was ten. I was still shining shoes after school down at the railroad station, and handing over the money to help in the house—holding out, it is true, an occasional cruzeiro or two in order to sit in the darkened auditorium of the local movie theater and see how life was in the rest of the world. (I didn't believe a word of it!) Inflation had put Dondinho pretty much back where he had been when he was only playing football for a living, and the shoeshining was a necessity. But occasionally, in order to find some free time for myself—since it couldn't be taken from shoeshining—I would cut class to go fishing. I never cut class alone, but at the same time I never lacked for others equally willing to cut class with me. After all, fishing was providing food, and this excuse was always a valid one with any of my friends.

There were usually four or five of us and we usually fished in the Rio Baurú, a swift-running stream that passed through our town. Our favorite spot was under the Soracabana Railway Bridge, just beyond the edge of town.

Our method of fishing would be called seining today. We didn't use a rod or reel; these sophistications were unknown to us. We didn't even use a line and hook. We merely dipped borrowed circular wood-edged screens into the water and caught whatever the rapidly flowing current delivered to us. The screens were large, flat, and round, about three feet in diameter, the type used for tossing coffee for drying. We would wade into the river as far as we could go, dip our screens down as far as we could reach without getting a noseful of water, and wait for the river to deliver its riches to us. The water being muddy kept us from having any notion of what we might get, but on the other hand we felt the muddiness kept us from being observed by the fish, so there were benefits both ways.

This day I remember very well; a soft summer day with fleecy clouds and the sounds of chirping insects to accompany the river's splashing and the occasional clatter as a train passed on the trestle overhead. I waded out, as usual, almost to my armpits—our clothes, of course, had been left on the bank, since wet clothes were always difficult to explain to Dona Celeste—and dipped my screen down as far as I could. Almost at once I felt something heavy strike it, and I yanked it up excitedly before my quarry could escape. It had not escaped—I had caught something, all right!—and it was staring me in the face. For one split second the tableau held. It was a huge snake, to my eyes the size of a boa constrictor, and after that split second we both reacted. The snake started to thrash wildly, its red mouth gaping evilly, its glistening fangs inches from my face. I screamed at the top of my voice and flung the screen as far as I could, twisting snake and all, and then started to scramble madly for shore, positive the snake was right behind me, positive I had earned the enmity of his entire family, who I could feel were striking at me blindly under the muddy water. We all knew, then, that snakes never traveled alone.

I reached shore, still screaming at the top of my voice, tears streaming down my face, trembling uncontrollably, and picked up my clothes to hold them to me as if for comfort, letting them absorb some of my shivering. For once my companions didn't laugh at my reaction: Snakes were one of the very un-funny things in our lives. They looked at each other in growing doubt as I struggled into my clothes, without bothering to wait to dry off, and then they began to scramble from the river as well. The snake I had caught undoubtedly was far downstream by now, together with any family he might have been traveling with, carried by the current, but none of the other boys could look at the muddy surface without wondering. We all went home together.

That affair brought three punishments: one, for having cut class; two, for losing the neighbor's screen, which Dondinho had to pay for; and three—by far the worst—the horrible nightmares that followed for months. Huge ugly snakes, some of them even hairy, some of them evilly and obscenely smooth, all of them terrifying, would come at me from the seining screen, or from the trees I walked beneath, or even from the tall grass beside a football field. They would take their time with me, toying with me as I stood petrified, and then they would attack, wrapping themselves around me, biting me; and I would start from my bed, screaming with fear, until Dona Celeste would come to my side to calm me and hold me until the trembling eased.

I am still deadly afraid of snakes to this day.

It was about this time that the gang decided to form a real football club of our own and call it the September 7th Club in honor of the street into which our street, Rubens Arruda, terminated and also—incidentally—in honor of Brazil's Independence Day. We decided to have a team that was properly equipped, with a real ball, real socks and shirts and shorts, and one that wore football shoes. In short, a real club.

The headquarters, we decided temporarily, would be in my own back yard—or in the back yard of one of the others if Dona Celeste had a negative reaction to the idea, which was extremely possible. Fortunately, Dona Celeste was more interested in seeing that I stayed around home to keep out of mischief, so this proved no problem.

Nor did the problem of the ball. That was resolved quickly.

"Let's put together some albums of complete sets of football cards for three or four of the top clubs of Rio or S□o Paulo," I said to my friends. "Big teams, like Corinthians, or Flamengo, or Vasco da Gama. We can sell them easily for enough money for a ball."

Football cards were like the baseball cards that were popular in the United States at an earlier time. They carried the picture of a big star from one of the clubs on one side, some biographical data or his professional statistics on the other, and were distributed in candy bars, cigarette packages, chewing tobacco, and just about everywhere. There was active trading in them by youngsters in every neighborhood, rich or poor, and four complete sets of players from different clubs would certainly have at least the value of a new ball and probably more. Everyone agreed it was a great idea and congratulated me.

"Now," someone else said, "what about uniforms?"

We talked that one over and came to the conclusion that we would need several strings to our bow if we were to raise the necessary money.

"I have an idea," one boy said. "Our kindling is delivered on Friday, and every Friday after school I have to stack it. If I manage not to show up at home Friday afternoon, and if you guys happen to walk past the house and offer to do it, like we do it for Pelé, I'm sure my mother will give you something. It won't be much, but it'll be something. Then if each one of you guys stays away from home when *your* kindling is delivered ..."

"Not me," I said at once. I could not picture Dona Celeste falling for anything that obvious.

"Well—everyone except you, then. You had the idea for the album."

It was discussed democratically, and agreed upon. We moved on.

"Downtown we could pick up cigarette butts and take the tobacco and roll fresh cigarettes and sell them one at a time," another boy said. This, we decided, was a good idea; the sale of cigarettes one at a time was a very common practice, although most of those sold by this method came from a package. Still, if we sold them at a reduced price we were sure we would find a market. The vote for this was unanimous. We moved on.

"How about collecting all the scrap metal, old iron, tin cans, empty bottles, and other rubbish and selling it to the junk dealer in town? He's always looking for stuff."

Again agreement, but after that our ideas ran dry. However, we felt we had enough to keep us busy, and we spread out to attack our projects.

But after a week it was plain that we needed further ideas. Most mothers thanked you profusely for stacking the kindling, and sometimes even offered a glass of lemonade, but very little money—and usually spanked her son for not being around when he was supposed to—so that endeavor brought little into the cashbox, and was quickly dropped. The market for reconstituted cigarettes brought in a bit, but nothing like what we had anticipated, while the junk we collected added almost nothing. In our neighborhood nothing was wasted and very little was thrown away. When we added up our take for the week we found we had enough for some poor-quality socks, and that was all. So we returned to the question of money for uniforms. The answer was finally given by a boy from the neighborhood named Zé Porto.

"We'll sell peanuts outside the railroad station," he said, "and outside the circus that's coming to town next week, and outside the movie house. The circus sells their own peanuts, but we'll stand down the road from them, and we'll sell them cheaper."

"Great idea!"

General hesitation.

"But—where will we get the peanuts?"

Zé Porto had the answer to that one all ready. In fact, he sounded as if we all had to be pretty stupid not to have seen the answer immediately ourselves.

"We steal them, of course. If we bought them, there'd be no profit. They've got tons of them down at the Soracabana Railroad warehouse."

I didn't much care for the idea. In my short time I had broken enough of Dona Celeste's commandments, but always only the minor ones. Stealing was one of the *big* commandments. It was a sin my mother would not treat lightly, and one she was almost sure to involve my father in. I couldn't picture what the punishment would be, but I was sure it would be horrible. Actually, I'm sure the huge majority of us were afraid of stealing, but Zé Porto ended the matter.

"Whoever doesn't go along with the idea is a *cagão*. A big shit!"

Naturally, nobody wanted to be a shit, big or little, so we agreed. Reluctantly, but we agreed. With what eventually turned out to be very tragic results. ...

Since the idea of the football albums was my idea, I felt it only proper that I take charge of the collecting of cards, and as a result that I be excused from any part of the peanut-stealing caper. But it didn't turn out that way.

We soon discovered, as we might have surmised, that we could easily round up about 75 per cent of the cards of any club without too much difficulty. The trouble came when we tried to find the balance. I know it's considered commercial for companies selling tobacco or candy to leave a few key figures out of the collections—or to put in just a few to keep on the right side of the law—since it increases sales as people search for the missing ones, but this tendency on the part of crass commercialism gave me a lot of problems. And I ran into even more trouble when I finally located some kids who had the rare ones we needed to complete our books. At the next meeting, called to discuss the dilemma, I explained the problem. Zé Porto listened with barely concealed disdain.

"What do you mean, they won't trade? You have to *make* them trade!"

"Fine!" I said sarcastically. "How?"

"Three or four of us will go with you, next time. You'll see—they'll trade. They won't argue."

I swallowed. I could picture the scene even before it happened. If one of the boy's parents came to Dona Celeste with the story that I was using muscle, and not even my own muscle, to force their beloved child to swap cards he didn't want to swap, I knew what would happen. I would be lucky to be walking again inside of a week.

"I don't like it," I said.

"I'll do it, then," Zé Porto said contemptuously, "and you can take my place stealing the peanuts."

"Wait—!"

"Yes?"

I shut my mouth. Stealing peanuts from the Soracabana warehouse had a slight chance of success. Not very much, in my opinion, but at least some; thievery from the Soracabana was not unknown. But I was totally sure that using muscle on kids to make them trade their rare and valuable cards for worthless ones was bound to have repercussions. I knew what my own reaction would be in the circumstance, and I was sure every kid with a rare card would feel the same. Guaranteed trouble.

"All right," I said sadly.

We gave the matter of the theft our totalized criminal knowledge and came to the conclusion that trying to steal from the warehouse itself was too risky; there always seemed to be someone around. Similarly, the trucks that brought the peanuts to the warehouse always had both a driver and a helper, and it was extremely rare when one or the other was not around; it would have been as easy to steal the truck as to touch its contents. The only thing left was the stationary freight cars in which the peanuts were loaded and eventually shipped.

We decided it would have to be a two-man job, one to enter the car and cut open the sacks, actually removing the peanuts, while the other would act as lookout and keep an eye open for possible trouble. I don't recall at the moment who my companion in crime was, but I do remember that we drew straws and I lost. I was elected to do the actual stealing.

We waited until lunchtime when the crew loading the cars had gone down the street for some food and beer, and then we went to work. I was almost dead with fear, hoping against hope that the crew would have closed and locked the heavy doors to the freight cars and that our mission would have to be aborted, but despite my fervent prayers, when we ducked down the narrow passage between the huge cars and the corrugated side of the warehouse shed, they were standing open, either because they were too weighty to keep sliding back and forth, or because the crew would have found an oven inside when they returned.

With no further excuse, I hoisted myself inside. I remember the smell to this day; I wondered why I had thought the odor of peanuts so tempting before. There were some loose peanuts on the floor and for a moment I considered searching for the bag they had come from, but then I realized that time was passing. The complete sacks weighed over two hundred pounds each, so we couldn't hope to move one of those intact; instead I had come equipped with my school satchel and some paper bags. I ripped open the nearest bag and was almost swept from my feet by the ensuing flood. In haste and in near-panic I crammed my bag full, stuffed peanuts into the other bags, filled my shirt with all it would hold, all the time trying to think of some logical explanation I might give if the crew came back and found me. I couldn't think of a thing. As soon as my shirt was rebuttoned I jumped down and with my conspirator ran around the corner, peanuts dribbling from my shirt. Once safe we stopped to stare at each other. We had done it! We laughed aloud in relief and went to join the gang.

The sale from that haul paid for shirts and for enough flour sacks so that our mothers could make fairly decent shorts from them. The shirts had no names or numbers on them, but they did look quite official, and since they were all the same, they made for a uniform. But there was nowhere near enough for football shoes for anyone. So we let Zé Porto talk us into the tragic decision to go back to the freight cars again.

Zé Porto did the stealing this time, saying he wanted to be sure it was done properly and this time we all assisted because he had brought along enough sacks and bags and even tin basins to be sure we would have enough, once and for all. He would come to the door of the freight car with a bag or a basin full, hand it down, and then go back for more, quite as if he worked there on a regular basis. I am amazed to this day that nobody saw us, that nobody came to the door of the shed and looked down the tracks; he could hardly have missed us. We must have looked like a trail of ants taking a dead cricket back to the anthill a piece at a time. When at last Zé Porto finished and climbed down, his own shirt stuffed, we felt we really had to have enough to pay for any equipment we might need. Now that the actual stealing was past, my only worry was how I could explain the possession of a complete football uniform to my parents.

That, however, was a problem for the future—I was sure I would think of something. At the moment a more immediate problem was where to temporarily store such a large quantity of peanuts. Certainly not at anyone's house; even the most innocent or trusting of parents would have to wonder if his son turned up with a hundredweight or more of peanuts. And we had to decide quickly, for a storm was coming up and we wanted to get rid of the peanuts and get home before it broke.

Zé Porto, the Brain, had considered this angle as well. Between the railroad yards and our neighborhood were some low wooded hills where we often played, and these hills were pockmarked with caves of all sizes. In their time they had served us as battlefields, as castaway islands, or more innocently as stadiums from which to watch either pickup games or the trains go by. Now Zé Porto saw no reason why they should not serve a more mundane purpose. He led us on a dash for the hills and got there just as the rain began to pelt down. The smallest of the gang was detailed to store the peanuts in the deepest recess of one cave as we handed the bags or basins to him, and he ran back and forth as quickly as he could, taking the peanuts from us and disappearing into the cave's depths to cache them. I don't remember his name and I suppose I should, because when the rain began to come down in force, the hill began to move! We all stood, amazed at first, and then scrambled for safety, but before the boy could make it back to the entrance of the cave, and even before we regained our senses and began to tear frantically at the sliding mud with our bare hands and empty basins, the hill settled and we knew the boy was lost.

I don't remember who ran for help, but the rest of us kept trying to scrape away the mud from what had been the entrance to the cave. Trees had slid down, their roots tangling in our feet; finally men came running, shovels in hand, and began to dig. We all stood back, silent, our hearts pounding, the rain soaking us to the skin, the misery of the day lending itself aptly to the misery we all felt, the guilt that attached itself to all of us. At last they brought his body out; the peanuts were not discovered. The boy had made it almost back to the entrance before he was caught in the slide.

One of the men wrapped the small body in his jacket and started toward the boy's home with all of us behind him, like a funeral procession. The tragedy was too great to think of escaping it by running home. I remember when we came to his house his mother came out, attracted by the commotion. She had been baking and her black hands were white with flour. She knew, long before the man laid the body reverently on the small porch. Her hands went to her face, leaving white streaks, ghostlike, through which tears left ragged trails. Her whimpers were accusing stabs I can still feel.

When I finally got home, trembling from the shock of the experience and soaked from the rain, I was given a stern lecture on playing in such a dangerous place, but the stolen peanuts remained a secret, locked in the hearts of all who had participated. But we were punished, every one: I still remember that small muddy body being dug from the collapsed cave, the ears and eyes and mouth clotted with the brown clay. I can still hear those agonized small whimpers from the white-flour-streaked face of his mother. The memory added to the many nightmares I suffered in those days. I would dream it was me in the cave when the roof began to descend; I would try to run for the entrance, which was clearly visible and seemingly attainable, but my feet would be unable to find purchase on the slippery floor, and even as I strained for the opening, the roof would come down and I would feel the crushing pressure, the taste of the mud pouring into my mouth and down my throat, strangling me, and I would sit up in bed, screaming, trembling, fighting for breath; and Dona Celeste would come hurrying in to hold me and comfort me.

So the September 7th team came into being with shirts and shorts, but without shoes. We therefore referred to ourselves as "the Shoeless Ones," considering it a brilliant nickname under the circumstances—only to discover, as we went around town trying to arrange games, that just about every other neighborhood in similar financial condition had a team with the same nickname.

We finally managed to complete two albums of football pictures and trade them for a football. It wasn't a regulation ball, but we didn't care about that. I remembered it was the kind that had no valve; the tube came out and had to be blown up, after which it was doubled, a rubber band was put on it to hold the air in, the tube was stuffed back inside the cover, and the cover laced. Whenever we needed to blow up the ball, we would take the valve from the tire of some car when the owner wasn't around, let the escaping air fill our ball, and then replace the valve, often leaving the owner with a flat. As I say, the ball wasn't regulation, but it bounced, which was more than could be said for a ball of rags. And it was all ours. I was the guardian of the ball and kept it at my house, and since I took care of the ball, I became, symbolically, the captain of the team.

We soon became known in Baurú. Among us were some very good players: Serginho, Zé Roberto (whom we called Toquinho), Nilo and Shôde—two very good Japanese players—Luisinho, Valdemar Mendes, Dino, Vado, Valdinho, Otelo, my brother Zoca, and many more. Zé Porto, oddly enough, liked to be in the gang but didn't particularly like to play football; it was probably the reason he hadn't kept the ball at his house.

Some of the nicknames of our team we had invented, some were copied from the names of great players in the big-city clubs, and some were merely inexplicable.

We were far more than eleven, and while this always led to strong arguments at the moment of picking a team to play a rival, it also gave us enough players to be able to put two teams on the field in a practice game among ourselves. At that time, as today, I played center-forward, but I also played defense at times, and even goalkeeper if we were playing a particularly strong team. But, easy teams or tough ones, I honestly cannot remember the Shoeless Ones of September 7th ever losing a serious game.

The influence of my father on me became greater and greater as I began to grow up. When I had been a youngster Dondinho had been content to leave Dona Celeste with the problem of raising me, but as I started to become more adult, he spent more time with me. Beside holding down his job at the clinic he continued to play for BAC in all their games. Still, in his little free time he would work with me and try to improve my game. He'd take me to the old abandoned Noroeste field at the end of our street and watch me try to dribble the ball and then kick it past him into the imaginary net where the old goal posts used to stand. I seldom managed to do it satisfactorily; Dondinho always seemed to know instinctively where to go to block. He would shake his head.

"You only know how to kick with your right foot. You lose time and rhythm trying to set the ball up to kick it with your right foot. It gives your opponent time to tackle the ball from you; you're off-balance. It also gives the goalkeeper time to get set to block you. Dico—here—watch this."

And he would demonstrate the proper method of handling the ball equally with each foot.

"Like this. If you ever want to be a decent player, you have to learn to use each foot equally. Without stopping to think about it. It has to be automatic. ..."

Or he would say, "Don't try to remember everything at one time. Forget your feet for a moment. Let's try heading. Remember: In the middle of the forehead, eyes open, mouth closed. Lean back and then come forward to strike the ball; the further back you lean and the harder you come forward, the further you can strike the ball. *Don't blink*! That's it—eyes open, mouth shut, middle of the forehead. That's it."

And he would toss the ball to me and I would bat it back with my forehead while he slowly backed away, making me strike it harder and harder. Then he would toss it to me higher and higher, making me jump up to head it back to him.

"All right. Now, back to the feet. Left foot, right foot. Like this. That's better. Again."

And again and again, with Dondinho always patiently correcting me.

"If you want to kick a low ball, you bend your knee so that the knee is directly over the ball, then you kick the ball with your instep. Remember, knee directly over the ball, kick with your instep. Your balancing foot must be in line with your target. Try it."

And I would kick and kick.

"To pass, you use your inside of the foot, or you can fool your opponent sometimes by pretending you are going to pass normally but nudging the ball with the outside front of your foot to a teammate on the off side. Like this. Now, you try it. Again."

And again and again, with Dondinho patiently correcting me, instructing me. And we'd come back to the house, sweating, tired, but happy. My mother would say to him accusingly:

"Very nice, Dondinho, eh? Your oldest son! Just remember: Don't come to me complaining later on when he wants to be a football player and starve to death, instead of studying medicine or law and amounting to something!"

Dondinho would laugh and put his arm around her.

"Don't worry, Celeste. If he doesn't learn to use his left foot, you have nothing to worry about!"

I always seemed to be fighting in those days, either in school or out, either on the football field or at home, either with kids bigger than me, kids my own size, or kids smaller than me. Almost any little thing seemed to get me started. Looking back now, I must have been much more insecure than I thought I was. Rather than trying to solve any problem, my first reaction was to strike out blindly, as if I could overcome the problem by hitting somebody or something.

In particular, I fought with Zoca, probably because I was fairly sure I could always beat him. When we didn't let him play with the September 7th team, Zoca and some of the others who also were left out more often than they cared for, formed their own team, calling it Rubens Arruda, after our street. Occasionally, when we couldn't find a better game, we would play them a fun game, almost a practice game, and on those rare occasions when Zoca's team would beat us—mainly because we didn't try very hard against them—he would rub it into me unmercifully. Until I'd tell him we let him win, at which he would call me both a liar and a bad sport and there we were, rolling around on the floor, punching at each other. This would go on until Dona Celeste took notice, after which I was sent into one room with a slap on the ear, while Zoca was usually taken into the kitchen and given a cookie.

We also fought over button football, a game we often played. It is a game that even today is quite popular among children—and even adults—in the smaller towns and cities in the interior of Brazil. Each player places eleven buttons on a table that represents the field of play. The buttons may be placed in whatever formation the player prefers; it gives him a chance to demonstrate his skill as a tactician. Something small and preferably square is designated as the ball—a sugar cube, a bit of whittled wood, or even a square button if one can be found. The players take turns snapping one of their buttons against the "ball," trying to knock it into whatever has been classified as the goal.

Zoca and I would play this game for hours, whenever a day was rainy and we were inside, or in the evenings before bedtime. Zoca developed into a great player and would beat me regularly, which would usually bring a cry from me that he was cheating, and a moment later there we were, rolling on the floor, punching. With the usual results: a slap for me and at most a chiding for Zoca.

One fine day I remember very well, when Dondinho came into the room where Zoca and I were playing button football, holding his spare pair of pants up with one hand. He picked up one of the buttons from the table, compared it to the spot where a button was obviously missing, and then merely stared at us.

"Dico took it!" Zoca said instantly.

I hadn't even known the button had been taken! But I had no time to think of that: Dondinho reached for me and I was around the table and out the door in a flash. Fortunately, the fence in our back yard had holes in it and I was small enough to slip through while Dondinho was not. I got away just in time and spent the afternoon plotting a revenge on my younger brother that would have made the *auto-da-fé* look like a reward for good conduct. Luckily, when I finally went home, Dondinho had discovered that the button we were playing with was *not* from his trousers, so I was saved. But I still had it in my mind to exact my just revenge on Zoca when the opportunity came up. It never occurred to me that I would have said, "Zoca took it!" if my brain had been able to think fast enough.

I remember another day when I was watching a game between BAC and some other team, where Dondinho was playing. On this particular play he dribbled down the field, evading the defense of the opposition with his usual skill, and then missed what surely seemed like a very makable goal. I was disappointed, but the reaction of a fan of BAC near me was worse. He started to yell.

"Dondinho, you bum! Dondinho, you clown! Your leg would make a good clothes pole! Hey, Wooden Leg!"

I instantly and unthinkingly lost my temper. The man was at least twice my size, but I was blind to everything except the wave of unreasoning fury that swept me, leaving me trembling. I glared at him.

"Who are you calling Wooden Leg? Who are you calling a bum? A bum is what your mother is!"

He looked down at me, surprised to hear all this noise coming from such a small size. Then he became furious as the meaning of my words came through to him.

"Why, you little black bastard, watch your mouth and get away from me before I kick your ass up around your chin!"

I picked up half a brick and sneered at him, the brick giving me courage. "Maybe you would," I said, "if you had balls!"

About that time one of the spectators, probably a friend of my father's, and aware that my father's son was about to be annihilated, entered the discussion.

"If you touch this boy," he said to the fuming man, "I'll make you wish you hadn't!"

The BAC fan had had about all he intended to take. He reached out and slugged my protector and the next thing I knew we had a real free-for-all going. I managed to escape with nothing more than a few bruises from blows meant for others, but I remember the fight was a big one. The police came but couldn't stop it; it wasn't until a group of soldiers who had been watching the game came over that the thing was brought under control. When I got home Dondinho was already there; he wanted to know what had happened. He obviously knew the entire story so there was no point in lying. Dondinho shook his head, sternly this time.

"You fight too much and it's about time you stopped," he said. "If you intend to play professional football"—I think it was the first time he spoke to me as he would to a man and not to a child; it was also the first time I realized he expected I would choose football as a career—"then you have to learn certain things. Controlling your temper is one. The Chinese say that when a man makes a fist, he has already lost the argument."

"He called you a name," I said simply.

Dondinho was not impressed at my championing him.

"There are two teams on the field, therefore there are two sets of fans. What makes one fan happy makes the other one angry. Someone on one side or the other will always call you names. Get used to it. And if you don't want to remember the Chinese proverb, remember that when you lose your temper on the football field you will play bad football. And you can also get thrown out of the game, and that only hurts you and your team. Besides," he added, "most of the time you lose your temper it's because you're angry at yourself because you know you're wrong. So go outside and kick yourself; don't start fights with strangers."

From the day of that fight, Dondinho seemed to pay more attention to me and my game. Even though he had little time with his job and his playing, he still managed whenever possible to come out and see our September 7th Shoeless Ones in action. And after a game, walking home with me, he would say:

"You tried to play that game all by yourself. It's a team sport. Don't lose goals because you want to be the big hero. If you had passed to Zé Roberto on that last play, he might have made a goal. He was wide open. He was calling for the ball."

Or he would say:

"Remember just after the second period started? Why did you pass the ball to Luisinho? He was covered. You had a clear road to go in and kick. Why didn't you?"

I would stammer and then fall silent.

"Admit why you passed the ball: It was to give you time to think. You can't pass off responsibility on a football field like that. You have to think at the moment, think before, or train yourself to make the proper play without thinking, or without conscious thinking. That's what makes crack football players."

And I, who didn't listen to many people, listened to him because I thought—and still think—that Dondinho was one of the best players in Brazil, even if an injury kept him from ever reaching the top. And I also listened because I knew he loved me and was trying to help me. Dondinho was a marvelous teacher.

One great example of his ability to influence me comes to mind. I have never seen my father with a cigarette any more than I have ever seen him drinking anything alcoholic. He always took good care of himself, watching his health and his physique, thinking this would be the best example to set for Zoca and me.

One fine day I was sitting with some of the gang in the shade of a tree far enough from our house not to be seen, when somebody offered me a cigarette. It wasn't a machine-made cigarette, but one made of *xuxu*, an absolutely tasteless Brazilian vegetable which kids rolled in paper to smoke, as American kids did with corn silk. After taking a careful peek around to make sure that Dona Celeste or Dona Ambrosina were not in sight, I bravely lit up. It wasn't my first cigarette, and while I had never inhaled the acrid smoke up to that point, I was beginning my first attempts. Our conversation became animated—I don't remember what about, but probably football or girls—and as a result my vigilance dropped. When I looked up, my father was passing by. He waved to us and went on his way without saying anything.

I jammed the remains of the cigarette down into the ground beside me and must have turned almost white with fright.

"*Criiiii*! I'll catch it when I get home!"

One of the gang scoffed.

"You'll catch nothing! He didn't see you smoking."

"If he had seen you," said another, "you wouldn't be sitting here right now. You'd be being dragged home by the ear!"

Their arguments seemed logical, and I certainly hoped their optimism was justified, but as soon as I walked through the door I knew it wasn't. Dondinho called me over at once, although to my surprise his voice was completely calm. He might have been talking to me about a recent game I had been in.

"I saw you smoking."

I didn't say anything. There wasn't anything to say. I just stood before him and tried to look anywhere except into his eyes. He remained patient.

"Well? Am I wrong?"

"No—no, sir."

"How long have you been smoking?"

Still completely calm. He might have been asking how long I had been shining shoes, or how long I had been going to school. The calm before the storm?

"I—only a few times. A few days."

"Does it taste good? Tell me. You see, I don't know. I never smoked."

I didn't tell him that I had never smoked a regular cigarette, that the *xuxu* cigarettes were the only ones I had ever tried. I didn't think it would make any difference to the discussion.

"I don't know. Not very, I guess."

I honestly expected a slap on the ear for such a dumb answer, but just the opposite happened. He pulled me to him, like a friend getting ready to speak to a friend, put one arm around my shoulder, his voice explaining something to me.

"You have a talent for football, you know, and in time you may even be a crack player. But you won't be any kind of a player if you smoke or drink. You won't be able to maintain the physical condition you need to play the way you want to play for a full ninety minutes. So you have to make the choice."

Then he put his hand into his pocket and brought out his billfold. It was worn and pitifully thin. He opened it; I stared at the few crumpled bills that were revealed as he went on.

"However, if you still want to smoke, it would be better if you bought your own. It's an ugly thing to always be borrowing from others. How much money do you want to buy your own?"

I didn't know where to turn. The fact that the cigarette hadn't been bought made no difference. I could see my father limping onto the field each week to play football, with a knee that was swollen like a melon; I could see him uncomplainingly cleaning bedpans and sweeping floors to support his family. I stared at the floor, wishing it would open up and swallow me, hiding my shame. Dondinho looked at me quietly for a long moment.

"That's all. For the pride of the family, for your own pride, don't borrow. When you want money for cigarettes, ask me. I'll give it to you."

And he would have, I know.

I've thought about that conversation many times since. Knowing myself and the confused tumult I felt inside of me at that age, had I been severely reprimanded I might well have revolted and been an inveterate smoker today. On the other hand, loving the game of football as I did and do, and knowing that smoking is truly harmful for any professional athlete, I might not have. I don't know. But I do know that since that day I've never touched a cigarette, or wanted to.

My reasons for never touching alcohol were based on a different experience, one as instructive but much more painful.

One of our neighbors, an Italian, used to make wine, and after bottling it, he would bury the bottles in the ground back of his house, and let the bottles stay there for many months, while the wine aged and got strong. One fine day his son, who was one of the gang and a friend of mine, told me when we were alone that he was sure his father never counted the bottles and would never miss one. The idea of experimenting with a new taste interested me. I had always wondered, when I saw the men down near the railroad station downing hard liquor at one of the stand-up bars, exactly what pleasure it gave them. Now I could find out for myself. The fact that we would be stealing the wine didn't occur to me at all; after all, the wine belonged to Antonio's father, which was almost the same as belonging to him.

We therefore waited until his father had gone off to work, went out in the back yard, and dug up a bottle. We were very careful to smooth over the area to leave no tell-tale marks of our raid, and then went off to the field at the end of the street to sample our booty. We sat down in the weeds on the far side of the field, out of sight of passers-by, wiped the dirt from the bottle, wrestled the cork loose, and finally got it open. It was a red wine, a nice cheerful color, and after admiring its beauty for a short while, we started taking turns tasting it. My first reaction was that it wasn't all that great; it seemed bitter to me. My friend, however, was drinking it with such gusto that I felt the trouble had to be with me and my lack of experience, and that practice would probably teach me to like it.

I must have drunk about half the bottle when it really hit me, and I suddenly felt awful. Cold sweat broke out on my forehead, my head ached, everything began to swing around and around, and I was suddenly sure I had been poisoned and was about to die. The next thing I knew I was on my knees, vomiting up everything I had ingested for the past month. To my amazement my friend wasn't affected in the least—they drank wine in his family all the time, children included—and he considered me with disgust, probably for having wasted half a bottle of good wine on me.

When I got home, Dondinho was there. He must have been able to smell me from the corner of the street; I stunk like a winery plus every other smell imaginable. He caught me by the arm as I tried to slip past him, attempting to escape to my room where I could lie down and pray for death, or anything else that might relieve that horrible feeling. Dondinho glowered.

"Where have you been?"

"I don't feel so good. ..."

"You've been drinking wine! You're drunk! Where did you get it?"

I told him. When Dondinho was in that mood it was not smart to lie to him.

"And I don't feel so good. ..."

"Maybe a spanking will help," he said unsympathetically, and walloped me.

But it wasn't the spanking that made me swear off liquor for life at that moment; it was that indescribable dizziness, that sick queasiness, that frightening feeling of insecurity, of not being in control. For many years, even after I was grown and traveling with the Santos team or the Brazilian Selection, if I sat in a restaurant and saw another patron pour any red wine, I would get that cold churning in my stomach, and I knew I couldn't tolerate the sight of food.

It was about that time that Zé Porto's family moved to another town in the interior, taking Zé Porto with them, of course, but before he left he gave me a legacy—his dog, Rex.

At that time Rex was just a puppy, some indeterminate combination of breeds that had resulted in this pathetically thin puppy, with fine hair, beige in color with brown splotches, shortened tail, and trimmed ears. Whoever had done the trimming of the ears had been careless and one ear stuck up above the other. He looked like that dog in the old Victor advertisement, with his head cocked to one side, listening to that big Gramophone horn. I fell in love with him the moment I saw him; he was going to be the first thing I had owned that I did not have to share.

When I got home, Rex trotting faithfully at my heels, my mother took one look.

"What on earth is that?"

"It's a dog. It's *my* dog. Zé Porto gave him to me."

"Well, you just march right back there and give him back! How are we supposed to feed dogs when we don't have enough in the house to feed people?"

"I can't take him back," I said desperately. "They're moving and they can't take him with them."

"What's that to do with me?"

"Please, Mama," I said. "I'll share my food with him. Nobody else will have any less. I promise!"

I must have sounded sincere. I'm sure that Dona Celeste, down deep, knew exactly how I felt. She frowned for a moment.

"Is he housebroken?"

It was victory!

"I'll house-break him, Mama. You have nothing to worry about. Honest!"

"All right," Dona Celeste said, "but he's your responsibility, understand that, Dico. I have enough to do without having to cook and wash and clean for a dog, yet!"

Which was fine with me. I didn't want anyone else taking care of Rex, or even touching him. Whenever Zoca would even try to pet him, I felt a wave of unreasoning jealousy. He was mine! And Rex seemed to understand that, and reciprocate. He followed me everywhere I went, hugging my heels, waiting outside the schoolhouse until I was liberated. When we went hunting, he loved running through the brush, and he was an excellent retriever, bringing back downed birds with care not to break the skin. When we went fishing he would stand on the bank, panting, anxious to join in but not too fond of the water.

But where his brilliance was best demonstrated was when we went to play football. If we wanted to plant some sticks as goal posts, all I had to do was point to a spot and say, "Dig!" and Rex went after that hole as if all the bones in the world were there. And when we went onto the field to play he exhibited an intelligence that is hard to believe. He seemed to understand that dogs were not allowed to be on the field amid all those running boys, and he would sit quietly behind the goal waiting for the halftime interval when he would come trotting up to the bench and sit at my feet, looking at me with those enormous eyes and that head half-cocked, as if waiting for me to say something. He was a marvelous friend.

Rex did much, I am sure, to get me through those tough years of childhood. When many years later I went to Santos, I was forced to leave him behind. When I came home for my first visit, I was told that he had disappeared soon after I left. Nobody ever saw him again, and I felt bad about that for a long time, wondering if anyone was feeding him, or if he might be hurt. But I think he probably wasn't hurt physically; he was hurt as I would have been hurt if he had abandoned me one day without explanation.

One day the September 7th team changed its name. It became Amériquinha.

It all came about when Sr. Nicola Avalone Júnior, the mayor of Baurú, decided to sponsor a football tournament among the various neighborhood teams of youngsters in the city. There was only one catch. The teams had to be properly uniformed, and that included football shoes. That left us out, as it left out most of the other "shoeless" teams in town. The fathers of the players of those teams didn't have money for food, let alone for football shoes.

We racked our brains trying to figure out how to get shoes, but we couldn't come up with a single idea. After the peanut tragedy, stealing was definitely out, and any honest way of getting enough money for eleven pairs of regulation shoes was beyond us. We didn't need shoes for our reserves; we would have taken off our shoes for any substitution and handed them over. In Brazil we have a saying, "*Pé de pobre não tem tamanho*," meaning that the feet of the poor man doesn't have size. He wears what he can get. We were about to give up when there appeared one Zé Leite, a salesman who was a friend of our family and also of many of our team. He made us a proposition:

"I'll get you shoes," he said, "but in return I get to be your coach. You'll have to train properly and you'll have to follow my orders. You must be disciplined, like a regular club. But if you do what I tell you, you can win this tournament."

"Great!" we all said. "But where will you get the shoes?"

"Leave it to me."

We felt a lot better with an adult on our side. I would have preferred Dondinho as our coach, of course, but he had no time, and he could never have gotten us shoes. But Zé Leite was not only pretty good as a coach, but he had a very good reason for wanting to help our team. He had three sons on it: Zé Roberto, Zé Maria, and Zé Luis.

"But we'll have to change the name of the team," Zé Leite added.

This was puzzling.

"Why?"

"Because your September 7th team is known throughout the city as a shoeless team. You are now going to have shoes, so we'll have to change the name. We'll call ourselves Amériquinha."

Amériquinha in Portuguese means Little America, but Zé Leite could have called us anything he wanted. The name meant nothing to us as long as we had shoes and got to play in the tournament. And Zé Leite lived up to his promise. He went to the Noroeste Club, sat down with the directors, and must have told a story that would have wrung tears from a rock, because he came away with all the used, worn-out shoes that most clubs seem to keep more for sentimental reasons than any other. As I said, Zé Leite was a salesman by profession. He brought them to our team, dumped them on the ground—a mountain of them—and smiled.

"There they are. Take your pick."

It was quite a sight. We would try on shoes, take off shoes, swap shoes, everyone wanting the least-used shoes, of course, regardless of fit.

Oddly enough, many of the shoes were too small rather than too large; going barefoot all your life tends to spread the feet, even if the rest of you is small and undernourished. But at least we were shod after a fashion and ready to play.

Or, rather, ready to train—because Zé Leite lived up to his promise on this, too. He trained us and he trained us hard, and he did not show the slightest favoritism to his sons. It took us awhile to get used to playing with shoes on, just as it took us awhile to get used to playing on the grass field Zé Leite found for us. On the old Noroeste field you breathed as much grime as you did air, and you often could hardly see your opponent through the clouds of dust. It also meant constantly exchanging shoes in hopes of eventually getting a pair that really felt good, but eventually we managed to reach a point where we could bring our minds to bear on football instead of constantly being preoccupied with just feet.

From the very first game to the last, we were sure we would win. We knew each of the other teams, having played them all many times before in our shoeless days; but we had the advantage of having played together as a team longer than any of the others. We knew exactly what each of us was capable of doing, and what each of us was *not* capable of doing. We could almost anticipate the play of each of us, but we played as a team from the very beginning. And having played on streets full of potholes and on fields that were either uphill or downhill but never flat, and having played without football shoes using a ball made with rags stuffed into a sock—well, playing with proper equipment on proper grass was as close to heaven as any of us ever thought we'd get. And our play improved accordingly.

I was only twelve at the time and the smallest on the team, but we all played a type of football that brought us the cheers of the crowds at each game, and not just because we consistently won. It was because we were exhibiting a style of football that was unusually advanced for a team our age.

And the crowds came out. Nicola Avalone Júnior, the mayor of the town who was sponsoring the tournament, also owned the Baurú *Daily*, our local newspaper, so we were assured of ample publicity. That, together with the word of mouth of our prowess, brought the people out. And we trained; how we trained! Every day between scheduled games, regardless of any other chores we had to do, regardless of school or shining shoes or any other duty to contribute to the family income—and we all had them—would find us on the field, doing the exercises proscribed by Zé Leite, practicing dribbling or tackling or ball control or heading or kicking penalty kicks or free kicks from every part of the field, hour after hour, left foot, right foot. Or playing as much of a practice game as the fading light would allow.

When the day came for our final game in that tournament, the game that would reward the winning team with the Nicola Avalone Júnior Victory Cup, I felt nervous for the first time in my life on a football field. The stadium where the final game was played was the BAC Stadium with a capacity of almost five thousand—and it was jammed! Every seat taken. And we were only kids. I was only twelve; the oldest on our team, Zé Roberto, was fourteen. What were we doing before this crowd? BAC had played before far less, as had Noroeste. And here we were, a bunch of kids, with a screaming bunch of fans treating us as if we were grown-up. It was a strange feeling. ...

Once the game started, however, all nervousness passed and I was in just another football game, like all the games I had ever played. I rapidly lost awareness of the crowd, although I remained aware of the importance of winning. I even was only faintly aware that Dondinho was there, watching. The only important thing was to stuff that ball past their goalkeeper into the net!

We won. We not only won but we overwhelmed the other team and I was the *artilheiro* of the game—the leading scorer. We were the champions! It was our very first trophy and we received it from the hands of the sponsor, the mayor, and then we made an Olympic march with it around the field, holding it high as we had seen champions do it on television, with the crowds standing and cheering, tossing money down from the nearest seats, as was the custom. Of the many memories I have of that glorious day, two things stand out: the crowd calling my name—"*Pelé*! *Pelé*!"—in a constantly growing chant while I no longer hated the name but actually began to like it; and my father holding me tightly after the game and saying:

"You played a beautiful game, Dico! I couldn't have played any better myself!"

When we got home and Dondinho proudly announced the victory, my mother for the first time smiled at something involving football. She hugged me tightly and congratulated me—but she hadn't gone to the stadium to watch me play.

To this day my mother has never seen me play, either in person or on television, nor will she ever listen to a game on the radio if I am involved. She says she gets too nervous worrying about my getting injured as Dondinho was injured, or in thinking of the heavy responsibility that is placed on a team or an individual by either the club or the fans. She has watched television reruns of some games, when she knows the game is over, knows the result, and knows I have not been hurt—or at least knows the extent of the injury if I have been hurt. Fortunately, I have never been so seriously injured in a game as to affect my career for any period of time.

It isn't that my mother dislikes the game of football itself. After all, she met Dondinho at a football game and fell in love with him there. It's just that football has caused her much suffering in her life, and no matter what my success in the game, she cannot forget the past nor help herself from worrying about the future.

That afternoon after Amériquinha won the championship of Baurú, I was wound up like a twelve-day clock. I couldn't stop talking. I must have been a nuisance!

"Mama, you should have heard all the people cheering, and for me! They were yelling my name! They were shouting Pelé! Pelé! Pelé!—like that! They liked me! And the ones near the field threw money on the field and the gang gave it to me because I was the *artilheiro!* Thirty-six cruzeiros! Mama, I was the star of the game! Ask Daddy! You should have been there! Thirty-six cruzeiros, Mama—!"

Thirty-six cruzeiros at that time of our lives was a lot of money. It would have bought three kilos of rice, three kilos of beans, a couple of kilos of coffee, and still left enough over to buy sugar for the coffee. But my mother, regardless of her personal feelings about the game, had lived too long in a household dominated by football not to know and respect the proper protocol.

"You didn't earn that money by yourself. After supper go out and share it with the others on the team."

She didn't say it, but I think we all knew that she was also thinking that if those thirty-six cruzeiros wedded me more firmly to football, it was a bad bargain. But she said nothing of this.

So I simply said, "Thank you, Mama," and loved her more than ever that moment.

And my brother Zoca, who hadn't played but had sat the game out on the bench, kept interrupting excitedly.

"Dico—hey, Dico!—do you remember during the game, when—?"

And we'd be off, replaying the game in all its aspects.

It went on like that during the rest of the afternoon until after supper when Zoca and I went out to meet the others from the team and spend that fabulous fortune we had picked up on the field. I imagine that Dona Celeste and Dona Ambrosina—and even Dondinho—while pleased to see us both so excited and happy, must have welcomed the silence that fell when we finally left the house!

Our Amériquinha team went on, as we say in Portuguese, "*de vento em pôpa,*" which is to say, with a tail wind. We would play any team our age that came along, as well as many older and more experienced teams, and we never lost a game. It got so that a tie would make us feel bad for days. Then, one day, Zé Leite up and moved to São Paulo and we lost at one time, our coach, our trainer, and also three of our best players: Zé Roberto, Zé Maria, and Zé Luis. In a very short time we fell back into being a team where everyone gave orders, a team without discipline, a team with eleven coaches, fifteen trainers, and twenty-two individuals. In short, a team that could not hope to compete properly. A short time later the defections began, and in a little while there was no longer any Amériquinha.

I was thirteen at the time and in my fourth year of primary school. I already had had to repeat my third year for being a poor student and for cutting classes, and it was already evident I would have to repeat my fourth year, as well. It was very discouraging. I was totally disenchanted with education in general and with this school and its teaching methods in particular, but Dona Celeste was adamant. She had reluctantly come to accept the fact that I would never be a doctor or a lawyer, but we still went to school, at least to the conclusion of primary, or else! So, of course, I went.

Fortunately, about the time our Amériquinha team was falling apart, the Baurú Athletic Club decided to start a juvenile team of their own and call it Baquinho—Little BAC. Naturally, many of our ex-Amériquinha team were asked to join, and I was one of them.

The day I was asked to join was one of the most exciting days of my life. All I could dream of was to play with this juvenile team until the day when I was adult enough to put on the shirt of the professionals, with the *BAC* in the fancy medallion over the left breast, and possibly even play at the side of Dondinho someday, which would have been the greatest thrill of my life.

We worked hard, training and getting used to each other so we could function as a team rather than as eleven individuals, for although some of our team were from the old group, there were also many we had not known before. But it was a pleasure to play on a team where, if a pair of shoes didn't fit, one had only to ask to be given another pair—and a new pair at that! Then, one day to our great surprise, we were told we would be getting a new coach—Valdemar de Brito.

Valdemar de Brito? We couldn't believe it! Somebody had to be pulling our legs! One of the great names in the history of Brazilian football, in his younger days a star for many of the top clubs in the country, a man who had played inside-forward on the 1934 Brazilian World Cup Selection, and now one of the top coaches of professional teams—to train and coach our small juvenile team? It was difficult to believe, but it was the truth, and I later grew to understand why Valdemar de Brito chose to coach our team. It was a remarkably simple reason: He liked youngsters and liked to work with them.

Today I can understand that much better than I could then, because I feel the same way. Youngsters can be taught; they don't have the habits ingrained in them that professionals do. After all, it's hard to tell a man—a man who has played for years with the best teams in the country, a man who, in addition, has cost some club a fortune of money—that he is doing something wrong, or even that he could do what he is doing better. All that results is that you have made an enemy and haven't gained a thing. Players at that age and with that background of experience either can't or won't change. But youngsters can and do.

And we found that out very quickly. We had thought we were pretty good, but we soon found out we could all be much better. We also discovered from the first day that Valdemar de Brito didn't stand for any fooling around. He talked to us like adults and expected us to listen and act as adults. He permitted no swearing, no temper tantrums, no fighting, no arguments of any sort either on the field or off, and definitely no disagreements with him. The first day he warned us that if we were going to train under him, the first thing we would learn would be discipline. And we quickly learned it.

He was stern but just.

"When you play for me," he would say, "you obey orders. You come to practice on time, you stay as long as I tell you to stay, and when you are here you do exactly what I tell you to do. Whether you are here or away from here you will not smoke or drink, and you'll get to bed on time to get your rest. I will make you tired enough—don't worry!—without you arriving here tired because you didn't get enough sleep!"

Then he would relax and add:

"What I have said goes for every man on the team; we'll have no prima donnas. Anyone who cannot stand this discipline doesn't have to stick around—but for those who do, I will teach you all I know about the game of football."

One day he added another commandment.

"I don't want you reading the sports section of the Baurú *Daily* any more. They've been running articles about some of you, as well as putting your pictures in the paper. When you see an article mentioning you, or see your photograph in the paper, your head gets all swollen and you figure if it was printed, you must have deserved the honor. Listen! When a player gets conceited, all he can see are his virtues; he cannot see his faults. That's bad enough in life, but it's fatal in a football player."

(But of course it was hard not to be conceited when you realized that Valdemar de Brito had chosen to coach your team when he could have been coaching any professional team he wanted.)

And at home Dondinho would say to me:

"Keep your eyes and ears open. Pay attention to every word he says: You're extremely lucky to get this chance; Valdemar's experience is invaluable. He is a great player and a marvelous teacher. Take advantage of your chance."

And heaven help the poor member of the Baquinho team who was caught breaking training, or any of the other of Valdemar's many commandments! The first thing would be a stern lecture, followed instantly by a visit of Valdemar to the family of the accused, in the hope that the discipline of the home might change the culprit. But if it didn't, and very quickly, the offender found himself off the team without the faintest hope of ever returning.

Valdemar was as black as Dondinho, if not blacker, and had almost the same build, and he had kept his physique so that his weight and condition were much as they had been when he had been on the Selection twenty years before. He tried to treat each team member equally, but I always felt he took a particular interest in me. It may have been because I was Dondinho's son and Valdemar and Dondinho were old friends; Valdemar had coached a state championship team that Dondinho had played on. Or it may have been because I was a forward and the forwards are the principal players upon whom a team depends for its goals. But in any event, he taught me—and the rest—many things.

His training methods were, for us, unique. He would have us stand in a circle, spread out with about five yards between us; then one player would be sent to the center of the circle to try and take the ball from us as we passed it or headed it or kicked it from one to the other. It developed rapid reactions, and in a short time we were prepared to receive the ball without warning and pass it off, all in a split second. For heading the ball, he had three balls hung up high above our heads, and we would have to run and jump up to hit the ball with our foreheads; the first ball had to be jumped for taking off with the left foot, the second taking off with the right foot, while the third ball had to be jumped for taking off with both feet. The result was that after weeks of this type of practice, one never even thought about which foot was forward when he had to leap for the ball. And, as I was one of the shortest on the team, and since the height of these balls was fixed, I had to leap higher than the others to reach them. I think this, more than anything else, trained me in leaping as high as I am able to do today.

He taught us how to properly trap a ball coming at us with our chest, or our shoulder, or our thigh, or even our foot. He impressed on us one thing that even today few coaches take the trouble to teach, and that is what to do *before* the ball comes at you. Most coaches are satisfied if a player stands perpendicular to the oncoming ball and stops it without having it bounce too far away, so as to lose control of it. Valdemar taught us to stand *sideways* to the ball until the last minute; this gave us the opportunity to observe the location of the other players, so that when we finally did square ourselves to the ball and trap it, we could instantly pass it off to a teammate without having to look around and discover where everybody was.

He taught us how to kick a ball so that it would curve, to either the right or the left, depending on the amount of "English" or spin one imparted to the ball. This was particularly important in free and penalty kicks for the goal, where the curve imparted to the ball could result in a goal where a straight ball could be intercepted by the goalkeeper. He taught us to always dribble with the body *between* the ball and the opponent trying to tackle the ball from us to prevent losing control of the ball. He taught us the need to learn how to place the arms when dribbling, so that they balanced you, especially at the moment of kicking. He taught us the tactic of feinting, to be able to swerve sharply around an opponent while having the ball go straight at the opponent, so that when the opponent attempted to swerve with us, the ball was already past him and ready to be picked up again.

And he taught us the famous "*bicicleta*"—the "bicycle kick."

People somehow have gotten the idea that I developed this kick. Actually, I believe it was developed by Leonidas, a very famous Brazilian player who played on the Brazilian Selections in 1934 and 1938, playing with Valdemar de Brito in 1934. Today, almost every Brazilian player is familiar with the kick, which, while actually not too valuable for making goals, is still a beautiful thing to see properly executed. The kick is executed by throwing your body in the air, horizontally, with the shooting leg bent at the knee. Then, just as the ball approaches, this leg is straightened up to propel the ball backward, over the head. The hands are spread to cushion the fall, and the play is finished. Actually, of all my goals, I think only four or five were obtained with the bicycle kick, but every Brazilian football player longs for the opportunity to perform this kick, if only for the pleasure of the fans.

In short, Valdemar de Brito taught us all he knew, as he had promised, and he knew a great deal.

And when I wasn't working on the football field, I was working in my spare time to earn money. The salaries Dondinho and Uncle Jorge brought home from their jobs, as well as Dondinho's earnings from football, bought less and less as time went on. Besides, there was a young lady growing up in the family, Maria Lúcia, and she needed clothes; and there was Zoca, who was turning out to be the student I never had been, and he needed books. And we all needed food.

But I was getting too old to shine shoes. The amount one earned shining shoes didn't amount to enough to really help at home and besides, the competition was too keen. I also felt ridiculous sitting on my shoeshine box next to a seven-year-old down at the railroad station trying to compete. It made me look as if I were trying to steal the bread from the little kid's mouth.

So the job I had in those days was selling meat pastries at the station to passengers when the train stopped; there were no diners on those trains. It was a poor choice of jobs for a growing boy—although I was still skinny as a toothpick and also quite short. Putting such succulent temptations under the nose of any boy was only asking for trouble. I would come back to the house of the couple who made the pastries—Sr. Rosalbino and his wife, Dona Filomena—turning in the remaining ones together with the money I had collected, and then wait for my share.

Dona Filomena would count the money, count the remaining pastries, and then look at me accusingly.

"You ate four of them!"

I would stare at her, shocked at the accusation. Pastries wouldn't have melted in my mouth.

"Who, *me*???"

"Then you stole some of the money!"

I would be speechless. Me, steal? The son of Dona Celeste, steal? The idea was enough to make the blood boil with indignation!

"Then where are the pastries? Or the money for them?"

I would consider the problem carefully. After all, there had to be a solution and I was obviously as interested in discovering it as she was. A possibility would occur.

"Some thief must have swiped them from the tray when I wasn't looking. ..."

She would sigh, take some money—not my full share, but some—and hand it to me.

"Pelé—please, eat at home before you come for the pastries tomorrow, *heim*?"

Chapter 7

I have often been asked if, being black, I ever faced racial prejudice. In Brazil there is very little racial prejudice; in our house we had friends visit who were black, white, mulatto, Japanese—you name it—and nobody thought anything of it. In Brazil very few people can tell how much black or Indian or white or any other kind of blood they have themselves. The early settlers came to Brazil without their women, and as long as there were native Indians to service them, they did not lead celibate lives. The same was true when slaves were first brought to Brazil, although the shame the American felt in his guilt at coupling with a woman of another color never seemed to disconcert the early Brazilian. Words like *caboclo,* a mixture of white and Indian; or *preto,* simply meaning black; or *moleque,* which means a street urchin but which today is universally considered to mean a black street urchin; or *crioulo,* a native-born black originally, but now any black—are not considered insults in Brazil, either by the giver or the receiver. Where an American might call a friend Shorty or Skinny, a Brazilian might equally well call a friend Crioulo or Moleque and nobody thinks anything about it. As a matter of fact, *morena*—dark-complexioned—is considered a high compliment to pay a girl (assuming, of course, that she isn't a blonde; calling a blonde *morena* might sound as if you thought her dye-job poorly done).

This doesn't mean there is no racial prejudice in Brazil, but it does mean that in Brazil there is far less than in most other countries. The majority of prejudice in Brazil is economic rather than racial, and since there are more poor blacks than whites in many cities, they suffer the most from this prejudice. The black man with money in Brazil—as in most places on earth—faces few if any restrictions; the poor man, white or black, faces many.

I do remember one incident that took place years later, when I was playing for Santos. We were to play the following day in Araraquara, a town in the interior of the state, and we all left in time to have dinner and a good night's rest in Araraquara. As usual, we left in six taxis, and the one I was in was the last one to leave. I was with another player and the driver of the cab when our car broke down on the road, and being the last one, none of the other taxis came to our aid. We appeared long after dinner was over, and when we explained the circumstances, someone asked:

"But why didn't you hitch a ride?"

I answered automatically: "Because who would pick up three black boys at night on a deserted road?"

It may be perfectly true that few people would pick up three white boys at night on a deserted road, but my reaction was instant; there was a difference and I knew it. As I say, I personally have never faced racial prejudice, but it is impossible not to recognize it exists.

I remember one time in Dakar, Africa. I was checking into a hotel and there was a crowd of people trying to peer in at the door to see me. The proprietress, a French woman, looked at them in disgust and then asked an African policeman to clear the "black savages" away from the door. She picked the wrong man, because rather than clear the people away, he instantly arrested her for her language. Later that day, other directors of the hotel, as well as the husband of the arrested woman, came to me and asked me to speak to the authorities, as they were sure my intervention on her behalf would get her out of jail. I looked at them with amazement. I told them the woman had offended the people I had come to play for, that she had offended them on the basis of their color, which was my color, and that I felt equally offended. She remained in jail until after we had left Dakar.

I also remember the polemic that developed when Rosemeri and I were married, for Rosemeri is as white as I am black. Some of the newspapers made quite an issue of it, which indicates that regardless of the Brazilian's boast of being prejudice-free, underneath there is a well of racial prejudice waiting to be tapped. As long as it is never tapped, though, and as long as common sense rules in Brazil, it will still be the best place for a black man to get along with his white neighbors.

I say I have never personally met racial prejudice—that isn't quite true. When I was twelve or thirteen an incident occurred that I shall always remember.

While my football prowess in those days made no impression on my teachers at school—and, in fact, seemed to weigh against me for some unknown reason—it did have a certain effect on other students, most of whom admired me for it. One student in particular seemed smitten either with me or with my football skills, and I like to think it was me. I should remember her name, since she was my first girl friend, but her name escapes me. It may have been Elena, but I'm not sure. Anyway, it was puppy love, I suppose, but to me it was quite important. For the first time a girl thought I was worth loving—for whatever reason, football or not—and there is nothing like being loved to boost the ego. The fact that she was white—her father was a Portuguese from Portugal, as we say—and I was black had nothing to do with it. We were in love.

Our love manifested itself in the most innocent ways. I would walk her home from school, she would come out to watch our team practice, we held hands as often as we could—I think

I stole an additional pastry from Dona Filomena for her once—it was wonderful. Psychiatrists would probably say the reason I cannot recall her name is Freudian.

One day her father showed up at school. He waited until we came out of class and took his daughter roughly by the arm. We had all come trooping through the doors as on any other day, school bags dangling, ready for adventure of any kind. My own thoughts were to walk down to the railroad station with Elena and watch the trains come in. But before the class could disperse, Elena's father swung her around with a jerk so she was facing me. Everyone stopped. She was pallid, frightened. I felt myself begin to get cold.

"You've been walking around with this black vagabond?" her father said, in front of the entire class. "You've been writing notes to this black tramp? This *negrinho*? This *moleque*? This *nothing*? I didn't raise a daughter of mine to be seen with trash like this! Now, let this be a lesson to you never to be seen with this *crioulo*, or any other!"

And in front of the entire school he swung her bodily over his knee and began to spank her.

I don't remember the girl's name but I remember the incident as if it were yesterday. I stood there, my ears burning, and did nothing. I knew that the class expected something more from me, the big football hero—that I rush in and tear his filthy hands from my darling, that I beat him to within an inch of his life as they did in the radio plays we listened to, or as the cowboys did in the films—but all I did was stand there, feeling sick. Everyone was looking, first at the father, systematically beating his daughter, and then to me for my reaction, their heads going back and forth. The girl made no attempt to protect herself, but merely cried silently, the tears running from behind her squeezed-shut eyes, probably shut against the sight of me standing there like a coward. Her books had fallen to the ground, scattered by her father's feet, but the only sound was his labored breath as he struck her again and again.

I turned and ran. I ran home, my heart pumping madly inside me. I threw myself on the bed and cried uncontrollably, Behind my closed eyelids I tried to picture myself knocking him to the ground, beating him down again and again every time he tried to pull himself erect, until he collapsed and begged for mercy—but no matter how many times I tried to conjure up the scene in this fashion, it was always wiped away by the real one of my beloved, her white dress wrinkled and hunched up over her father's leg, her books scattered in the dust, being beaten unmercifully while I stood by and did nothing. It was useless to tell myself that he was an adult, that he was twice my size, that he was merely exercising his parental authority and prerogative—I had stood there like a stone and had done nothing. That was the picture that remained—and, to a certain extent, still remains. She never spoke to me again, but whether out of fear of her father or disgust with me, I shall never know.

Fortunately, there was always football.

When the Baquinho team finally took the field for their first official game in competition, it was, properly enough, for the Nicola Avalone Júnior tournament again, now in its second year. Our team was really something; it had to be seen to be believed.

The fans in town, not completely kidding, would say, "The directors of BAC ought to put this bunch of youngsters on the field instead of the professionals, sometime. Maybe they'd win, for a change!"

It wasn't true, of course, but it was lovely to hear!

It was a remarkable team, thanks to Valdemar de Brito, and we didn't dare lose and make him look bad. But there was never any danger of our losing; we won the championship handily and came home with the cup. When the final game was over and Baquinho had taken the tournament, the BAC fans went crazy—you would have thought we had won the World Cup.

Baquinho went on to win the following year, as well. It was a sensational team!

And then, after what seemed a lifetime, I finally managed to complete school. It had taken me six years instead of the normal four, and I was sure the staff watched me leave with much relief, although nowhere near as much relief as I felt. Now I had to face the probem of making more money than I could selling meat pastries, especially with my appetite. I took a job in a shoe factory, sewing welting onto boots, and on the side I helped a Japanese friend in his dry-cleaning store and his family in their vegetable market, principally because he had a sister I thought was beautiful. Her name was Neuza Sakai, and I was sure my feelings for her were adult. However, since I was too shy to mention my adoration, I doubt if she even realized it existed. But despite all the work and the secret yearnings, I still basically lived only for football, playing for Baquinho in all their games, training in my little spare time, and dreaming of the day when I would get to play with BAC as a professional.

Then, again, bad news!

One not-so-fine day, Valdemar de Brito announced that he was leaving Baurú and our juvenile team and going back to the big city to coach professionals again. I imagine it may have been the money, or possibly because Baquinho was now as good as it was going to get and the challenge of building us to where we were was largely gone. Or maybe it was because we weren't youngsters any more. Whatever the reason, Valdemar never explained. We were all afraid that once Valdemar was gone the team would disintegrate as Amériquinha had done, and we were right. The BAC assigned other coaches, but they lacked the authority of Valdemar, nor did they have his knowledge of skills and tactics, and we rapidly went downhill. We were still a team, but not a very inspired one.

At this time, two things happened: The Noroesten Club beganto push juvenile football, forming a team called —naturally—Noroestinho, or Little Northwest. The club wanted to sponsor a tournament of juvenile games to precede their professional games at night. At the same time, *futebol de salão* made its appearance in Baurú, sponsored by the Radio Club. *Futebol de salão*—indoor football, really—actually started outdoors, being played on small courts with reduced teams. The first games were actually played on basketball courts, outdoors, and because of the small size of the field, made for a very fast game. Today, indoor football is common, and is actually played indoors with six players on a side. Since today it is played in a limited arena, like hockey, there are no out-of-bounds, so that the play never stops except after a goal is scored. It makes for a very fast game, but even the outdoor version was extremely fast.

The Radio Club called its team Rádium and I was asked to play for them. I was the only nonprofessional on the team and was fourteen years old at the time. I played center-forward, my usual position, and that season led the league in scoring forty goals. In addition, I had been asked to play for Noroestinho, and had happily accepted. So between my work at the boot factory and playing on two teams, one juvenile and one adult, my work with my Japanese friends had to stop. It was just as well; I had decided never to marry, and seeing Neuza Sakai very often had a tendency to weaken that resolve.

The reason for never intending to marry grew from the conviction that at last I now thought I knew where I was going in life. I was going to become a professional football player like Dondinho, moving naturally from the juvenile team at Noroestinho to the professional team at BAC as I grew older, but I would also hold my job at the boot factory, so that Dona Celeste would have no reason to complain. I would also give all my earnings to my mother all my life, which would preclude giving them to a wife; besides, I had seen the problems that existed for professional football players in the interior, and I knew if I ever married I would have to choose between my wife and the game. And I knew the game would always win. Besides, I thought that when I became a star at BAC, my mother would forget about her feelings and come out to see me play. That alone would have been worth any sacrifice.

Then, one day, Senhor Tim came to Baurú.

Tim was a very noted name in Brazilian football. He played forward for the Brazilian Selection in 1938, beside the famous Leonidas, and was now the coach of the prestigious Bangú Club in Rio de Janeiro. Apparently word of our juvenile teams in Baurú, and my particular talents, had reached as far as the nation's capital, because Tim wanted me to return with him and try out for the Bangú Club. If accepted I would become a professional, not at a small-town club like BAC, but at one of the big ones!

My head was spinning! I was still a minor, of course, so Tim had to discuss the matter with Dondinho. I listened to their discussion and in my head I saw pictures of me playing in the giant Maracanã Stadium with Bangú, against teams like Vasco da Gama, or Flamengo, or Botofogo—with me scoring goal after goal, being paraded around the huge stadium to the wild cheers of the crowds, and being showered with tons of money from the stands, which would make Dona Celeste proud and happy. I remembered the pictures I had seen of Rio, nestled between the mountains and the sea, one of the most beautiful cities in the world. There was the magnificent statue of the Christ on top of Corcovado, arms outstretched, blessing the city spread out beneath it; there was the rock of Pão de Açúcar—Sugar Loaf—out in the bay, with the spidery cables of the cable car reaching to its summit; there was the wonderful Copacabana beach, with the wriggly mosaic design of its sidewalks skirting the wide sand leading down to the ocean. There was always warm weather, palm trees, soft breezes. ... My head continued to whirl—until Dondinho said:

"It's fine with me. I know Dico has talent, and Bangú is a first-rate club. I'll take the matter up with Dona Celeste and if she agrees, it's all set."

That ended it, naturally. Mama looked at Dondinho more with curiosity than anger.

"Are you feeling all right, Dondinho? You should see a doctor at that clinic where you work, because you are losing your mind! Dico is a baby. Go live in Rio de Janeiro? Alone? What nonsense!"

Nor would she even discuss it further, and that was that. Actually, to be honest, I wasn't too unhappy at Mama's decision. Of course when I thought of playing with a major club like Bangú in a big city like Rio de Janeiro, it was a very exciting thought, a wonderful dream come true—but on the other hand, when I thought of having to live alone, in a place where I didn't know a soul, and after practice or after a game going alone to a small room someplace with an unfamiliar bed, with no Dondinho, no Dona Ambrosina, no Uncle Jorge, no Zoca, no Maria Lúcia, no Neuza Sakai, even though we would never marry and she didn't even know I loved her, or especially, no Dona Celeste to scold me or darn for me or cook for me or love and calm me when I had my frequent nightmares—when I thought of that angle I was secretly pleased that Mama had put her foot down.

So things went on in much the same fashion for another year. Football and work; work and football. Then, one day when I was fifteen, Valdemar de Brito reappeared in Baurú and came to visit my father. He made it clear at once that his was not a social call.

"Dondinho," he said, "I know all about Tim and Bangú and that Dona Celeste wouldn't hear of Pelé going to Rio. But he's a year older now, and anyway, Bangú wasn't the proper club for him. And I agree with Dona Celeste that Rio is too big a city for a young boy. Pelé should be trying out at Santos. They have a young team, but they are a fine ball club. The city is not much bigger than Baungú—and I'm sure he could be very happy there."

Dondinho looked doubtful. Valdemar pressed on.

"If Pelé could qualify there, he could play with their juvenile team. In fact, he's still young enough to play with their infantile team. And in time he would have an excellent chance to play for their professional team. They're very good—state champions in the first division—and he would have wonderful opportunities there. I've spoken to the top people there and they are anxious for him to come down for a trial."

Dondinho was no problem, but there was still Dona Celeste.

"Dico's still a baby, Valdemar," she said. "I don't want him to leave home yet. What if he gets in with a bad bunch of boys? Who is going to see that he behaves properly? Who is going to see that he eats right? Who is going to look after his clothes, because they're always having to be darned? Look at him—he still wears short pants. You want to take a young child like that to Santos and leave him to run loose like a vagabond? And you expect me to agree? Nonsense!"

But once Valdemar de Brito made up his mind he wasn't as easily put off as Dondinho, or myself, or Tim of Bangú. He left our house without any further argument, but a week later he was back in Baurú, and this time he asked my mother and father to accompany him downtown to his hotel. There would be a long-distance call that afternoon, he said, and he wanted them both there when it came through.

Later I learned the call was from the president of the Santos Football Club in Vila Belmiro, a neighborhood of Santos. I don't know exactly what he said, but whatever he said must have been convincing because when Dona Celeste came back she was crying.

"Dico," she said, "to me you're still a little boy, but everyone else seems to think you're grown-up. Maybe I'm wrong. Maybe I shouldn't stand in your way if this is really a chance for you. But I don't want you to be hurt, injured like Dondinho was. I don't want you to suffer in your life as we have because of football. On the other hand, you were never a good student and I don't want you sewing boots for a living the rest of your life."

I could hardly believe it!

"You mean—I can go?"

"Yes. But they tell me it's only for a tryout. And Valdemar promises to watch out for you. And the man at the Santos Club said they would make sure you don't get into bad company and that you eat properly and get to bed on time and stay out of mischief—"

She wiped her tears away and got down to business. Once a decision had been made, Mama never wasted time on useless regrets.

"You'll need clothes. Look at you! You look like a pig. You can't go in short pants—the people on the train will laugh at you. You'll need long pants, at least two pair, and new shoes and shirts."

Which raised the question of money. But eventually we managed to raise it. My boss at the boot factory, almost as excited at my chance as I was, loaned me some money; Dondinho and Uncle Jorge both got advances on their salaries, and when we finally managed to scrape enough together, we went out as a family and bought the shoes and shirts. Then Dondinho proudly took me to a tailor to make up two pair of pants for me from strong denim. They were my first long pants and the first time I had visited a tailor, and the night I tried them on to see how they fit, I was as happy and excited as I had ever been. I wanted to go right out and show all my friends how grown-up I looked. But Dona Celeste would have none of it.

"You want to ruin your new clothes even before you've had them an hour? Take off those clothes until it's time to wear them! With you, you could get dirty taking a bath!"

And then, with time seeming to stand still from day to day, to my amazement the final night for me to sleep at home finally arrived. I remember it was a Saturday and I was to leave the next morning before dawn. Dondinho was going with me, and Valdemar de Brito had arranged to meet us at the central railway station in São Paulo and go the rest of the way with us to Santos, to present us at the club. Dondinho had been gone all day on errands and also to stop in at the Noroeste Club because they had sent him a message they wanted to talk to him. When he came home his face was grim.

"The directors of Noroeste don't want you to go to Santos, Dico. They say they'll give you a small salary to stay here and play with them as a professional. They also said I'd lose a lot of friends if I let you go."

I stared at him, confused. I didn't know what to say. I didn't want my father to suffer just because I was going to Santos. Dondinho had always only played for BAC, never for Noroeste, but I knew the enmity of the directors of a big club in a small town like Baurú could be prejudicial. Dona Celeste started to beam.

"Fine! Now you can stay, Dico! I never did want you to go."

But Dondinho's face got hard. It is very seldom that Dondinho disagrees with my mother, but when he gets that look on his face, Dona Celeste knows that argument is useless.

"If those are supposed to be my friends," he said, "losing them will be no loss. You gave your word to Valdemar and to Santos. You will go to Santos. You owe Noroeste nothing. Don't worry about us. You take your opportunities when they come. Don't end up like your father."

He looked over at Dona Celeste. There was nothing she could say to that; it had been her own argument for too many years.

We stayed up half the night, sitting in the kitchen and talking while Mama made a light lunch for us to take on the train. Everyone from my grandmother, Dona Ambrosina, to my sister, Maria Lúcia, was giving me endless bits of advice on everything under the sun, but I heard only about one tenth of what was being said. I couldn't really believe I was actually going away from home. All the doubts that had assailed me when I thought I might go to Rio and Bangú with Tim a year before now returned, multiplied because the hour of departure was so near. When I finally did go to bed, I couldn't sleep.

I tried to think of Neuza and how much I would miss her, and if she would be impressed if I ever became famous; but then I knew that if she ever was, it would only be because I was a friend of her brother. Anyway, my mind could not stay on Neuza; it kept veering to think of all the big names at Santos I would meet and train with and maybe—unbelievable!—even play against. I knew them all from football cards and from radio games and from the exhibition games Santos had played in Baurú that Dondinho had taken me to see. All of a sudden I was caught up by doubts, desperately afraid. It was this fear my mind had been trying to save me from, by trying to concentrate on Neuza.

What would I do against a player like Zito? Or a Formiga? Or—my God!—a Vasconcelos? Would they laugh when I came onto the field? Or would they refuse to play with a skinny little *moleque* like me, as being beneath their dignity? What if I went all the way to Santos and then they refused to play with me? What if they considered it an insult to play with someone who was young enough to qualify for their infantile team? How could I ever come home and face my family and my friends if anything that embarrassing happened?

Or what if they condescended to play with me just to make me look foolish by their superior play? What if they merely made me the butt of some horseplay on the field and then sent me home for the presumptuous idiot I was? After all, they were big stars, and who had I ever played either with or against of any stature? All young kids like myself, except at Rádium, and what was Rádium but a small-town club in a nothing place like Baurú? Whatever made me think I was qualified to play on a team like Santos? Whatever made Valdemar de Brito think so? Or did he really think so? Suppose he just wanted to embarrass me for some unknown reason. Had I done something to make him angry at me? Going to Santos was asking for rejection, asking for trouble, asking to be slapped down, to be put in my place. Going to Santos was madness!

When Dondinho came in to wake me it was still dark but I hadn't closed my eyes. I got up silently and got dressed in my new clothes. When I came into the kitchen the others were all there, already dressed, even though the sun hadn't scratched the horizon. My grandmother, Ambrosina, was crying softly and didn't stop crying even when we were leaving; Maria Lucia was also crying, but more to keep my grandmother company, I suspect, than because I was going.

And then, suddenly, the time which had dragged for the past two weeks began to race, and it seems that in seconds we were at the railroad station: Dondinho, Zoca, Uncle Jorge, my mother, and me. Dona Celeste held me close and then tried to smile as I climbed onto the train and looked down at her through the open window, but she couldn't keep the tears back. I had a lump in my throat that threatened to choke me, but I was determined not to cry and embarrass everyone in front of the passengers. And then the train started and I leaned from the window trying to keep their waving hands in sight as long as I could. And when at last we had passed a curve and they were out of sight, I turned to my father and said fiercely:

"The first money I earn I'm going to send to you to buy a house for Mama!"

Dondinho smiled, his usual patient smile.

"It's a bit early—both in the morning and in your life—to dream," he said. "Lie down and try to get some sleep. You've had no rest and it's going to be a long trip."

I lay down and curled up on the seat, closed my eyes and tried to sleep, but sleep wouldn't come. All I could think of was that I was going to be all alone. And that I was desperately afraid.

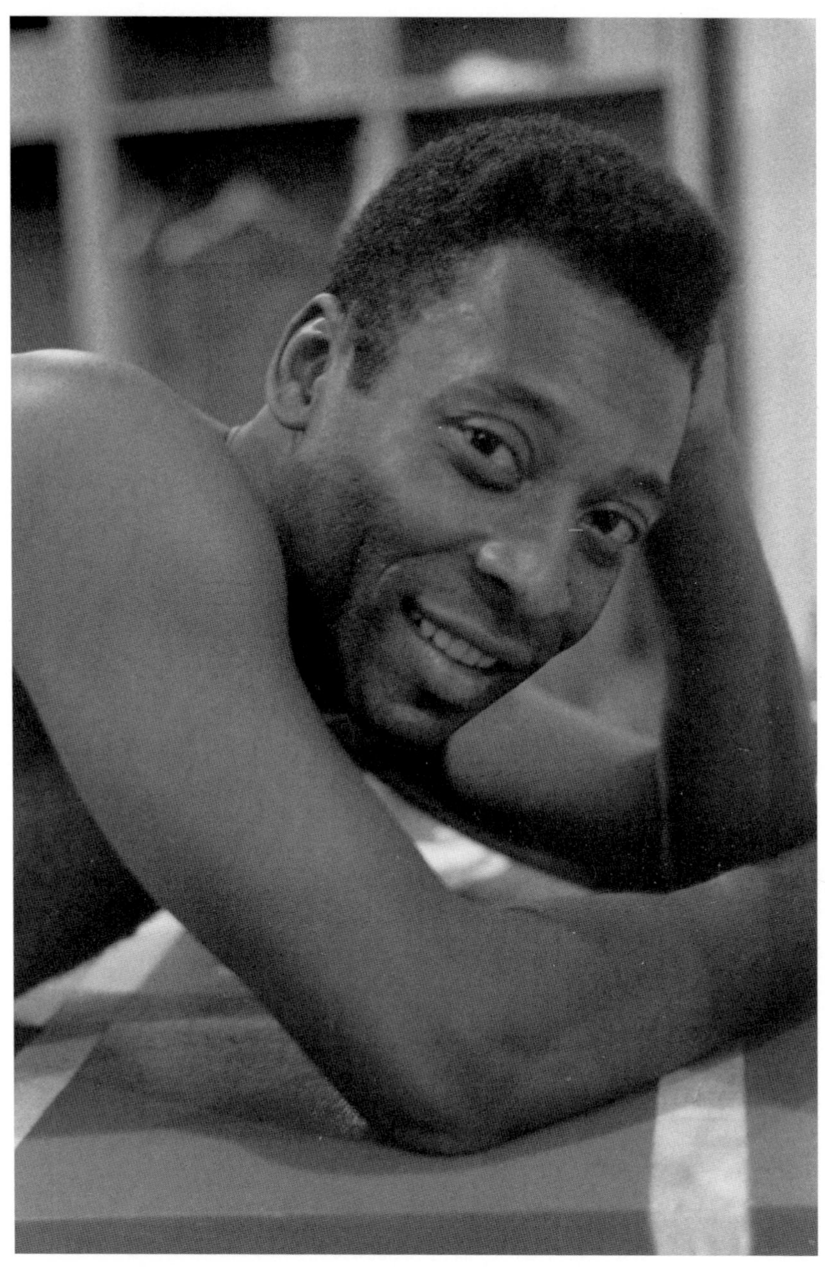

Downing Stadium, 1975
Pelé relaxes after a Cosmos practice session.

Downing Stadium, 1975
Fans and press anxiously await Pelé's first appearance as a member of the New York Cosmos.

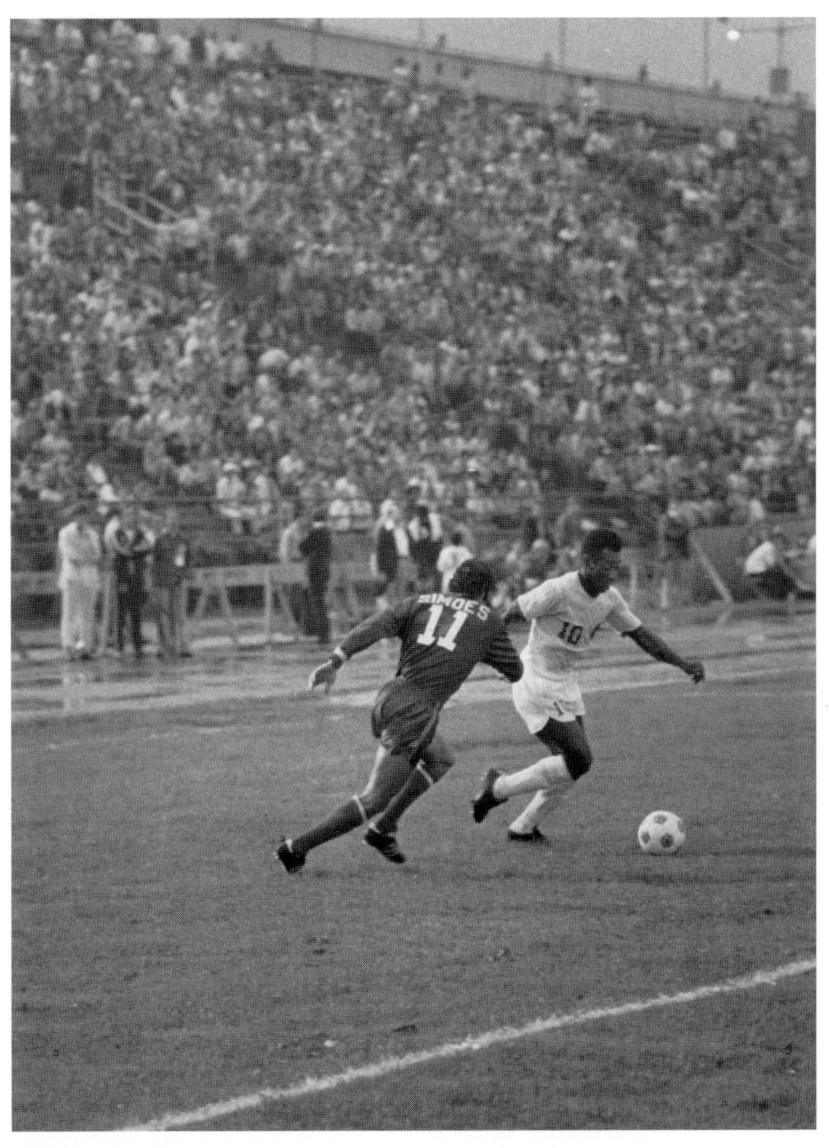

Downing Stadium, 1975
António Simões marking Pelé.

Nickerson Field, Boston, 1975
Pelé and António Simões competed against each other when Simões played for Lisbon's Benfica team and again in the 1966 World Cup. In 1975, they met once again, this time on the Astroturf of a Boston soccer pitch.

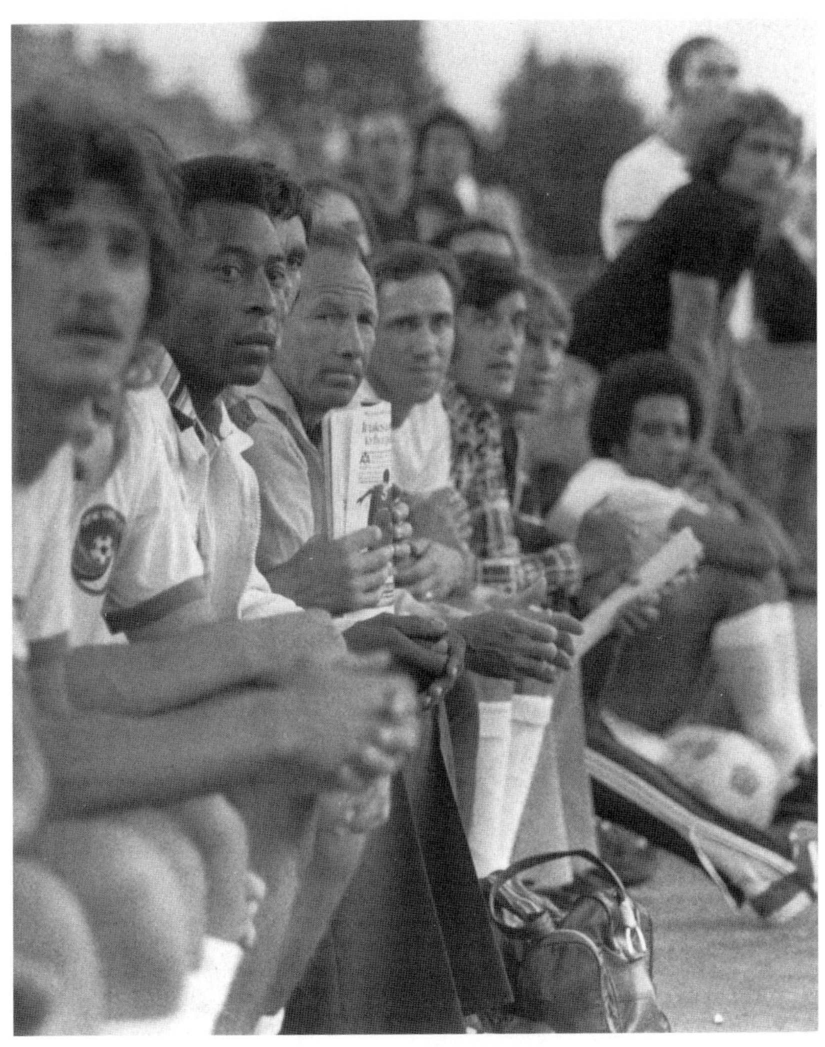

Downing Stadium, 1975
An injured Pelé is forced to sit on the bench and watch his team get along without him.

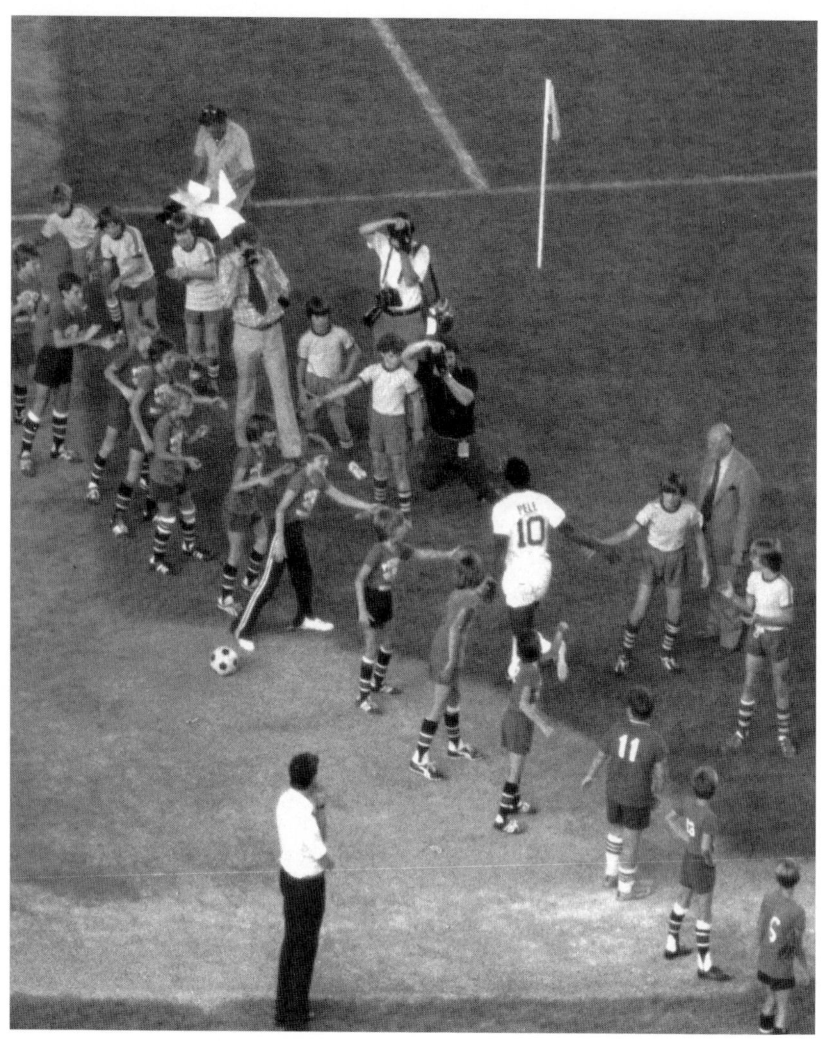

Shea Stadium, 1976
Pelé runs through two rows of youth soccer players during player introductions.

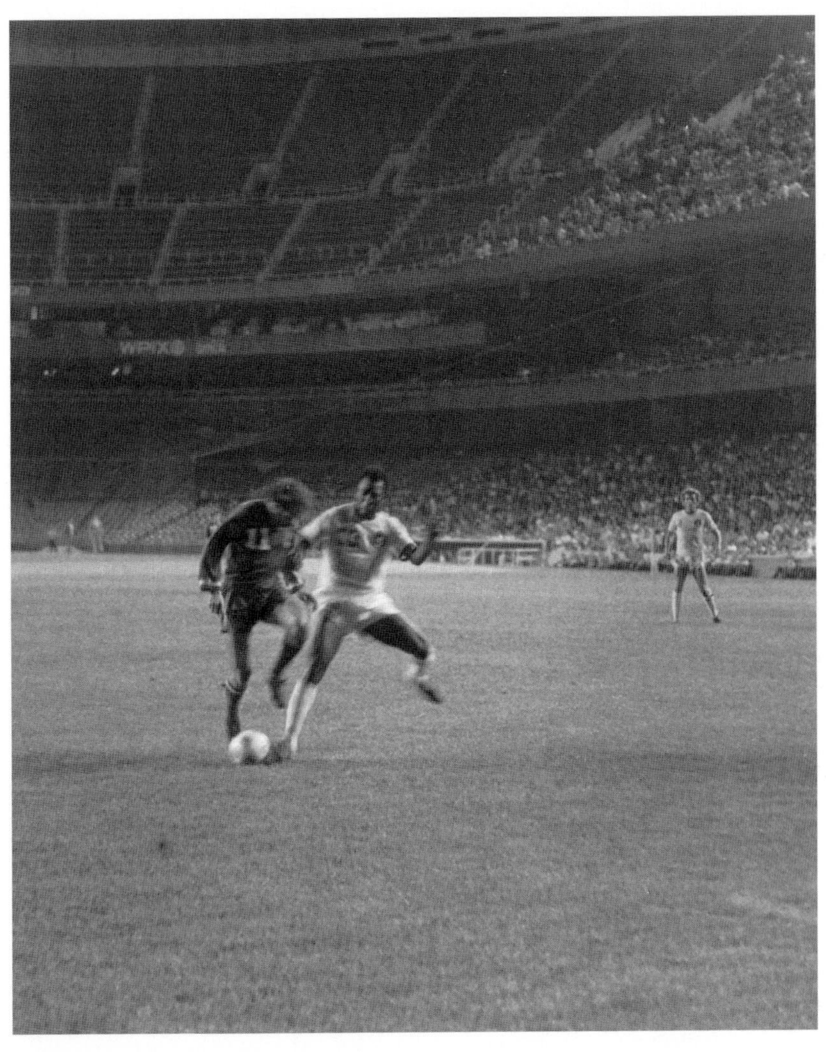

Yankee Stadium, 1976
An unaccustomed sight: Pelé is playing in front of a half-empty stadium.

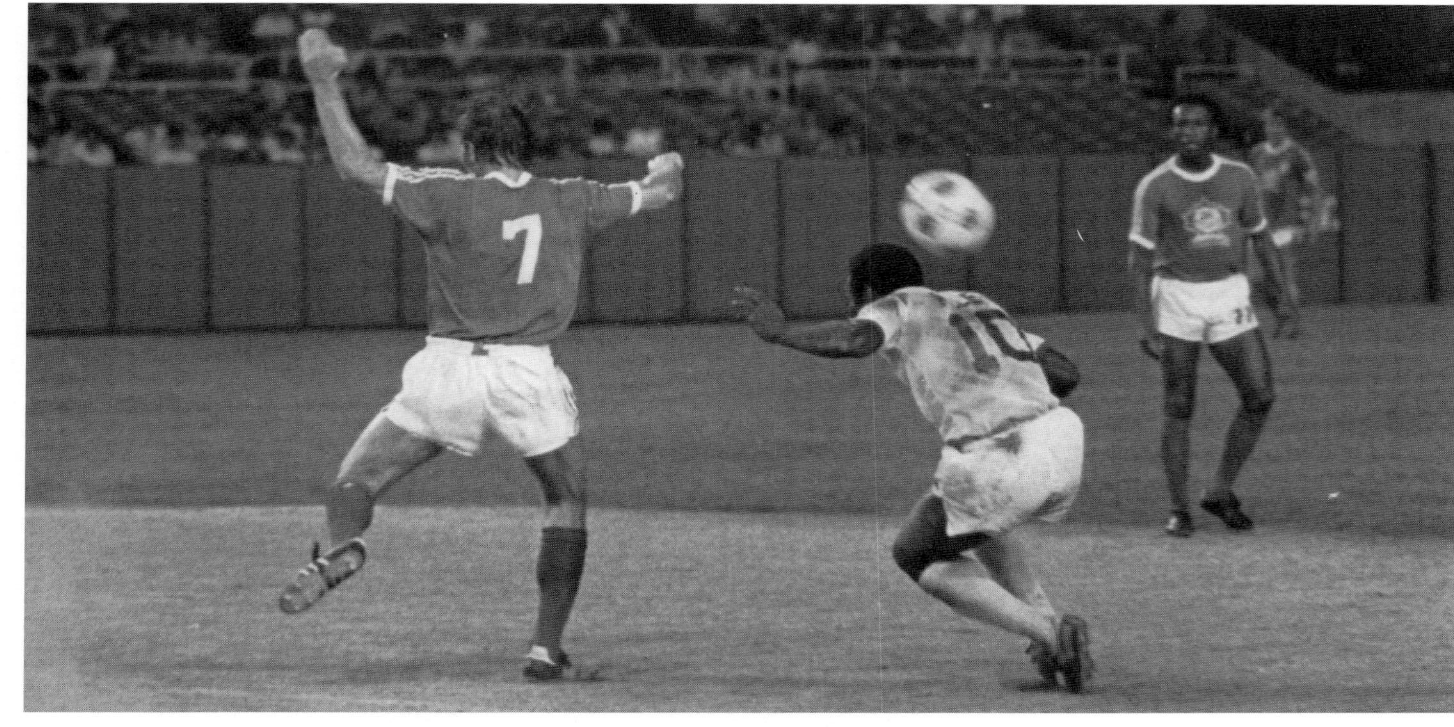

Yankee Stadium, 1976
The strange sight of Pelé trying to control the ball in the area of second base.

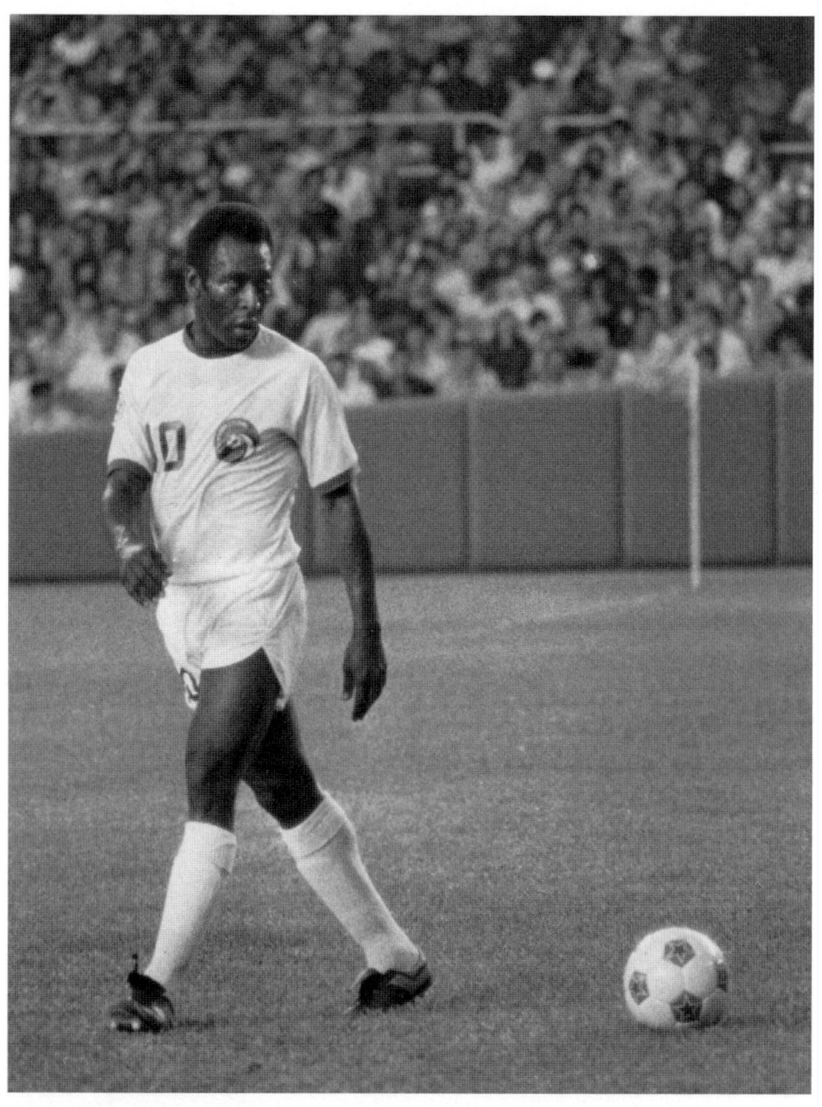

Yankee Stadium, 1976
Pelé addresses the ball before attempting a free kick.

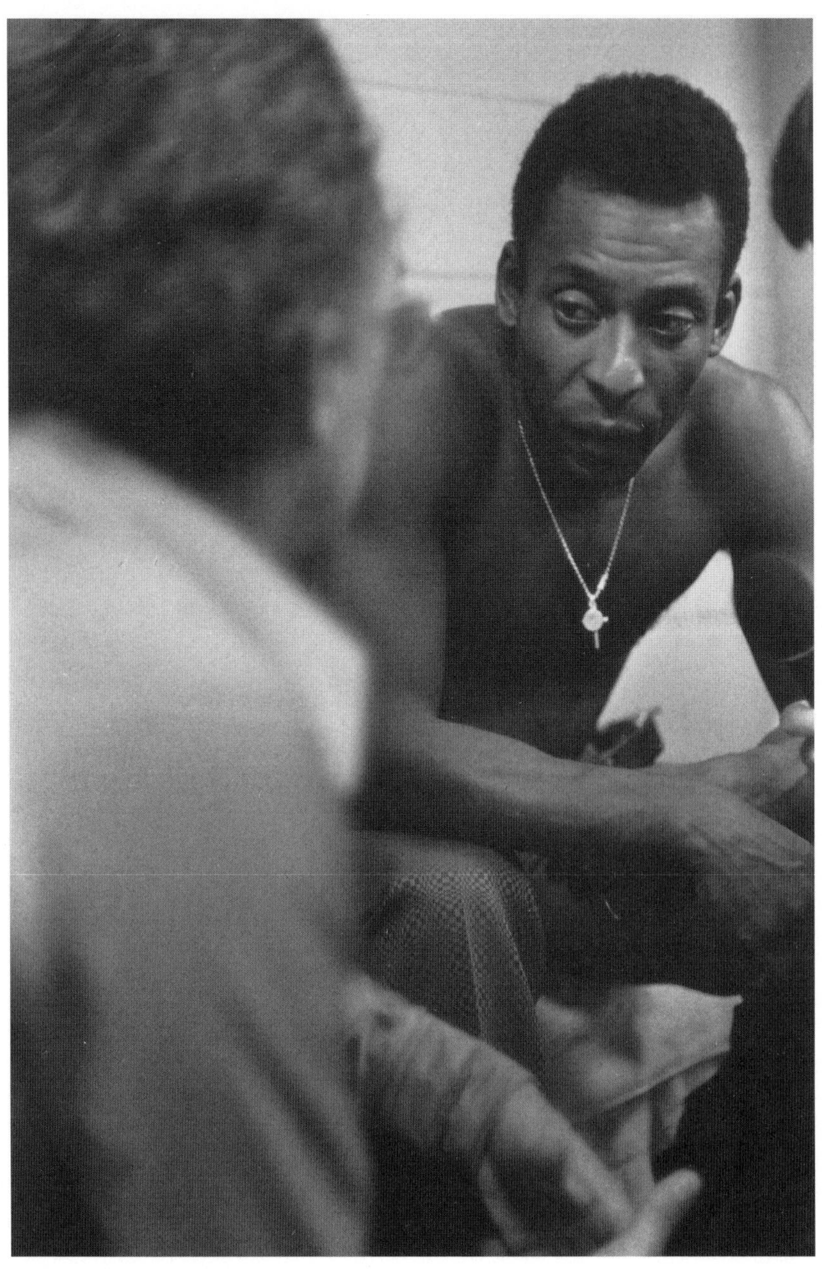

Yankee Stadium, 1976
Pelé gives an interview after a game.

Yankee Stadium, 1976
Pelé running on the field.

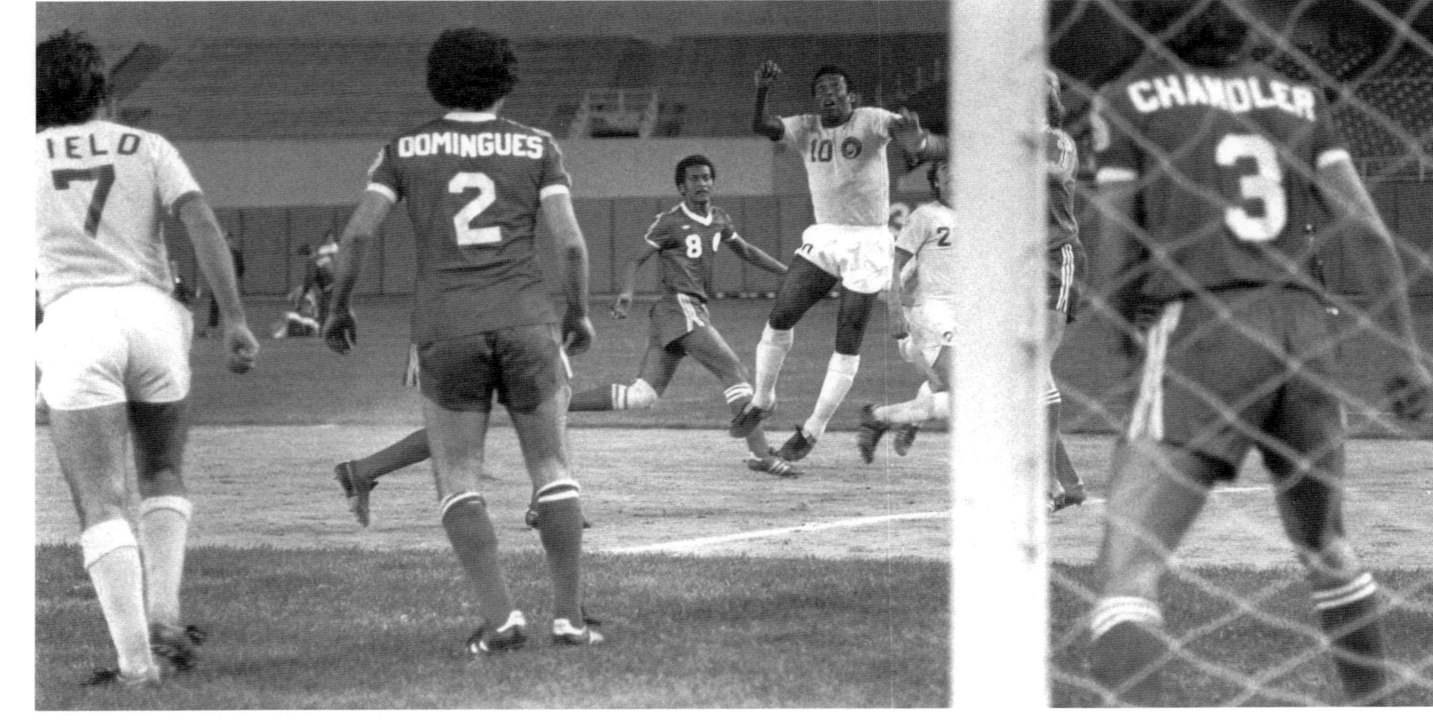

Yankee Stadium, 1976
Pelé waits to pounce on the ball for an attempted header.

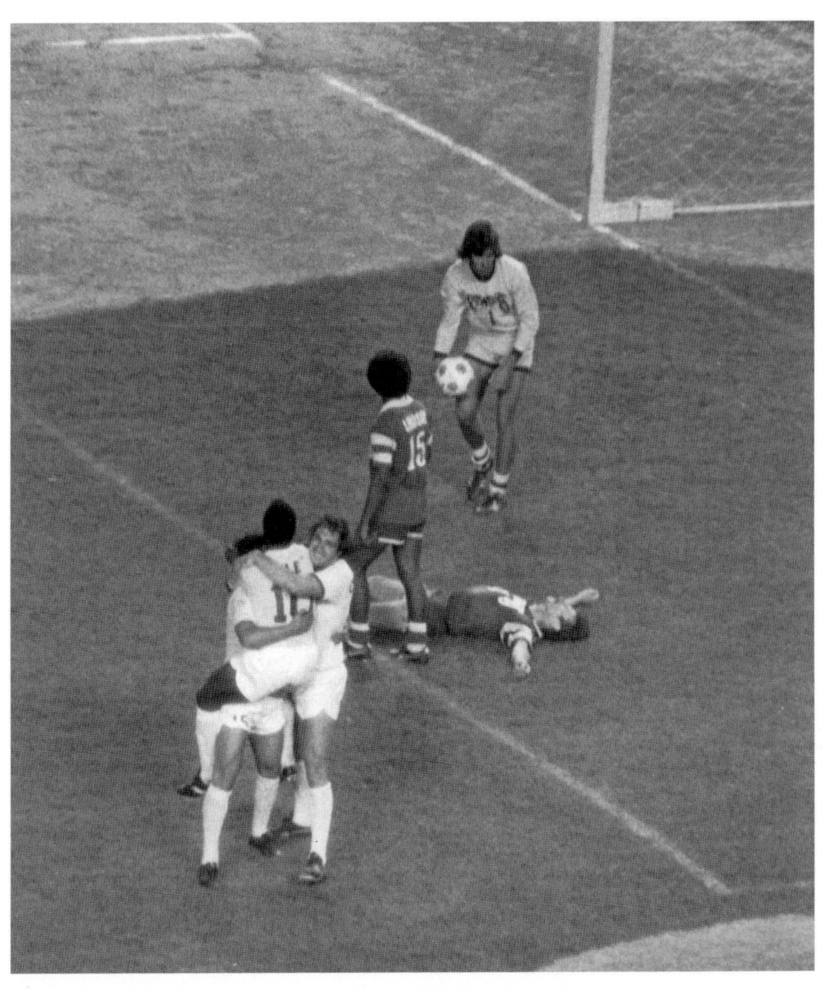

Yankee Stadium, 1976
Pelé and Georgio Chinaglia celebrate a Pelé goal.

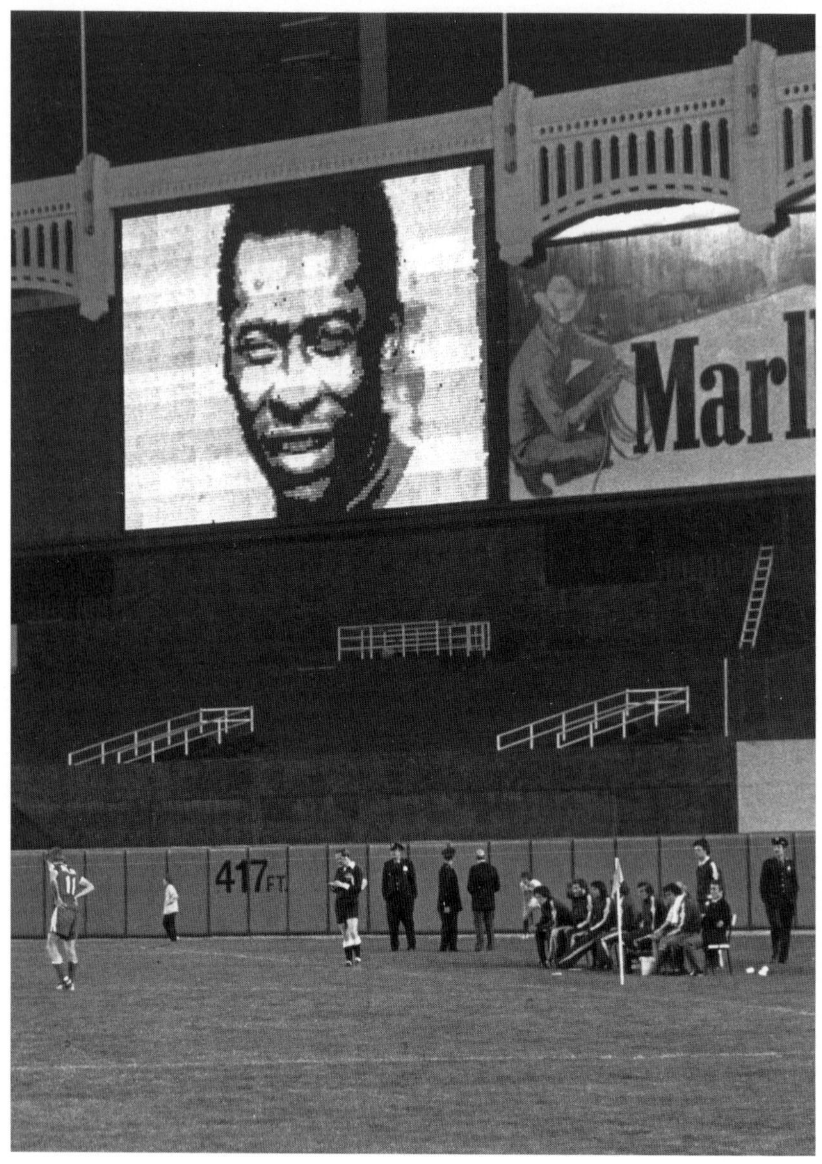

Yankee Stadium, 1976
The electronic scoreboard celebrates the main attraction.

Yankee Stadium, 1976
Pelé scores off of a dramatic header.

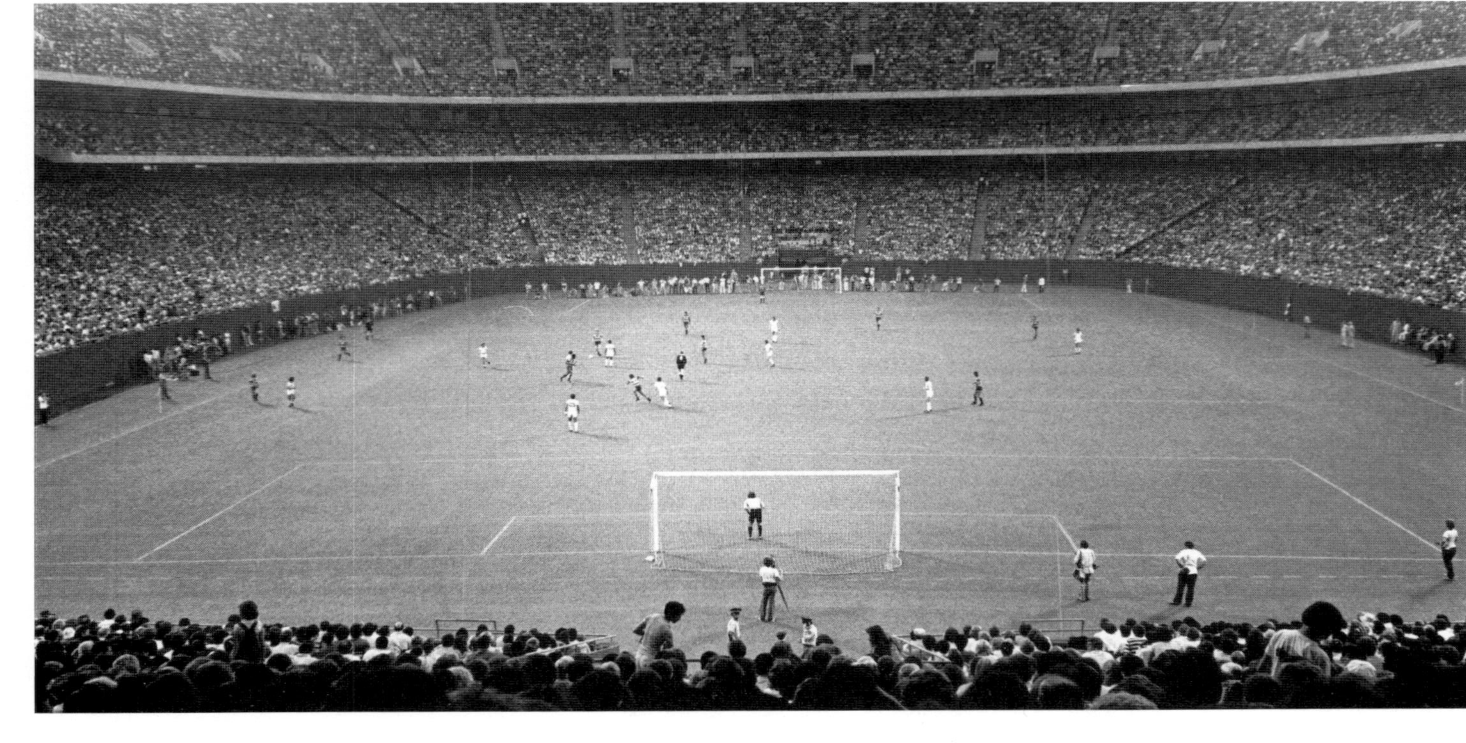

Giants Stadium, 1977
A record crowd of nearly 80,000 spectators.

Chapter 8

There are few views in this world as spectacular as the one that spreads before you from the top of the plateau overlooking the city of Santos. The drop is sheer and the height is more than half a mile. The highway that twists its way down the face of the cliff—the Via Anchieta—is a marvel of engineering. In places it carries you on cantilevered bridges hung from the cliff face; in places you wind through tunnels cut in the rock to come out again and see the same breath-taking view, foreshortened. The road has two levels, one above the other, the one descending the other going up. As you drop down the three thousand feet to sea level the air gets warmer and more humid; not far away, dropping precipitously down the mountainside you see the large covered spillways that drop water from the São Paulo lakes on top of the mountain to feed the Cubatão power complex which furnishes electricity to Santos, and to the city of São Paulo, as well.

I have seen that view hundreds of times in the past twenty years, and it never fails to impress me, but never quite as much as the first time I saw it with Valdemar de Brito at my side on the bus, and Dondinho sitting behind us, as impressed by the view as I was. Valdemar had met us at the railroad station in São Paulo as he had arranged. We had eaten at a small restaurant nearby where I could hardly swallow, I was so overwhelmed by the enormity of the city in which we found ourselves. I had always known that São Paulo was the largest city in our country, but it was one thing to know it and another to experience it. The streets were bustling, even on a Sunday. After lunch we had taken the bus to Santos. For almost an hour we had wound our way through the streets of the huge sprawling city, an endless procession of block after block, each crowded with houses or apartments, the roads filled with thousands of cars, but with the same brown dirt as Baurú where an empty lot appeared. It was almost comforting to see that dirt; it tied one to the earth and to Baurú.

At last we were out of the city and on the highway on top of the São Paulo plateau, passing the great factories that lined the road, each with extensive green lawns smooth as the finest football field, and every now and then a town in the distance where the workers lived, visible in the afternoon sun. Mile after mile we crossed the plateau until we had come to the sheer drop that marked the descent to Santos, and now we were on our way down.

Valdemar was talking, but I was only half aware of his statements or his questions, answering him automatically, my nose pressed tightly against the closed window, not wanting to miss a single moment of the view as the bus negotiated the sharp twists and hairpin turns on its way down the mountain. I remember we passed people climbing laboriously up that incredibly steep road, stepping aside to let the bus pass, looking at us impassively. I wondered where they could be going, what they could possibly be doing in a place as isolated as that. But then we would pass some thatched hut, clinging to the mountain, with a tiny patch of cultivated garden, almost vertical, beside it, and I knew the people must live in these, although why they did evaded me.

Valdemar was speaking.

"There's no need to be nervous, Pelé. I know it's only natural, but the thing to do is simply pretend you're playing in a Baquinho or a Noroestinho game back in Baurú and forget who you're playing with. ..."

"Yes, sir—"

To the left I could see the sheer fall of the mountain following but stepped back from the ocean until it faded into a violet haze in the distance. Between the wall of the cliff and the faraway sea there was a long flat stretch of green, broken only by a series of low hills, all deserted, and leading to a stretch of sand, barely visible, that I was later to know and enjoy as Guarujá. As soon as I got the chance, I knew I would want to explore that deserted-looking beach, appearing from the bus almost like a place where pirate ships might put in to bury treasure.

"... and don't let the big names of the players you'll meet and train with get you rattled. They're just people, like you and me. You can play the game as well as any of them. Remember that."

"Yes, sir—"

There seemed to be a channel of water running all the way around the city of Santos, making it an island. The sun glinted from the windows of tall buildings far away; in the channel there were ships that looked like toys from where we were. And beyond everything there was the ocean, stretched out like rippled glass under a high blue sky and a blazing sun all the way to the horizon. I knew the Atlantic Ocean was big; I knew from school that it ran all the way from our coast to the coast of Africa—but who would ever have imagined it *looked* so big?

"... don't let it bother you, feeling strange, or out of place, at first. You'll get used to the club and the men. Feeling strange is only natural. Even when a professional changes from one club to another it takes time to get used to his new teammates, even though he's probably played against them before. You'll be fine. The men on the Santos squad are a great bunch. You'll like them and they'll like you."

"Yes, sir—"

We were getting lower on the mountain. Just beneath us I could now see that what I thought had been a huge stand of palm trees was actually a large banana plantation, running for miles toward the distant city. To our left some sort of construction was going on where the spillways came to earth, diving into the top of a large building. The banana plants had been laid out in even rows, with planning, not at all like the haphazard *bananeiras* we saw in the interior, growing at random. Here the buildings of the power complex looked much more haphazard.

"... and nothing of bad companions away from the club, you hear? I feel responsible to your mother and father. No smoking, no drinking, and no chasing after girls, either. ..."

No chasing after girls ...

I remembered all too clearly an incident that had occurred just after I turned fourteen, when a friend of mine called Zinho talked me into going out with him one night to visit a local prostitute, who he assured me would not only teach me the facts of life—which I thought I knew but obviously didn't—but who would demonstrate how wonderful the lesson could be. As I sat in the shabby front room of her small shack, smelling the combination of stale cooking and cheap perfume, waiting for Zinho to finish and my turn to come, I was torn between the fear of going ahead with the adventure and the shame of running away. Besides, down deep I was consumed with curiosity as to what it was really all about. So, when Zinho came swaggering out of the bedroom, winking at me lewdly, I girded my loins, as they say, and in I went.

The episode was a combination of unrelieved terror and incredible sweetness, but in any event it was quick. As soon as it was over, however, and I was dressing, I realized I had taken a grave chance of getting infected with venereal disease. No sooner had the thought come to me than it solidified into an assurance, and as we made our way home I could almost feel the little bugs at work. I turned pale. How would I ever be able to explain my disease to my parents? I couldn't keep it a secret forever; how could I hide it when I went blind, or my nose fell off? I spent an agonizing two weeks before I tentatively accepted the assurance of the more experienced Zinho that if there was no tangible evidence of any disease by that time, I was free and clear. But that sick fright was such that no other feeling, sweet or not, could possibly compensate for those two weeks of unrelieved terror.

So I smiled at Valdemar, taking my eyes from the view for the first time.

"Chasing girls? Don't worry!"

I must have sounded sincere, because he merely nodded and said:

"Good!"

When we got off the bus in the center of Santos, far from the beach I had hoped we would at least pass, I had to admit there was a certain resemblance to Baurú, but it was basically the same resemblance almost all cities and towns of medium size bear to each other in Brazil. The bus station was in an older part of the city and the narrow cobblestone-paved streets, the plaster-faced buildings built in rococo Brazilian colonial style, the soft but worn pastel shades, the wooded plaza, the ancient church, were really not too different from the town where I was raised. It wasn't until later, when I got to see the busy docks and their monstrous cranes, the huge ships looming over the quays, and the beaches and the residential sections that I realized the vast differences. Baurú was a small town and Santos was a big city, and the designation had nothing to do with their populations.

Valdemar carried my bag and we took a cab to the Vila Belmiro, where the Santos Club was located. It was, as I said, a Sunday afternoon and Santos was playing a game against Comercial of Ribeirão Preto as part of the tournament for the state championship. The stadium was of fair size, but nothing too impressive; I had seen games on television that had taken place in Maracanã and in Pacaembú, and this was disappointing in comparison. Still, it was in this stadium that players like Jair and Formiga played, and it was in this stadium that the state champions played.

Valdemar, after leaving my bag at the office, managed to arrange excellent seats for the three of us, although the place was crowded, and before the end of the game I had forgotten all about the size of the stadium and found myself cheering wildly for Santos and their excellent play, as if I were a member of the team already.

When the game ended and Santos had won, Valdemar led Dondinho and me down to the dressing rooms. There was the usual happy confusion that always animates a dressing room after a victory, and Valdemar presented me to Luis Alonso, the coach, who was known to all as Lula. He was also known as a fine coach. Lula smiled.

"So you're the famous Pelé, eh?"

I didn't know if he was kidding or trying to put me at my ease. If he was trying to put me at my ease, he wasn't succeeding. I knew I wasn't famous, certainly not outside Baurú, and never would I have even faintly considered the word "famous" in the face of the number of truly famous names who were in the locker room with me at the time, changing clothes. I didn't know what to do or say. All I could do was swallow.

"Yes, sir."

Lula laughed, and I realized what I had said. But I also knew he hadn't been trying to put me down, but only to make me feel welcome.

"We've been expecting you. Let me introduce you around."

He took my arm and led me around the room, introducing me to the others on the team. I could hardly believe I was actually there, meeting and shaking hands with the famous names I had only known from football cards or from hearing their names on the radio or reading of them in the Baurú *Daily*. It was an odd feeling, as if I might wake up at any minute and find myself in my bed at home, dreaming. It seemed totally unbelievable that I would actually be on a football field training with them.

But it was also nice to know that many of them had heard of Dondinho, some had seen him play, and many came over to tell him how sorry they had been at his accident. Dondinho waved this all aside in favor of something more important to him.

"Look," he said. "This boy is going to stay with you here at Vila Belmiro. I have to go back to Baurú, and Valdemar has to go back to São Paulo. So he'll be here all alone. I'm asking you to take good care of him, for me. *Heim*?"

Vasconcelos was the captain of the team, a big man with an equally big heart. He put an arm around my shoulders.

"Put your mind at rest. He'll be safe with us."

The whole thing looked like a part of a movie I was watching from the balcony of the picture house in Baurú. Among all those big names I was tongue-tied. Zito was there, Jair, Formiga, Pagão, Pepe. This was the team that had taken the São Paulo state championship the year before and was successfully defending it this year. Dondinho and Valdemar came over to me.

"We're leaving now. You'll be all right. Don't worry."

Dondinho put his hands on my shoulders.

"Do what Lula tells you. Behave as you would if you were home with your mother and me. No bad companions. No—"

He stopped and drew me to him, hugging me tightly, and smiled apologetically.

"No more lectures, Dico. You're grown-up, now."

But I wasn't grown-up and I knew it and I knew Dondinho knew it, too. Much as I liked the idea of training with the Santos team, and much as the idea of being on my own should have appealed to me, I was already ready to go back to Baurú. But I couldn't say so in front of so many people; I couldn't admit to anything as childish as homesickness, not the first day! So I just hugged my father with all my might, and wished to heaven I was getting on the bus with him.

I spent that night and the nights that followed at Vila Belmiro. There were rooms enough to accommodate the entire first team; when an important match was to be played the following day, the entire first team was required to stay at the clubhouse in what was called a *concentração*—which means "concentration" and it would not surprise me if that is where the phrase "concentration camp" came from, because that is what it was. A *concentração* put the players under the watchful eye of the coach, limiting them to the premises, and was meant to keep them out of any trouble they might get into away from the club that could prevent their appearance at the important game. But even when the first team wasn't being held in quarantine, many of the players lived at Vila Belmiro; certainly all the single players. It cost nothing, and as football players, none of them could afford to throw money away. None of them made all that much.

The rooms were small but clean, with either two or three cots in each room, nails on the back of the door for clothes, and with a chair or two for those too neat to sit on an already-made bed. In a way they were austere, with no decorations on the walls and no mats or rugs on the floors, but they were filled with friendships, which is what counted. The first team of Santos in those days was made up of Manga, Helio, Ivan, Ramiro, Formiga, Zito, Tite, Jair, Pagão, Pepe, and with either Vasconcelos or Del Vecchio playing the center-forward position; and many of them were permanently housed at the Vila Belmiro stadium. In addition many of the reserves lived there: Cássio, Raimundinho, Hugo, Dorval, and even me.

Everyone did his best that first night to make me feel at home, but it took a long time to get to sleep in the unaccustomed bed, my head whirling with thoughts. I had had dinner at a nearby boardinghouse with the others from the clubhouse; there was a full kitchen in the section of the stadium that held our rooms, and we always had breakfast there and many of our other meals, but when the cook had her day off or was away for any other reason, we took our evening meals at Dona

Antonia's or at the Louis XV, a combination bar-restaurant across the street from the club. The food had been good—far different food from what we had at home—but I had not been too hungry. I lay in the strange bed wondering, even if my football turned out to be enough, whether I would ever be able to overcome the homesickness that was already beginning to haunt me.

Eventually I fell alseep, and the next morning I walked the mile or so to the beach, realizing a dream I had had since I was a youngster. I'm sure it must be the dream of every Brazilian who does not live near the ocean, although they are in the minority, since Brazil, to this day, has concentrated itself along its Atlantic beaches. But I felt if I failed with Santos, or if my homesickness overcame me, I certainly didn't want to go home without seeing at close up the ocean I had dreamed about for so long.

It was everything I had imagined it to be, and much more. The Santos beach is one of the most beautiful in the world. Wide colorful flower gardens separate the two roadways that front the beach, carrying traffic in each direction. In those days there were few apartment houses along the shoreside of the beach; instead, large stately homes lined the mosaic walks, with low stone walls that added rather than detracted from their impressiveness. They had evenly clipped lawns that were like green carpets, multigarages for the many cars they owned, balconies and turrets, like castles. Occasionally I saw maids and cooks, neatly uniformed, coming to the wide verandas to enjoy a view of the beach and excite the imagination of a youngster from Baurú. I had never seen anything like this. I later learned that many of the homes were only vacation places for businessmen who lived in São Paulo and came to the beach on weekends only. I could hardly imagine wealth that could permit only partial use of such palaces; in Baurú, not even our mayor, Nicola Avalone Júnior, had a home like these.

There was a small island off the shore that I particularly remember; it was the only one near shore and looked as if one could walk there at low tide. Beyond it, at the southern end of the beach, rock walls came out of the water as if to contain the scene, give it a margin, making it appear unreal, like a picture postcard. Through the years since then the large homes have gradually disappeared, replaced by elegant apartment buildings, but otherwise the Santos beach is the same. The island off the shore still entices—and one *can* walk there at low tide—the wall of rock at the southern end still encloses the beauty of the beach, the wide gardens still line the roadways. It is still the most beautiful place I know.

The sand was warm and I took off my shoes and socks and walked down to the water. One thing I clearly remembered from school was that the ocean was supposed to be salty, a statement I had always considered with suspicion but one which I could now easily verify. I bent down and scooped up a handful, tasting it. It *was* salty! I sat down and considered the vast reaches of the sea before me. It must have taken a fantastic amount of salt to salt it all! And how had it possibly been done? It was hard to imagine such a task. And *why*?

I spent the rest of the day at the beach, enjoying the view, enjoying the feel of the warm sand between my toes, and the water against my ankles, glad that I had had a chance to see the ocean at last—and wondering how long, despite the beauty of Santos, I could manage without Baurú and my family.

Tuesday morning, two days after my arrival, I trained with the Santos team for the first time. I recall there was a slight drizzle and for a moment I hoped the practice would be postponed and I wouldn't have to face the others on the field, but nobody seemed to even think about the drizzle, changing into uniforms and trotting out to the field. Although I did everything I knew to keep calm, when I pulled on the uniform of Santos for the first time, my legs were trembling. Pepe walked out to the field with me, smiling down at me.

"Nervous?"

"A little."

"There's not a thing to be nervous about. You're among friends."

And I was. It was very interesting. When I left Baurú many people came to me to say:

"You won't have a chance with those big shots down in Santos, you'll see. They'll boycott you. They won't let you touch the ball. It'll be like that training of Valdemar—you'll be in the middle and they'll keep the ball from you. They'll do everything to make you look bad. They worked too hard and too long to get where they are, to let some fifteen-year-old kid walk in and start where it took them ten years to get. They'll kill you. You'll see."

Well, I saw. The players could not have been more co-operative or more friendly if we had played together for years. If anything, they went out of their way to try to make me look good. We started out with calesthenics to loosen our muscles, and after an hour or so of practicing passing to each other, and trapping balls, Lula separated us into teams for football practice. He walked over to me.

"You play center-forward, I understand?"

"Yes, sir."

"All right. You play that position today. First team."

I was almost paralyzed with fright at the thought. I had thought that after practicing the dribbles and the traps and the tackles, he would have me sit on the bench while the teams had their practice game. Formiga, standing next to me, laughed.

Under his breath he said, "Don't let our side down, kid!"

It has been said and written in newspapers and magazines that the first time I walked onto the field for Santos I played phenomenally, that I scored many goals, and that the next day I was made a member of the professional team. It actually didn't work out quite that way. I was very nervous among all those top stars and I began very badly. But as the game went on I started to loosen up and forget I was playing against such stars as Vasconcelos and Pagão; I wasn't in Santos at the moment, I was back in Baurú, playing for Baquinho, and I was Pelé! My dribbling got better, my tackling less timid. I didn't score any goals that first training game, but at least I felt at home with my game. And, as I said, rather than "boycott" me I felt they co-operated fully. They passed the ball to me when the play indicated they should, and they passed it to someone else when it was better to do that. They played like the professionals they were.

When we finished the day's training, Lula called me over.

"I liked the way you played today. The only thing is, you're still very small. Too small to play with the professionals, I'm afraid. We'll just have to wait until you're bigger and a little older and then we'll see. What do you weigh?"

I looked down at the floor, feeling as if my lack of weight was something I should have rectified a long time before, something I should be ashamed of.

"I—I weigh almost one hundred thirty pounds. ..."

Lula nodded.

"Well, you can play with the juvenile and the amateur team and get good practice and experience with them. Actually, you would even qualify for the infantile team. They play until age fifteen."

Santos supported four teams, as most of the major clubs did: an infantile team, taking players from age nine through age fifteen; a juvenile team, from age fifteen through eighteen; an amateur team where age made no difference; and the professional team. I swallowed. I don't know what had made me dream I might start right out on the professional roster. Still, there wasn't very much I could do or say.

"Yes, sir ..."

"Good! Go in and take your shower. Afterward we can discuss it in greater detail."

In the dressing room all the players came over to congratulate me on my play during practice. Zito was there, Dorval, Jair, Pagão, Del Vecchio, and the rest. Pepe came over and patted me on the shoulder.

"You're good, kid," he said. "You're going to be very good!"

"Great!" I said bitterly, "except I've just been told I've got to play on the juvenile team—maybe even on the infantile! Lula says I'm too small, too light. ..."

Pepe grinned at me.

"So we'll feed you, son—day and night!"

The days managed to go by, with calisthenics, training, and eating mammoth meals at the boardinghouse, the club, or the restaurant-bar across the street. But before those mammoth meals began, I had to take medicine for *lombrigas*—worms—a very common infestation of the poor in Brazil. Almost all players from the poorer sections of Brazil, or the interior, or the northeast, suffered from this common complaint, and when they first arrived in Santos their first medical checkup usually revealed the *lombrigas*, and an awful-tasting medicine was always prescribed. But once the problem of the worms was cleared up, then I really began to eat!

Foods we had rarely been able to afford in our house in Baurú became common; meat as often as I wanted, chicken every day if I wanted—all high-protein foods rather than the starches on which most of the poor in Brazil existed. Wonderful fish from the beaches of Santos, in sauces I had never imagined, let alone experienced. And after those enormous meals we would sit around and talk until bedtime, of football, of our homes, our families, all warm and friendly.

But the nights were awful. My room had two cots in it but I had no roommate, which was just as well as I would have kept him awake with my crying. I was homesick and nothing anyone could say or do could make it any better. Besides, what was the use? I had been told I was too small for professional football, and I had been eating myself sick for four or five whole days and could see no appreciable change in my proportions. I was small and skinny and I was going to stay small and skinny my entire life. It was obvious I would never make the first team but would play with the juvenile or the amateur until I was too old even for them, or until Santos got tired of seeing me around and feeding me those enormous meals, at which point they would send me home.

So why wait for the inevitable and suffer in the meantime?

One morning, about five o'clock, the fifth or sixth day after my arrival, I got up, dressed quietly, packed my few belongings into my bag, checked to see that I still had the money Dondinho had left to cover my fare home if I ever needed it, and sneaked from my room and down the stairs on tiptoe.

And ran into a young fellow named Sabú, whom we called Sabuzão, or Big Sabú. Sabuzão worked at the clubhouse doing odd jobs, cutting the grass on the field, picking up in the locker room, or whatever else had to be done. His mother ran the kitchen and cooked us our breakfast as well as other meals. Sabuzão was on his way to the market for our fresh fruit and hot rolls. He saw me with my suitcase and frowned.

"Where do you think you're going?"

"Back to Baurú," I said stubbornly. "I'll never make the team. I'm too small."

Sabuzão smiled.

"Of course you're small. You're only fifteen years old. But if you keep on eating the way you're going, you'll be the fattest man in Santos inside of six months."

He took the suitcase from my hand gently.

"Anyway, I haven't been given permission to let you go anywhere, and I don't want to get into trouble. Go upstairs and take it easy. Breakfast will be as soon as I get back."

So I went upstairs, feeling a little foolish.

I had been participating in training sessions with the Santos team for over a week when Sr. Antonio, the Director for Sports for the Santos Football Club, came to me and asked me if I wanted to sign a contract. Before I could get too excited—pictures ran through my mind immediately that Lula had changed his mind and needed me desperately on the professional team—Sr. Antonio indicated that I would still be playing with the juvenile and amateur teams, at least for the time being, and besides, it wouldn't be a *contract* contract. Since I was very much underage, it would be what they called a *contrato-de-gaveta*—a "contract-hidden-in-a-drawer"—until I was older and could sign a proper contract. Of course, contracts-in-the-drawer were illegal, and most clubs will deny they ever signed any, but almost every football club holds promising young players with something of the sort.

Well, of course I had come to Santos with the original intention of staying, regardless of my homesickness. And I did want to keep training with Santos and eventually play with them. So I agreed. It meant that Valdemar de Brito had to come down to Santos to advise me, and then he and I went to Baurú, because the final decision had to be with my parents.

It was a wonderful feeling being back in that house with my father and mother, my grandmother, uncle, sister, and brother, believe me! I had been gone about two weeks but it seemed like ages, and from the reunion we had one would have thought it had *been* ages. When I told everyone that Santos wanted to sign me to a contract, my father was delighted; but Dona Celeste was something else. It seems that Dondinho had assured her my very first trip to Santos was only for a brief training period, and she was under the impression I had come home to stay.

"If you go," she said sternly, "then go to stay! You'll be no son of mine, if you can disregard my feelings this way!"

She was so upset by the news, in fact, and carried on so, that I was about to decide to stay in Baurú and forget about Santos. I hated to see my mother so unhappy. Besides, when I thought of those lonely nights in the small room at the club, home looked better and better.

At this point Valdemar de Brito started to talk. He went through the entire story again, how well I was treated by everyone in Santos—which I could not deny, since it was the truth—the great opportunity I had there, playing with their juvenile and amateur team now, but with time I would assuredly make the first team.

"And there's the money, too," he said. "This 'contract-in-the-drawer' will pay Pelé five thousand cruzeiros a month, and that's only until he gets a little older and heavier, when they'll give him a regular contract at more money. He'll also be earning bonuses when the teams win, even the juvenile and amateur. The bonuses won't be large, but it all adds up. And where else could he be making money like that at his age? Certainly not working in a factory sewing boots—or playing with Noroeste or BAC or any other professional team around here. And he's eating properly, for once; and he has his room thrown in."

It was a potent argument, and eventually won over my mother. Five thousand cruzeiros in that year, 1956, was worth about sixty dollars American, and that was far above the minimum wage, which is the most I could have hoped to earn in the boot factory. And room and board—especially the way I was eating—were worth a lot, too.

So back we went to Santos, this time with a "sort-of" contract, but at least with the assurance of being paid something each month. Of the five thousand cruzeiros, I kept one thousand and sent the other four to Dondinho with the suggestion that he investigate the possibility of putting the money down on a house for Dona Celeste, so that the worry of having to pay rent could be eliminated for her for all time. Dondinho found a small house on September 7th that was for sale, and started to make payments on it; it was much the same as the house we rented on Rubens Arruda, but at least it was going to be our own.

I continued training with the first team, but I still only played with the juvenile and the amateur. The fact that I was receiving money did not bar me from playing with the amateur team; only members of the professional team were barred. Nor did it prevent me from receiving bonus money, together with the other players, if we won a game.

The way bonus money is paid in Brazil is fairly standard: A certain amount of the gate is put aside to pay the winning team. This money is divided among the team members on the basis of two shares to a player who was actually in the game, and one share to a player who sat on the bench as a reserve. In World Cup games, however, the shares are alike, whether a player plays or not—and equal shares are also given the trainer, the coach, the masseur, the doctors, and all others who form a part of the commission.

A certain Nenê was in charge of the three groups other than the professionals at Santos, and I played under his orders. And it was under his direction that I played for the Santos colors for the first time, in a juvenile game against another local club called Vasco da Gama. (Readers should not be confused by the duplication of club names in different cities. Vasco da Gama is a popular name and there are dozens of clubs throughout Brazil with this name. Similarly there are many Corinthians clubs in various cities in the country.) In any event we won and I scored three goals that day, and we later won the juvenile championship of the state, as well as the amateur crown. Since Santos was the state champion in the professional class, it meant that this one club held three of the four possible titles.

But the fourth—the infantile—looked to be in jeopardy. The team needed strengthening and since I was technically able to sneak under the wire as a fifteen-year-old, and therefore eligible to play, Nenê decided that I would play in this important game. Nobody, least of all myself, had the slightest doubt that with my vastly greater experience, and playing in a game where for a change I would not be the smallest player but one of the largest, we would win in a breeze. It was felt, and I agreed, that I should be able to make as many goals as I wanted whenever I felt like scoring them.

It didn't work out that way. Either because I was secretly ashamed to be playing against a team that included some nine-year-olds, or because I was having a bad day, or because the opposition, young or not, was simply playing good football, the fact is I couldn't get a goal to save my soul. And the harder I tried the worse I played. My passes went to the opposition, ten-year-olds tackled the ball away from me; eleven-year-olds dribbled right through me. It was awful!

But then, with time running out and our youthful opponents one goal ahead, one of the youngsters fouled one of our players in the penalty area and of course I was the one called upon to make the kick and tie the game. To make a long story short, the ball was placed on the penalty spot, the players of both teams stood back, and I smiled to myself as I saw the tiny goalkeeper there, his little feet planted, and his short outstretched arms not covering a tenth part of the goal. I stepped forward and kicked—and the ball went completely over the crossbar! The *Booooo*!!!! that rose from the stands I shall never forget, and one which I try to recall whenever I get a tendency toward a swelled head.

The score ended that way, and the Santos Infantile had lost. The great Pelé had done absolutely nothing—unless one counted missing a very easy penalty kick. My ears were burning when I left the field.

I did not shower with the others but took my clothes from my locker and ducked up to my room. I locked the door and then lay down on the bed and cried as I hadn't cried in a long time. It was obviously impossible to continue training with the professionals after the sorry exhibition I had put on that day. The booing I had gotten from the stands would be nothing compared to the ridicule I would face from the team members if I ever saw them again. Beaten by a bunch of infants! Beaten by babies! Besides, if I couldn't play any better against a bunch of kids half my size, what made me think I would ever get to play with the Santos first team, whether I gained weight or not? Or grew to be eight feet tall?

I had been living in a dream world, I told myself sternly, and the sooner I got myself out of it, the better. My place was Baurú, playing with teams whose skills I knew. Or maybe not playing at all, after today. The Santos directors would have no trouble canceling a contract that legally didn't exist—in fact, they were probably doing that right this moment.

I fell asleep, still snuffling, still in my sweaty uniform, and woke up to find the room pitch-dark. I turned on the light, dragged my suitcase over from the corner, and started to pack. I changed my uniform, leaving it on the unmade bed, climbed into my regular street clothes, unlocked the door, and sneaked down the stairs.

And ran into Sabuzão again. He shook his head in disbelief.

"Not again!"

"You don't understand—"

"I understand. You missed a penalty kick yesterday. Against an infantile team."

"You see?" I said furiously. "You're making fun of me!"

"I'm not making fun of you," he said calmly. "I'm telling you what happened. When you miss a penalty kick it doesn't make any difference against whom. You would have missed that kick against Gilmar. I've seen Vasconcelos miss penalty kicks. I've seen Del Vecchio miss them. You can miss them, too."

He reached over and took the suitcase from my hand.

"Now, go back to your room. If you try running away again, I'll have to take your suitcase away from you."

And that was the last time I tried to run away.

When I first started to train with Santos, a lot of the members of the team began to call me Gasolina instead of Pelé. Whenever they wanted someone to go out for coffee, or to run any kind of an errand, they'd call on me as being the youngest and newest, and they'd tell me not to spare the *gasolina* in getting there and getting back. Thus the nickname Gasolina, which at least had some logic to it. But by now I had become accustomed to the name Pelé; it was the name by which I was known in football circles in Baurú and I didn't like the idea of changing nicknames. But I also didn't want to argue with the top players in the top team of the state. So I tolerated it, especially since not one player ever said a word about my performance in that awful infantile game I lost for our club.

Santos had, at that time, one of the finest teams ever assembled. They were young, hard-working, extremely skilled individually, and excellently coached. Lula was a strong advocate of an attacking game, one where rigid ball control was essential, and his style of play required great imagination on the part of his players, inventiveness and quick responses to any situation that might arise. Santos, at that time, was well on its way to repeating the victory of the year before in the state championship, and the players all received plenty of publicity. At times Alfredinho would substitute for Tite at right-wing, and Alvaro would alternate with Jair, as Vasconcelos did with Del Vecchio, but the rest of the team played their positions regularly, barring unforeseen injuries. Vasconcelos—whom we all called Vasco—and Del Vecchio were the stars, the chief goal-getters, and they played a marvelous game. I knew, therefore, that it would probably be a very long time before I would get a chance to play, as they played my position and played it very well, indeed.

But not every game saw Lula calling on all his stars to play. One day, for example, Santos was scheduled to play against Cubatão, a team from our neighboring town, and since Cubatão was a small club and a weak one, and not involved in the state championship, Lula decided to give some of us second-stringers a chance. The game was actually considered a practice game, a training game—what we in Brazil call a game of *amizade*, a "friendship" game, and not one for the record. But it was the first time I pulled on the black-and-white-striped shirt of the Santos Club to defend the first team in any game. I recall that Dorval, Fiote, and Raimundo were also given a chance to play, at long last. Since the game was for *amizade* it was considered unofficial, and therefore does not appear on my record as my first professional game with Santos. For the same reason the four goals I made in the game, which we won 6–1, do not appear on my record nor on my lifetime total. Still, to those of us who played, it was an exciting event, and my four goals raised me in the opinion of my teammates. It got me a little publicity in the local papers and it also allowed me to say to the older and better players:

"All right. I'll still get soda for you and coffee, and run errands, but from now on, no more Gasolina. I'm Pelé in the newspapers and I'm Pelé here, too. ..."

And it's been Pelé ever since.

I shall never forget the afternoon Vasconcelos was injured. It was in a championship tournament game against São Paulo, and São Paulo had come down the mountain to Santos intent upon whipping us in our own Vila Belmiro stadium. The stadium was packed, mostly by Santos fans, and I was one of them, watching the game from the stands. Actually, there was little point in any reserve sitting on the bench since in those days no substitutions were allowed, so one might as well sit up in the stands and get a good view of the game, rather than on the bench at field level.

São Paulo was in top form that day and everything they did seemed to work while everything Santos did went sour. The game hadn't been on very long when São Paulo scored, and a short time later scored again. Santos retaliated with a goal, but moments later São Paulo made their third goal, and if I'm not mistaken that was the score when the half-time period ended. The mood in the stands was of solid gloom.

In the second half Santos came out all fired up, ready to tie the score and go ahead to win, but São Paulo seemed equally fired up not to let it happen. Then, about halfway through the period with the score unchanged, Vasconcelos passed the ball to Pepe, ran for the goal area to take the return from Pepe, and was about to kick when Mauro ran into him. I do not think that Mauro's charging Vasconcelos so hard was calculated; I'm sure that what happened next was not. The two tangled and fell to the ground, and Mauro, quite by accident, fell on top of Vasconcelos' bent leg. When Mauro got up, Vasconcelos was still down on the field, his face distorted in agony.

They carried him from the field amid a general booing for São Paulo from the fans, and Santos had to play one man short for the rest of the game. The ten men played well, keeping São Paulo from increasing its lead, but it is almost impossible to play catch-up football with a man missing, especially against a team as strong as São Paulo. The game ended and Santos had lost, 3–1. When I went down to the dressing room after the game, I heard the bad news.

"Vasco broke his leg!"

It was true, my very good friend Vasconcelos had indeed broken his leg. At the moment I honestly did not realize that this accident meant there was a chance I might play on the first team; my only thoughts were of him. He stayed in the hospital for a few days, and when he finally came back to Vila Belmiro with his leg in a cast and hobbling along on crutches, he waved the whole thing aside lightly.

"It's nothing. A few months and I'll be back, better than ever for the rest!"

Well, the months passed and eventually Vasconcelos returned to train with the team. But he wasn't the old Vasco we had all known. He seemed a bit hesitant in his attacks. None of us considered this strange; after all, he had been inactive for a long time with his leg in a cast. It took time to get a broken leg feeling just right again. But it was more than that, and we soon saw that, too. He had been badly and painfully injured, and it had to be in the back of his head every time he saw another player coming down to tackle the ball from him, or every time he charged down the field to take on an opponent. Slowly, however, he began to fight the fear, trying to conquer it, and while he soon regained all of the physical prowess he had always had, he never returned to be the great Vasconcelos he had been before the accident. He ended up by leaving the Santos Club to try his luck at other clubs.

That accident, of course, gave me a chance to play but it also made me realize fully for the first time what the life of a professional football player could be. I had grown up with the example of Dondinho and his injury before me—and constantly referred to by my mother—but I don't think I really understood what it could be like until that accident to Vasco. One day he was the idol of the fans—then, as soon as he was injured and could no longer score goals for them, he was effectively forgotten. It led to many discussions in the club in the evenings. Usually, since I was very young and these were adults speaking, I kept quiet—but I always listened.

"Football doesn't last a lifetime. The thing to do is try to make some money while you can and save as much of it as you can."

"Maybe there ought to be some sort of insurance so that when a player is hurt he can still collect."

"Maybe there ought to be some sort of *sindicato*—some sort of union—for football players, like they have down at the docks."

"Maybe we should all be in some other business."

"Sure—but what?"

"Look, it's the same thing in a factory! If you get hurt it's just too bad for you!"

"True—except in a factory nobody is jumping on you with spiked shoes, breaking your leg!"

"No—the only answer is to make as much money as you can, and save as much of it as possible."

I think the majority of the players felt like this underneath, but they only discussed it when something happened such as Vasco's broken leg. A number of the members of the team were married and had families, and very few of them had any reasonable amount of savings in the bank. None of them could or did throw their money away. I, of course, with my five thousand cruzeiros under the table, earned less than the others, but at the same time I had my room and board and didn't need much money.

So my life fell into a pattern. I went to the beach either mornings or afternoons, depending on the training schedule, I played with the juvenile team and the amateur team, I spent hours talking with the fellows at the club or at the Louis XV restaurant-bar where we often ate, and occasionally I would go to a movie with Dorval or one of the others of our clubhouse live-in fraternity. On occasion I would get homesick, but no longer with any idea of running away and going back to Baurú. Sabuzão, and the chance of playing on the first team, had effectively cured me of that.

Lula was more a father to us younger players than he was a coach. You could take your personal problems to him as well as any technical ones, and he always did his best to find an answer. On the other hand, nobody tried to take advantage of his willingness to give a player time off to solve his personal problems, and as a result we all got along very well. Lula gave his players excellent treatment and understanding, as well as fine technical advice, and as a result could and did demand top performance from each man. And he always got it.

My first game with the first team of Santos was against the AIK Club of Sweden, visiting us at Vila Belmiro. For the first time I played beside all the big names instead of just training with them, and to my surprise when I went out onto the field I didn't feel nervous at all. Actually, it seemed like just another practice game, with the same players beside me, except this one didn't end until the full ninety minutes were up, this one had strangers opposing us, and this one counted.

It was a hard game. The Swedish team played very well, especially on defense, but their offense was weaker and unable to penetrate our backfield. The game was very even. We finally won, thanks to a goal by Feijó on a penalty kick. In the dressing room after the game, while I was changing. Lula came over.

"Everything all right?"

"More or less ..."

"What's the trouble?"

"I didn't make a goal ..."

Lula laughed.

"You don't make goals every day. It would be nice, but it just doesn't happen. Unfortunately."

The first game in which I actually scored a goal for Santos—against a first-rate Brazilian team, that is—was on September 7, 1956. I think it may have been in celebration of our Independence Day, or in celebration of our new house on that street in Baurú. I was still only fifteen years old, I had been with the club for several months and had trained religiously, hoping for a chance to play. I was beginning to fill out in the shoulders and legs but I was already accepting the fact that I would never be very tall.

We played Corinthians of Santo André, a suburb of São Paulo. Lula decided to put me into the game instead of Del Vecchio, saving his big star for more important games; with Vasconcelos lost to the club, Del Vecchio became even more vital to the overall strategy of Santos. However, as good as Del Vecchio was, and that was very good, we didn't need him in that game. We won, 7–1, and while I made only one goal, it was my first professional goal and was enough to keep me walking on air for days.

Following this game I started to alternate with Del Vecchio—whom we called Deo for short—just as Vasco had alternated with, him before his injury. We played Jabaquara and beat them, 4–2, and again I scored a goal. We played Guarani de Bajé, a small unknown team, and while I scored a goal we only tied them! We played Renner of Pôrto Alegre and they beat us, 5–3! Well, it happens. ... We played Corinthians, São Paulo, and many more, winning or tying them all with the exception of the upset handed us by Renner. In my first games I scored several goals and started to get my name and picture into the Rio and São Paulo papers more and more.

About this time it apparently occurred to the Santos directors that we had no legal contract, so once again Valdemar de Brito and my father came down to Santos to negotiate a proper and formal contract, legally binding on both parties. As I was now sixteen this was possible, even though I still needed Dondinho's permission. I expected that with my record on the field up to that time, I could expect a major raise, bringing me closer to the other players, but the Santos Football Club didn't see it that way. They pointed out that I was still only sixteen, that I was still small and therefore easily injured, in which case they would have to still pay me as long as I remained with the club, as they had to pay Vasconcelos after his injury even though they did not have the use of his services. They pointed out that I had played for a very short time—and that in view of all these reasons, I should be more than satisfied with a simple raise to six thousand cruzeiros. After all, they said, a raise from five to six thousand was an increase of 20 per cent, which was generous by any standards. How often did anyone get an increase of 20 per cent at one time?

Valdemar de Brito was not too happy, either with the sum offered or with the reasons for not offering more, but to Dondinho, six was better than five, and either was better than I could earn in a factory. To me it made little difference. All I wanted to do was to play football, and it was very nice to get paid for it.

So my first real contract was signed with the Santos Club on April 8, 1957, to run until August 8, 1958, a period of sixteen months. The salary came to about seventy-five dollars, American, a month—and we went back to playing football.

In June of 1957 we came to play in the Maracanã Tournament. Santos and Vasco da Gama of Rio were to make up one composite team in the tournament and I was selected to play center-forward on the team, a distinguished honor for a sixteen-year-old. The tournament was never finished—I don't remember what caused its interruption—but I recall the tournament principally because it was in that tournament that I got to play, for the first time, in the giant Maracanã Stadium in Rio. It was there, before the largest crowd I had ever seen, let alone played before, that we beat Belenense, of Portugal, 6–1, and I made three of our goals. In our next game, we faced Dynamo of Zagreb, Yugoslavia, a game we tied, 1–1, and I scored our lone goal. Four days later we faced Flamengo, again tying them 1–1, and again I scored the lone goal for our side. We were in a rut, I guess, because three days later we played the noted São Paulo Football Club and once again we tied them, 1–1, and once again I scored our only goal. We were in first place when the tournament was discontinued, and we received a great deal of publicity as a result. I was the *artilheiro* of the tournament—the leading scorer—and so a good part of the reporting covered my play. I am sure that this had much to do with Silvio Pirilo selecting me to play with the Brazilian team against Argentina in the Copa Roca that followed shortly thereafter. I was sure my folks in Baurú were hearing of me and my progress and I was sure they would be proud.

It was on that trip, also, that I first had a chance to really see the then capital of our country, Rio de Janeiro. Santos had played there before, but they were overnight trips; now, during the Marancanã, Tournament and the Copa Roca I was there for a longer period, and I enjoyed every minute of it. Rio was everything I had always dreamed it to be, and much more. The tourist sights were everything the posters proclaimed, but in our free time we saw much more; Gavea, with its huge rock standing above anything around it, its side glistening with the water of the springs far above; the Forest of Tijuca, a jungle within mere minutes of downtown Rio; the Barra de Tijuca, a long spit of deserted sand that today contains some of the most valuable land on earth, but which in those days boasted the best shrimp restaurant in the area, plus undisturbed swimming in a fresh clean surf. I wondered if I would have been as enchanted if it were my home; if I had come here before with Tim and played for Bangú. I do not know. I love Santos as a Santista; I love Rio as every Brazilian loves Rio. They are not the same, but they have much in common, mainly tropical beauty, friendly people, and wonderful weather.

When I was alternated for by Deo, or he by me, there was never any resentment on either side; the same was true when Tite stepped aside for Pepe, or Pepe remained benched while Tite played. This is not always true of many clubs. After all, a player gets to be known and his value enhanced only to the degree that he has a chance to demonstrate his skills on the field before the fans, the press, and the radio. Nobody knows how good or bad a player is, if he always sits on the bench; they merely assume he's bad. And, too, his share of bonus money is cut in half if a game is won while he is on the bench with the reserves. So playing is important.

But Lula disciplined us well. The object was to win games, not to show individual talent. On the other hand, he always managed to give everyone a chance without in any way endangering the winning of a tournament, or even a game. In every case Lula had to take into consideration a player's physical condition at the moment, his mental condition, his relationship on the field with the others of the playing team that day, and all the other multiple factors that might be involved in any set of circumstances. Coaching is far from an easy job.

So life went on—the beach, football, an occasional movie, and our life at the club. One day a former basketball player of some renown in Rio de Janeiro—his name was Raimundo—came to me and suggested I might be happier living in a family atmosphere. Raimundo had been injured playing basketball in Rio much as Dondinho had been in football, and had come home to Santos where he coached the Santos Club's fledgling basketball team, and also occasionally helped out in our training program. His wife, Dona Georgina, ran a boardinghouse and Raimundo thought I would be happier there, as well as less homesick. So in the middle of 1957 I moved to Dona Georgina's, a move that greatly pleased my mother—for Dona Celeste had immediately come down from Baurú to visit the people who were to be her surrogate to her son—and where I found a real home away from home for the years I spent there. Dona Georgina and Raimundo became my second family.

When the World Cup games in Sweden were finished, life returned to normal with surprising swiftness. We played our first match, against Jabaquara, on July 16; it had been exactly seventeen days since we had won in Stockholm, and it seemed like seventeen years. Göteborg, the Nya Ullevi stadium, the Solna stadium, Lena, the pretty girls, the excitement, the thrill of returning as champions of the world, the wild welcome we had received—none of it seemed to have happened at all, or if it had happened, to have happened in a long-ago dream.

Within days we were back at our old schedule, playing every three or four days. Del Vecchio had taken an offer in Europe and the club had released him, so now I played center-forward full-time. That year, 1958, following the World Cup, I played an additional forty-four games with Santos, with our team winning thirty-one, tying eight, and losing five. I was the *artilheiro* of the state championship, with fifty-eight goals in thirty-eight games.

Santos had raised my salary from six thousand cruzeiros to thirteen thousand as soon as we returned from Stockholm, and in August of that year, when my contract terminated, we wrote a new contract giving me a monthly salary of fifteen thousand for another year. In addition, there were the bonuses for winning games, and these were amounting to more and more. Our house on September 7th Street in Baurú was now paid for—it wasn't a very expensive house in that neighborhood—and with the specter of rent eliminated for all time, I asked my father to start making any improvements my mother might want. The money also allowed my parents to begin visiting me on a fairly regular basis, so life was very good.

In fact, after one bonus I felt so rich I went right out and bought my mother a gas stove and had it shipped at once to Baurú. I remembered all too well having to lug the kindling in and stack it every Saturday; I remembered shivering in a cold house until my mother got up and started the wood fire in the old stove; I remembered the jockeying for position when we slept around that old stove on winter nights, and how someone had to remain at least partially alert to keep feeding the monster. With a new gas stove I was sure Dona Celeste would be the envy of the neighborhood, as well as being relieved of much of the work of getting a fire started for heating or cooking.

She thanked me in a letter and repeated her thanks profusely when she came to visit me. What nobody told me—apparently Dona Celeste had passed the word that I was not to be told—was that Baurú at that time had neither piped gas nor bottled gas, and the nice new stove, therefore, was merely a conversation piece that took up room.

Chapter 9

And then, one wonderful day in 1958, some times after the World Cup, something happened that, for me, dwarfed even that momentous occasion. I first met Rosemeri. ...

It was a Saturday night and we were in "concentration" for an important game the following day, which meant that the first team had to spend the night at Vila Belmiro and not go out and get into trouble. We were to play Corinthians the next day, and I have no recollection of how the game came out, but I remember that night very well. It was early, we had eaten and were sitting around being bored with each other's company, when somebody suggested we go downstairs to the gym and watch a girls' basketball game that was to be played there that night. Since our own gym was not out of bounds for concentration, and since we had nothing better to do, four or five of us went down to the gym to see if watching girls' basketball could be more interesting than sitting and looking at each other upstairs.

We sat on the bleachers and watched the two teams warm up before the game started. The scoreboard advised us that the teams represented Alético of Santos and Corinthians of São Paulo, apparently down to watch their football team the following day, and taking advantage of the trip for the basketball contest. Some of the girls recognized us and came over to speak to us, but there was one girl who was sitting on the bench as a reserve who caught my eye. She didn't come to talk to us at first, but she turned and kept looking in my direction. At first I thought she might be looking at someone behind me, but when I turned around I saw there wasn't anyone behind me. When I looked back I saw she was, indeed, staring at me. I waved to her and motioned for her to come up and join me. At last she did.

"Hello," I said.

"You're Pelé, aren't you?" she said.

"That's right," I said, basking in contentment.

"Well, just don't beat Corinthians tomorrow," she said, and went back to the bench.

I kept looking at her, or at the back of her head, rather, since that was all she presented to me from then on. I had been very impressed by what I had seen of her—her beauty, in fact, impresses me to this day. She stayed on the bench throughout the game, so I had no means of judging her basketball skills, but the truth is I wasn't interested in her basketball skills. (I saw her play later, and she was quite good; but then Rosemeri is quite good in anything she tries.)

In any event, after the girls had all disappeared into the locker room we went back upstairs to our concentration. I must have been mooning, because they asked me what I was thinking about.

"It couldn't have been the basketball game," one of them said. "You didn't watch that at all. All you kept doing was looking at that girl on the bench."

"The one on the bench that came up and talked to you?" another said. "She was only a kid! She couldn't have been more than thirteen or fourteen. You're getting to be a dirty old man, Pelé!" (I was all of seventeen at the time.)

And that's how matters stood when we went out on the field the next afternoon to play. I kept looking up into the stands to see if by some odd chance I might pick her face out in the crowd; it's a wonder I managed to play at all that day. When the game was over and we were released to go home, I asked Raimundo at Dona Georgina's if he knew the girl who had been sitting on the bench, second from the left, the night before. He looked at me as if I were crazy!

Then one day by pure accident, I ran into several of the girls from that basketball game on the street. They recognized me and we began to talk. I asked them what they were doing in Santos, and they looked at me in surprise.

"We live here."

"You live here? But I thought you were with Corinthians, from São Paulo?"

"No, we're with Atlético of Santos."

Well, that was fine! That meant that my girl friend—I had already begun to think of her as my girl friend—also lived in Santos! I continued the subtle approach to my main interest.

"There was a girl on your team. She didn't play in the game. She was one of the reserves. Brown hair—"

One of the girls laughed.

"You mean the one who went up and talked to you? That was Rosemeri. All she talked about after the game was you."

So much for subtlety. So she had only talked of me? Well, that was certainly good news. But, on the other hand, why shouldn't she talk about me? I was Pelé, champion of the world! The girl went on.

"She works in a record shop in Gonzaga after school. She's probably there now."

Since Gonzaga is a section of Santos which was about ten minutes from where I was talking to the girls, I excused myself and got there as quickly as I could without running, afraid I would find the elusive Rosemeri had disappeared again. But there she was, indeed, back of the counter. I walked up to her in the shop, trying to think of something clever to say to impress her, but the best I could do was:

"Hi!"

"Hello."

"I—do you remember me?"

"Of course. You're Pelé."

"That's right. I—say, why did you ask me not to beat Corinthians? If you're not from Corinthians, that is?"

"I'm for Corinthians when they play against Santos," she said.

"Oh!" Not a very good start. An enemy. "Did you see the game?"

"No. Football doesn't interest me."

I sighed. This wasn't going the way I had fantasized.

"Look," I said, "I'd like to see you sometime. I don't mean around here."

Rose shook her pretty head.

"I'm only fourteen. I don't go out with boys."

"But—the girls said you talked about me after the game—"

For the first time Rose looked a little flustered.

"The girls talk too much," she said.

I sighed again. This was hard work.

"Look—"

"If you'd like to visit me at home," Rose said, "that would be all right. I'm always home on Saturday."

"Saturday it is, then! Expect me!"

My tone was triumphant. I winked at her, man-to-his mate, and strode from the shop, shoulders back, walking on air. And then returned a moment later, a bit deflated.

"I forgot to ask—what's your last name and where do you live?"

And that was how I met and wooed Rose. At least that was how we met; the wooing went on for many years and was an extremely slow process. That Saturday I showed up at Rose's house dressed in my best clothes, my face bright and shining, my fingernails trimmed and clean, my behavior at its best. Rosemeri's parents were very nice, considering I was probably the first boy Rose had invited to her home, and almost certainly the first black boy. Dona Idalina, her mother, had baked some pastries and we sat around while I stuffed myself and talked of everything under the sun. It was a lovely day. Rosemeri's father was an official at the Santos docks and a football fan; their home was comfortable, and throughout the day I was aware of Rose's presence whether I was looking at her directly or not—although for the most part I had trouble keeping my eyes from her.

It was only the first of many visits to her home, nor were our meetings limited to those, although whenever we met away from her home it was always in an offhand manner and with the connivance of her aunt, who always came with her. After all, Rose was very young and I was quite well known in Santos, and we were both very sure her parents would not be pleased if the newspapers began to speculate on the relationship between what young black football star and what underage white girl?

So Rose and her aunt would go to the movies and after the lights went out I would slip in and sit next to her, whispering to her, or trying to hold her hand. Or we would meet accidentally at the beach when Rose and her aunt or Rose and her schoolmates would just happen by that portion of the beach occupied by me and some of the others from the club. Somehow the boys would get talking to the girls, all quite naturally, and Rose and I would be able to exchange glances or manage to brush hands once or twice. And as time went on I became more and more convinced that eventually I was going to ask Rose to marry me, although we both knew she was too young for the question.

I will admit that when I first started going with Rosemeri—if seeing a girl as infrequently as I did, or under the restricted circumstances, can be called "going with"—I was a little afraid that possibly Rosemeri might be attracted to the football player, Pelé, rather than to me as a person. I'm sure this is a thought that haunts many name athletes or movie stars or other so-called important persons. I never had any illusions about myself as a person; I'm not tall, I'm not handsome, although I am dark. On the other hand I remembered the girl who had gotten a spanking for liking me, and I remembered Neuza and her family, who I was sure liked me for myself and not my football prowess; and the same was true of Lena in Göteborg. Still, that fear of having a reputation admired rather than the person is one that was naturally in the back of my mind.

I need not have worried. In a very short time I became aware that the fame of the name Pelé meant very little to Rosemeri. I think in this regard she is quite a bit like my mother; they both think it very odd that people will pay money to see grown men in short pants kick a ball around a field. In fact today, after more than eleven years of marriage, I still wonder if my Rose appreciates that her husband is Pelé, the man who plays football, and who everyone thinks is a great star. ...

There are many people who travel—salesmen, sailors, airplane pilots, railroad men—but I doubt if anyone travels as extensively, or as continuously, or to as many different places in such a short space of time, as a player on a professional football team. Even before traveling to Sweden for the World Cup games I had seen much of my own country and had come to appreciate it far more than I could simply by reading about it in books. Playing for Santos was a great education in geography and sociology, and I took advantage of it. Every moment not training or playing on the many trips we took saw me wandering the streets or beaches of the places we visited.

I saw Pôrto Alegre, in the south of Brazil, in March of 1957; a city then of over half a million, built on the sloping sand hills that rise from the Guaíba River—which I discovered wasn't a river at all, but a lake. I recall being surprised at the number of ships in the lake, until I was told Pôrto Alegre was the largest port for inland navigation in the entire country. But the ships were smaller than those I was used to seeing coming into Santos to unload and load up on coffee; the outlet of the lake is too shallow for deep-draft ships. The architecture was different, too; not the Brazilian or Portuguese colonial I was used to in Baurú, or Santos, or even the older sections of Rio de Janeiro. This was more European, one saw chalets like one would expect to see in the Swiss Alps. I also remember walking the streets of Pôrto Alegre and looking for a black face, but seeing very few.

And then, in contrast, there was Salvador of Bahia, where a white face is rare, and where the two levels of the city were joined with a huge elevator, called the Lacerda, large enough to carry huge throngs up and down. I spent one whole morning in the church of São Francisco, all decorated with gold, and an afternoon at the market in the lower city, where one could see foods we never saw or tasted in Santos. Salvador was the first capital of Brazil—we learned that in school—and it is a fascinating place. The lower city is completely different from the upper city; one might be visiting two different towns that happened to be next to each other.

Then even further north, we played at Recife. To me Recife is one of the most beautiful cities in Brazil, which makes it one of the most beautiful cities in the world. It has been called the Venice of Brazil because of the many canals and rivers that crisscross the town; one can get from almost any part to any other part by water. Some of us on the team would go down to the beaches at the southern end of town and walk the long dirt road that skirted the ocean there. There is a reef only a hundred yards or so from the sand; it separates the rougher ocean from what has become a quiet, shallow lagoon. The water there is warm as bathwater and it makes a perfect place for mothers to let their toddlers learn to swim.

There are coconut stands all along the beach, where an attendant will lop the head off a coconut and give it to you to drink. They are artists with that heavy, razor-sharp machete; if I had tried to use it on a coconut I would have cut off my arm. We would stand and drink coconut milk and watch the fishermen take out their *jangadas*, which are sail-driven rafts made by tying a few logs of balsa together with vines, and hoisting a sail on a thin pole. These fishermen have to be the bravest—or the most foolhardy—men in the world. When they are in their boats they seem to be standing directly on top of the water. Yet they have taken these flimsy craft as far as a hundred miles out to sea, and have even sailed them as far as Rio de Janeiro, more than a thousand miles to the south. I'll stick with football!

We saw Curitiba, in the heart of the pine country of Paraná; we saw Fortaleza, where I remember walking past a *cachaça* factory, where they made that crude brandy from sugar cane, and almost being knocked down by the smell. We saw Brazil from one end to the other—we even saw Baurú! We played Noroeste there in August of 1958—and they beat us, 1–0!

It was a great experience, but above all it was an education; I came to learn to love and appreciate my country and its people. From the extreme north, with the foliage of bamboo and cetigo, to the south, with its pine and oak and birch, with the differences in foods and customs, we found friendship and welcome wherever we went. That never varied.

By the end of 1958 Santos had achieved a formidable reputation (despite the loss to Noroeste!) that made every team in the world want to play us. We had former world champions like Zito, Pepe, Pelé; we had a team that was considered the best in Brazil, where top teams were common. We had the flair of the Brazilian style of attacking football and superb ball-handling and ball control that other countries found intriguing. And we had the box-office appeal that filled stadiums and club coffers. We received more invitations to play than we could actually accommodate, and after picking the cream of the crop our directors sent us out into the world to make our—and Santos'—fortune.

We started 1959 with a trip around South and Central America, playing in Peru, Ecuador, Costa Rica, Guatemala, Mexico, Curaçao, and Caracas; we played at sea level one day and then at eight thousand feet the next. We played before

Indians wearing derby hats; Mexicans in sombreros; Dutch islanders with peaked caps; in six weeks we played fourteen games in seven countries, winning thirteen and losing one to a Czechoslovakian team we met in Mexico. As soon as we returned from that trip I was selected to play in the São Paulo State Selection in a series of games against a Selection from Rio de Janeiro, and then against the World Cup teams of Peru, Chile, Bolivia, Paraguay, and Argentina. We tied in the Rio tournament but we won the majority of our games against the best of the other South American teams. With our reputation enhanced by these victories, in May of 1959 we set off for Europe.

Santos had already played twenty-two games that year when we left for Europe, and our schedule there was unbelievable. We were scheduled to play almost daily, and in different countries. We played the Bulgarian Selection two days in a row, had a day for travel, and then played in three Belgium cities three days in a row. Sight-seeing was out, other than what glimpses we caught from the window of the train, or what little we could see going from our hotel to the stadium on the bus. It was a merry-go-round. We would play, eat, sleep, catch a train—and sometimes sleep on the train, having to get out in the middle of the night with about two minutes' notice, stumbling onto a platform in some strange town, half-asleep, our bags in one hand and, at times, our pants in the other, while the conductor waited impatiently for these foreigners who didn't speak German—or Flemish or French or Swiss or Italian or whatever—to get down so the train could continue. And then it was try to find six taxicabs to take us to some hotel for a few hours' rest before we had to go out on some field and play again.

Football stadiums are remarkably alike; hotel rooms the world over are remarkably alike. And football fans, too, are remarkably alike. That trip to Europe, my first since the World Cup matches in Sweden, left little impression on me, other than constantly being taken from one place to another with no time to see anything, and therefore no time to learn anything. It was a brutal schedule, designed to make the Santos Club rich, and with small regard for the players. And it was at the end of that trip that we came through Spain and found an extra game had been added to the already demanding schedule—to play, the very day of our arrival, Real Madrid.

In those days there had always been speculation as to which club team was the better—which in the eyes of the world would make it the unofficial best in the world—Real Madrid or Santos. Apparently some impresario felt such a game would be sure to draw the maximum crowd, and he convinced the directors of Santos. They really needed little convincing; it was more money and they could not have cared less that the team had had a very hard trip and needed rest badly. We were exhausted. Some of the players had problems with their stomachs as a result of differences in the food and water and with no time to get accustomed to either. Many of us had played with injuries and bad bruises that should have had treatment, because we knew that had we failed to play the loss of our names from the line-up would have meant reduced fees plus a lack of interest at the box office. Many of us were simply exhausted from lack of sleep, having had trouble accommodating ourselves to mid-European beds where the feather quilt either roasted you or, if removed, allowed you to freeze. What we all needed was a long rest rather than a game with a very tough team. We had played fifteen games in the past twenty-two days in nine different countries, while Real Madrid had avoided other games once they knew they were going to play us, and had trained extensively for this one game.

Well, to make a long bitter story short, they beat us, 5–3, and it was a defeat I have never forgotten. On the other hand, it was apparently a victory Real Madrid has also never forgotten, because they have consistently refused to play Santos from that day to this, and I am speaking of a game that took place eighteen years ago! Still, I'm sure Real Madrid had good reasons for refusing to play Santos since that day—under normal conditions Santos had always been a better team, and with proper rest we could have wiped them out in 1959 and they knew it. In fact, in a tournament in Argentina some years later, Real Madrid actually withdrew rather than play Santos when the respective victories of each team matched them against each other in the tournament ladder. No, Real Madrid beat Santos once and they are certainly not going to jeopardize that record!

We returned to Brazil after two months of constant football in Europe. It had not been as educational as I had hoped, and it had been very tiring. We were all very happy to be home. I was especially glad to get back to Rosemeri. I had written her postcards from our various stops in Europe, but our schedule was such that it was almost impossible for her to write in return with any assurance that I would ever get any of her letters. The mail system of Brazil, plus the mail systems of some of the countries we visited, plus the fact that we only stayed in one place a day or two at the most—and half the time nobody was sure which hotel we would be in—all these made contact difficult. I used to wonder if I would get back and find that Rosemeri had fallen in love with someone. I could picture him: He would be tall, handsome, and blond. It was a very disturbing thought. I would sit at the window of the train, looking out at neat yards and organized factory storage areas without really seeing any of them, and torture myself with dark thoughts of Rose at the movies, or the beach, with another.

But Rose was still there when I got back, no new boy friend around to threaten my security, and we took over where we left off. The travel had been fine—it had been lucrative, at least, because my bonuses that trip amounted to a lot of money—but it was still wonderful to be back in Santos and to be near Rosemeri.

Toward the end of 1958, even before our trip to Europe with the heavy feather quilts and the almost-daily games, I had passed my eighteenth birthday and thought that other than my family, or maybe Rosemeri, nobody would have noticed. But I was wrong. The Brazilian Army, seldom lax in such matters, remembered very well, and when I returned from the trip to Europe they decided it was time I spent my year in the armed services, as all Brazilian men are obligated to do after the age of eighteen. And off I went to be inducted and fitted with an itchy uniform.

When I was first called up for my military duty, I smiled to myself. I had been assigned to the 6th Group, Motorized Coast Artillery, stationed at Santos—and this group was under the command of Colonel Osman, now General Osman. Colonel Osman, in addition to being a career soldier, was a director of the Santos Football Club, and I was certain he had to be an ardent fan of one of their stars. Life, I was positive, would be a pleasure. I had already been informed I would be expected to play on the barracks football squad, and I quite naturally thought this would relieve me of such flunky duties as drilling or peeling potatoes or even making my bed.

What a dream!

Colonel Osman did indeed expect me to play football for the barracks team—as well as for the Army Selection of Brazil in international play, as well as for the Santos Club in any games they might need me, as well as for the Brazilian Selection were we ever called together during my army career, as well as any other time he wanted me to do anything, anywhere. But Colonel Osman was also an officer who staunchly believed in allowing his subordinates full authority over their recruits, and Captain Aurino, who headed our battery, liked to do just that. He was an officer who felt that no man could be prepared to defend his country who did not know in detail how to pick cigarette butts from a company street; that no man could be depended upon to give his life for his nation who had not already demonstrated his sacrificial willingness by learning how to sweep a squad-tent floor with military precision or dig grass with a hoe from a company street, or from the potential garden of an officer's wife, if it came to that. So I found myself doing everything other recruits did, plus playing football.

Still, I learned many things and made many friends in the army. The coach of our barracks team was a Lieutenant Falcão and he was as tough as any coach on the outside, being armed, as he was, with far more authority over personal life than any coach in civilian life. Fooling around during training brought extra duty, often guard duty at night, which was no joke when you had to play a full ninety minutes the next day. A poor showing on the field could result in restriction to barracks except, of course, for the time spent in an actual game. But Lieutenant Falcão was a fair man and a good soldier and we became good friends.

We had a very good team in our barracks. Among the players were Lorico, who later played for Vasco da Gama in Rio de Janeiro; Célio, who went to Jabaquara; Hélio, a goal-keeper for Portuguesa Santista; and poor Lara, who later had a heart attack and died during a game because he refused to advise the club doctor of the pains he had been experiencing. Our team won the military championship of the entire Santos garrison, and I was picked for the Military Selection in the inter-South American championship games that year.

In the game against the Military Selection of Argentina I was thrown out of a game for the first time. I have been thrown out often enough since then, but usually for arguing with a referee over a decision; this was one of the few times I have ever been expelled for fist-fighting. But there are certain teams and certain players who still feel the best way to win is to disable some of the most effective players of the opposition, and an attitude such as this needs to be discouraged thoroughly and quickly. Valdemar de Brito taught me that fighting on a football field is foolish; but he also taught me that when a player is subject to constant attacks that could cripple him, the best way to stop it is to retaliate instantly and in no uncertain manner.

Unfortunately, he never taught us how to do so without getting called for it by the referee.

People have often mentioned how pleasant I am on the field, how I smile at the opponent who bumps into me, accidentally or on purpose, how I help him to his feet. They ask me, Don't you ever lose your temper? People who ask this question haven't followed my career very closely. I lose my temper very often, but I try my best not to show it, especially not to an opponent during a game. It gives him an advantage to know you're angry, and he may well make you pay for showing your temper. Losing your temper with a referee is more allowable, if one watches one's language. A sharp protest at a poor ruling may make the referee more careful when the situation is duplicated. Far better than getting in a fight with an opponent is to force that temper down, and play more intently, scoring on him, or making him look foolish so he will lose *his* temper. Then the advantage is with you.

In any event, this Argentinian back concentrated on me, kicking me viciously every time the referee wasn't looking, which seemed to me to be about all the time. I decided there was only one way to end the attacks, and the next time he came at me I let him have one right in the shins. The Argentinian back got angry and started to swing. I swung back. The referee, who had been blind to the constant attacks, now suddenly got eyesight and we were both thrown out of the game and sent to the showers. Since it harms a team much more to lose a center-forward than a defensive back, Argentina still gained from the fracas, but not enough to win the game. The Brazilian Selection won, 2–1. And it was a good thing for me we did; as I left the field Lieutenant Falcão called me over.

"If we lose, you just got yourself one week in the brig," he said, and he meant it!

The following day I was in Pôrto Alegre, playing against the Grêmio Club for Santos in defense of the Brazil Cup. It wasn't the first time I played two games in less than twenty-four hours, playing one at night under lights and the next one the following afternoon, sometimes miles away. That year, 1959, I played in over one hundred games, which I believe is the record for a player on a major team, and many of the games were played with bruises and aching muscles. But I was obligated to play for Santos as their professional, and one didn't argue in the army when told to get out there and play. In addition to playing more than one hundred games that year, I also learned how to dig grass from a company street, sweep a floor, make a bed—knowledge which I hope I never have to use. I also learned how to take a gun apart and put it back together again—knowledge I hope even more I never have to use. ...

The year 1960 saw me out of the army and traveling once again, playing for Santos in some games, for the São Paulo State Selection in others, and for the Brazilian Selection in still others. The travels once again took me throughout South America and once more to Europe, although this time on a far less frantic trip than the one we made in 1959. In Egypt, for example, we spent eight days and only played three games; the time between games gave me a chance to see all the sights I had read about in school and had heard about throughout Europe. We saw the pyramids, a far more impressive sight, standing out on that barren plain, than one would imagine just from photographs, and we climbed them to the top, which is almost as much work as playing a full game. We managed to get on top of camels, an even more difficult ascent, and had our pictures taken, tourist-fashion, hanging on for dear life, and feeling as if we were fifty feet off the ground. We walked through the crowded streets of Cairo, shopping in the bazaars. The games in Egypt and the ones we next played in Denmark, Italy, and Portugal were with the Brazilian Selection, and in Cairo, Djalma Santos had to be restrained from punching some enthusiastic football fans—males—who would grab him and suddenly kiss him on the lips.

The food was, of course, different, and one meal I shall not forget. We had completed a very fine dinner at the hotel where we were staying when the head waiter, obviously proud of the cuisine he had presented us with, explained that the delicious meat we had just eaten was camel. Well, anyone who has ever smelled a camel for the first time can hardly get excited about eating anything that smells like that. A goodly number of the players turned slightly green and asked where the rest room was. After that, for the rest of the trip we all made inquiries as to the contents of any proffered exotic dishes before tasting them.

From Egypt we went to Malmö in Sweden; it was a strange feeling being back in Sweden for the first time since the World Cup games; I wondered if Lena was still there, and then put the thought away. Rosemeri was my girl now and would be for all time, if I had my way. Besides, there was no time to even consider a trip to Göteborg; we were off to Copenhagen the next day. Copenhagen is just across a narrow strait of water from Sweden, a short ferry ride, and I remember it very well. It was May, there was a chill still in the air, and I felt wonderful. We had swamped the Malmö team, 7–1, I had contributed two of our goals, and I was looking forward to seeing the famous Tivoli Gardens in Copenhagen as soon as our game there was over.

When our seven games with the Brazilian Selection were finished, games in which we won six and tied one, I joined the Santos Club again, which was arriving to tour Europe. We met in Brussels, a city I have always enjoyed not only for its clean streets and orderly ways but for the excellence of its food. I have also always enjoyed visiting the Grand-Place and listening to the chimes on the bell tower of the City Hall, watching the heavy metal figures come out and march around the tower, striking the hour as they march. It seemed to me hard to believe that when that tower was constructed so many years before, the engineering ability existed to make such a mechanical marvel.

Once I was playing with Santos, of course, the leisurely schedule of the Brazilian Selection became a thing of the past. Once more we were playing almost daily, one day in Poland, a day for travel and then Germany and Belgium again, a country a day, bringing in the crowds as fast as the Santos directors could arrange it. But it was worth it when we got to France; we were there five whole days, and enjoyed every second of it for several reasons. We came to France from Italy, where Fiorentina had handed us a 3–0 loss, the largest on our entire tour, so it was nice to come to a country where we could be fairly sure to win our games, as we did. It was also good to see Paris, the City of Lights, and deservedly named.

I was nineteen at the time, and Paris at any age is beautiful, but at nineteen it is breath-taking. I was introduced to an actress and fashion model named Kiki, and she showed me the town. We saw the Champs Élysées, the Left Bank, Montmartre; we rode to the top of the Eiffel Tower and saw all Paris spread out beneath us, and the Seine wriggling through it, the sun glistening on it, reflecting back to us on the tower, and the long flat barges on it looking like black beetles. They say that Paris in September is lovely, but this was June and I found it irresistible. When the photographers asked me to pose with Kiki I did so gladly, and was pleased to see myself beaming from the front pages the following morning, with Kiki cuddling up to me and with me obviously enjoying every minute of it. What I couldn't have known, of course, was that the pictures were taken by a wire service that also served the Brazilian press. The caption under the photograph suggested that marriage was imminent between Pelé and the Parisian model, Kiki—and I heard a good deal about that picture from Rose when I got back. On any trips in the years after that, I was far more careful with whom I allowed myself to be photographed, or what was in the captions under the pictures.

I think the travels of the Brazilian Selection and the Santos team served many purposes, but to me one of the most important ones was educating the European public as to where Brazil was and which cities were a part of it. When we first played in Sweden in 1958 it was very common to have people come up and say they had heard how pretty our capital—Buenos Aires—was. Or to think we spoke Spanish. When we said our language was Portuguese, or that Buenos Aires was indeed pretty but it happened to be in Argentina, not Brazil, and that our capital (in those days) was Rio de Janeiro, they were truly amazed. They acted as if we were telling them something quite at odds with what they had learned in school. And maybe it was, for all I know. But one thing was certain: As uneducated as many of us were, we had a far more thorough knowledge of Europe, its countries, capitals, and languages, than they did of South America and particularly of Brazil. I think they expected to see Indians from the Amazon on the field, Indians who had been taught by European missionaries to play football as a means of keeping them from scalping the settlers.

I believed then as I do today that one important purpose of our trips was to publicize Brazil and put it in a more realistic light for Europeans. When we told them that our country, Brazil, was larger than all of their Europe without Russia put together, they flatly disbelieved us. When we told them that the Amazon River carried more cubic feet of water than all their rivers put together, it merely proved our casuistry to them. When we said that São Paulo was a city at that time of over four million inhabitants—today it is over eight million—they knew we had to be pulling their legs. A village in the interior of a small South American uncivilized land, to have four million inhabitants? Impossible! They would all get lost trying to find their way through that many thatched teepees! I'm sure that if we had had pictures of São Paulo to show them they would have sworn we were trying to fool them with photographs of New York or Chicago.

The year 1960 also saw the beginning of a business partnership that was to have a great effect on my life. The money I was beginning to earn was assuming important proportions by any standards. After 1959 my contract had been adjusted to 80,000 cruzeiros per month with a 60,000 cruzeiro cost-of-living allowance, while my bonuses came to almost a million cruzeiros a year. All together this was in the neighborhood of a yearly income of about $75,000 to $100,000. But just translating it to dollars does not give the proper picture. The devaluation of the cruzeiro in those days would make it seem that the purchasing power of the cruzeiro was being reduced proportionately, and this, of course, is not true. It is true that it took more and more cruzeiros to buy dollars, but I wasn't buying dollars. In terms of what this sum would buy in Brazil, it was worth far more than $100,000 would buy in the United States.

That was just the money earned in football. In addition I was able to command large fees in advertising for endorsing every kind of product from trousers to soft drinks. It was obvious some sensible arrangement of investment was sorely needed, because I was still spending almost nothing, and the money was accumulating.

I spoke to Zito and asked his opinion as to what I should do with the money, how best to invest it. Zito and I had been close friends as well as teammates since my earliest days at Santos. He said he was going into business with a few friends, and why didn't I join them? I spoke to my father about it, but Dondinho had no opinion. I was growing up, he said, the money was mine, he knew very little about business in general and even less about business in Santos, and he thought I should seek and follow more mature advice.

As a result, Zito put me in touch with his major partner, a Spaniard named José Gonzales Ozoris, whom everybody called Pepe Gordo, and who at the time seemed to me to be more Brazilian than Spanish. In fact, we were so compatible that shortly after entering in partnership with Zito and Pepe Gordo, I left Dona Georgina's boardinghouse and moved in with Pepe Gordo, his wife and family. Their home was quite large and Dona Georgina's boardinghouse had become very crowded, so to me everything had worked out well. I was traveling almost constantly, and since I had total confidence in Pepe Gordo, I gave him my power of attorney. This permitted him to make any financial decisions for me, to sign checks that needed signing, to withdraw and deposit monies for me, to pay my bills and collect money due me, to sign advertising contracts in my name—in short, to handle my affairs as if he were me, myself.

The major business in which we first invested was a large store—Sanitaria Santista—which handled the sale of construction materials: pipes, bricks, tiles, lumber, plywood, nails, even interior fixtures such as toilets, bathtubs, and sinks. Zito traveled as much as I did; we usually traveled together, so Pepe Gordo was left to run the business and handle the finances, while Zito and I kept paying and the money kept rolling in.

With the store as a base, our company soon began to expand into construction, building small buildings of rental apartments, each holding nine or ten small rental units. With our connections in the field of construction materials we were able to build relatively cheaply, and at last I could stop worrying about what would happen when I could no longer earn a living playing football. Merely letting the money accumulate in a bank would be no assurance, even if one found a bank where one could be sure of continued liquidity, which was not always the case; with the continued inflation one could only be sure of the future by investing in it. True, when we started the business I was only nineteen years old and when we started the construction phase of the business I was only twenty—but I had seen what had happened to Vasconcelos and to Dondinho. I had no intention of starving if I suffered a major injury at age twenty-one, for example, and was forced to start living on capital. Even large sums wouldn't last forever. Besides, only a few days earlier, the fans of Corinthians had booed Gilmar for long, long minutes when he left the field at Pacaembú—Gilmar, the goalkeeper champion of the world and one of the greatest ever produced in Brazil, to be booed like that? I swore it would never happen to me. I would leave off playing when it suited me, when the fans wanted me to stay—not when they booed me off the field! But to be that independent one needed money, and I was ensuring myself of its continuance after football, by my investment in the business.

Besides, I had a growing feeling that one of these years I would be thinking seriously of marriage, and I knew from bitter experience in my childhood that nothing could threaten the happiness of the home, or the love between two married people, like the lack of money. Rosemeri and her family were pleased to see me get involved in a steady business, although I am sure that at that time neither Dona Idalina nor Sr. Guilherme, Rose's father, had any idea I was anything more than a friend of the family who stopped by occasionally to eat cookies, drink milk, and chat. Whenever I would mention to Rose the possibility of speaking to her father seriously, I was always met with:

"No, no! I'm only fifteen—" or sixteen, or seventeen, as the years went by—"wait awhile. ..."

So I waited and continued to play football and add to my growing equity in our growing business, and to visit Baurú whenever I could, or to see my parents on their ever-increasing visits to Santos. Life was good and looked as if it could only get better. I had been *artilheiro* of the São Paulo championship in 1960; I had played a total of eighty-two games that year and had scored seventy-two goals. And on March 5, 1961, I made what is now referred to as "the Goal of the Plaque." We were playing in Maracanã Stadium against the Fluminense Club of Rio—a game we won, 3–1—when I took the ball in our own penalty area, dribbled it past their entire team unassisted, and scored the goal. To commemorate what they called "the Most Beautiful Goal Ever Scored in Maracanã" the sports newspaper *O Esporte* of São Paulo had a plaque cast and mounted at the entrance of Maracanã, the world's largest stadium. It was a great honor and one I am very proud of.

So everything was fine; it could not be better. The newspapers gave me a good deal of favorable publicity, my health was excellent, and I had not suffered a major injury for a long time. There seemed nothing that could possibly mar the horizon. And, too, I—together with all Brazil—was looking forward to the Selection in preparation for the World Cup matches that were scheduled for Chile in 1962. Then Brazil could repeat its victory of 1958 and become champions of the world for the second time. And I could only enhance my growing reputation. ...

Chapter 10

The Brazilian Selection for the World Cup of 1962 was almost the same as the 1958 Selection, with a few changes. Our coach and manager, Vicente Feola, was in poor health and was replaced by Aimoré Moreira, brother of Zeze Moreira, who had managed the 1954 team. Of the players who had been in that final game in Stockholm we still had Gilmar, Nilton Santos, Djalma Santos, Zito, Didi, Garrincha, Vavá, Zagalo, and myself. Belini was in reserve and Mauro took his place on the first team. Orlando was playing in Argentina and was replaced by Zózimo, while Mazzola—whose real name was Altafini and who held dual Italian-Brazilian citizenship—played for Italy that year.

The rule as to eligibility in World Cup football is quite different from that of club games—or of most other sports, as far as that goes. American baseball, for example, uses many players from Cuba, Puerto Rico, Venezuela, or Mexico, and they are certainly not barred from playing in the World Series—if they were, the World Series would probably be won by a Little League team from Logansport. But in the Jules Rimet Trophy competition, a player *must* be a national of the country for which he plays. Where a player holds dual citizenship, which is rare but which occurs at times as in the case of Altafini, he can play for either country. There are also cases where a player will change his nationality to play for a certain team, but again these cases are rare. It is a very good rule and prevents any wealthy country from "buying" the championship simply because they may be able to afford to purchase a player's contract from clubs in other countries for large sums of money.

In addition to those who played in that final game in Stockholm we also had Pepe, who had been on the Selection twice but who had never managed to get into a final game because of injury, or because Zagalo was doing too good a job to be replaced. There was also Castilho, a carry-over from 1954 who also had no chance to play, and we had many new players, many young players—because at age twenty-one I now considered myself an old boy, especially since I had more than five years of professional experience plus one World Cup behind me. We had players like Amarildo, Jair da Costa, Coutinho—one of the very best and with whom I paired so well at Santos—Mengálvio, Zequinha, Jair Marinho, and Jurandir. The head of the commission remained Dr. Paulo Machado de Carvalho, and Carlos Nascimento remained his assistant; our technical staff also remained the same, with Paulo Amaral our trainer, Mário Américo our head masseur, Dr. Mário Trigo still our dentist, and Dr. Hilton Gosling still our team physician.

Brazil, by winning in 1958, had automatically qualified for the finals, as had Chile, which was to be the host country. We had qualified as one of the sixteen finalists, but we still had to win our key group in order to go on to the quarter-finals. In our group, which was scheduled to play our games in Viña del Mar, were Brazil, Czechoslovakia, Spain, and Mexico, none of them easy.

And as in 1958, Paulo Amaral was a martinet on training.

"If you can walk, you train! If you can't walk, don't tell me—tell Dr. Hilton Gosling!"

Nor could anyone argue with him, neither Feola in 1958 nor Aimoré Moreira in 1962. They could have gone to Dr. Carvalho and asked that he be replaced, of course, but nobody even faintly considered doing this; he was too valuable. But other than replacing him there was nothing anyone could do. If Aimoré Moreira tried to say anything, Paulo Amaral would get very irritated.

"I say that everyone trains equally! I know what I'm doing and I don't let anyone interfere in my job, which is exactly why I don't interfere in anyone else's job! My training won for the team in 1958 and if you just leave me alone I'll win it for you again in 1962!"

Since there was a good deal of truth in his statement, everyone left Paulo Amaral alone and we all trained equally. In general I agree with the philosophy that it is wrong to allow differences in the way different players are treated, but I also believe there should be exceptions. Paulo Amaral insisted that a small man such as Zagalo—or myself—should do every exercise and put in as fully a strenuous training period as, say, Nilton Santos, who towered above us and was probably the strongest man on the team. When a day's training was over, Zagalo and I would have lost precious weight, while Nilton wouldn't have worked up an appetite. And so, partly because of Paulo Amaral's philosophy of training, and partly because I wasn't very bright and was too reticent about bringing my problem into the open, I managed to get myself into trouble.

As I said, we didn't have to play any qualifying games, but Aimoré Moreira had nothing against playing training games against the Selections of other countries—and they, of course, were only too happy to play against the world champions, since a loss to us wouldn't make them look too bad while a victory over us could make us appear in a poor light when the actual cup games came along. Fortunately, we won all of these training games, the first two against Portugal and the next two against Wales, but at the end of the first game against Portugal I left the field with a slight pain in my lower abdomen, where the trunk joins the thigh. And the day following the day of the game, as we did every day when we were not actually playing, we went back to Paulo Amaral's exercises and training. The groin continued to be sore, but I thought the training itself might work itself away, and therefore said nothing.

I played in all four of the training games, scoring four goals and winning two of the games with those goals, and the groin continued to hurt and kept hurting throughout our daily training sessions. Each day as I limped off the field I tried to decide whether I should mention it to anyone or wait for it to disappear by itself. As I said, it was not a very brilliant decision.

Our first game of the World Cup matches, in our group, was against Mexico. We won, 2–0, and Zagalo and I each scored a goal. I left the field feeling happy, of course, but also extraordinarily tired, considering the extensive training and physical preparation we had undergone. In addition my groin hurt even more than usual. At long last I went to speak to Dr. Gosling about it. He examined me and asked how much it hurt.

"A little ..."

"How little? Or how much?"

"Very little ..."

It was feeling better every minute I was with the doctor, like an automobile engine that begins to run well as soon as you drive it into the garage, or a tooth that improves in the dentist's outer office. Dr. Gosling studied me with half-closed eyes.

"How long has it been bothering you?"

"Oh—for a while ..."

"Can you train?"

Well, knowing Paulo Amaral and his theories, if I didn't train there was certainly no chance of my playing.

"Oh, yes, sir!"

Dr. Gosling didn't look too happy about the whole affair.

"Well, all right," he said half-grudgingly. "But if it continues to hurt, if it doesn't improve, and soon, you'll be excused from training."

Which would certainly mean being excused from playing.

"I'll let you know, Doctor."

But I knew I wouldn't.

Our second game was with Czechoslovakia, always a tough team and known to be exceptionally tough this year. And we definitely had to get past them, either with a win or a tie, if we hoped to reach the quarter-finals. The game was played, as all our group games were played, at Quilpué, just outside Viña del Mar, and when we came out onto the field the crowd stood and cheered. We were the favorites and we had the fans with us, which is always a bigger advantage in a game than many realize. There was a Brazilian samba band playing and for a moment I forgot my groin, forgot everything else. We were the world champions and nothing was going to stop us!

I began playing with complete confidence, overlooking the pain in my groin, and then decided to test myself on my next kick. The ball was passed to me by Garrincha. I dribbled downfield, avoiding several defense men, brought it into the penalty area, feinted another defender away, and kicked with all my strength. The ball struck a side post and bounded back; I was ready for it and I kicked it toward the goal again, again using all my effort. Only this time when I kicked I felt something in my groin give way and I found myself stretched out on the ground, my one leg pulled up tight against my stomach.

Mário Américo was on the field in an instant, bending over me anxiously.

"What is it?"

"My groin ..."

"Can you stand? Here, let me help you up."

I came to my feet slowly, bending over to reduce the pain. There were no substitutions in those days, and even a crippled body on the field was better than no body at all, since even a crippled body requires at least a little attention from the opponent's defense. I nodded to Mário Américo.

"I'm all right."

Mário looked at me a moment in doubt, but I waved him away. He walked from the field, still not sure, and sat on the bench, watching me. I smiled at him and we went on to play.

That day I witnessed and experienced something I had never seen before and very seldom have seen since. I saw three Czech players who were really and truly sportsmen: Masopust, Popluhar, and Lala, the Czech lateral. They saw I had been injured; they must have suspected I had pulled a muscle since there was no one near me when I went down, they must have known how desperately I wanted to remain in the game, and they also knew I was in poor condition to defend myself against rough tackles. They also knew that any brutal attack could easily cripple me, not only for the length of the tournament, but possibly for life—and all three of them avoided any roughness that could hurt me. At no time did they allow me to threaten them with goal possibilities—at that time I couldn't have threatened an infantile team—but while they protected the interests of their team, they saw to it that I was protected. There are few players and very few teams that would not have taken advantage of a star player when injured, to make sure he would not threaten them in the future, but Masopust, Popluhar, and Lala did nothing to harm me. The Czechs were also fighting to classify for the quarterfinals; they also could not afford to lose the game, but those three players put the well-being of an adversary in proper proportion. This is one of the things I shall always remember with emotion, and one of the finest things that happened in my entire football career.

When the game ended in a scoreless tie and we went back to the hotel, I could hardly walk. Still, I remembered other injuries, principally the one that kept me from the first two games in 1958, and I was sure that with my youth and my condition, I would soon recover. Now that the muscle distension had actually occurred and I could admit the pain, I could get proper medical treatment and be excused from training, which would clear up the trouble in short order. But when Dr. Gosling finished with his examination, he shook his head.

"You should have mentioned this a long time ago. The way it is now, I doubt that you'll play in any more of the games."

I smiled, knowing Dr. Gosling's psychology.

"Don't worry, Doctor, I'll take any treatment you prescribe. But the games are going on for a long time yet. I'll play in some of them, you'll see."

Dr. Gosling merely looked at me with his usual expressionless look, and then shrugged. Then he gestured for Mário Américo to come over and receive instructions for my treatment.

The days went by and the treatments were followed religiously, but the muscle didn't seem to get any better. When the game with Spain was to be played the following day, I asked Dr. Gosling to come and see me. He walked into the dressing room and looked at me questioningly.

"Look, Doctor," I said, "it's only a muscle. If I don't strain it, it doesn't hurt. If you give me an injection of something to deaden the pain, I won't even feel the muscle, and I can play."

For the first time I saw expression on the doctor's face; he looked as shocked as I have seen him, and angry, too.

"As if you were a horse? No, Pelé—you're talking to the wrong man. If I gave you an injection and you played, you could be crippled for life. And that would end your career in football. Do you think it would be worth it? What made you think I would allow such a thing?"

He shook his head and glared at me.

"I have never given a player an injection to allow him to play, and I never will. Now, go back to your treatments and don't get any idiotic ideas any more!"

So I went back to my treatments and spent the time when I was not under Mário Américo's ministering in bed. I watched Brazil beat Spain on the television. Amarildo had taken my place and had played spectacularly. Despite the excellence of such Spanish players as Puskas at center-forward and Paco Gento at outside left, Brazil won, 2–1, with Amarildo scoring both of Brazil's goals, bringing Brazil from behind to win in the last four minutes. Amarildo was twenty-four years old, an inside left from Botafogo; his first goal was made by converting a pass from Zagalo through the center, his second was made when Garrincha got away from the opposition, crossed the ball to Amarildo who darted in to head the ball into the net. I must admit it was a tough game for Spain to lose, but all I could think of was being very happy that Brazil had won.

Still, as I lay in bed I couldn't help but wonder if possibly Pelé was all through at the age of twenty-one, and if Amarildo would be the next Pelé. He had certainly played as brilliantly as Pelé, or anyone else, in that game, and deserved all the credit he received. All finished at twenty-one! I gritted my teeth and told Mário Américo to make the towels hotter. I had to get back on the field for at least one of the last two games!

But the days went by and the groin responded to treatment far too slowly for me. I began to wonder if I would ever play again, and not just in the last two games. I remembered 1958 and wondered if possibly I was accident-prone, or at least accident-prone at important times. It was a very disquieting thought.

And then one day I got out of bed and found that the groin did not hurt! I tested the muscle with my fingers, probing it, and then pressed my foot against the floor, tensing the muscle—there was no pain! I had done it! I would play yet! I got dressed and went out with the others for a training session, practicing with the ball, running slowly but running, dribbling the ball with no attempt to make any spectacular movements, any sudden feints, but dribbling the ball just the same. The groin felt good. By God, I'd done it. I'd still play!

The days went by and I continued the hot towels and all the other phases of the treatment, but I also trained daily. When the semifinal game against Chile came along, I was still not in top condition and I watched from the stands with the other spectators, but I didn't care. I knew I would be in the finals if we won, and win we did, 4–2, with Vavá and Garrincha each accounting for two goals. It was a rough game, and one it was better I was not in with a pulled muscle. Garrincha, finally tired of being constantly kicked, kicked back and was sent from the game; as he was leaving, a fan threw a bottle that struck him on the head, which required stitches to close. The South Americans take their football seriously, and Chile hated to lose—although why they should have gotten so worked up when they obviously had a far weaker team than Brazil is hard to understand. But at least Brazil would go to the finals now, and the way I was feeling I was positive I'd be on the field for that game.

And then, three days later when I was feeling fine, I went to practice corner kicks with Paulo Amaral beside me, and at the very first kick I felt that wave of pain that told me in no uncertain matter than I had pulled that same *filho de mãe* muscle again!

I cried. I didn't cry from pain, or from the thought of the blistering hot towels I knew I would now have to endure for a very long time, if I ever expected to play again. No—I cried out of frustration, because if I hadn't cried I might have punched somebody just to get it out of my system. The final game was to be against Czechoslovakia for the World Cup championship, and I wanted to be in the game! I had looked forward to these matches since 1958, determined this time to play in all of them, and this time I was going to miss the last four. How was it, I thought bitterly, that I could play between eighty and a hundred games a year for Santos, or for the army, or even for the Selection, and never miss a game—and every time a World Cup match came along, there I was on the sidelines? Nor could I even blame the injury on anyone; no one had been near me when I pulled the muscle. I had had more than sufficient warning that something was not right in my groin, and I had stupidly refused to report it to the doctor. If my career was ended, I would have nobody but myself to blame.

I sat in the stands for that final game, sure that Brazil would win and become a two-time champion, but I wouldn't be on the field and this hurt more than my groin. And we won, 3–1, in a bruising game, with Vavá, Zito, and Amarildo each scoring a goal, and were world champions for the second time—and all the old fears of being replaced in the eyes and the hearts of the football world came flooding back. We had played Czechoslovakia with Pelé on the field and only managed a tie; with Pelé off the field we had beaten them with a two-goal margin. That was a hard game to sit and watch. ...

It was almost two months after pulling that muscle before I came back to play, and once I was back in a game and knew my fears of being permanently side-lined were baseless, I stopped thinking about the 1962 World Cup games and concentrated, instead, on playing for my club. That year Santos won the World Interclub title, playing thirty-four games, winning twenty-seven, tying six, and losing only one. The final game was one I shall always remember; it was against Benfica, of Portugal, and Coutinho and I made it our personal game, with me scoring three of our goals and Coutinho the other two. We beat them, 5–2, and it took a little bit of the sting out of having played only two games in Chile, because I played in every one of the World Interclub matches and was the high scorer with fifty-two goals.

And 1963 and 1964 followed in much the same manner. Again the Santos team traveled throughout the world, building up its reputation as one of the greatest teams ever formed, once again I saw new countries, or at least new cities in countries already familiar. Even returning to a familiar city, I would see it through older eyes, and would see it in a different, more adult way, so that the travel never ceased to educate. And once again I would sit in some foreign hotel room at night and wonder what Rose was doing, and if she was meeting new people, and if she might find someone while I was gone who was taller, richer, more interesting—or more *present*—than I was. After all, traveling most of the time was no way to maintain constant relationships. Rose was growing up—in 1965 she would be nineteen—and getting more attractive and desirable every day. But I kept alive the hope that one day soon she would break down and let me speak to her father about my honorable intentions. And when that day came, we could get married and live happily ever after. Pepe Gordo was handling my business interests which he reported were booming, money was rolling in from all sides, so what was there to stop us from getting married and living happily ever after?

Chapter 11

The year 1965 was an extremely provocative one for me. There was good news and bad news.

First, the good news. To begin with, that was the year that a new physical-conditioning trainer came to the Santos Club, Professor Julio Mazzei. A cultured and educated man who had studied his profession in the university and finished it with postgraduate work at Michigan State University in the United States, Professor Mazzei spoke many languages and presented a far-different picture from most of the trainers in Brazilian clubs at that time. He had, and continues to have, an important influence on my life. He had come to Santos after serving Palmeiras in São Paulo; it was a big catch for Santos. Besides being an excellent physical trainer who knew exactly how to get each man in the squad into his own individual best physical condition, Julio Mazzei also understood the necessity of getting to know the inner man, to understand his personality and appreciate his personal problems; to consider a man's way of thinking, the motivations that activated him. His advice to me in many matters beyond the scope of football helped me a good deal in those days and since, and we became the good friends we are to this day. It was because of the example I saw daily of Julio Mazzei that I later went back to studying and eventually obtained my university degree. Many other players on the Santos squad owed him equal debts.

(Seven years later, the fact that Professor Mazzei did not hold himself aloof from the players as most physical trainers do, considering themselves a part of management rather than feeling themselves a part of the playing team as Julio Mazzei did, led to his dismissal from the Santos Club. But more of this later.)

Nineteen sixty-five was also the year that I included in my contract a house that was available from one of the directors, and a lovely house it was and is. It is huge, located a few blocks from the Santos beach in one of the finest of neighborhoods, with a kitchen alone almost as big as our entire house in Baurú. There is a patio, a wide veranda, and the house is walled from its neighbors, as is common in Brazil. With all that much house available I could no longer see any reason for my family not to move to Santos. Dondinho, who insists upon working whether he needs to or not, could transfer from the job he had to a similar one in Santos if he still insisted on working; his job was a state job and Baurú and Santos were both in the same state. And Dona Celeste, who was traveling down to Santos at least once a month to see to my well-being, would be saved the trips, as well as have that lovely kitchen at her disposal. My brother Zoca had already moved to Santos and was living with me at Pepe Gordo's. He was also playing on the Santos football team and playing very well, although—unlike me—he never allowed football to interrupt his continued studies. Zoca had decided to become a lawyer, and after playing professional football for Santos for several seasons, he gave the game up to concentrate on law school. So there was no reason not to get the family together once again. Pepe Gordo argued against the move; he was strongly opposed to bringing my family to Santos. It would be distracting, he said. I'm sure, however, it was only because he was afraid his influence over me and my affairs might be diluted—and since I could see no chance of that, I disregarded his arguments.

So everyone moved in and got settled: Dondinho, Dona Celeste, Dona Ambrosina, Uncle Jorge, Maria Lúcia, Zoca, and myself. It was like old times in Baurú, except now we actually had room for everybody, and I was pleased to be going home each night to my own home and my own family. And it was in the neighborhood where I intended to find an apartment when and if Rosemeri ever got around to saying yes.

I went and talked to Rose, seriously this time.

"Look, honey," I said, "we've been going together for years and years, and we're not getting any younger. I want to be formally engaged to you so we can plan our wedding. I want to be engaged to you so we can go where we want when we want without having to bring your aunt with us. I want to marry you as soon as possible. No more of this nonsense! I'm going to talk to your father."

"No, no! Wait awhile longer. It's too soon. ..."

I decided to be firm this time.

"It's not too soon at all. Do you love me?"

"Of course."

"Do you want to marry me?"

"Of course."

"Then it's all settled. I have a date to go fishing with your father next Saturday. I'll talk to him then."

And the following Saturday I went fishing with Sr. Guilherme Cholby, Rosemeri's father. In those days we used a rented row-boat, taking it from a dock at the beach and rowing it out into the ocean until we were almost out of sight of land before baiting and tossing over our lines. This particular day the sea was rough and it suddenly occurred to me that if Sr. Guilherme didn't care for my proposition he could easily throw me overboard and let me swim back to shore. Still, I had come here with the intention of asking for Rosemeri's hand in marriage, and even the possibility of having to swim was not going to deter me.

I waited until he had landed his first fish—always a better psychological moment—and then got down to it.

"Senhor Cholby, I want to become formally engaged to Rosemeri. I want to marry her. As soon as possible."

I don't suppose he was really very surprised. After all, I had been eating his wife's cakes and cookies and drinking his soft drinks and milk for a good many years, and one has to wonder at such devotion to snacks. Still, I was surprised at his reaction. Somehow I had come to expect one of two attitudes on his part: either to drop his fishing gear and throw his arms around me, saying, "My boy! My boy!" or something like that; or to raise his gear threateningly and say something like, "You have to be out of your mind to think I'd let my daughter marry you!" He did neither. He looked at me a moment unemotionally, shrugged noncommittally, and turned back to his fishing line.

"We'll see."

"What's to see?" I asked impatiently. "Why can't we discuss it now?"

"Because my wife isn't here. When we get back after fishing, we'll go to the house and sit down with Rose and her mother and discuss the matter in detail."

There wasn't much I could say to that. It hadn't been a refusal nor an acceptance. But I couldn't concentrate on fishing after that. The day dragged on interminably. On the other hand, if Sr. Guilherme had adopted the "My boy! My boy!" routine, I suppose it would have been even harder to wait to get back to land and tell Rose the good news, because Sr. Cholby hadn't rowed halfway to Europe to go back without getting in his full day's fishing. So there we sat in the rocking boat, each with his own thoughts, while the day never seemed to end.

Eventually we got to shore and went to the Cholby home, to discover that Dona Idalina was not at all surprised at the request; she said she had been wondering when I'd get around to it. And Rose and I were formally engaged to be married.

We celebrated the occasion later, when I threw an elaborate party for my twenty-fifth birthday, as well as for the engagement. There was one slight hitch as a result of the party, but it was a minor one, at least for me. Some myopic photographer, probably drunk, took a picture of me talking to Rose's sister, and it was printed the next day in a local newspaper purporting to be of Pelé and his bride-to-be. A minor mistake to be chuckled over, one would think, and then to be tucked away among light memories—but nothing that simple occurred. Rose's sister happened to be engaged to a man who refused to believe that where there was smoke there could not be fire; he had more faith in newspapers than most people, and obviously more than he had in his fiancée or in the word of her family. Or, as I suspect, he simply may have used the occasion as an excuse to break off the engagement, not wishing to have a black brother-in-law. But he did break off the engagement, which could scarcely be classified as a loss to the family, under the circumstances.

Now for the bad news:

One day, several months before the date Rosemeri and I had set for the wedding, Pepe Gordo came to me and said he needed money for the business. I looked at him with a frown.

"Money? Aren't the banks open today?"

But of course the banks were open that day and I knew they were. Rosemeri was working in a bank at the time, as secretary to the head of the bank, and she was working that day. Pepe Gordo admitted that the banks were open.

"They're open," he said, "but your account is depleted. We've had a few poor investments, and there have been several small reversals in the business. ..."

One could scarcely accuse Pepe Gordo of exaggeration. A few small reverses, eh? When I pressed him for details, I discovered that everything had been going poorly for a long, long time, but nobody had bothered to inform me of the fact.

I can't honestly say that nobody had bothered to inform me, because Rose had mentioned more than once that from the little she saw of our accounts—our business, Sanitaria Santista, did a major part of its banking business at the bank where she worked—she felt that Pepe Gordo was not doing a very good job of protecting my investments. But I had paid little attention to her, having complete faith in Pepe Gordo, and now I found that not only was Rose perfectly correct, but that the situation was far worse than even she could have imagined. Once again I had been stupid, not only for not having listened, but for not having taken corrective steps a long time before.

It seems that properties had been purchased that were unsuitable for construction. Construction materials had been purchased from fly-by-night outfits who took payment for their shoddy goods and then either went into bankruptcy or disappeared before they could be brought to account. Apartment buildings had been built at sites where nobody wanted to live. Roofs leaked from bad materials and poor workmanship; sanitary facilities were of poor quality and had to be replaced while practically new. Everything that could go wrong had gone wrong! Bills had piled up and now the creditors were threatening to sue me. I couldn't believe it! I stared at Pepe Gordo in consternation.

"*How could this have happened?*"

Pepe Gordo merely shrugged.

"It's only a temporary thing. If we pay off the most insistent creditors—"

"That's not the answer! We're in deep trouble! What can we do?"

Another shrug.

"Go into bankruptcy, I suppose. ..."

I stared at him. Go into bankruptcy? Everyone in Brazil was positive that Pelé was one of the richest men in the country; that compared to Pelé the Count Matarazzo was ready for the poorhouse and the Rockefellers in need of handouts. And that "everyone" included my family and Rosemeri's family. Rose might have an idea that things had not been going well, but even she had no idea of the full extent of the disaster. But I knew my family and Rose's family would understand; I had no fear of their not understanding. I knew equally well that the rest of the country would not understand. If I knew my fellow Brazilians—who only differ from their counterparts in other countries in degree—they would smile up their sleeves and say that Pelé was a pretty sharp character, pulling this bankruptcy gag to avoid paying taxes, and that the money was undoubtedly in Switzerland in a numbered account, or in real estate in the United States. And the Brazilian tax department could well believe the same nonsense. And it wasn't just the loss of the money—which was sickening—it was also the fact that I had worked very hard for many years to make the name Pelé mean something. It not only had a very definite financial value, but it also had a certain moral value to the youth of the country. *Bankruptcy?*

"I'll think about it," I said.

And I did. I thought about my blindness in trusting Pepe Gordo and in not paying the slightest attention to the business. I thought about Rose's warnings. I thought about the fact that six months before this debacle, Zito had come to me and said he was separating from the company, that he was having disagreements with Pepe Gordo, that he didn't like some of the things that were being done in the company. He said he had bought a dairy farm and wanted to concentrate his attention on that, as his only interest outside of football. I should have asked him in detail exactly what things he didn't like in the way the company was being run—but I didn't. I merely assumed that if Zito knew anything he felt I should know to my advantage, he would tell me. He may have told me, and I hadn't paid any attention, even as I sloughed off Rose's warnings. I'm sure that if Zito had known the full flimsiness of the company's financial position, he would have said so. He was, and is, my friend.

I thought of the punishment I had taken on the football field, the target of kicks from every defense man who wanted to be a hero to his fans and put me in the hospital. I thought of the bruises that had kept me from sleep on many nights, the burning towels I had suffered, the weariness, the years of training and constant practice. I thought of playing those two forty-five-minute halves without a second's rest, running myself ragged, just to build for a future. The future? What future? It was all in some set of accountant's books I could not pretend to understand, and it wasn't a future at all. It was a past, and a painful and expensive one at that.

Not knowing what else to do, I went to talk to Rose's boss, Sr. José Bernardes Ferreira. Bernardes, in addition to being a banker, was also a member of the Santos Club. I told him the entire situation, although he already had a fair idea of it from his dealings with Sanitaria Santista.

"I have to know exactly where I stand," I said. "I want to know what happened and why. And I have to know what the situation is right now. I want someone to go over the books—everything!—the papers, the accounts, the inventory. Everything! I have to know where I stand, what I owe. ..."

He agreed and did just that. When his survey was finished he called me in.

"Pelé, things are bad. Worse, in fact, than I thought."

I looked at him.

"How bad, exactly?"

"About as bad as they could be," he said somberly. "If you sold all the properties you own in Santos, plus the ones you own in Baurú and even in Três Corações; if you liquidated your holdings in stocks and sold the house in Baurú and the house here in Santos—even with what you could get from complete liquidation, you still could not pay off the people Sanitaria Santista owes money to."

I didn't know what to say; I had no idea what to do. It seemed impossible that all those years of making large amounts of money, and spending very little of it, could be wiped out by a simple statement of a bank officer trying to help me. I stared at him unbelievingly.

"It's true," Bernardes assured me. "It's also true that we could find no evidence of criminal behavior on the part of Sr. Ozoris—Pepe Gordo. You've canceled his power of attorney, which you should never have given him or anyone else in the first place, but that's about all you can do. The books have been kept so badly, in fact, that there is hardly evidence of anything, except for the money your company undoubtedly owes to many people. And you are personally responsible for the company, because Pepe Gordo, in your name, signed the papers making you so."

I felt sick all over again.

"Is anything salvageable?"

"There are a few apartment houses, but the rents barely pay for the maintenance and the taxes. Still, it might be wise to hold them. And there are some empty buildings which cost a small amount to maintain but which might—some years from now—be worth something. As for Sanitaria Santista itself and its inventory—nothing."

"Is there anything we can do?"

"Well, there's always bankruptcy—"

My reaction to this was almost violent.

"No! What can we do to avoid bankruptcy and still settle those debts?"

He hesitated a moment and then answered me.

"There's only one thing: You can borrow. You can borrow and hope to be able to pay back the loan before it just adds to the chances of a future bankruptcy on an even greater scale. Today's interest rates are extremely high, you know—they are averaging over twenty-four per cent a year. Also, I must warn you that with the present inflation you'd be lucky to arrange a loan for more than two years, and even then I doubt if any bank would loan you the money you need on the collateral you could offer." He looked a bit embarrassed. "I know this bank would not be able to do so."

I nodded. At least I knew exactly where I stood. I shook his hand, grateful for his help, thanked him for his kindness, and went in search of a loan—not from a bank.

The obvious place, of course, was the Santos Football Club, many of whose directors could have paid my debts without making the slightest dent in their standard of living. The club itself, as far as that goes, I thought, could also hardly have been poverty-stricken. After all, in the years I had been playing for the club we had played over six hundred games, many of them away from Santos, nearly half of them in foreign countries, and each of these foreign games had earned the club thousands of dollars in fees, much of which—without necessarily being modest—had been earned because Pelé was in the line-up. And from the physical appearance of the club itself, which hadn't been improved in any way since the day I first came there—and which hasn't been improved even to this day—the money they earned, largely through my name, had to be someplace.

So I went to Vila Belmiro, sat down with the directors, and explained my problem. It took them awhile to believe it was not some fancy scheme to avoid taxes, and that I really was broke and in debt, but once they finally accepted the fact, they went into a huddle. They came out of it to offer me a proposition.

"Pelé," they said, "you have a contract with us that still has one year to run. We will put up the money to pay your debts. In return we want you to sign a three-year contract with us; the second year at no increase in pay and no increase in bonus, and the third year free."

This time I stopped to figure out exactly what the offer meant. With the normal increase I could have counted on, considering the increased fees Santos was demanding and getting for games away from Vila Belmiro, with the increased fees at the gate which were raised periodically to keep up with the galloping inflation, and considering the increased bonuses that would have resulted from those increased fees, and considering the salary and bonuses I would lose by playing that one year free, Santos would get a very nice return on their loan to me. On the other hand, I had no choice. It was accept the offer of Santos, or go into bankruptcy and have my name ruined. In the long run it would cost me more, I was sure. So I agreed to their terms and signed the contract they presented.

But I refused to allow the loss of money to affect my plans for getting married. I still had my income for the year and the next, I still had my properties, and I knew I would earn money, whether from my salary or not. I also knew I would never give power of attorney to anyone in the future. And I had my health, I had my youth—I was only twenty-five at the time—and above all, I had Rosemeri, who never even said "I told you so" once during the entire affair. What man could ask for more than that?

The newspapers were overjoyed at the thought of my marriage. It gave them an excellent opportunity to fill their pages with wild speculations. After all, we were getting married the Monday of Carnival, when government offices and all factories and business would be closed, and during Carnival there is a traditional shortage of news. So the journalists went to town on my wedding. The stories in the papers were incredibly inaccurate, which is not news in itself.

One story had it I was to be married in Pacaembú Stadium in São Paulo, the only place (they said) which was big enough to seat all the guests I had invited. (In Rio de Janeiro the story had me being married in Maracanã, as Pacaembú was too small.) Other reports had me flying off to Rome with Rose to be married personally by the Pope, others said it would take place in either the São Paulo Cathedral or at the Gloria in Rio, with Dom Helder Camara officiating. Still others had it taking place in Brasília, with the President of the Republic doing the honors.

The fact is we had always planned a very small religious wedding at home, and that is what it was, held in my parents' home in Santos, with our own parish priest officiating, and with only the immediate family and a very few close friends in attendance. In Brazil it is common to have a "godfather" for a wedding just as one has for a child—he more or less takes the place of the best man in the United States—and years before I had asked Pepe Gordo to do me the honor. Rose was amazed when she learned of it—amazed and far from pleased; in addition to losing me my money, Pepe Gordo had been quite vocal in his opposition to our wedding, predicting darkly that a marriage between a black Pelé and a white Rosemeri would lead to all sorts of problems. This was before the disaster of Sanitaria Santista, and I correctly assumed that again he feared loss of control over me and my affairs. But, in any event, I had asked the man to be the godfather of the wedding when we were the best of friends and I could not back out and refuse him the honor now. So Pepe Gordo was there, quite unperturbed at his errors, and the wedding went off without a hitch.

In the street beyond the wall, kept at bay by police, were mobs of people, all trying to get a glimpse of the bride, the groom, or anyone else who might have been a member of the small wedding party. We had a small reception there in the house, one at which red wine was not served—it would not do to get ill at one's own wedding!—and once the crowd had gotten tired of hanging around, and went on about the usual business of Carnival, Rose and I made our escape.

For our honeymoon I must thank an old friend who is still a close friend today, Roland Endler. Roland Endler was a German who lived in Munich; he was an important industrialist, but the love of his life was football. He was president of a large football club in his home town, and his pleasure in life was traveling around the world and watching important games being played. He had once traveled throughout South America with the Santos Club just to watch us play, for he considered Santos, at that time, the finest team in the world. When he heard I was getting married, he insisted upon giving me an expensive wedding present. I refused.

"Then you must come to Europe on your honeymoon with Rosemeri," he said. "As my guest. I insist!"

It is very difficult to refuse Roland Endler when he insists, so off we went to Europe on our honeymoon. We stayed in Munich with Roland, and then toured the Continent, staying either at some of the guest homes Roland has in Germany and Italy, or in hotels. The guest homes were better, less hectic; the hotels were always crowded with reporters and people asking for autographs—which I did not mind giving at all, even on my honeymoon, since they impressed Rosemeri that her husband was, indeed, a great star known throughout the world. Rosemeri was not all that happy with the attention, though. She was, and is, an extremely private person. But I am still sure she enjoyed seeing her new husband besieged by crowds, all wanting to touch him, or get his signature on a piece of paper.

For me, the honeymoon was the culmination of years of pursuing Rose, and I was never so happy in my life. It was an even greater thrill to show Rose places I had been, hotels I had stayed at, stadiums I had played in, than it had been when I had seen them for the first time. It was an infinitely greater thrill than I could have imagined. We traveled through France to Paris, accompanied by our driver and a young man named Helmut, a friend of Roland Endler's, who worked for Channel 2 of German television, and who smoothed many of the obstacles of the trip for us. In Paris we saw the famous Sacré-Coeur, walked the boulevards and along the Seine, saw the Left Bank; in short, had the relaxed pleasure of acting like typical tourists—which we were, of course. We traveled through Switzerland, seeing the Alps—which impressed Rose the most, I think, since the highest mountain we have in Brazil would be called a hill in Switzerland. For the first time we could take our time and see things properly, and not have to rush off to be in a different town for a different game the next day. I wallowed in the pure luxury of simply not having a rigid schedule.

In Vienna we received a great surprise, and a great honor, too. One day in our hotel we were told there was a carriage awaiting us, with the mayor of Vienna present. We looked at each other wonderingly. What was this? An old custom, we were told. When we came downstairs there was, indeed, an old-fashioned carriage, of the type used for royalty before World War I, I imagine, with six huge horses standing patiently before it, hitched in three double spans. The mayor of Vienna escorted us into the carriage and we were off, driving smartly through the streets with crowds on both sides cheering as we passed. At last the carriage drew up before the City Hall and Rose and I were taken inside and given a second "wedding"—where we stood before the mayor, repeated our vows, and then signed the special guest book. It was, apparently, a ceremony reserved for special guests of the city, and was one of the highlights of a honeymoon filled with highlights.

We traveled down to Italy, then, to spend a week at a small village on the Adriatic Sea, called Riccione. Roland had a guest house there which he put at our disposal, and we looked forward to the first real rest we would have on our honeymoon—but we had not counted on the enthusiasm of the mayor of Riccione, as well as the populace. The first morning, far before any decent hour for tired travelers to be wakened, we heard the blaring of a brass band, come to honor us. And it went on that way most of the week. Between the band and the parties the mayor insisted on throwing for us, we got very little rest there. Still, I must admit we got as much in Riccione as we did anywhere else, that trip; and we have always appreciated, and will always remember, the hospitality of that small town.

Then on to Rome. Our escort, Helmut, had heard that the Pope was interested in knowing I was married and planning on visiting Rome; through the apparent intermediary services of a Brazilian priest who was part of the Vatican staff, a meeting was arranged between the Pope, the Brazilian priest, and Helmut, Rose, and myself. The emotion generated by meeting the head of our church in person can only be imagined by another devout Catholic. I had met Pope John XXIII in 1961 when I was traveling with the Santos team and we had been presented to him in a group. That had been a thrill, but this time the feeling was more personal, because I was also able to present Rosemeri, my wife, to Pope Paul VI.

We were driven through Rome to the Piazza of St. Peter at the appointed time, and then proceeded on foot to the Palace of the Holy Office, where we met the Pope in the Vatican Library. I had visited the Vatican before, with the Santos team, and at that time we had seen the various buildings and the wonderful Vatican gardens to the west of St. Peter's Basilica. But this visit was even more impressive, being able to speak to the Pope personally, carrying on a conversation half in my very poor Italian, and then falling back on the services of the Brazilian priest as interpreter when my Italian failed. Both Rose and I still speak of that memorable visit. It was one neither one of us shall ever forget. (The newspapers in Italy claimed the Pope declared himself more nervous at meeting me than I was at meeting him—but I sincerely doubt this story.)

We ended our honeymoon travels where they had begun, in Germany, driving there along the Italian coast and then over the Alps. We might have done better, possibly, to have picked a small town in the United States where I was unknown. In Germany it was impossible to go anywhere, or even to eat in a restaurant, without having a crowd appear instantly, usually accompanied by reporters, all asking for autographs, or wanting to know my opinion on everything under the sun, mostly on subjects I had no opinion on, or trying to practice their school Spanish on me—because to this day people think we speak Spanish in Brazil, which we do not. I'm sure that Rose was proud of her husband and pleased at the attention we received. After a month in Europe on our honeymoon, our audience with the Pope, not to mention our reception by the mayors of Vienna and Riccione, she had come to accept the fact that I was known outside of Santos. But she was also beginning to find the constant attention restrictive. As I say, Rosemeri always was and still is an extremely private person, and her privacy is valuable to her. I also like privacy, but I understand how crowds feel about the stars the public, itself, has created; they feel they have a right to their time. Besides, I was used to reporters and to people asking for my autograph, and I truly do not mind them. As long as you make your living in the public eye, you should never be bothered by people asking for your autograph. It's when they stop asking that you ought to be bothered.

But it was nice to escape to the privacy of our rooms at night, away from the crowds, and be alone with each other, to discuss the events of the day, or the program for tomorrow, or look forward to Santos and our own apartment and eventually a family. Or just to sit together and be together. It was a wonderful honeymoon, even though some things happened which I would have preferred did not happen.

For example: One day I went shopping, and of course gathered an entourage as soon as I left the hotel; as usual there were reporters there among them. I have a feeling they slept in the hotel lobby, waiting for Rose or myself to appear. In any event, I went into this store, found what I wanted, but when I went to pay for it the proprietor held up his hand.

"No, no, Pelé! It's a present!"

"I don't want it to be a present," I said patiently. "I want to pay for it."

"But I insist! For your wife—from us."

I tried to continue to be patient, but it wasn't easy.

"Look, sir," I said, "if I accept this as a gift, I won't be able to shop in your store any more. I would be afraid your hospitality might be repeated, and that would be embarrassing for me. But I would stay away from your store, and that would be embarrassing to you—and also unfair to you. So please—let me pay."

He waved my argument away as being specious.

"Of course you can shop here in the future. Anytime! We hope you do!"

"And in the future you'll let me pay?"

He smiled at me.

"We'll worry about that when the time comes. ..."

And that was that. He refused to take the article back and he refused to accept payment for it. That night the story was in the newspapers and the next day we found ourselves inundated with presents: certificates for washing machines, refrigerators, stoves, even automobiles; we would have needed to hire a ship to take even a part of it home. However, in addition to not wanting the presents, the Brazilian import regulations are very strict and forbid bringing many of these things into our country. It meant a very confusing and embarrassing few days getting the gifts and the certificates and the presents back to their owners, and meant hours of explaining that we appreciated their hospitality, but our government forbade, etc., etc. They were hours we would have much preferred spending with each other, just being in love.

And then at last the wonderful honeymoon was over and we were back in Santos, happy to be home again, in our own and first apartment. Rose had always been an avid photographer, a photographer of professional ability, and in Europe she had taken mountains of pictures. So while she got down to the job of developing and printing them, her husband, the breadwinner, went back to work. And work at that time, in addition to playing for Santos, was the Brazilian Selection for the World Cup matches of 1966.

Chapter 12

There is only one way to describe Brazil's 1966 World Cup effort, and that is to openly declare that from beginning to end it was a total and unmitigated disaster. It was true that since 1958 and 1962 many new and talented players had appeared, but one doesn't readily find men like Didi, or Garrincha, or Gilmar, or Mauro, or Belini, or Nilton Santos, or Djalma Santos, or Vavá, or the others. True, we still had some of the old bunch; we had Garrincha, Gilmar, Belini, Djalma Santos, and Orlando, not to mention myself—but eight years had passed since 1958. I was still relatively young, but I had only been seventeen in Stockholm; the others had been older and now the years were beginning to wear. But our major problem was that the entire nation had been led to believe, by the radio and the newspapers, that winning the championship for the third time in a row was practically assured and would be no task at all for our formidable Selection. And here I cannot honestly fault the media, because they were merely repeating the statements of the Brazilian Sports Federation and the officers of the Technical Commission of the Brazilian Selection.

Naturally, when winning is guaranteed there is no need for the complicated organizational plan that carried us to victory in 1958 and 1962. As far as the directors of the Technical Commission were concerned, it was simply a matter of appearing at the various stadiums in England where the cup games were being held, accepting the trophy when it was presented by the Queen after we won it, politely thanking her, and bringing it back to Brazil without scratching it, if possible.

I believe we began to lose the title at that point, well before we even began our training and months before we set foot on English soil. Nor did we ever do the slightest thing to overcome the many difficulties placed in our path by this completely unfounded and totally idiotic optimism. To begin with, an extraordinarily large number of players were invited to try out for the Selection. Normally, between twenty-two and twenty-eight players are asked to appear, of which the best twenty-two will remain—or at least the best twenty-two in the eyes of the coach and the Technical Commission. This year the directors chose to call forty-four players, which meant that a full half of them would be dropped after training.

Some, like Jair da Costa, were called even though they were obviously in poor physical condition and had to be dropped almost immediately. Others, like Amarildo, who had starred so spectacularly in 1962 and who was now playing for Milan, were brought from these contracts in foreign cities, only to be dropped after their absence had jeopardized their jobs. It was a completely unthought-out manner of selection and did nothing to help the selectees maintain confidence in the Technical Commission in charge of their fate. Nor did it in any way indicate that we were on the right road to win the trophy for the third time. Nor did the decision of the directors to divide the unwieldy mob of forty-four players into four separate teams, and then to train them separately in different locations.

This decision alone was ridiculous, but they compounded their folly by training the four teams not merely at four different places, but at many more. Before we were through, our four groups had trained at different times at Lambarí, Três Rios, Caxambú, Teresópolis, São Paulo, Belo Horizonte,

Serra Negra, Niterói, Rio de Janeiro, and many others. It sounds inconceivable, but it is true. We had an excellent opportunity, it is true, to visit and admire most of our vast country; we also had a chance to train and play before many of our fellow Brazilians who previously had not had a chance to see us—but as a means of determining which twenty-two players could best defend the country as a team in a World Cup match, it made no sense. And when, at long last, we finally left Brazil for Europe, we still had nothing resembling an organized team, nor had many of the players been cut from the squad as yet. We were traveling with far more than we were allowed to enter in the finals, which merely meant that many of the players, particularly the newer ones, were far too nervous and fearful of being eliminated abroad, to demonstrate their true ability.

There were many other things in the handling of the team that were in error. Those in charge would come to me or to one of the other more experienced players, and ask our opinion as to the ability of this new player or that, as if we were responsible for judging the newcomers or determining which should be cut and sent home. All this did was to lead to friction among the players. Where our opinion might have been asked—on questions such as physical preparation procedure, or training methods, or field tactics for play—we were ignored; but judgments were asked which we were in no position to give. To begin with, such judgments were not our responsibility, but even more important, we had only trained with our own eleven-man squad, and were in no position to make such judgments. Vicente Feola was back as our coach, but he was a far different man from what he was in 1958. He didn't seem to wield the power he once had, nor did he seem to want to. The steadying hand of Dr. Paulo Machado de Carvalho was no longer at the head of the commission; this position was now held by Carlos Nascimento, and Carlos had distinctly opposite views from Feola on which players should be kept in the final Selection. And when they could come to no agreement, they could come to me or to another elder member and ask for our opinion, which we would not—or in fairness, could not—give.

Nor was Paulo Amaral the physical trainer any more, although he was still on the Technical Commission. The post of trainer was held by Bruno Hermany, whose background had nothing to do with football. Paulo Amaral wanted to run the team as coach; between 1962 and 1966 he had been in Italy, coaching teams there, and he flatly stated he was no longer a trainer but a coach, and that he should be running the team rather than Feola. Since Paulo Amaral was a strong personality, we found ourselves with two coaches—which is to say, with almost none. And while Bruno Hermany was new and had little experience, Paulo Amaral refused to help him or to give him advice on the best methods of training a team; as he said, he didn't mix in other people's business. So our training suffered. Unfortunately, the directors didn't consider putting Julio Mazzei in charge of physical preparation, even though he handled the training of the Santos team, which was considered at that time to be the best trained team in the world.

When we finally flew off to Europe and began a series of training games with various countries there, the confusion deepened. We played a game in Madrid, followed by one in Scotland, and then a series in Sweden, and in none of the games did we field the same team or anything even approximating the same team. And cuts continued to be made throughout our tour. Carlos Alberto and Djalma Dias were cut, although they were without a doubt among the best we had, and certainly were in the best of physical condition, which was not true of many others. When we played in Scotland, our attacking line consisted of Jairzinho, Gerson, Servilio, Paraná, and myself. I thought we all worked together very well, even though the best we could do was a 1–1 tie, but after the game Servilio was cut and sent back to Brazil without an explanation. As were Valdir and Dino Sani after the games in Sweden, both great surprises to the rest of us. So when we finally started for England and the finals, we still did not have a set group of first-string players and a set group of reserves, and all the players who remained were uncertain of their own security.

As a result the players lost confidence in the Technical Commission, if they ever had any, as well as confidence in themselves as a team. The directors, on the other hand, were still so blithely sure that Brazil was going to walk away with the trophy that they spent little time worrying about exactly which eleven men they were going to field for any game. They acted quite as if it made no difference, since the tournament was in the bag. But at last, somehow, a little intelligence filtered through; someone had claimed the team was unhappy. So they called a meeting, to calm us down, they said. That meeting, like everything else connected with the Brazilian effort in that tournament, was a waste of time. The directors refused to believe there was any problem at all. We were reasonably nervous before the matches, but all it was was imagination. We should relax. All we had to do was to win the next five games and we could go home with the trophy and be heroes, so what was the fuss all about?

When I walked out of that meeting with Garrincha, the two of us looked at each other. If I had been a drinking man, that would have been the time! So many errors had been made at this point that I wouldn't have minded being cut myself, since I was ready to concede our not winning a single game. There had been the overinvitation of players, the divided training in Brazil, the ridiculous selection of our European pretournament schedule, with endless travel and the constant changes in climate and food. There had been the inadequate physical preparation, the ever-present and continuing uncertainty as to who might still be cut, the continuing squabbles between our two coaches and between our head coach and the head of the commission. The sum of all these mistakes had to spell disaster.

But we were far from being finished with mistakes. ...

Our first game of the official tournament was against Bulgaria, and our team consisted of Gilmar at goal; Djalma Santos, Belini, Altair, and Paulo Henrique at defense; Lima and Denilson at mid-field; and Alcindo, Garrincha, Jairzinho, and myself as forwards. We were all experienced players, all good players in my opinion, but the fact is we had not trained together as a team. Still, we managed to win, 2–0, on a free kick in the first half by me, and another in the second half by Garrincha. The result was that our directors now had a victory under their belts to boost their already overinflated confidence, and that did not help matters.

I was exceptionally tired after that game, the result of three things: the insufficient and even erroneous physical preparation, the six warm-up games that had foolishly and needlessly been scheduled in the order and the places they had been, and most important, the fact that I had been the target of merciless attacks from Zhechev of Bulgaria throughout the entire game. I have heard it said since, and I firmly believe it, that Sir Stanley Rous, the British president of FIFA at the time and the man who selected the referees at Liverpool where the game was played, had instructed those referees to go easy on the "virile" game played by the European teams against the South Americans, with the result that Zhechev did everything he could to physically cripple me, and the referee, Jim Finney, gave neither me nor any of the others on our team the protection we had a right to expect from an official in a game.

My legs ached as a result of Zhechev's constant tripping and kicking, and our directors therefore decided I should stay out of the next game, with Hungary. I think this was another mistake. To their minds Hungary would present no problem and we could therefore rest some of our better players, saving them for future matches. What they overlooked was, whether Hungary was weak or not, winning against them in this particular game was essential to qualify for the quarter-finals, and every effort should have been put into that game. And while I had taken a beating from Zhechev, my legs were still in shape to play against Hungary.

However, players do not order nor do they decide strategy or tactics, and so Brazil put another strange team on the field that day and I watched the game from the stands. Even after the first period, when Tostão managed to score and tie the game, we still had a chance to qualify. All that was required was to play for a tie, which was the best we could have hoped for against a team as strong as Hungary, but the order was never given. Florian Albert, the versatile center-forward of Hungary, dominated the field, while Ferenc Bene, the small but agile right-wing, seemed to be all over the place, scoring the first goal, assisting on the second, and being fouled to let Hungary score on a penalty kick, to finish the slaughter. Hungary won, 3–1, and watching the game from the stands was a bitter experience, with the crowds cheering for Albert and Bene and the Brazilian team walking from the field, beaten for the first time in over twelve years of World Cup football.

Now Brazil was in a precarious position. Hungary had accumulated four points, Portugal had four points, and we had only two. Our only hope to remain in the tournament was to beat Portugal by a very large score, which was a lot to hope for against a well-rested, well-prepared, and well-organized team like Portugal, with stars like Eusebio, the fantastically skilled inside-forward, Coluna, Portugal's splendid black captain and left-half, and Morais, Portugal's tough, conscienceless back. And now that we were in this poor position, our directors suddenly woke up to the fact that we were an improperly trained team, quite disorganized, and that there was now no time left to rectify the many errors that had been made. When I say our directors recognized this fact, you may be sure I do not mean that they ever made any statement to the press to that effect. The fault was never theirs; the players merely played poorly.

Nor were the mistakes even finished now. Until the very last minute nobody had the faintest idea of who was going to play against Portugal. The team was constantly being changed on the bulletin board, and when we finally ran out onto the field, there were very few veterans on the team. That day the men we fielded were Manga at goal; Fidelis, Brito, Orlando, and Rildo as defense backs; Lima and Denilson at mid-field; and Jairzinho, Silva, Paraná, and myself as forwards. We had made seven changes in our line-up from our previous game, an almost unheard-of thing in World Cup competition. Among others, Gilmar, Belini, Djalma Santos, and Garrincha, all world champions, were replaced. Manga came in for Gilmar and was obviously very nervous to be put on such a spot. We had never come close to playing together as a team, nor had we ever even trained together as a team. It would have been a ridiculous situation on the most inexperienced team in an infantile league; here, in World Cup competition against one of the strongest teams of the tournament, it was suicidal. But I suppose our directors put their faith in the old dictum that "God is a Brazilian," forgetting that God also helps those that help themselves.

The results were foreordained. Manga gave our first goal away at fourteen minutes into the game, knocking Eusebio's kick through the center, back to where Simões could head it into the net. After twenty-five minutes, another goal, this time when Coluna, the black left-half for Portugal, sent over a free kick which Torres sent back into the area in order for Eusebio to head into the net. Rildo, one of our defense backs, managed to make a goal for Brazil with a magnificent run and kick at sixty-four minutes of the second half, but before we could get any hopes up, Eusebio ended any chance we might have had when he kicked past Manga for their third goal. And that's how the game ended, Portugal 3, Brazil 1.

Morais, of Portugal, had a field day fouling me and eventually putting me out of the game. He tripped me, and when I was stumbling to the ground, he leaped at me, feet first, and cut me down completely. It wasn't until I actually saw the films of the game that I realized what a terribly vicious double foul it was. The stands came to their feet screaming at the foul, but the English referee, George McCabe, allowed Morais to remain on the field, although again, even in the most inexperienced league in the world, he would have been thrown out for either one, let alone the double foul. Dr. Gosling and Mário Américo came to help me from the field, and Brazil went on to play with ten men, and to end up eliminated from the tournament.

In the quarter-finals that year, England faced Argentina, Uruguay faced West Germany, Russia faced Hungary, and Portugal faced North Korea. In that round, unquestionably the best and most exciting match was between Portugal and North Korea at Everton. In this match, the beginning was as galvanic as any beginning in the entire tournament: North Korea scored their first goal within a minute, an amazing exhibition by Pak Seung Jin, a mid-fielder, coming in to score after a sensational feint put the Portuguese off-balance. This was followed in short order by subsequent goals by Li Dong-Woon and later by Yank Sung Kook, the outside left for North Korea. Within twenty minutes, North Korea was leading 3–0, and it looked as if nothing could stop them. But Eusebio proved almost enough, alone, to do just that. His first goal was made at twenty-eight minutes, followed, a few minutes before the half, by a penalty kick when one of the North Korean team took Torres down illegally. Then, fifteen minutes into the second period, Eusebio scored again, tying the score, and then went on with another penalty to go ahead. Augusto, of Portugal, put the finishing touches on the reversal by scoring from a corner kick before the game ended, and Portugal had gone on to the semifinals, winning the game, 5–3.

England had beaten Argentina in a game that became famous for its roughness, as well as its poor refereeing—nothing strange in that tournament of 1966—while West Germany had beaten Uruguay, 4–0, in an equally rough game, in which two Uruguayan players were sent from the game. Russia beat

Hungary, 2–1, largely due to the excellent goalkeeping of Iachine, now playing in his third World Cup tournament.

The semifinals pitted England against Portugal at Wembley Stadium, and Russia against West Germany at Everton. In the earlier game, that of Russia against West Germany, the game lacked any skill on either part, other than the excellent play again by Iachine, the Russian goalkeeper. Russia had two men sent to the showers for fouling, and with nine men had no chance. West Germany won, 2–1, in a very undistinguished game, other than the poor refereeing, if this could be called distinguished. At least it was consistent. England beat Portugal by the same score, 2–1, in a game that was a little more civilized. The Portuguese, apparently irritated by the comments they had received in the press for the way Morais played against me, were on their best behavior, and on their best behavior could not win. Still, only the excellent defense of Stiles in containing Eusebio kept England from losing.

In the final, England against West Germany, England practically conceded the first goal after only thirteen minutes. Wilson, a back, inexplicably headed a ball to an opponent rather than a teammate, and the opponent, Haller, was nothing loath to kick it past Banks for the goal. But England equalized within six minutes, and then went ahead in the second half, after a heavy rainstorm, to lead by one goal. But a foul call on Charlton, with less than a minute left, allowed West Germany to tie on the penalty kick, and the game went into overtime. And then England finally woke up and scored twice before the final whistle, to finally win the game and the tournament, 4–2.

I was completely disgusted with what had happened in 1966, and today, more than ten years later, I still am. After that game I swore I would never play in another World Cup game. I would stay in Santos and play for the Santos Club; I might or might not play with the Brazilian Selection in other than World Cup games—but the thankless job of playing for the Jules Rimet

Trophy under the inept leadership of the Technical Commission such as we had suffered in 1966 could be left to others. I had competed in three World Cup tournaments. That was enough.

Besides, who needed to face the type of refereeing we faced in England that year? And when I say "we" I mean not just Brazil but all the South American teams. The play of Zhechev in the game between Brazil and Bulgaria led one French journalist to say he was sure that, being the target I was and with the refereeing that was in evidence, I wouldn't last throughout the tournament—and he was right. Another journalist wrote that the play of Morais in the game between Brazil and Portugal was "... the most scandalous of World Cup play." But the referees, under orders in my opinion, managed to overlook every infraction, and I was left with a leg that could well have meant the end of my football career.

And who needed the criticism we players received from the press at home, as well as the media commentators and the general public, just because we hadn't won? Little of the blame and none of the scathing remarks fell where they belonged, on the terrible organization, the overconfidence, the internal bickering of the directors, or just their lack of common sense. The players did their best; they played their hearts out. And they lost, but not through any great fault of their own.

I know there are many who will say this is dodging responsibility, passing the buck; that if eleven top stars are on the field and they fail to win, then they obviously haven't played all that well. To these people I can only repeat what every football player knows: Stars don't win games, teams do. Football is the ultimate in team sport, and no individual can win a game by himself. In baseball it is possible for a pitcher to win a game with his infield and outfield sitting on their hands, but not in association football. Pelé is a famous name, but Pelé made his goals because another player passed to him at the proper time. And Brazil won games because Pelé didn't try to make all the goals by himself, but passed the ball to others when it was indicated, so the goal could be made—and that's the way games are won.

And as for physical preparation: In association football there are no rests between innings, or standing around the outfield waiting for something to happen, as in baseball. Nor are there endless substitutions, with offensive teams and defensive teams, as in American football; one cannot even foul an opponent to get time-out in the penalty box, as in hockey. In association football a player runs for ninety minutes, and anything less than perfect physical condition will result in lost games. And when I say we played our hearts out against Hungary and Portugal in 1966, I don't mean I think we deserve any special credit for it. I only mean that playing your heart out, by itself, does not win games. You need a trained and physically prepared *team* to do that.

Chapter 13

I must admit that when I first came back to Brazil after the World Cup games of 1966, my heart wasn't in playing football. The games had been a revelation to me in their unsportsmanlike conduct and the weak refereeing. England won the games that year, but in my opinion she did not have the best team in the field. Not that Brazil did, because we certainly had one of the poorest—but neither did England. And the refereeing helped her win, without a doubt. I have played a lot of football in my time, and I have been the target for attacks many times, but seldom as often or as viciously as in those games.

I was also convinced that I was not meant to play in World Cup games, that injuries would always keep me from playing in all of the games, and maybe that was the way it was meant to be. And each injury meant months of painful treatment before I could play again, and each injury also seemed to take a bit longer to heal as time went on, and it was only a matter of time before I received that final injury that would put me out of the game forever. It was a disquieting thought.

That year, once my leg healed from the damage done it by Morais in the game with Portugal, I played in a total of only fifty games and scored only forty-two goals, the lowest of my career. That year, though, did take me to the United States for the first time. The Santos Club played Benfica, of Portugal, at Randall's Island in New York, beating them, 4–0; and later we played Internazionale of Italy in Yankee Stadium winning over them, 4–1, and setting an American record for association football attendance up to that time. There were 42,000 there that day, and the record stood until 1976, when there were 58,000 at a game in Seattle. But even the trip to the United States could not snap me out of my distaste for the game, and I suppose that was the reason for my poor showing.

At home, however, things could not have been better. Rose was pregnant and we looked forward anxiously to the arrival of our first child. We gave much speculation as to what we would name our son, as well as to what future a boy might have growing up in the shadow of a famous father. Would the world expect him to play football whether he wanted to or not? Would he constantly be compared to his father and would he feel the pressure of such constant comparison? If he wanted to play football I would be more than willing to help him as much as I could, as Dondinho had helped me, but if he never wanted to see a stadium or kick a ball, that would also be fine with me.

All I wanted was for him to have a normal childhood, a happy one, and for him to grow up with a feeling of security. In our home in Baurú when I was a child, we often lacked things, but we never lacked security. We knew our parents loved us and that they were there, always ready to help us as much as they could, and that's what security is all about. It isn't merely money. And I wanted my son to study, like his Uncle Zoca rather than his father, regardless of whether he ever played football or not. But there was always the question of whether the newspapers and the other media would permit him to grow up normally, or whether they would force him into competition with his father, which could be traumatic for the boy.

It was a real problem, but like so many of the problems I faced in those days, Rosemeri solved it for me—by presenting me with a little girl. Kelly Cristina was born in January 1967, on Friday the 13th, and was the luckiest thing that could have happened to us. With both Rose and Kelly Cristina to greet me at home after a hard game or a bad afternoon at Vila Belmiro, the knots in my stomach slowly unwound and I began to regain my love of the game, and consequently to play it with more enthusiasm. That year, 1967, I played in sixty-seven games with Santos, scoring fifty-five goals, and the only thing I continued to resent as my love of the game returned was the constant travel that kept me from my family for long periods of time. That year the Santos Club seemed to be traveling more and more.

The first two months of 1967 were spent in our usual South American tour, then at the end of May the directors scheduled a trip to Africa and Europe that covered two additional months. It was back to one-night stands, playing in different stadiums in different countries with little time between games and insufficient rest, but I must admit that the trip to Africa, at least, was worth it to me.

It was with very strong and strange emotions that I first saw Africa. I had never visited it before, despite all my travels, other than the trip to Egypt years before. But this trip brought me to entirely different regions; we visited places like Libreville, Kinshasa, Brazzaville, Abidjan, Cotonou, Lagos, and many more. It was a completely different experience from seeing the cities of Europe for the first time. Everywhere I went I was looked upon and treated as a god, almost certainly because I represented to the blacks in those countries what a black man could accomplish in a country where there was little racial prejudice, as well as providing physical evidence that a black man could become rich, even in a white man's country. To these people, who had little possibility of ever escaping the crushing poverty in which they found themselves, I somehow represented a ray of hope, however faint.

Wherever we went we faced the same thing: thousands and thousands of people waiting at the airports, crowding onto the runways as the plane taxied in, ducking under still-turning propellers to maintain their place so they could reach out and touch me as I came down from the plane. The stadiums were filled with people who had been there from earliest dawn, or who had even been there throughout the night to be sure of seeing me and knowing that this black athlete who had won fame and fortune really existed and was not just a story made up by the newspapers or the radio. Many times crowds were held back by police or soldiers so that the President of the country could make his way through and greet me personally, or ask for a few minutes where we might speak through interpreters. But then the mob would pour back in, eager to touch me or hear my voice, as if I could somehow save them.

It was a very intensely emotional scene for me, and I remember that first trip to Africa very clearly. As well as one particularly disturbing event.

We were playing in Dakar, in Senegal. The stands were packed, the aisles filled, people standing, all come to see the great Santos team and their famous black star, Pelé. They had come to cheer us on, even against their own team. That particular day I was in rare form, charged with emotion, determined to give them as fine an exhibition of football as I could. Twice in the first ten minutes I took the ball, dribbled it down the field through their defense, and then simply faked the goalkeeper out of place and dribbled the ball around him, rolling it into the net. Suddenly, after the second goal, I saw him raise his hand for the referee and I saw he was crying as if his heart would break. I had never seen a goalkeeper cry before, except in happiness at winning an important match; the next thing I knew, the goalkeeper had walked dispiritedly from the field, still crying uncontrollably, and a replacement had to be found before the game could continue.

I suddenly realized I had done more than merely score two goals against him. I had made him look foolish before his own people. I had made him lose face. After the game I went to their dressing room, wanting to see the man and try to explain that I was sorry. I wanted to tell him that it was only a game, that Santos had a better team with much more experience and could only be expected to win. I wanted to do or say something that would make him feel better, but he refused to see me or speak to me. I felt bad about that incident for a very long time. It was the only thing I felt bad about on the entire trip, other than being away from Rose and Kelly Cristina for so long.

The year 1968 passed as most years passed in those days —more games, more goals, and with Kelly Cristina getting bigger and prettier, and with my life at home more than compensating for the occasionally missed goal, or the far more frequently bruised leg or twisted knee. That year was the best year Santos ever had; we played in eighty-one games, I scored fifty-nine goals, and Santos won the five major tournaments in which she entered. My business interests were also increasing, and I was considering opening regular business offices as soon as I found the time and the proper place.

It was also in that year that we made our second trip to the United States, and this time we played in cities other than New York, playing in Boston, Cleveland, and Washington among others. I found to my surprise that I wasn't totally unknown, even in the heartland of America. It was true that I could walk down the street without having anyone recognize me, which was a pleasure, and I could eat in a restaurant without having a crowd besiege me for autographs, and without the waiter pointing me out to the other patrons, as if I were a special attraction brought in by the management. Still, the name Pelé was known to far more people than I would have imagined.

I came to realize that America was a vast reservoir for future association football. Soccer had been played in America, of course, as early as the mid-nineteenth century; it has always been claimed that the first game of American football played at Rutgers University was actually a combination of rugby and association football. I also came to realize there were many people in the United States who remembered football from their childhood in Europe, or who had been introduced to the game in junior or senior high school. I could tell there was a feeling among many of them for the game that would have been expressed in attendance had there been teams to play the game or fields on which to play it.

My name was known wherever we went. I was traveling at the time with the Santos Club and the team was also known wherever we went. Actually, while most people either do not know it or have forgotten it, when the World Cup games were first started in 1930, the United States had a team entered, long before many of the European countries—before England, as a matter of fact, although the English take credit for the invention of the game. The United States, in the cup games of 1930, beat both Belgium and Paraguay by identical scores of 3–0, and were only beaten in the semifinals by Argentina.

No—I could see that despite the seeming lack of interest in the sport in the United States, all the game needed was an impetus to bring the United States back into the fold, to make the game as popular here as it was in the rest of the world. That was quite interesting, since at that time I had no idea nor any intention of ever coming to the United States to play on an American team.

By the year 1969 I had finally finished my obligations and responsibilities to the Santos Club for paying off my debts from the disastrous Sanitaria Santista adventure, and was on my way to building up my equity once again, although with a good deal more care than before. Through the offices of a television entrepreneur I had met at a Santos game, a man named Marby Ramundini, I had been offered the leading part in a television *novela*—the Brazilian equivalent of an American soap opera—and managed to find the time to do it, although it very often meant getting up extremely early to tape an episode before training session began, or staying up late at night after a game, to film what we could. In addition, Marby Ramundini arranged a sports program for me to announce.

It was interesting work and helped me replace some of the money Pepe Gordo had lost for me; besides, I actively enjoyed working before the cameras.

Ramundini was an interesting person who, in addition to his work developing television properties, also acted as an agent for many television and sports personalities. We had first met in 1967 or 1968, and after getting me the part in the soap opera and the sports announcing spot, he suggested acting as my agent for the endorsement of products, since the name Pelé at that time was thoroughly known throughout Brazil. I agreed. Rosemeri, as usual, looked on the idea with a jaundiced eye; she had never forgotten Pepe Gordo and seemed to automatically suspect anyone who got any money from me whether he earned it or not. Still, with the help of Ramundini we went ahead with the endorsements with a great deal of success.

Ramundini taught me two very important lessons in business: Never underestimate the power of a well-known and respected name; and never be afraid to charge an appropriate fee for its use. When I compared the fees he demanded for the use of the name Pelé in an endorsement with the fees Pepe Gordo had charged, I almost felt ashamed—but the sponsors not only paid the fees gladly, but hurried to renew at even higher fees as soon as a contract was terminated. As a result I was endorsing everything from bicycles to flashlight batteries, from shoes to wrist watches, from sporting equipment to coffee, and earning large sums of money for doing so. I will say that I turned down as many products as I accepted; I never endorsed a product I did not believe in and use, and I never endorsed any product that had any connection with tobacco or liquor of any type.

With the money that came in from these endorsements, I began to widen my investments in real estate, believing then—as I still do—that land and property are excellent investments in Brazil. I realized that eventually, as my investments grew and as the endorsements continued to grow, I would need an office, but at that point I was too busy to think of taking the time to look for one, rent it, staff it, and all the rest of the headaches that would be involved. So I continued to make my business deals at home, or in some friend's office, or in my car. But wherever the deal was made, it always turned out to be profitable. Ramundini was involved in most of them, and was always very correct in his dealing. He did not, however, ever sit in on any of my contract talks with the Santos Football Club, and I am sure I would have done much better if he had.

Chapter 14

Early in 1969 I was asked to join the Brazilian Selection for the fourth time, in preparation for the World Cup games which were to take place in 1970 in Mexico. My first reaction had been to refuse, as the memory of 1966 was still fresh in my mind. Also, although I am not superstitious at all, I could not help but consider in each of the previous three World Cups I had suffered injuries that kept me from play.

However, several things combined to make me change my mind. The newspapers, for one thing, had finally begun to properly analyze the reasons for our defeat in the 1966 matches, and under their pressure the mistakes were not apt to be repeated. Then, too, the personnel of the commission had been changed, although the CBD—the Brazilian Federation of Sports—was still under Dr. João Havelange, a most knowledgeable man. A further influence on my decision was the fact that the games were to be played in Mexico. Many of the European teams were violently opposed to the selection of Mexico as the site of the games, complaining of the altitude of Mexico City and Toluca, where many of the games were scheduled to be played, and also complaining about the terrible heat there in the summer.

To most of the Latin American countries, of course, the heat would be no disadvantage; we Brazilians played with it most months of the year, and often under temperatures that would probably make Mexico seem cool by comparison. And as far as the altitude was concerned, while Brazil has no major city with any altitude to speak of, I had played in Mexico City many times, both with Santos and with the Brazilian Selection, as well as in cities even higher, such as Bogotá, Colombia, or La Paz, Bolivia. I knew that with proper training and a proper period for adjustment, we could easily acclimatize our people to the altitude.

So if the other teams were upset by the selection of Mexico and we were not, we would start with an advantage. There was a further point: In Mexico we Brazilians had always been well liked and well treated, and we felt at home there. The Mexican fans had always cheered us and acted toward us as if we were guests, rather than opponents—which was not always the case in Uruguay or Paraguay, for example. So we knew we would have the additional advantage of a friendly crowd, which helps a team more than one might think. England, for example, had made the mistake of calling the Argentinians "animals" in the games of 1966; all Latin America resented it, especially in view of the poor judging they faced from English referees in those games.

I must admit that the English had partial reason for their condemnation of Argentina, although a large part of the fault for the discontrol of the Argentinian team was due to the poor refereeing of Herr Kreitlein, of Germany. The saddest part of the affair was that I thought that Argentina might well have won that match with England had they played more seriously. There were endless fouls on the part of Argentina, seemingly on purpose, to distract the English team, and Kreitlein ran all over the field putting names in his book, but doing little else. Nine minutes from half time, the Argentina half, Rattin, was sent from the field—and refused to go! The game stopped while the arguments started. At the game's end, which the English won, 1–0, the Argentinians attacked the referee, made a shambles of their dressing room, kept banging on the door to the English dressing room, and in general made themselves unpleasant. But the reaction of the Latin Americans to calling the Argentinians "animals" remained to plague England in future World Cup matches anywhere in Latin America.

So in view of the fact that the commission had been changed, that the newspapers recognized the errors of 1966 and now placed the blame where it belonged, and with the possibility of being on the team that would finally win for the third time and retire the Jules Rimet Trophy, I changed my mind and decided to accept the invitation. Besides, I wanted to put to rest, once and for all, the idea that somehow I couldn't enter a World Cup series without getting hurt. Add to this the fact that I would be playing with Tostão, the other center-forward of the team, and it was impossible to refuse. Tostão and I always played well together, almost as well as I had combined with Coutinho at Santos, and that is saying a good deal.

The Selection had originally begun with Aimoré Moreira as coach, but he had been replaced as early as February 1969 by João Saldanha. Everyone was quite surprised by the choice of Saldanha. True, he had managed the Botafogo team in Rio for a year or two back in the 1950s, but João Saldanha was primarily a journalist. Still, as a sports reporter specializing in the game of football, he was not only familiar with the sport in all its phases, but he knew every major player in the country. He was thoroughly knowledgeable regarding the strengths and weaknesses of them both as individuals and as team members. But Saldanha had a reputation of being a man with a quick temper, very opinionated, and nobody knew how the team would fare under his direction. However, I had always admired Saldanha and saw no reason why I couldn't play under him with no trouble at all.

Saldanha based his first team on the Santos Club as the point of departure for building his selection, and added other players sparingly. There was to be no repetition of the excessive invitations that had damaged the morale of the 1966 team. Brazil, having been eliminated in 1966, had to qualify for the 1970 matches, and Saldanha knew precisely which twenty-two players he wanted for those qualification matches. As a matter of record, the same twenty-two men played in all the elimination rounds. Nor was Saldanha averse to asking our opinions, not on another player's ability, as had been done in 1966, but on more important issues, such as training methods, field play, and so forth.

When we played our first qualifying round we fielded a team that consisted of six players from the Santos Club, two from Cruzeiro, and one each from the São Paulo Football Club, Fluminense, and Botafogo. Some of the other clubs claimed there had been favoritism shown to Santos, and a few of the newspapers from Rio de Janeiro and São Paulo echoed the charge, but Saldanha never minded a fight, either verbal or physical, with the media or with anyone else, and he made it plain he was running the team, not the newspapers, and if he were left alone he would not only qualify Brazil, but would win the Jules Rimet Trophy as well.

We had no problem at all in becoming qualified. On August 6 we played Colombia in Bogotá and beat them, 2—0, with Tostão making both of our goals. Four days later we defeated Venezuela on their home grounds of Caracas, 5—0, with Tostão making three of our goals while I made the other two. Our morale was high; we moved on to Asunción in Paraguay for our third game with no doubts as to our ability to easily win the game and return to Rio for the last three games with three victories under our belt.

But when we walked out onto the field at Asunción to begin the game, I wondered. The crowd looked surly, ready to start a war rather than watch a football game. It was not unusual in either Paraguay or Uruguay, and I wondered if we'd have a repetition of a riot. I remembered being involved in one Montevideo ten years earlier. That day both teams, both benches, the referee and linesmen, plus the fans, had a free-for-all that took most of the city's police to settle, and the game was never completed. I wondered, now, if a similar scene was about to be enacted—but before the Paraguayan fans could build their booing of our team to a proper pitch, half the stands stood up to cheer us, and we saw they were Brazilians. They brought out Brazilian flags and started to wave them. Whether they had come to see the game, or to make sure their team returned to Brazil in one piece, I do not know; but I know it was a comforting sight to see all those flags being waved, and to know if there was a riot, at least we stood a decent chance of coming out whole. After that we beat them easily, 3–0. Jairzinho and Edu each scored a goal, while Mendoza of Paraguay inadvertently aided our cause by allowing the ball to bounce off him into his own net. The self-goal, I'm sure, did nothing to ease the pain the Paraguayan fans were suffering that day, and I've often wondered what reaction poor Mendoza received after we left the country.

We came back to Rio de Janeiro with extremely high morale. We were playing together as a team, and rarely did Saldanha make substitutions. In that year, 1970, the rules of the game were changed to permit two substitutions per game, rather than none, as before; in the first game against Colombia, Paulo Cesar had replaced Jairzinho for one half of the game. Similarly, in the game against Venezuela, Everaldo had replaced Rildo for one half. Otherwise the team played as a unit. What a difference from 1966, where nobody knew until game time who was going to play, and where six or seven changes in the starting line-up was not unknown! And the result of Saldanha's strategy could be seen in our continuing victories.

Back in Brazil, in Maracanã Stadium in Rio, we met Colombia for the second and last of our series with them, and beat them, 6–2, with Tostão scoring twice, and Edu, Rivelino, Jairzinho, and myself each accounting for one. In that game Gerson and I stepped aside in the second half for substitutes. But we didn't leave the game until after it had been won, not as in 1966 when the game was still to be won. It was a pleasure to sit on the bench and watch that superb team at work! Three days later we met Venezuela for the second time and defeated them, 6–0, with Tostão scoring three of our goals while I scored two and Jairzinho one. Now only Paraguay, still smarting from its defeat in Asunción and that embarrassing self-goal, stood between us and qualification in a clean sweep.

The team we put on the field that last day of August was, like the teams we had fielded throughout the qualification, still part of the original twenty-two men with which Saldanha had started: Felix at goal; Carlos Alberto, Djalma Dias, Joel, and Rildo at defense; Piazza and Gerson at mid-field; Jairzinho at right forward, Edu at left, and Tostão and myself being the center-forwards. It was as strong a team as we could field, and we had no doubt at all of an easy victory. But Paraguay was determined to defeat us, and they played impressively well. Their defense was unbeatable, and only the fact that their attack was not as strong as it might have been kept them from winning. Time was running out and neither Jairzinho, Edu, Tostão, or myself had been able to penetrate their defense and score. And then, with little time left, I received the ball, managed to dribble through their defense into the penalty area, feint the goalkeeper out of position, and boot the ball past him into the net. And the game ended that way: Brazil 1, Paraguay 0.

We had qualified and we had done it with a clean sweep of all six games! Saldanha had fulfilled his promise to qualify Brazil and he had done so, mainly by keeping the same squad from start to finish. Brazil had scored twenty-three goals and had given up only two. Many people were saying that our defense was weak; that Felix in particular was nothing like Gilmar at goal—but we had played each of three tough teams twice and only Colombia had been able to score against us. Our defense, we felt, couldn't be all that weak!

But that was in August, and the World Cup games were not until June of the following year. There was still a lot of club football to be played. And there was also the matter of the thousandth goal. ...

Toward the middle of October 1969, the Brazilian press discovered that the number of official goals I had scored since beginning my career with Santos twelve years earlier was approaching the magical number of 1,000. They wrote in their columns that Jimmy MacCrory of Celtic F.C. had acquired immortal fame in Britain for having scored 500 goals, and they also noted that when he had done so, defenses in general were weaker than they were at the moment. They said that for any player to score 1,000 goals would be to immortalize him, as well as the country that had produced him and his football.

The story was picked up abroad. In the United States the marking of 1,000 goals in soccer was compared to hitting a home run in every game, and that if Babe Ruth had maintained that pace he would have hit more than 2,000 home runs in his years with the Yankees. At that time I had approximately 990 goals in fewer than 900 games, or an average of better than one goal per game, so they felt the comparison was just.

In England it was compared with the records of other great players of the past, and none of them had come close to 1,000 goals. It had always been believed that 1,000 goals was an impossibility, and here was the young Brazilian, Pelé, getting very close. I am sure it was a great story for the press and for the sports fans throughout the world, but personally it made me very nervous. I would have been pleased to have been informed one morning that the day before I had scored the thousandth goal, but to have it ahead of me, and referred to daily in newspapers or on the radio, was unnerving.

Still, as long as we were reasonably far away from the magic number, things continued to go well. On October 15, playing against Portuguesa—a game Santos won, 6–2—I scored four goals, which were duly enumerated in the media as numbers 990, 991, 992, and 993. The pressure began to build. A week later, playing against Coritiba in the state capital of Paraná, I scored numbers 994 and 995. Now the press came around in force, represented by correspondents from all over the world. Every time I approached the goal area there would be a battery of cameras aimed at me from all sides of the net, and it became quite irritating. In our next game, against Fluminense, our entire team, including myself, went scoreless—but fortunately for us, our opponents did the same. And then, on November 1, I did manage to score number 996 against Flamengo. But after that there was a dearth.

On November 4 Corinthians of São Paulo beat us badly, 4–1, and I scored no goals. The pressure was getting to all of us. Five days later the São Paulo Football Club tied us, 1–1, and our lone goal was not mine. I imagine the newspapers and the radio stations throughout Brazil and the rest of the world must have started to get worried; after all, they had limited budgets and it had begun to look as if they might be paying out travel and per diem expenses to a mob of correspondents for a long time without getting a story in return. In addition, I know the entire Santos team was hoping for the magic number to be reached to permit us to go about our business of playing football without feeling like something on a slide under a microscope.

Then, on November 12, playing against Santa Cruz in Recife, I scored two of our goals in a 4–0 victory, and we were up to number 998. The reporters and television men, the photographers and the radio men, swelled even further at our next game. Number 999 was scored in Paraíba in the northeast, two days later. So when we came to Bahia to play the Esporte Club of Bahia on November 16, I think we probably had every radio in the country tuned in to the game.

When I came out onto the field, I felt nervous. I had long wished the thousandth goal was over and done with, but never as much as on this day. I had a sudden cold feeling that I was doomed to go for years and years without scoring another goal, that the elusive Goal Number 1,000 would always be in front of me, taunting me, and preventing me from playing proper football. Nor did the hundreds of cameras that followed every play in which I was involved help in any way. They looked to me like Martian monsters with their single expressionless glass eyes watching me emotionlessly. The Bahian newspapers had bragged that when I made my famous goal that day, the celebration they would throw would shame anything that Rio de Janeiro or São Paulo could possibly have offered. It would demonstrate to the Paulistas and the Cariocas—our word for people from Rio de Janeiro—that Bahian hospitality. There was the only true hospitality. There was even to be, the newspaper noted, a special thanksgiving mass for the event.

I tried to put my fears aside and play my best, but there is no doubt the constant pressure was having an effect on me and on my game. I never got what I considered a first-class opportunity until just before the game ended, and then I thought I really had it! The ball was passed to me and I dribbled it down the field, avoiding the defense, and then when I was sure I had the goalkeeper beaten on a feint, I kicked as hard as I could without breaking stride. Unfortunately, it struck the crossbar and came bounding back, but before either I or the goalkeeper could get to it, my teammate Jair Bala was there and did what had to be done; he kicked the ball into the net. The game eventually ended in a tie—1–1—and the thousandth goal still evaded me.

Our next game was against Vasco da Gama in Maracanã Stadium in Rio, and the Cariocas were overjoyed at having the opportunity of seeing the thousandth goal kicked in their home town. I was far from all that happy. In the first place, I was beginning to think the number 1,000 was a jinx and that maybe God never intended that anyone should ever score a thousand goals. And in the second place—confirming my feeling that God was against the idea—that day, November 19, it rained as only it can rain in the tropics when it makes up its mind to rain. The sky seemed to open up and everything wet that had been held up there for a long time came down. One could have cut that rain with a shovel. Still, there were 80,000 spectators who had braved that storm to come and witness the event, and for that number of soaked martyrs one had to do one's best.

Rene, of Vasco da Gama, was guarding me, and Rene was built like Nilton Santos, with legs like tree trunks and a body to give authority to any defense effort he made. On that slippery field, with the rain pelting us in the eyes, and with Rene apparently on every side of me no matter where I turned, I barely touched the ball for the first thirty minutes. Then, at last, I caught him off-balance for a split second, feinted him out of position, and then was off for the goal area, splashing through the rain, before he could recover. I avoided the other defenders who ran to intercept, and kicked with all my force, positive as I watched the ball rise and heard the scream start building up from the spectators that the goal was assured, the jinx licked, the ordeal over! Flash bulbs almost blinded me, but I could still see what I had been hoping I would *not* see—Andrade, the international Argentinian goalkeeper for Vasco, leaped into the air as high as he could and managed to divert the ball over the crossbar with the tips of his outstretched fingers.

I was desperately disappointed, but the play had done one thing for me—it had completely evaporated my nervousness. The thousandth goal, I now realized, was a goal like any other goal; it was simply a matter of putting the ball in the net. The number made no difference. There were no jinx numbers, and God undoubtedly couldn't care less about one football goal. Rene had demonstrated that he could be feinted out of position, and now the thing to do was to calm down, get the goal, and end the nonsense of the magic number once and for all.

I was passed the ball again, once again feinted Rene out of position, and started for the goal area. Once again I dribbled through their defenders and once again I had a good shot and took it. The ball was high and struck the crossbar, but I was prepared to head it in on its return, when Rene, also leaping for the ball, accidentally headed it instead—and the ball bounced into the net for a Santos goal! Making a goal for the opponents always makes a player, as well as his team, feel foolish. I was sure that the mistake would upset Vasco and that opportunities to score would come often that day, despite the weather and the condition of the field. The crowd booed Rene, but not for scoring a goal for us; it was for preventing me from scoring that magic number 1,000.

There was still plenty of time in the game. Once again I was in mid-field and Clodoaldo of our team made a beautiful pass that split the Vasco defense, and then I had the ball with only the two backs, Rene and Fernando, between me and Andrade, their goalkeeper. And Fernando and Rene were split! I took off as fast as I could, intent upon going between them before they could join forces. Fernando, though, was taking no chances of my getting closer to the goal and scoring; he dove at me, sliding to trip me. The crowd rose with a scream at the referee's whistle: a penalty kick!

A penalty kick certainly wasn't the way I had hoped to make my thousandth goal, but at this point I would have taken it any way I could, just to get the affair over with! I don't know how long I stood over the ball with Andrade watching me intently; I was trying to clear the cobwebs from my mind, trying to forget the importance of this one goal to me, to my game, to my team. I was trying to relax and regain the calmness I had felt only moments before. For one split second I remembered missing that penalty kick in that long-ago infantile game in Santos, but I forced the thought away. Instead, I told myself that just standing there could only increase the chance of missing, and that if I missed, what the hell! I'd get the thousandth goal another time. Then, almost as if my body had gotten tired of waiting while my mind was still discussing the matter, I found I had kicked the ball and was watching it curve nicely past Andrade's outstretched fingers, into the net.

The roar that rose from the crowd was almost enough to hold back the rain; the photographers and reporters mobbed me at once, coming from behind the goal; they were joined almost at once by hundreds upon hundreds that poured from the stands, disregarding the police, and raced across the wet grass to reach for me. My jersey was being torn from my shoulders; I squirmed out of it only to have someone press another jersey on me—this one with the number 1,000 on it. Then I was raised to shoulders and being carried around the field, the tears in my eyes testifying to my emotion. The crowds cheered as we passed them. Then, once I was on my feet again, they demanded that I trot around the field so everyone could admire the new jersey. I jogged slowly past the crowded sections of Maracanã, my heart beating rapidly, pleased the ordeal was over, and happy that I was the man who had done it; the crowd stood and screamed as I went past them.

Then, into the dressing room, and a substitute sent in for me; and I sat there, drained of feeling; then I slowly took off the new jersey with the number 1,000 on it, folded it neatly, and laid it down on the bench beside me to be taken home and treasured forever.

The next morning the front pages of the Brazilian newspapers were divided equally between my goal number 1,000, and the second landing on the moon by the American astronauts Conrad and Bean. To me, the relative importance of the two events could hardly be compared. Certainly putting men on the moon, not once but twice, was far more important than anything that went on on a football field. But at that point I was just happy the entire quest for the thousandth goal was over and done with. The goal had come in my 909th game, and allowed me to clear my mind of the pursuit, once and for all, and get back to the more important event that was coming up—the 1970 World Cup matches.

Chapter 15

While João Saldanha, following his methods, had qualified Brazil as he had promised, in the pre-World Cup period, however, he began to demonstrate a restlessness, an unsettled state of mind, that began to worry us all. Where he had always been short-tempered and even insulting to newsmen, he now began to resort to his fists more and more to settle disputes. There was even one day when he took a gun and went in search of a detractor; fortunately the gun misfired and no harm was done before bystanders took the weapon away from him.

I must say that in the case of his losing his temper with some newspapermen, I can hardly blame Saldanha. Too many of the media came to our practice sessions to try to find some cheap story that could raise a one-day sensation, whether there was any truth to it or not. It came to a point where any conversation between our coach and a journalist would end up in a fight, whether the reporter was reputable or not; whenever we saw a group in one corner of the field we automatically knew that João Saldanha had invited someone there to settle things with fists. If a fan said something that Saldanha didn't like, then he went for the fan, ready to beat him up. The directors of the commission began to get tired of excusing Saldanha's conduct; from that point on Saldanha began to lose control of the Selection.

Antonio do Passo was the head of the Technical Commission, and when he finally had had his fill of Saldanha's antics, he went to João Havelange, the head of the Brazilian Sports Federation, and said it was either Saldanha or him, that he could not continue to work with Saldanha as coach of the team. Havelange, quite naturally, went along with the recommendations of his head of the commission, and that meant Saldanha was finished. And, being no fool, Saldanha was aware quite early that he was going to be replaced. He could not, however, permit himself to leave with no glory, without some justification for being replaced, and he therefore decided to charge me with the responsibility for his fall.

He claimed to the press that the reason he was being let go was that he had decided to drop me from the Selection—but that the directors of the commission were quite wrong in replacing him, since the fact was he was correct in dropping me. I was in no condition, physically, to be on the team since I was suffering from a bad case of myopia, and my vision was too poor for proper or safe play.

The charge that I was suffering from myopia was certainly not a new one. When I had first come to Santos as a boy of fifteen, I had been given a thorough physical examination, and the physician reported a slight case of nearsightedness, which technically is known as myopia. The myopia had never changed in all the years I had been playing, and had never interfered with my play, as Saldanha knew very well. He also knew, speaking of eyesight, one of the reasons often given for my ability at the game of football was because I was supposed to have extra-peripheral vision, so that of all the excuses he could have picked, the one of my "suffering" from myopia was the weakest.

The newspapers were not slow to expose this charge as a false one, so Saldanha changed his story. He now said that even if the myopia were not enough, I was being dropped from the team because my general physical condition did not warrant my remaining. At that time none of us were in our top playing condition; we were just starting our training for the actual World Cup matches, but at the moment I was in no worse condition than the others on the squad. When this was also exposed as a false argument—because the polemic of my being dropped and of Saldanha having dropped me was a major one in the papers and on the radio—Saldanha changed his story for a third time. Now he said—on a television program that I watched—that the truth was I had a very serious disease, but that he was not at liberty to disclose what it was. He seemed so positive on the point that I became worried. Was it possible that while he had been coach, Saldanha had seen physical reports on me that were being kept secret from me? Did I, in truth, have some terrible disease that the directors of the commission, out of pity, did not want to tell me about?

I went to Antonio do Passo and to our club doctor, demanding the truth—was I seriously ill or not? They assured me the whole story was nonsense; that João Saldanha had to find some excuse for being fired, and the easiest one for people to believe was that he had had a fight with me because he wanted me off the team. But it was not until I had personally examined all the results of my past as well as my latest physical tests that I knew for sure that there was nothing to the story of my poor health. As for Saldanha and *his* health, I wish him well. I simply hope he never gets a chance to do to others as he tried to do to me with his ridiculous charges. For a while he had me actually believing I was suffering from cancer, or something equally frightening.

The odd—and disturbing—thing was that so many people belived Saldanha's charges. And even more disturbing was that many newspapers wrote that whether I had myopia or not, or whether I had a serious disease or not, Saldanha was correct in dropping me from the team. They said I was in no condition to play in the World Cup matches, that I was past my prime, all burned out at twenty-nine years of age, and that if I went to Mexico at all, it should be as an individual, not as a team member. At least the most outspoken of my detractors had the courtesy to come to me after the games in Mexico to apologize.

But I do not want to complete the story of João Saldanha without giving him the great credit that is due him. His limiting the number of the players invited, for example, was an excellent change from 1966; his leadership during the qualifying games was undoubtedly basic in getting us through the matches without losing a game; his idea of basing the team primarily on the Santos squad and adding other players sparingly helped us with the qualifying games and brought us to Mexico with a strong team that had worked together both in training and in play. It is a pity his personality, undoubtedly affected by personal problems, led him to be dropped as coach of the Selection.

With Saldanha out, the question of a replacement arose. At first the commission asked Dino Sani if he wanted the job, but Dino did not. The coach of a country's selection gets little credit when his team wins, but takes an unfair amount of criticism when his team loses. It can and has ruined many a coach's entire career to take on the job of training a World Cup team. There are sixteen teams in the finals and only one can win, so the percentage is greatly against the chance of being that one; many feel the job isn't worth it. Oto Gloria was the next to be asked, but he felt the same as Dino Sani. The commission then went to Zagalo, who accepted. They could not have been luckier when he took on the job.

Mário Lobo Zagalo was not only an excellent player, but his manner of handling the players was completely different from Saldanha's manner. To begin with, Zagalo had played on two World Cup teams, both of which won for Brazil—in 1958 and 1962. He knew how the players felt, on the field and off; he had been one of them. When he spoke to the team, he spoke with respect from a position of respect, and this makes a great deal of difference. Zagalo had been raised in the poverty-stricken laying in friendly games in Europe, I had noticed that uropean goalkeepers had a tendency to stray from sition in front of the goal whenever the play was in the it's half of the field. In this particular game I noted Czech goalkeeper, Viktor, had this same tendency. ned assured that there was no danger as long as the was so distant, and that he had more than ample time ack to his position to guard the goal area if the play come close.

particular moment I had the ball in my possession our side of the mid-field stripe, and the defense was ; no great attempt to tackle the ball from me, seemingly ; until I attempted to dribble through them into their ry. Viktor was off to one side, watching the play, ready rn when required; the moment I had been waiting for l. It was a moment to demonstrate Dondinho's advice y instinctively, almost without thinking"—and almost t thinking, but with full knowledge of what I was doing, ched a powerful kick for the goal.

n sure that most of the spectators must have thought insane, to turn the ball over to the opponents when was no need to, especially in a game of such caliber and tance—but they changed their minds when they saw the urving in toward the goal and Viktor many yards away, ss, without the slightest chance to defend. Unfortunately, all just slid by the corner post on the outside, but the roar proval from the crowd at least partially compensated for niss. It was the most commented-upon play of the 1970 s. The tragic thing was that from then on Viktor kept near et no matter where the play was, as did the goalkeepers of ubsequent opponents, so that I later wished I had saved a like that for the game with England, or for a more difficult rsary than Czechoslovakia.

xty-five yards and almost in the net! So much for myopia!

he second half was all Brazil. I caught a long, high pass n Gerson, trapped it on my chest, and volleyed it into the

northeast, and had learned his great physical endurance swimming in the rough waters of the ocean there; he knew the tough training needed, and had suffered through those two long forty-five-minute halves of play that Saldanha had never personally experienced. That also made a difference. And where Saldanha was peppery, ready to fight at the drop of a criticism, Zagalo was the calmest person I have known, and this steadiness did much to bring our team together again.

When we finally went to Mexico, there were many both at home and abroad who felt Brazil didn't have a chance in the games. They felt we were insufficiently trained, that the disagreements that had led to a change in our coaching staff, even though resolved, had led to dissensions that would be difficult to overcome. These critics also had an unfortunate tendency to believe the statements of the managers of competing teams. In our group, for example, were Czechoslovakia, England, Romania, and Brazil. The head of the Czech commission, Joseph Marco, made endless statements to the press that his team was unbeatable, certainly in our group eliminations; Sir Alf Ramsey, of England, never noted for modesty, insisted that England would not only win in our group, but would go on to repeat their victory of 1966. But Zagalo never said a word about our chances; he was a firm believer in the old proverb that a shut mouth catches no flies. If Saldanha had been coaching us, he would have taken Marco's bragging and Ramsey's boasting as a personal insult, and probably asked the two men to step outside into the alley. And the animosity he would have earned us with these tactics would scarcely have helped our cause.

We played training games in Guanajuato, Irapuato, and Guadalajara. In every city where we played we were met with that wonderful friendship of the Mexican people we had always enjoyed before. Unfortunately, when we remained in Guadalajara for the first official game of our group, I discovered that many Mexicans were still quite concerned about my health, and particularly my myopia. It seems that the América Club of Mexico had been considering buying my contract from Santos, and they certainly didn't want to put up all that money for a player who couldn't see the ball properly! Saldanha was in Mexico for the games, and had repeated his charges endlessly, predicting the failure of Brazil because I was on the team and had not been dropped as he had recommended. And since Saldanha was an excellent speaker, and very convincing, a great many people in Mexico continued to believe his nonsense.

The constant necessity of explaining to journalists the story of my myopia became tiresome and began to get on my nerves; it also began to upset some of the players. Felix, our first-string goalkeeper, was also nervous; the newspapers at home, never too favorable to his selection, continued to pour doubts on his ability, which does very little to increase a player's confidence in himself. I noticed that Jairzinho was also on edge, although in the end he proved to be one of the best in the tournament. Oddly enough, the younger and newer players on the team seemed the least disturbed, and the tranquillity, as opposed to overconfidence, of the commission never wavered. Antonio do Passo and Brigadier Jerônimo Bastos never had the slightest doubt that we would win in our group and go to the quarter-finals. Their confidence, we felt sure, was based on their opinion of our abilities, and was not the false confidence of 1966. This helped us greatly. It's always supportive to know that you are not the only one who thinks you may win.

Myself I was most preoccupied with Tostão. Tostão, playing for Cruzeiro of Belo Horizonte against Corinthians in the Brazil National Cup toward the end of 1968, had been struck in the eye by a ball kicked by Ditão, the fullback of Corinthians. As a result of the blow, Tostão had suffered a detached retina. An operation at Houston, Texas, put the retina back in place and Tostão's play returned in time to the perfection he had demonstrated during the qualification matches, where his play had been spectacular and had resulted in his being the leading scorer of the six games, with ten goals. But then, after we had

qualified and in our training perio
Houston for a further operation. No
but he had shown a great aversion to
of being struck in the same eye again,
damage resulting. It was a perfectly
but very disturbing to those of us w
his ability so much, and who found i
partner on the field.

He demonstrated his preoccupatio
ever anyone spoke with him. It mac
Tostão, one of the finest players in the
would be unable to play. Or, if he did p
from the ball at a crucial moment, w
Tostão had made the majority of our
rounds, but he had also assisted, creatin
that I had made, or others had made,
play, and the thought that he might not l
fine play in the World Cup games was m

But we really need not have worried.

The first game of our group was again
June 3. Czechoslovakia had been called
teams at the games by the press, and th
start by a goal by Petras just eleven minut
moved past Brito and feinted Felix out of
ball in the net. But I was not worried. It
after play began that the Czech team, reg
nouncements of Joseph Marco, was certain
team they had fielded in 1962, eight years
I knew our defense had its weaknesses,
that our strong attack could not more tha
those weaknesses. And, as if to prove my p
a swerving free kick, equaled the score not l
game was tied, 1–1.

It was during this game that I came close
the most unforgettable goals of my career. I

and in
many
their p
oppone
that th
He see
activit
to get
should
This
well o
makin
waitin
territc
to ret
arrive
to "p
withc
I laur
I a
I was
there
impc
ball
help
the l
of a
the
gam
his
our
shc
adv
fro

net before it touched the ground, or before Viktor knew what was happening. Then, a short time later Jairzinho, certainly not nervous any more, took the ball down the field after Czechoslovakia had given over the ball on a corner kick, and broke through to score our third goal. Before the end of the game, Jairzinho did it again, shaking off three defenders and an attempted foul to cut back in smartly and shoot the ball past a frustrated Viktor for our final goal. And that was the way it ended: Brazil 4, Czechoslovakia 1.

So much for the exaggerated confidence of the Czech manager, Joseph Marco! Now we had to worry about the confidence expressed by England's Sir Alf Ramsey, which was another matter entirely. England had beaten a tough Romanian team, 1–0, at Guadalajara, and they were still the champions of the world from their victory in 1966. And we knew their defense was formidable; it always had been and still was. If they managed to score against us, I was afraid that Brazil might never reach the quarter-finals. ...

We met on June 7, again in the Jalisco Stadium in Guadalajara where we had met Czechoslovakia, and to most of us—as it was to most of the spectators and the radio and television audience around the world—this was really the most important game of the tournament. This was the "final," so to speak. This was the meeting between the champions of 1958 and 1962, Brazil, and the present world champions, England, and it promised to be a great battle. People were looking forward to seeing how the Brazilian style of football—an attacking game—would fare against the English style of football, which was primarily defensive. But Zagalo decided that we would play their game. It would be a game of patience, he told us; a game like chess. The first one to make a mistake would pay for it, probably by the championship.

It was a day of extreme heat, bothering the English much more than it bothered us, and to add to the problem for our opponents, the game was scheduled to begin at noon, because of television commitments. It was the hottest hour of the day, and the English later complained bitterly. But, as they say in the game of golf, it was the rub of the green. We certainly had nothing to do with either the weather or the prior television commitments, nor would we have even thought to complain if we had to play in very cold weather anytime or anywhere. And the altitude of Guadalajara favored neither of us particularly, since we both were acclimated to playing at sea level. Guadalajara's elevation of five thousand feet was generally considered rather ideal, being high enough to avoid the really oppressive humid heat of the coastal lowlands of Mexico, while still low enough to avoid any thin-air problems.

The stadium was jammed when we got there, and we arrived feeling in a festive mood. In the bus from our hotel to the stadium we had a little *batucada* going; *batucada* is the Brazilian word for the Carnival rhythms beaten out on any object by any other object close at hand, such as fingers drumming against a matchbox, or hands slapping against a window sill, sometimes while one is humming a Carnival tune as accompaniment, sometimes not. *Batucada* has a beat to it; it is always morale-building to a Brazilian—and we needed all the morale-building we could get. True, we had beaten the Czechs by a large margin while England had just managed to squeeze by Romania; but we were not deceived by these statistics. We were all aware of England's defensive strength, and we would also be playing without Gerson, who had been injured in the previous game. On the other hand, Gerson had been replaced by Paulo Cesar, whose true value was unknown to the English, so that, at least, was a plus.

The game had not been in progress very long when we knew our worries about England were fully justified. I had this excellent opportunity to score: Jairzinho took the ball past Cooper, the strong English back, in a rush and sent it to me in a perfect high pass. I leaped for it and headed it perfectly toward one corner of the net while Banks, the English goalkeeper, was at other corner. I was already shouting *Goooaaallll*!!!!! when Banks, like a salmon leaping up a falls, threw himself in the air and managed to tip the ball so it slid over the crossbar! It was, in my opinion, the most spectacular save of the tournament, an impossible play—but Banks made it. And soon afterward he made an equally impressive save on a free kick which again I was sure would be a goal. For me, Banks was the leading goalkeeper of the 1970 games, and quite possibly the leading defender in any position.

The first period ended with neither of our teams having scored; we had dominated the ball for most of the period but we had been unable to break through and score against that tough defense. In the interval between halves we discussed the possibility of returning to our normal attacking style, but Zagalo would have none of it. The type of tactics in the second half, therefore, was a repeat of the first. The English called for two of their forwards to drop back to stiffen the defense whenever the ball was in their territory, so that while it made it more difficult for us to get through and put the ball in their net, at the same time it eased any great pressure on our defense. In fact, it appeared to me that England was playing for a tie, possibly hoping to beat Czechoslovakia by a large margin while Romania contained us, thus putting England into the quarter-finals.

But the English team overlooked the individual skill of the Brazilian player, whether playing a basically defensive game or not. Tostão gave the impetus to our winning play; he dribbled past three defenders and, without even glancing in my direction, sent the ball to me in a perfect pass. I could have attempted to kick, but it was obvious both Banks and Cooper were sure I would, as they shifted position to block. It was a fatal mistake. I sent the ball to Jairzinho in the same motion and he put it past a surprised Banks into the net.

We led, 1–0! It was a great feeling. Ramsey immediately made his two permitted substitutions, putting in Jeff Astle and taking out Charlton for Bell, hoping to get that goal back, but our defense held and the game ended with that score. It was the superb dribbling of Tostão that made that score possible, and I had wasted time worrying about Tostão? Not any more in that World Cup!

That victory over England was an extremely important one; to most observers it was the most important one of the tournament. To these fans it was a contest, not merely between two previous winners, or even between what many of them considered to be the best two teams there; to these people it was a contest between two different styles of football. It wasn't, really, since we tried to duplicate their style as closely as we could. But it was generally considered in 1970 that England had the best defense, while Brazil had the best attack. People said that if a team could he made up of the English defense and the Brazilian attack, it would be the perfect unbeatable team. Possibly. Or possibly not. One has to remember that England's defense was strong precisely *because* their attack was weak. With only two or three men in front it automatically gives the defense one or two more men Conversely, critics of Brazil's style of play constantly claim that the defense is weak. This claim is based on the fact that Brazil puts four men on the line, thus depriving the defense of the possible assistance of those men. But the difference in style between the European type of play and the South American style of play is far more than the difference in one man more or less on the line. Regardless of style it must always be remembered that the object of the game is to score goals, not merely to prevent your opponent from scoring them. Scoreless ties do not win games, or tournaments—nor interest most spectators. And it is the fan who supports the game and keeps it going.

But credit must be given where credit is due. The English team had players on it who were outstanding. Men like Banks, and Bobby Moore, and Cooper and Bobby Charlton and Jack Charlton. They can play on any Brazilian team at any time—and that is no light compliment.

However, England came into this game with a further disadvantage: They were actively disliked because of their calling the Argentinians "animals" in the 1966 games. In our game with England the stands were full of Brazilian flags, held not just by Brazilians, but by Mexicans who wanted to see England beaten. The effect of those flags boosted my morale in that game, even as I'm sure it had to have an adverse effect on the English.

When we got back to the hotel after the game, happy and excited, there was a mob of Brazilians and Mexicans there, all wanting to continue the celebration through the rest of the afternoon and far into the night. Sleep was almost impossible; automobile horns never stopped blowing, the crowd never stopped singing and shouting. One would have thought we had already won the World Cup, whereas we hadn't even made the quarter-finals with any assurance. And although we felt confident, we didn't feel overconfident. After all, England had proven a very tough opponent, and they had barely managed to beat Romania—so our upcoming game against Romania could not automatically be guaranteed a victory. It would not be—as we say in Brazil—*sopa*.

On June 10, three days after defeating England, we met Romania. Romania had beaten Czechoslovakia in the interim, to everybody's surprise, and had automatically gone up in everyone's estimation. Dembrowski and Dumitrache, two powerful forwards, were proving themselves to be players of international caliber. We were fortunate that their fine goalkeeper, Raducana was not in for the full game; rumor had it he was still being disciplined for having pushed someone in the hotel pool in a moment of high spirits. When Romania had first appeared in Mexico they had been an unknown quantity, and everyone automatically assumed they didn't even deserve to be among the final sixteen teams; now they were proving themselves a very good team, indeed. But Zagalo was not worried, and he proved it by giving Rivelino a rest and allowing Gerson more time to continue to treat his injured thigh. Piazza was put in mid-field, although the rest of the team remained intact.

We started off playing excellent football against a team that quite obviously was nervous to be playing us, with our record and reputation. With the game only nineteen minutes old, the ball was passed to me; I took it through the Romanian defense and kicked our first goal, an easy goal, and just one minute later Jairzinho took a pass on the by-line, dribbled it through the Romanian mid-field and secondary, and easily scored our second goal unassisted. It appeared to us we could make as many goals as we wanted, whenever we wanted, and we allowed this feeling to relax our guard somewhat. Shortly thereafter, Dumitrache made a brilliant goal, passing our defense as if they were not there and completely fooling Felix at the net. We did our best to get back our two-goal advantage, but the Romanians had discovered that the Brazilians were only human, Pelé and all, and the half ended that way, with Brazil leading by only one goal.

The second half had scarcely started when I scored our third goal, and immediately we became the same euphoric team, convinced of some divine inspiration that would lead us to an overwhelming victory—but after that the Romanian defenses tightened and we could make little headway against them. Then, with eight minutes left in the game, Dembrowski took a high ball perfectly and headed it past Felix to score the second goal for Romania. The game ended that way, with Brazil winning, 3–2, but it was far from the runaway we had expected, and I am convinced that a bit more of that euphoric overconfidence in the first half could have led to a tie, or even to our defeat. I was left with a strong admiration for this team and the conviction that with time they will be a formidable opponent in future World Cup games, and a reconviction that overconfidence can be as deadly to a team and its chances as inadequate physical preparation. We had also been told that in the game between England and Romania the Romanians had constantly fouled the English, but we faced none of this in our game.

Still, we had made the precious quarter-finals, and our first opponent there was scheduled to be Peru.

We were to meet Peru in the Jalisco Stadium in Guadalajara, which was a recognized advantage to us. Peru had been playing in Group IV in León, and had to travel to what we had come to think of as our "home" stadium, while we could remain where we were, rested and happy. Almost all of us were personally familiar with the Peruvian players; in 1968 we had played the Peruvian Selection twice in Lima and they had come to Brazil to play, as well. Names like Cubillas, Perico León, Baylon, Chumpitaz, Ramon Mifflin, and Gallardo were well known to all our players, and for this reason we had little fear of Peru. We knew they had grown stronger in recent years, and we also knew they had beaten Bulgaria and Morocco in their group, but we still felt sure we could beat them.

If we had any preoccupation with Peru at all, it was not because of the team as much as because of their coach. They were being led by Didi, our old friend from the Brazilian Selections of 1958 and 1962, who not only was a fine player but had turned out to be an excellent coach, bringing Peru to the finals here in Mexico. Didi, having played with us for many years, knew all our strengths, our weaknesses, our strategies. It was strange, picturing Didi sitting across the field when we finally met; I wondered how he would feel, seeing his old friends and teammates facing him instead of sitting beside him. I tried to put myself in his place, but couldn't. But one thing we all knew—Didi would do his best to beat his old friends and teammates, and Didi's best was very good, indeed.

In the evenings between our game with Romania and our coming game with Peru, as we did between all games, we held nightly meetings at our hotel. There, led by Zagalo, we would watch the television tapes of our past game, as well as tapes of our opponent's games, and then discuss our future tactics. These discussions were completely frank, and every member of the team, whether a first-string player or a reserve, was encouraged to give his opinion. Nor was criticism rare, although we made sure it was constructive. There was a feeling of "family" that came from these meetings, and from this feeling of togetherness, another parallel activity each evening developed. And that was prayer.

It all began with a telephone call to me from Rosemeri one night.

"Here at home," she said, "we all pray for you. My family, your family, Kelly, myself. Not just for you, personally, but for all the men there in Mexico. Why don't you also pray? All of you?"

I didn't know how to answer. I was tangled up emotionally, just from speaking to her, knowing her thoughts were with me. I was lonely for her and for Kelly Cristina, for home in general. I don't know now what I said, but from that telephone call came the idea. I spoke to some of the players individually, not feeling it was a matter for our evening strategy meetings, first with Rogério and Carlos Alberto, and both of them thought it was a good idea. The three of us then went to the head of our commission, Antonio do Passo, with the idea, and he liked it. The four of us, therefore, began regular prayer meetings in one of the hotel rooms every night after supper and before our strategy meeting. Afterward Tostão came in, then Piazza, Mário Américo, Marco Antonio, and before we were through at least half the delegation of forty members were attending our daily prayer meetings. There was nothing obligatory about the meetings. Not all the delegation were Catholic, and not all the Catholics felt like joining us, nor was there ever any pressure on them to do so. The idea was to unite us, not to separate us.

We never prayed that we might win, either the World Cup or any game; to have done so would have been to degrade the meaning of prayer. But every evening we found a different motive as the basis for our prayers. We prayed for the poor, for the crippled, for the sick; we prayed for the victims of the war in Vietnam, for the innocent victims of all wars, for the health of loved ones. And while we never prayed to win, we did pray that nobody would be hurt in any game, on either side.

I am convinced that those prayer meetings helped us to win, and certainly not because any of us prayed for that outcome. But those meetings helped to unify us as a family. They increased our mutual respect and strengthened our understanding of each other.

The game with Peru came on June 14. The well-liked and friendly Peruvians had come from a terrible catastrophe in their country, the earthquake that had killed thousands of their countrymen, and they were in the finals of a World Cup tournament for the first time in their history. For this reason, in addition to the natural backing of those Peruvian fans who came for the game, the team from Peru also had the enthusiastic support and sympathy of the Mexican crowd. Nor did we from Brazil fail to understand this; we sympathized with the Peruvians, too. But that did not mean we could afford to lose to them.

The game itself was a joy to play in. Both teams, being South American, refused to play the defensive game preferred by the European teams, and it was attack followed by attack from both sides. Zagalo, who had come to like the defensive game, at last gave in to our arguments that a defensive game against a South American team—especially a team led by Didi—was a mistake. He allowed us to play our usual game, and the results justified the decision. Since Didi had always liked an attacking game, it was, as I say, one that was a joy to play in.

We had Gerson back, as well as Rivelino, and we were emotionally prepared to play and win. Not long after the game started, Campos, the Peruvian fullback, slipped while trying to chest-trap a pass, and Tostão was there in an instant, passing the recovered ball to Rivelino, who had the ball into the corner of the net before Rubinos, the Peruvian goalkeeper, could defend. As if inspired by his quick thinking on that play, a short time later Tostão, playing with all the brilliant flair he had exhibited in the qualifying games, feinted one opponent out of position on one side, feinted Rubinos out of position on the other side, and kicked the ball into the net. Peru came back with a goal before half time when Felix misjudged a lone curving shot from Gallardo, and the half ended with Brazil ahead, 2–1.

The second half had not been on for more than a few minutes when I had the ball and saw Tostão free near the goal mouth. I lofted a high kick in his direction; it curved in and Tostão, as usual, was prepared for it. He raised his foot and deflected the ball, rather than kicking it, and it flashed past a confused Rubinos to increase our lead to two goals. Sotil, who had replaced Baylon at forward for Peru, came back almost at once, taking the ball downfield, passing it past Brito, our half-back, to Cubillas, who drove the ball into the net from at least twenty-five yards out, an excellent shot. But Jairzinho gave us back our two-goal advantage soon afterward with a brilliant shot past the Peruvian goalkeeper, leaving him stretched out helplessly on the ground, and we had won the game, 4–2.

We were now in the semifinals, and when we went back into the dressing room we had no idea who our next opponent would be. Uruguay and Russia were still playing to determine that, and the game was still in progress. Without showering or changing, we all sat down to listen to that game on the radio. The score was still tied after regulation time, and we waited throughout the overtime. Then, with only seconds remaining in the extra period, Esparrago of Uruguay, a mid-fielder, slid one past the Russian goalkeeper for the winning goal. I finally went in to shower and change, pleased with the result of that game. I looked at the others as we went into the shower; we all smiled grimly.

We had been waiting for a game with the Uruguayan Selection for a long, long time. Twenty years, in fact. ...

It is the winter of 1950—July 16, to be exact, and a date that few Brazilians, if any, will forget. It is chilly in the house, because, as I have said, not all Brazil is hot all year around. In the *planalto* where Baurú is located, winter can bring bone-chilling temperatures. But we have guests in the house, all of my father's friends that can crowd in and share the radio, so the stove is blazing and the cost be damned! I clearly remember that for some reason the small two-button radio receives Rio de Janeiro better than the much-closer São Paulo, so we are tuned to Rio. It makes no difference, though—every radio in the country is broadcasting the same glorious event: the World Cup Finals being played that afternoon at Maracanã Stadium in Rio de Janeiro.

Each person in that room—together with the other seventy million Brazilians through our vast country—would have given everything he possessed to be able to be a part of the huge mob that jammed themselves into Maracanã that afternoon. Maracanã, the largest stadium in the world, built just for this particular World Cup series; and while it was designed for a previously unheard-of 200,000 spectators, today it is crowded far beyond that capacity. We listen to the announcer describe the mad scene before the game starts, the people fighting for inches in the aisles, paying not the slightest attention to the attendants intent upon keeping passage open; people standing on the walls, so far away they look like ants; people on the roof, on the broadcasting booth, risking a fall that would be certain death. And we envy every one of them.

The emotion in Maracanã as well as in our house is intense. For the first time in football history, Brazil is finally in the finals of the World Cup! To get there we have won our Group, beating Mexico, 4–0, tying Switzerland, 2–2, but then going on to beat Yugoslavia, 2–0. Then, in the quarter-finals we wiped out Sweden 7–1, took Spain, 6–1, in the semifinals, and now we were up against our ancient rivals, Uruguay, in the finals! Uruguay had won the Jules Rimet Trophy in 1930, twenty years before in the initial World Cup games, but they were not a strong team this year. In the considered opinion of most impartial observers, Uruguay had been extremely lucky even to have qualified, let alone managed to squeeze into the finals. But Brazil would end that lucky streak! This was going to be *sopa*—duck soup—for Brazil.

To have been at Maracanã in person that day, for an adult, had to guarantee him endless free drinks in any *botequim* in the interior, just for the telling and retelling of the fabulous day when the Brazilian Selection brought the Jules Rimet Cup home to Brazil for the first time, and he was there! To have been there for me, at the age of nine, would have been the highest point of my life, higher than any I have attained since, I swear!

The men in the room are all taking advantage of the time before the game actually starts to speak excitedly of the huge celebration downtown in Baurú when the game is over and Brazil will have won. I tug at my father's sleeve.

"Papa ..."

Dondinho looks away from his friends and their discussion, frowning at the interruption.

"Yes? What is it, Dico?"

"Can I go downtown with you to the celebration?"

Dona Celeste starts to shake her head violently no but Dondinho pretends he doesn't see her.

"All right," he says, smiling in understanding. "Not for long, but for a little while."

I never love my father as much as that moment. My world is complete. I try to hold back the tears of happiness but it is difficult; I've always been prone to tears at an emotional crisis. For this privilege I swear I will never cut classes again, I will study like a fiend, I will become a doctor or a lawyer or whatever anyone wants me to become. I won't give up football completely, of course, but I will put it into its proper perspective. I will do whatever my mother tells me to do, I will obey, I will not lie, I will stop fighting all the time, I will not—

But then the game starts and all else is forgotten as we listen feverishly. Barbosa, my idol, is the Brazilian goalkeeper; for backs we have but two, Augusto, our captain, and Juvenal; midfielders we have three: Bauer, Danilo and Bigode; and five forwards—five!—and what great ones: Friaça, Zizinho, Ademir, Jair, and Chico! With the roar of the huge partisan crowd urging them on, Zizinho, Ademir, and Jair work their way magically through the Uruguayan defense time after time, only to be frustrated by Andrade or Varela, the Uruguayan backs, or by their goalkeeper, Maspoli, who seems to be everywhere at once. In the sixteenth minute there seems to be an excellent chance for Brazil, but Andrade charges in, tackles the ball clear, and kicks it from the danger zone. Seven minutes later Jair lets loose a fabulous kick only to have Maspoli make a sensational save. You had to give Maspoli credit—he is playing well, but he cannot possibly ward off all attacks all day. Any lingering doubts we might have had as to the eventual outcome are long gone now. Brazil is dominating the play entirely, and Barbosa, our goalkeeper, has almost nothing to do. There can be no doubt that with such domination it is only a matter of time before we score.

Now Brazil is applying the pressure once again! Friaça takes Brazil's third corner kick of the game and when it comes back to him he kicks it expertly toward the goal. But again, Maspoli saves. *Filho de mãe*! Why doesn't Maspoli break a leg! But with all his saves, Uruguay is still only playing defensively, and this doesn't win games—especially not this game! Because even a tie here will win the championship for Brazil on points. So what is there to worry about? Certainly not the fact that Uruguay seems to come to life a bit just before the half ends, for Barbosa makes an easy save from Miguez and another from a kick by Schiaffino as the whistle blows and the half ends in a scoreless tie.

The men sit back, relaxed and smiling, waiting for the interval to end. Then the announcer is back, the men are lining up on the field, and we are hunched over the radio once again. We are sure Uruguay will not stand up long under our attack, and as if to prove it, just two minutes after the half begins Zizinho and Ademir, working the ball between them skillfully, draw the Uruguayan defense to the left; then there is a short pass to Friaça, who has been waiting for it. He runs in and shoots the ball past a startled Maspoli, into the net!

Goooooooaaaaaaalllllll!!!!!!!Brazilllllll!!!!!Goooooooaaa-aaaallllll!!!!! Friaçaaaaaaaa!!!!!!!

Everyone in the house is screaming madly! Maracanã is exploding! The radio announcer is going insane! The house is too small to contain our joy so we run out into the street to celebrate. Our neighbors are there, fireworks are going off everywhere, everyone is pounding everyone else on the back. We see rockets from every corner of town, blazing into fiery trails that light up the distant hills; somewhere someone must have found a cannon, for its dull *boom* is heard at regular intervals. Children run between their parents' legs, not understanding the excitement but wanting to join in. But if we want to hear the game we have to hurry back to the radio; there are no time-outs and the game is going on.

We crouch over the radio once again, grinning to ourselves like idiots. Uruguay is now pressing our team more and more but with a goal advantage, where did they think they were going? Then suddenly Varela has the ball and is leaving his mid-field position to attack, bringing it to our half of the field, passing it to the forward Ghiggia, who brings it past our defense and slips it to Schiaffino, who kicks it past Barbosa into the net!

We stare; then we shrug. The score is tied again, 1–1, but Brazil will win the championship even with a tie, so why worry? Besides, Brazil is bound to score again if they keep the pressure up—but the pressure seems to have shifted. Now Ghiggia has the ball and sends it to Perez. Perez feints Jair, shaking him off, and returns the ball to Ghiggia; once more they have turned our flank. Ghiggia takes the ball alone, feints Barbosa out of position while running, and shoots. And Uruguay leads, 2–1.

And the game ends that way and we have lost.

Brazil has lost. ... It is a day I shall never forget, an emotion I shall never feel duplicated. It is as if Brazil had lost a war in which they were in the right, and not only lost it, but lost it with ignominy and many dead. The general grief is inconsolable. I cry and I cannot stop myself, but I am not the only one crying. For the first time I see adults cry, I see tears in Dondinho's eyes. I have seen my father play with his knee so swollen every step had to be torture, but I have never seen tears in his eyes before.

I go into my parents' room where there is a figure of our Lord on the cross, hung on the wall, and I say to it:

"Christ, how did it happen? Why did You let this happen to us? We had the best team, everyone knows that—even the Uruguayans know that—how could we lose? Why were we punished? What did we do wrong? Is being the best team a sin?"

And I keep on sobbing, the tears running down my cheeks.

"Christ," I say, "if I had been on that field today, I swear we would have won. If I had been playing forward today, we would never have lost this championship. We would have beaten them, badly! Or if Dondinho had been playing, he would have marked a second goal for Brazil, easily, and we would have won."

And I know then that my profession has been chosen. I want to be as good as Dondinho and someday I want to avenge myself on Uruguay. Someday, I swear, I *will* avenge myself on Uruguay!

There is no celebration that night; the streets are empty. And the next day nobody feels like playing football. Nobody wants to talk about football. We only want to forget.

But we never forgot.

Now, after twenty years, the chance to redeem my pledge had finally come. Brazil had not faced Uruguay in a World Cup match in all those twenty years, and now at last we would. Nor could we afford to lose, or we would have trouble facing a single soul when we got back to Brazil. There were some on the team, of course, like Clodoaldo, twenty-two years old, who could not possibly appreciate the feeling that loss to Uruguay left in the hearts of all Brazilians, but to most of us it was something we had lived with for a long, long time. In Mexico there were, I knew, two men from that Brazilian team of 1950 who would certainly never forget that day: Zizinho and Ademir, both in Mexico as commentators on the games. I was also sure they were also happy that Uruguay had beaten Russia, and that now we could get our hands on them.

The night before the game was something to remember. Everyone from the commission, every commentator from Brazil, every Brazilian newspaperman and radio announcer, made a special trip to the hotel to tell us the same thing, as if we didn't know.

"You can lose the championship—it's important, but we can live with that. We can live with the fact that a team plays their best and still loses. *But you must not lose to Uruguay*! They've been a bone stuck in our throats for twenty long years, and you have to get them out of there. They're going around telling people that just the sight of the Uruguayan uniform is enough to make all Brazilians tremble in their boots; that you are so afraid of them that only the police will be able to get you onto the field at all! You have to make them eat those words!"

We had the good fortune of being scheduled to play this match in Jalisco Stadium again, at our home base of Guadalajara. The Uruguayans complained bitterly about being moved from their base in Mexico City, where they claimed they were now acclimated, to Guadalajara, three thousand feet lower—but when the game started no one would have suspected that the Uruguayans were preoccupied with anything. The game started out completely different from the game twenty years before, when Brazil had dominated the play and scored the first goal. Now, although Uruguay was not playing particularly brilliantly, Brazil played so poorly as to make Uruguay look marvelous in comparison. With the game only eighteen minutes old, Clodoaldo, in control of the ball but very nervous, pushed it into the path of Cubilla, the left-forward of Uruguay, who instantly took advantage of the gift. He brought it down the right side, where he faced Piazza. Rather than pass the ball off, he tried what appeared to be an impossible shot from an extreme angle, and the ball slid into the corner of the net almost under Felix's nose. Felix, expecting a bomb he was sure could never go in, was simply unprepared for a soft shot that did.

Uruguay 1, Brazil 0!

Uruguay held that one-goal lead until almost the end of the first half. Then Clodoaldo, now more relaxed, made up for his previous error by taking the ball on a pass from Tostão, coming through the Uruguayan defense, and kicking the ball past Mazurkiewicz, the Uruguayan goalkeeper, and the score was tied. It was an extremely important goal for us, breaking us out of our lethargy, and we went into the dressing room for the interval between halves in a much better frame of mind.

It was also in that half that I came close to making another goal I will always remember. Mazurkiewicz had a habit of kicking the ball out short to his backs after making a save in the penalty area. I had watched him do this time and again on television tapes and in person. This time I was waiting for him! Just as he kicked I turned and raced past his defense to kick the ball toward the goal with all my force before it reached the waiting back. It was only a remarkable save by a startled Mazurkiewicz that kept us from leading at the half. From then on, of course, the Uruguayan goalkeeper was a bit more careful when and where he released the ball.

The second half saw Brazil constantly on the attack, despite a roughness of play that even exceeded the first half—and in the first half the Uruguayans, always noted for their rough play, played as if there were no referee on the field. But there was—Sr. Ortiz de Mendibil, of Spain, and a very good referee. Still, although we were awarded free kicks for the fouls, the excellent performance of Mazurkiewicz kept them from becoming goals. But they could not avoid our attacks forever, and thirty minutes into the half, Tostão passed the ball to Jairzinho, who ran it past two defenders to kick the ball into the net. Then, with one minute left to play, I drew the defense to me, passed the ball to Rivelino, and he shot it past Mazurkiewicz into the net.

Brazil 3, Uruguay 1! Final score!

I could picture the excitement throughout all of Brazil at the victory, and particularly I could picture the excitement in Baurú. The Uruguayan defeat of 1950 had been avenged at last, and I was very happy to have been a member of the team that did it.

It had been a rough game, but fortunately nobody had been seriously injured. Of the Uruguayan team I must say I thought Mazurkiewicz did an outstanding job at goal, making many saves for his team. I was also very impressed by the Uruguayan defense back, Matosas, as well as Cubilla, the attacking forward. In general the Uruguayan team was a strong team, but again they depended too much on defense, in my opinion. They often withdrew all but one forward to have ten men defending, to prevent us from scoring. It didn't prevent us from scoring, and once they were on the offense again they failed to send the proper number of attackers back to the front, reducing their own chances of scoring. Defense is essential, of course—but it must be balanced with attack. One cannot win games by defense; the best one can hope for with defense is not losing. And not losing is not winning.

There was now only one game left between us and our third World Cup championship, and the retiring of the Jules Rimet Cup. Italy had defeated West Germany in Mexico City by a score of 4–3 and would be our next and final adversary. We had no intention of coming this far and then going home without that trophy.

Italy had also won the World Cup two times, once in 1934 and again in 1938, and for them to win this game would mean they would retire the trophy and we would have to start over again. Better them to start over, we felt, than for us.

Besides, in 1958 when we left for Sweden and the World Cup matches, many at home said we had no chance. We were too young and inexperienced. In 1962, on the other hand, many of these same people said we had no chance because we were too old and worn-out. In 1966, when everyone was sure we could not lose, we fell apart. Now, in 1970, when the Selection left for Mexico, many of these same people at home said, again, that we had no chance since we were too young and too inexperienced.

There seemed to be only one way to answer those eternal critics.

Chapter 16

The final game of the 1970 World Cup was to be played at the colorful Azteca Stadium of Mexico City. We were not at all disturbed by the altitude; before moving to Guadalajara we had played our training games in León, Irapuato, and Guanajuato, almost at the same altitude as the capital. We were fully acclimatized and ready to play. When we first arrived in Mexico it is true that some players felt themselves short of breath, probably more for psychological reasons than physical ones, but this feeling passed quickly and by the time we came to Mexico City for the final, we were in excellent shape. Still we had to remember that Italy had trained and played their early games at Toluca, the highest city in Mexico, and had played their last game in Azteca itself, so they would have even less trouble with both the stadium and the altitude.

We arrived in Mexico City two days before the final game was to be played. I was the most experienced man on the team, and I did my best to calm the younger and newer players who were about to play in their first World Cup final. The pressure one feels in the final is many times the pressure one feels in any of the games leading up to the final. The final is everything; it is for the championship. And the championship is all that counts. Second place may seem like a reasonable award to be proud of, but who remembers who placed second to Italy in 1938? Or even to England in 1966? Or who will remember one week later who finishes second to the winner in 1978? First place is all that counts.

In addition, as one nears the final, one begins to meet teams who have also won their Groups, and their eighth-finals, and their quarter-finals, and when you come to the final you are facing a team that has also won its semifinals. The teams get better as you climb the ladder; the competition gets stiffer.

We avoided the many parties to which we were invited on our arrival in the capital, remaining strictly in *concentração*, although I did consent to give several newspaper and radio interviews, mainly in the hope that some of the confidence, the assurance, I voiced to the reporters might rub off on the younger members of the team, and reduce their nervousness. Actually, I honestly believed we would have little trouble. I was familiar with Facchetti, Burgnich, Mazzola—not our Mazzola, who was now playing under his real name of Altifini, but the son of the famous Italian inside-left, Valentino Mazzola, who captained his country's Selection in 1950. I also knew Domenghini and some of the others. I had played against them and had studied their moves on tape, and I knew how they played. Besides, on June 17 in winning over West Germany, Italy had to go to overtime and had played a full 120 minutes on a wet field, and this had to take a lot out of a team.

To me, beating Italy would complete the third "revenge" of the 1970 games. The first had been in beating England, in retaliation for the refereeing we had suffered in Liverpool in 1966. The second, of course, was in beating Uruguay. And the third, I kept telling everyone, would be in beating Italy for their win over Brazil in 1938. None of us had been born in 1938, but anything to boost morale, no matter how far-fetched; why explain that Italy hadn't beaten us in the finals but had eliminated us in the semifinals?

Still, despite my self-confidence—and for the first time in my football career—on our way to the Azteca Stadium that rainy morning of June 21, 1970, I had a sudden attack of tears that was without explanation. We were having our regular *batucada*, bringing up our spirits, preparing us for the game, when without warning I felt my throat choke and the flood of tears come. Nobody saw me cry; I had a rattle in my hand with which I had been beating out the rhythm of the *batucada* against the palm of my hand, and I pretended it had slipped and fallen to the floor of the bus. I remained, bent over as if searching for it, until I felt myself under control. I didn't want anyone else to see those tears. They were sure to be misunderstood, and could make the others more nervous than they already were. I have no idea what caused the sudden breakdown, but it seemed to have cleared the air for me, because when we had changed and went out onto the field, I felt completely relaxed and totally sure of our victory.

The team we put on the field that day consisted of Felix, at goal; Brito, Carlos Alberto (our captain), Piazza, and Everaldo at defense; Gerson and Clodoaldo at mid-field; and Jairzinho, Tostão, Rivelino, and myself in the front. The Italians fielded Albertosi at goal; they had five defenders: Cera, Burgnich, Rosato, Bertini, and Facchetti; at mid-field they had Mazzola and De Sisti; and they had three forwards: Domenghini, Boninsegna, and Riva. The referee for that game was Mr. Gloeckner, of East Germany, and we were playing before a crowded stadium filled with 110,000 people. The television audience was calculated at over 900 million—ten times the number ever to watch a sports event before.

The game had been in progress only seventeen minutes when we first scored. Rivelino crossed a high ball over the heads of the Italian defense and I jumped as high as I could, higher than the defender, and headed the goal over the fingertips of Albertosi. I leaped in the air, striking it with my fist, screaming *Gooooooaaaaaallllll*!!!!!!! until I was almost hoarse, while the others smothered me under them in congratulation. It was our first goal of the game, but it convinced me that between the accuracy of our attack and the defensive nature of the Italian game, only a gift from us would ever earn them a goal. And at thirty-seven minutes into the period, that's exactly what they got! Clodoaldo, without thinking, back-heeled the ball, intending it for Brito, but he missed him entirely. Boninsegna swept in instantly! Felix dashed out to save, which had no chance at that distance, and Boninsegna was on his way. He passed our goalkeeper and put the ball into the unguarded net with no effort. And the score was tied!

If that goal had been made by the superior play of the Italians, instead of being handed to them by a gross error compounded by the poor defensive tactic of Felix, I might well have worried about our chances of maintaining our drive and eventually winning. Or, if the Italians had capitalized on our momentary demoralization, I might have wondered if we had come this far only to lose—but neither was the case. The Italian team made no effort to attack but retreated to their normal defensive game, and it gave us the chance we needed to recover our spirits and our morale.

Then—at what at the time I was sure was forty-four minutes and thirty seconds of the first period, with what I was positive was a full half-minute yet to play—I was in possession of the ball and was prepared to kick what seemed to me to be an almost sure goal, when the whistle suddenly blew and the period was over. The official time is never what the clock says, but is kept by the referee in a major game of football—but for a moment I had that old, cold feeling. Were we going to be victimized by a referee from Europe in favor of a European team, as had happened in the past? I went into the locker room at half time nursing this fear; but the second half proved it to be unfounded. The refereeing in the game was very good and totally impartial as far as I could tell.

Twenty-one minutes into the second half, with the defense intent upon bottling up Jairzinho and me, they allowed Gerson to come through the center from mid-field and boot a powerful kick past a surprised Albertosi. From that point on there was no doubt as to what the final result would be. Five minutes later, Gerson took a free kick, passed it to me, I touched it to Jairzinho, who was momentarily unguarded, and he slid it into the net. Then, with only three minutes left in the game, Jairzinho found me with a pass. I laid the ball off to my right as Carlos Alberto drove in at top speed; he kicked the ball on the dead run past Albertosi for the final goal. And the game ended.

BRAZIL 4, ITALY 1!!!!!

We had won the World Cup for the third time, retiring the Jules Rimet Trophy! I was the only three-time champion of the world in football! And I had played in every qualifying game, in all the training games, and in every World Cup game, and had come out without injury! A superstitious fear was put to rest at long last!

A comment on the play of the Italians in that game:

It was good, far better in fact than the score makes it sound. They had a strong team in 1970, within the style of European football that they play. They also had much individual talent. To my mind, their forward Domenghini was the best of the team, attacking as much as he could, always trying for a goal, giving us the most trouble of any player on their team. Riva was having a bad day; he was not playing as well as he could. He was known as a most dangerous attacker, especially when coming down the center, and he must have been a disappointment to his fans that day. Facchetti was a great player; Albertosi deserved little blame for the goals we scored. And Bertini, their defense back, worked hard for his team, even though—or possibly because—he gave me a lot of trouble.

Bertini was an artist on fouling a man without getting caught. Whenever he came close, he managed to dig me in the ribs, or put his fist in my stomach, or kick me in the shins during a tackle. He may well have been hoping I would lose my temper, try to teach him a lesson, and end up being thrown out of the game. And whenever I fell to the ground after he had kicked me someplace he shouldn't, he would run for the referee, screaming "*Cinema*! *Cinema*!" as if I were merely putting on an act in the hope of drawing a free or a penalty kick. Bertini was an artist, I must admit. He got away with quite a bit, for which I do not particularly blame the referee; he cannot be watching everyone on the field at the same time. Bertini was very subtle. But he did not manage to make me lose my temper and kick him back. I was credited in that game with one goal and two assists, and being thrown out of the game for the dubious pleasure of kicking Bertini where he ought to have been kicked, could have made a difference in our victory. I had learned a great deal from Dondinho and Valdemar de Brito; I had the experience of four World Cups behind me. Did Bertini honestly think I was stupid enough to lose my head at a time like that?

But after the game the Italian team acted very well; everything was sweetness and light. They came over to congratulate us on our victory, and there was no indication of the ferocity with which they had played. One might have thought Bertini was my brother from the way he shook my hand enthusiastically and hugged me. Which, I suppose, is the way a game should end.

Also extremely important in our victory was the one I call Player Number Twelve—the fans. Not just the Brazilians, who would go to Mexico on any excuse just to enjoy that wonderful country, and especially during a World Cup—but the thousands upon thousands of Mexicans who transformed the Azteca Stadium that day into another Maracanã, vibrating with their constant screams of encouragement. I think a good part of our final victory was due to their enthusiastic support.

What happened when the final whistle blew and the game was over is indescribable. Happily, this game had been televised to the entire world, including Brazil, even including Baurú. People there could see and at least partially share in our triumph and the emotions that were evinced that day. The crowds poured from the stands, brushing aside the police as if they were not there, tearing at us like hungry wolves. I was without clothes in seconds, except for a small pair of underpants I wore under my uniform, and I'm truly grateful to the fans for leaving me those. Of course, as soon as I saw the screaming mob come boiling out of the stands, I instantly took off my shirt. I had no intention of being strangled by some delirious fan intent upon taking a piece of my neck along with a piece of my shirt! I was right—shirt, shorts, socks, and shoes were gone in an instant. I had started the game with high spiked shoes, to compensate for the heavy slippery turf, but at half time I had changed to lower spikes, and that pair of shoes remains my only souvenir of the game.

The second that final whistle blew, I began to think of so many things all at the same time that my thoughts were completely disorganized. When the crowd finally allowed us to get to the dressing room, I went into the shower as being the most private place I could find; there I started to pray, thanking God for all the many things he had done for me. But even there I was not to be allowed any privacy; I was immediately invaded by an army of newspapermen who came in, clothes and all, even under the shower. It was a mad day!

When we went back to the field to receive the Jules Rimet Trophy, which was now ours for all time, most of the crowd had returned to their seats for the ceremony, and this time the clothing we had put on in the dressing room was allowed to stay on us. Everyone was laughing, everyone was hugging everyone else—players hugging fans, fans hugging fans, journalists hugging journalists—a rare sight in Brazil. I thought of my wife and Kelly Cristina, of my mother and father, of my grandmother and Uncle Jorge, of Zoca and Maria Lúcia, of my many friends back in Santos. I thought of the many years that had led me here, and wondered what the future years would bring me. I thought of so many things that in truth I don't remember exactly what I thought!

We received the Jules Rimet Trophy from the hands of the President of the Republic of Mexico, Gustavo Diaz Ordaz, and we gave an Olympic march around the huge stadium, with the confetti and streamers falling like snow and with the constant beat of a samba band mixing with the most enthusiastic ovation I can remember. As we marched I remembered 1958, with Belini holding the cup proudly aloft; 1962, with Mauro grinning and holding the cup over his head. Now it was Carlos Alberto, giving it a loving kiss before holding it as high as he could, his eyes glistening between tears and joy.

It was a long day. The festivities simply would not stop in the stadium, and when we finally made our way to the bus to take us back to our hotel, the crowds almost prevented us from getting in. They swarmed around the bus, trying to touch us, to kiss us, and then almost prevented the bus from leaving by refusing to get out of the way when the bus driver let his clutch out and edged forward.

When we got back to the hotel, I disappeared without excusing myself, and went to my room to pray. Photographs of the festivities upon our return to the hotel will show that I was not present. It was not that I didn't want to be there, or that I thought myself different from others. It was that I felt a more important responsibility, and that was the promise I had made to God. I thanked him for our health; I thanked him for the health of our opponents. I asked for a safe journey home, for all who had participated in the tournament. And then I had to stop, because my room was being invaded. It was time to leave for the banquet which would mark the close of the 1970 games.

The banquet was held in the Hotel María Isabel on the Reforma, in the center of Mexico City. There was a show starring our own Brazilian star, Wilson Simonal, and everyone was very pleased with the entire evening. The show went on until one o'clock in the morning, but the party in the streets went on all night, despite the rain that had returned. One would have thought it was Carnival in Rio. The streets along Reforma were jammed with people singing, dancing, drinking—a mixture of Mexicans and Brazilians showing their pleasure that we had won.

Then the telephone calls and the telegrams began to arrive. The first call was from the President of Brazil, Emilio Médici. He spoke with me, with Gerson, Carlos Alberto, Rivelino, and others; as President he had managed to get the call through, which was a miracle that night. The press and radio personnel had the lines tied up with stories to the networks and papers of the world. I had been trying all evening to call home to speak with Rosemeri, but it was impossible. It was just as well; the call from President Médici was barely understandable, not only because of the poor connection, but because all around us everyone was trying to talk at the same time.

I received telegrams of congratulations by the hundreds, from mayors of Brazilian cities, from governors of Brazilian states, from Europe, from Africa, even from Asia. As I said before, I later learned that nearly one billion people had seen that final game on television, the most people to witness any event, sporting or not, in the history of television!

Then, at last, we were on our way home. Normally, I find it easy to sleep on airplanes, but not this trip. First, because the celebration and the *batucada* continued all through the flight; second, because I found myself strangely tense, as if we were on our way to the games rather than returning from them, a winner.

Our first stop was Brasília, which had taken over as our nation's capital ten years before, and our reception there was spectacular. President Médici received us at the palace with high honors; as a Brazilian he had, of course, always loved football, and as President he saw in our victory an affirmation of the importance of our country in the eyes of the world. And from Brasília we flew to Rio de Janeiro, repeating the madness there of our trips following previous World Cup victories. The personnel carriers of the bombeiros were barely able to creep through the jammed streets; the noise was deafening. When at last we arrived at the Plaza Hotel, we needed squads of police to assist the firemen in getting us through the crowd to reach the safety of the lobby.

Ever since setting down in Brasília I had been trying to call home, but without success. Now, when Sr. João Havelange told me that Rosemeri had called and wanted me to call back, I determined to stay at the telephone as long as necessary until I got my call through. It was three o'clock in the morning before I finally managed to be connected, and then only after repeated arguments with a number of operators, who didn't seem to care whether we had won a World Cup or not. Then, at last, we were speaking to each other.

It was an emotional moment. Rosemeri was expecting our second child and was understandably nervous. She was in her seventh month and needed her husband at her side, with which I was in total agreement. When we left Mexico we had been told that after our reception in Brasília and Rio, we would be free to go home; now, in Rio, we had been told we were also expected to make an appearance in São Paulo the following day. But I thought that Rosemeri's need was greater than the need for more celebration, and at dawn I rented an air-taxi and had the pilot fly me to Santos, to my home and my family.

To this day I am surprised at the repercussions that resulted from my departure from the Selection without visiting São Paulo with them. I suppose, in a way, I will always be surprised at the animosity I seem to raise in the hearts and words of a few commentators and newspapermen, almost always in my own country. We, in the Selection, had given up six months of our private lives for the training, for the qualification games, for the training games, and for the actual World Cup matches. Now, when we had won the cup, when we had fulfilled our commitment, I was practically an ungrateful traitor, according to these newspapers and radio stations, simply because I had gone to my wife, who needed me, rather than to São Paulo, where only the newspapermen and the commentators needed any of us.

But I was sure that the Brazilian people, themselves, would understand, regardless of the comments in the papers and on the radio. Because I am sure that under the circumstances, each one would have done the same.

Chapter 17

On August 27, 1970, our second child and first son was born. He was christened Edson Cholby Nascimento, and as quickly nicknamed Edinho by the family and his godfather, Professor Mazzei. I'm sure I didn't pinch his fat little thigh and say, "This one will make a fine football player," because if Edinho wants to play football, he will; and if he doesn't, he won't. But I did realize that with his birth, regardless of Edinho's eventual career and life-style, my own life-style would have to change radically. Rosemeri and I spent many hours discussing it.

One thing was certain: The endless travel which kept me away from home the major part of each year would have to be sharply reduced. My family wanted me to spend more time with them, and I wanted the same thing. By concentrating on my growing business, I could remain in Santos with them. This meant several things. First of all, I had to plan to stop playing with the Brazilian Selection, since all of their games were away from my home in Santos. It also meant eventually stopping playing for Santos, as well. Even though half of their games were played at home, the rest had taken me all over the world more times than I could count, and I had enough travel to last me several lifetimes. I was tired of living in airplanes and out of suitcases. Besides, I had finally returned to school with the aim of obtaining a university degree in physical education, and traveling meant missing classes. And of all the students in the world, I was surely the last one who could afford to cut classes and expect to end up earning a degree.

I had decided to return to school for a very good reason.

During the playing season I was often called upon to speak at various universities, or high schools, or even hospitals, telling those who attended these lectures all about football, its history, its skills, my travels, and anything else they cared to question me about. I always had to ask Professor Mazzei to accompany me to handle any questions I was unable to handle; and these proved to be more than I cared to admit. I had always realized my education was inadequate, but these lectures and seminars proved it in a most embarrassing manner. Besides, I was determined that my children would be given every educational advantage, and I felt it would be more of an example for them to have a father with a university degree, rather than one who was merely a fourth-grade drop-out. So, when the professor pressed me to return to school, and when he was backed up strongly by both Rosemeri and my studious brother, Zoca, who was now in law school, I made no attempt to argue.

But merely wanting to return to school was one matter; getting accepted was quite another. In order to qualify for entering the university, one had to show he had passed both secondary and preparatory, and even then he had to pass examinations which are similar to the Regents in the United States, and can be classed as university entrance exams.

It looked like an insurmountable task, but this time my mind was as set on learning and passing as it previously had been set on not learning and not passing. First I had to prepare for the examination granting me a diploma from secondary; to accomplish this I hired a tutor and together with Professor Mazzei, I got down to serious studying. It took a full year of study before I felt I was prepared for that examination. When

I went into the room to take it, Professor Mazzei patted me on the back.

"Relax, Pelé," he said. "Don't be nervous. You've worked hard and studied hard. You are completely prepared. Don't think of failing and you'll have no trouble."

It made me remember the trip to Santos by bus with Valdemar de Brito beside me trying to build up my confidence. Well, Valdemar had been right and the professor was probably also right. I *had* studied hard. And the professor was proven right, because I passed.

The diploma from secondary permitted me to study for passing an examination for preparatory, and this took a second year of constant study in all my free time, with the help of both the professor and my tutor. But at last the year was over and I felt I was ready. This examination was scheduled to be held in Aparecida, a pretty little town nestled in the Paraíba River valley, about halfway between Rio de Janeiro and São Paulo. My old friend Zito had a farm near Aparecida, and I stayed there the night before the exam, sleeping little and worrying a good deal. In the morning I remember I borrowed a horse from him, and came trotting into town early on the morning of the examination, probably looking like Don Quixote. I remember hitching the horse, taking a deep breath, and walking into that room. I tried to smile as I entered, but the smile disappeared as soon as the door closed. Still, the studying paid off; when I walked out of the room several hours later, I felt sure I had passed. A week later the precious letter arrived, advising me that I was now permitted to take the entrance examinations for the university. Exams, exams! I sighed and went back to my books.

The final examination was taken in Santos, and by now I was weary with studying, but I knew I would not stop now until I had that precious diploma in my possession. And this time when I went down to the University of Santos to take the examination, I knew I was going to pass. I had worked too hard not to pass; two solid years of constant study on top of all my other activities were not to be thrown out! And I did pass, not, perhaps, at the top of the list, but I was on the list, and that was what counted! The examination consisted of many subjects, such as Brazilian history, mathematics, and other humanities courses; in addition, since I was to enter the Physical Education College, I had to pass a test of running, jumping, chinning, rope climbing, and many other tests of physical ability. Unfortunately, one of them was swimming! Like many Brazilians who spend a lot of time on the beach near the water—or like many sailors, I have been told—I had never learned to really swim. Now I had to swim twenty-five yards without drowning! Well, after those past two years I certainly was not about to be stopped by twenty-five yards of water. I took a day off, had the pool to myself, and by the end of the day I was swimming. Nothing to make Johnny Weissmuller envious, but at least I made the twenty-five yards without having to ask somebody to haul me to the edge and revive me. And I was in the university!

While I was preparing for the examinations for secondary, preparatory, and the university entrance exams, my studying time was more or less my own; but when I entered the university they expected me to be at class on time when a class was scheduled. It is true that when one travels with a professional football team and is a student at the same time, the state allows the missing of classes without penalty, and examinations can be made up at a later date. Still if one misses too many classes one is not going to pass those made-up examinations—and this the university does *not* allow. There were several players besides myself on the Santos team who were also students at the university, and we were fortunate in that Professor Mazzei made sure none of us lost out because of our travels. When we were on a trip, or in *concentração*, the professor would make sure we studied. He would hold classes and give us short exams so that we would not be behind our classmates when we returned. Often we found ourselves ahead of them after a protracted trip. I believe the professor deserves a good deal of credit for the fact that many of us on the Santos team eventually ended up with our university degrees.

One real drawback at the university—at least for me—came in my very first year when I, together with the other first-year men, had to undergo the standard freshman hazing. The upperclassmen, in their wisdom, decided that my punishment in the hazing was to have my hair cut extremely short. I explained to them that I had many contracts for the endorsement of products, and that my sponsors liked to have me look the same in all my pictures. However, I said, if they chose another punishment, I would be more than willing to undergo it. My eloquence, plus the logic of my position, can be judged from the picture of me taken at the 1970 World Cup matches in Mexico, where I looked as if I had been scalped.

The three-year course at the Faculdade de Educação Física—the College of Physical Education—at Santos University was surprisingly well rounded. It included many humanities courses seemingly unconnected with physical education. We studied psychology, physiology, Brazilian history, and many other courses meant to broaden us in general. Classes began at seven-thirty in the morning, and there was nothing that impressed the professor of a class less than the fact you had been up the previous night running your legs off on a football field. And if any of my teachers were excited or thrilled to have the great star Pelé in their class, they disguised the feeling very well. I was resolved not to repeat the errors of my youth. This time I took school seriously, with the result that eventually, five years after I had first started to cram for my secondary certificate, I put on my cap and gown and graduated with my class.

I was determined to end my playing career with the Brazilian Selection at the end of their season in 1971, and definitely not to accept an invitation to play in the 1974 World Cup games. It was not a matter of age or physical condition: My condition was excellent as evidenced by my performance at the 1970 games, and as for age, in 1974 I would still only be thirty-three years old, and Djalma Santos and Nilton Santos had both played World Cup football at the age of thirty-eight. Several things led to this decision. I felt a player should leave the game when he was in condition to continue, rather than when the fans drove him from the game; I remembered all too clearly the booing Gilmar had taken that day in Pacaembú Stadium, and this less than a year after he had won the World Cup. Also, to play with the Brazilian Selection after 1971 would have been to deprive some younger player of the berth, as well as of the experience that went with it, experience he would need to properly prepare for the 1974 games. A final reason was that accepting an invitation in 1974 would mean another six months or more of separation from my family. I had been in four World Cups; it was enough.

As far as the Santos Club was concerned, my contract ran until the latter part of 1972, and I felt I could renew that contract once more, for an additional two years, without excessive personal sacrifice. I felt this would give Santos ample time to find a suitable replacement, and I felt they would want this extra time.

So I continued to play for Santos and to plan for the future, when all playing would be behind me, and I could go to the office at nine in the morning and come home at five or six in the evening, kiss my wife at the door, play with the children, sit down to a quiet meal and talk of normal things—instead of strained muscles or torn ligaments—and relax in the evening; a life I had envisioned ever since Rosemeri and I were married. But in the meantime there were still the years to be spent playing whenever and wherever Santos wished. I had made my plans for retirement public enough—there was no secret about them—but Santos made no effort to find a replacement. Instead, they tried to schedule as many games abroad as possible, to earn the maximum number of dollars while the golden goose was still on their payroll.

The first six weeks of 1971 were spent in a swing around South and Central America, as well as through the Caribbean. In that time we visited Bolivia, El Salvador, Martinique, Guadeloupe, and many other places; and it was when we were in Jamaica that I first met Mr. Clive Toye.

We were sitting round the hotel swimming pool, relaxing the morning before a game, when three men approached and introduced themselves: Clive Toye, head of the New York Cosmos; Phil Woosnam, who today is commissioner of the North American Soccer League; and Kurt Lamm, secretary of the U. S. Soccer Federation. Clive Toye is a tall, curly-haired, genial man with a cigar usually clamped between his teeth. He sat down on the lounge chair next to me and started talking. Since Clive spoke with a broad British accent, and since my English at that time was almost nonexistent, I didn't have the faintest idea what he was talking about until Professor Mazzei was kind enough to interpret.

"Mr. Toye is explaining," the professor said in Portuguese, "that the game of soccer in the United States is having a difficult time. A league was formed in 1968, using imported players for the most part, but the league failed. This year, 1971, they are forming a new league, better financed and with greater possibility of success."

He turned to Toye to indicate he had translated as far as he could. I looked on politely. The other players on our team, none of whom speak English, got bored; some lay back on their lounge chairs and closed their eyes, some jumped into the pool, and some simply wandered off. I envied them all. I wondered why this blond curly-haired giant was giving me the sad story of his failures.

Through the professor's translation efforts, the conversation continued.

"We feel sure," Toye said, "that with the proper encouragement, the proper public relations, soccer can become as important a sport in the United States as it is everywhere else in the world."

"I agree," I said. "I felt that when I first went to play in the United States some years ago, and had it confirmed for me at my last trip there." But I kept wondering why Mr. Toye was telling me all this. The clock over the entrance to the hotel from the pool was approaching noon, and I dislike missing meals.

"What we feel," Toye continued, "is that in order to make it that big a success in the shortest period of time, we need some truly big foreign soccer stars to come to the United States and popularize the sport—"

"It would help," I agreed.

"—and since the biggest name in the world of professional soccer today is Pelé, we wonder if you would be interested in coming to the United States when your contract with Santos is finished. And signing up with the New York Cosmos."

When the professor finished putting that into Portuguese, I stared at Clive Toye a moment. The New York Cosmos? He had to be joking!

"Tell him no," I said to the professor.

Toye frowned. No is pretty much the same in any language.

"Are you saying no without even wanting to know what we would be willing to pay you?"

Through the professor I tried to explain.

"If I'm not interested in going to New York, or in playing with your club, what difference does it make what you are willing to pay? I've been offered very large sums to sign with Barcelona, and Real Madrid, and several Italian teams, and the answer has always been no. I was offered a blank check by a Mexican club and told to fill it out for whatever I wanted, and the answer was no. When I finish playing for Santos I intend to remain there, in Santos, living like a human being, spending my time with my business and my family. My family is there—"

Toye interrupted.

"We'll go down to Santos and talk to your family."

I smiled.

"My family has an influence on me, to be sure, but they don't make my decisions for me. I make those. And I have no intention of going to the United States, or anywhere else, to play football."

The three men got to their feet. In their jackets and ties, they looked uncomfortable under that hot Caribbean sun. But Clive Toye smiled his usual relaxed smile.

"Well, you don't mind if we don't give up, do you? We'll keep after you. Maybe you'll change your mind."

When the professor had finished translating, I shrugged.

"Maybe," I said, "but I doubt it."

And then they left and I could go into the pool for one final dip before lunch.

Shortly after our return to Santos from that trip, I was approached by a Henry Stampleman for the Pepsi-Cola Company, who—quite unlike other sponsors—did *not* want me to say I drank their product and loved it. Instead they wanted me to teach football to children around the world. I was intrigued by the uniqueness of the approach by a commercial company, and even more intrigued by the idea. It would mean, of course, an even more complicated and crowded schedule, but I felt it would be well worth it. By co-ordinating these football seminars with Santos' travels abroad, it would merely fill the time between games when we were in a foreign country. I would be teaching children instead of sitting around a hotel lobby, or watching television in a language I probably didn't understand.

Our initial contract was for one year, mainly to see if the program was working out, and if the Pepsi-Cola Company and I were compatible. After that first year it was obvious the answer to both was yes, and the program was expanded and a five-year contract signed between us. To handle the physical-preparation aspects of football training for children, Professor Mazzei was also signed by Pepsi-Cola, and thereafter we traveled together to all of the seminars, dividing the time given between proper training methods and proper football skills. It made for a busy schedule, playing football, training, studying for my degree, and traveling, but I had always wanted to teach children and I enjoyed the seminars very much.

To add to my labors, the year 1971 also saw me finally opening my own offices on the fifth floor of a building at 121 Rua Riachuelo, in Santos. Ramundini was opposed to the move, claiming that with an office, people would know where to reach me; that I would be so busy with people asking for favors or donations that I would end up with much expense and nothing to show for it. I knew that Ramundini's objection was based on the knowledge that, with an office of my own, I would no longer need the services of an agent. He was quite right, nor do I blame him in the least for trying to protect his interests. I could certainly never blame him; he had always protected mine. But I felt I no longer wanted an agent, even an honest and efficient one, as Marby Ramundini was. I wanted to handle my own affairs, with my own employees. I couldn't go on forever depending on others to make my business decisions for me. The Pepsi-Cola contract was the first I had made, other than football, without Ramundini's assistance, and I felt the proper time to open the office and start on my own had arrived. And in fact, business grew so rapidly that we moved from the small offices on the fifth floor, taking over the entire third floor of the building—and the Pelé Administration and Advertising Company was born. I brought in José Rodrigues Fornos—Pepito to all—to manage the offices; my Uncle Jorge, long an expert on figures, came to handle the accounting, and I knew we were on our way to success. And Marby Ramundini and I remain good friends, if not associates, to this day.

On July 18 of that year, 1971, I played my final game with the Brazilian Selection. We played against the Yugoslav Selection in Maracanã in Rio, before 180,000 people. It was not the best game of my career; I was too emotionally involved, knowing I would never again wear the yellow and green colors of Brazil on the football field. Nor did it help my concentration to have 180,000 fans standing and shouting in rhythmic unison: "*Fica*! *Fica*!" meaning: "Stay! Stay!"

But, as it says in Ecclesiastes in the Bible, there is a time to laugh and a time to weep, a time to be silent and a time to speak, a time to be born and a time to die. I had been born into Selection football fourteen years before; now, in a way of speaking, it was a time for my playing days with the national team to die.

It was an intensely emotional moment for me. When the game ended in a tie, 2–2, I ran around the field, my arms up, trying in some way to tell the fans of my love for them, to thank them for their support throughout the years. The crowd stood and chanted with growing volume: "*Fica! Fica*!" and the tears ran down my cheeks like rain. I took off my uniform shirt with the number 10 on it, the shirt I had worn with such great pride for fourteen years, and held it up to the crowd; then I had to bring it down to my face and try to dry my tears with it, but they would not stop. I shall never forget that day.

That year, 1971, was also the year when there was a most important election at the Santos Football Club, and most of the old directors were replaced. The new directorate was of the opinion that a new broom ought to sweep clean, whether the floor needed it or not. They immediately began to make changes, and the first one was to replace Antoninho, our coach. Antoninho had taken over in 1967, when Lula had retired, and under his direction the team had continued its success, winning the São Paulo state championship twice, as well as winning most of the other tournaments in which we entered. Now the directors were firing Antoninho and replacing him with Mauro.

It was not that we had anything against Mauro. Many of us had played with him—I had played in two World Cups with him—and we knew him to be a great player and we also knew he had developed into a fine coach. But we could see no reason for the change unless it was simply for change's sake, which is always disturbing to a winning combination. We were further disturbed when Mauro later told us the new directorate had asked him to fire Professor Mazzei, without giving him any reason.

Mazzei was considered to be the best physical trainer in Brazil, and under his training program Santos had continued to win games and tournaments. Firing him made no sense to us; again it looked like change for the sake of change. I did admit to myself that if the professor had one fault, it was that he liked to talk—and he may have said the wrong thing at the wrong time to Dr. Clayton Bettencourt, the new director of sports for the club. Or, as many of us suspected, it may have been that in most clubs the physical trainer considers himself a part of management rather than a part of labor—which is the team. Mazzei always acted as a part of the team, and the new directors may have considered him an opponent automatically, for this reason. In any event, Mauro refused to fire Mazzei—with the almost predictable result that about a year later, again despite a winning season, Mauro himself was replaced.

This time the new coach was Jair da Rosa Pinto, the same Jair who had played in that game against Uruguay in the final of 1950, the same Jair who had been at Santos when I had first arrived there. And Jair da Rosa Pinto finally completed the job the directors had had in mind for over a year—to rid the club of Professor Mazzei. My complaint wasn't that Professor Mazzei was fired; every new coach has every right to bring in people in his own confidence, his own people as trainers, masseurs, or anything else he wants. It was the manner in which Professor Mazzei was released that disturbed me and the entire team. This particular day, after the professor had changed into uniform, he stopped in Jair's office to discuss the training program with the new coach.

"Jair," he said, "as the new coach I'm sure you have your own ideas on physical preparation. If we can sit down and talk it over, I'll be glad to get your program started."

But Jair da Rosa Pinto shook his head.

"That's really no problem for you, Professor."

"I beg your pardon?"

"I mean, you no longer work here. You've been terminated by the club. So you can change back into your street clothes and go home."

Which is what the professor did; there was little else he could do. We saw him come out of the dressing room in street clothes, but before we could ask him why he wasn't in uniform, he disappeared through the front door of the club. As soon as training was over that day, some of us players, friends of the professor's, went over to his apartment to find out if he was unwell, or what had happened. The professor shrugged.

"No, I'm well. It's just that I've been fired by the club."

We stared at him.

"What! By whom? Dr. Bettencourt?"

The professor smiled sourly and shook his head.

"No. Not one of the directors said a word to me. You would think that after seven years with the club, they could at least have given me that courtesy, but they didn't. They left the dirty work to poor Jair."

And when the others had left, I stayed behind.

"Professor—what do you plan to do?"

"I haven't thought about it."

"Professor," I said, "you know how my business is growing and how I need experienced, intelligent, and honest people. How would you like to come to work with me in my office?"

The professor didn't hesitate. He shook his head at once.

"Pelé, we've been friends ever since I came here over seven years ago. We've never asked each other for a single favor—not a single thing. That's a very good way to keep a friendship. I value yours, so let's keep it that way."

"But what will you do?"

Mazzei smiled.

"Well, I'm still working with Pepsi-Cola, as you are. And there are books I want to write, on which you could help me. And actually, I've been collecting newspaper articles and magazine articles and just about everything I could find on the subject of Pelé for a long time. Now, maybe I'll get time to put them all in order."

"There's one thing, Professor," I said. "Consider it a favor to me, not to you. My new offices, as you know, have more than enough room. Why don't you use one of the offices there for whatever you want to use it for? As you say, we're both working with Pepsi-Cola. This way we can be in constant touch."

"Fair enough," he said, and put out his hand.

And we shook on it.

That scene took place in April of 1972. In October of the same year my contract with the Santos Club came up for renewal, and while the rest of the world may know little of it, in Brazil the resultant polemic kept the newspapers in headlines for weeks, and gave the radio and television commentators something they could really get their teeth into.

There seems to be a love-hate relationship between the press and the idols that are made in a large way through the efforts of the press. It is as if, having built a person up, they feel a driving need to tear him down. This is particularly true, in my case, of a certain section of the Brazilian press. Not all of the press or radio, obviously; a good part of the newspapermen and radio commentators always have been and, I hope, always will be my friends. But certain sections of the Brazilian press have lost few opportunities to take me to task for something I did or didn't do to their complete satisfaction.

In any event, the newspapers printed stories saying my demands for renewal of my contract were nothing less than insane; I wanted everything, and the poor Santos Football Club, broke and starving, was to be left with less than nothing. They simply could not afford my outrageous demands, and

I was being very selfish not to remember that it was Santos who had given me my first chance to play professionally. I was a dog in the manger. I was biting the hand that fed me, etc., etc.

Actually, my demands were far from unreasonable. For many years I had provided Santos with an income greater than any other Brazilian team could have hoped to enjoy, through earning hard currency in foreign countries in large amounts—but the newspapers that criticized me failed to mention this fact. And when I say that "I" earned the money for the club, I mean the name "Pelé" earned it for them; in every contract Santos signed for our appearance in a foreign country, there was a clause reducing the fee by half if Pelé did not play. Nor did those newspapers, while crying poverty, ever bother to ask where all those foreign-earned dollars went. At the time of our discussion over the contract renewal, I had played in over eleven hundred games for Santos, over half of which had been abroad, and which had brought the club an average of approximately $20,000 per game. And where had this money disappeared? Nobody even bothered to ask. Nobody even bothered to ask if it had disappeared, at all. Santos was broke, said these papers, and that was all there was to it. And Pelé was rich and wanted to get richer at the expense of the club and the game of football in general.

Well, what were the facts? One of the things that made the monetary difference between the present contract and previous contracts appear so great when only the figures were shown without explanation was that in previous contracts Santos had taken the responsibility for paying my income tax. The law no longer permitted this, insisting that the tax fall on the individual, and I now had to pay the tax that Santos had previously withheld. And many of the demands the press managed to make appear ridiculous had a logical explanation. One was my demand for a suite rather than a single room at a hotel, when we traveled abroad. The press suggested that I suffered from delusions of grandeur, that I had forgotten my humble beginnings in Baurú, and that now only the royal suite would do. They never mentioned that when we traveled abroad the directorate of the club expected me to entertain the heads of state or other VIPs wherever we went, as part of the public relations of the club. To do this, a suite was necessary. I could hardly entertain the President of France, for example, standing in one corner of the room while the maid straightened out the bed, or ask him to step out into the hall while my wife dressed.

All these facts could easily have been explained in the press had the press so desired, but they obviously did not. And they might have added that many times I played with injuries that should have been treated, just so the Santos Club would receive the extra income. That I had remained loyal to one club throughout my entire career, despite much higher salary offers both inside and outside the country—and that I was probably the only one of the top players in the country who had played for only one team. They might also have added that, quite contrary to popular belief—largely developed through articles in the press—I was *not* the highest-paid player in the world, or even in Brazil, nor had I even been the highest paid at Santos during my career. But not one word of this was published by this section of the press.

When my friends asked me why I didn't answer the charges in the press and on the radio, I pointed out that answering would only lead to continuing debate, and I had neither the time nor the desire for that. One newspaperman, in fact, printed an open letter to Pelé—an entire page of questions—that came close to being libelous, but to have answered it would have been to extend publicity to it. By ignoring it, I knew it would be forgotten as soon as the contract discussions were ended.

The directors of the Santos Club were not being honest in holding back many facts from the press, and both the directorate and the representatives of the media acted like amateurs in the entire matter. I had signed contracts with

Santos at their terms for years; now, with two years left, I wanted to sign one on my terms or not at all—and I didn't much care if it was "not at all" or not. For years I had signed whatever Pepe Gordo had put in front of me in contracts with Santos, and Pepe Gordo was a great fan of Santos and never wanted to hurt the club's purse. Now it was time for a change. If Santos earned an extra $10,000 or $15,000 because Pelé was in the line-up, then Pelé deserved a portion of this money. And if I didn't get it, I would quit. I was tired of arguments.

I was also tired of seeing the Santos team degenerate from the finest team in the world to a rather mediocre one, through attrition of one sort or another. Men were either being fired or quitting for a better job or leaving simply because they were disgusted. The first had been Antoninho, but since then Formiga had left, Macedo and Zito were gone, Lima had taken a job in Mexico, and with the departure of Professor Mazzei the last of the gang that had brought Santos its world championship was gone, and I felt very much alone. Nor had the club made any effort to find a replacement for me, even though it should have been fairly obvious that once I left the game they would need a Tostão, or his equal, to fill the stands. But they did not. And in response to the question of what value Pelé had for the Santos Club, I can only say that since I finally left in 1974, Santos has not played one single game abroad—and that is three years ago.

But at last I made my final offer to the club. I said I would play two years more, one year on my terms, and one year free. But by "free," I explained, I meant I would get nothing, but the club would have to pay the amount to charity. It was a hard offer for them to refuse without looking very bad, so they accepted and the controversy was finally over. With the matter settled I once more became the darling of the sports writers—until the next time, that is. ...

The next time was not long in coming.

I had learned many things during those contract negotiations with the Santos Club. Or, rather, I had been forcibly reminded of things I had always known but had not sufficiently remembered over the years. One was that the professional athlete in Brazil at that time had no protection of any kind beyond what he could provide for himself. I remembered Vasconcelos and what had happened to him when his leg had been broken and his career effectively ended; nor had conditions improved since that time. The Brazilian social laws, like the social laws of most Latin American countries, give a factory worker a certain amount of protection, or job security, a guarantee of a month's severance pay for every year he has worked, guaranteed service after ten years with a company, a thirteenth month's pay as a minimum year-end bonus, a medical center where he and members of his family can go for treatment—but the professional athlete in Brazil at that time did not come under these laws. He was a nonperson as far as the law was concerned.

It was also true that many players, and not just the successful big-name players but even many unknown players, were not interested in being members of any organization that looked like a syndicate or a union. They felt it was beneath their dignity to be classified in the same category as a common laborer. As a result they lived much more precarious lives than any workman. An attempt had been made some years before in São Paulo to organize the football players of the clubs there, as had also been tried once in Rio, but both attempts fizzled out, more of disinterest on the part of the players, I will admit, than from any concerted efforts by the club directorates to stifle the movement.

But I felt times had changed, that we had now brought a third world title to Brazil, that we had demonstrated the importance of the Brazilian football player to the country, and we would now have a sympathetic ear from President Médici and the Ministry of Labor. After all, the President was an ardent football fan, and had indicated to us when we visited Brasília on our return from Mexico that we should come to him with any problem. I felt sure he would agree that the professional athlete deserved as much protection as a factory worker. Possibly he would be surprised to hear the argument coming from me, but I was sure he would agree with the premise. But I knew that to present our best case, we would need the top names in the game, and when I spoke to them, I found them in agreement. We made up a committee, which included myself, Gerson, Gilmar, Carlos Alberto, and others, and went to Brasília, where we were given an audience with the President as well as the Minister of Labor. Our case was listened to, and we left with the assurance that the matter would be studied and some action would be forthcoming to change the status of the players.

It took five years before positive results were obtained, but better late than never. Today the professional athlete in Brazil comes under the social laws. True, there is still the matter of the reserve clause, which the American baseball players have finally managed to get modified, and which still leaves the Brazilian player almost a slave to the club that holds his contract, but at least, with the present law, the first steps have been taken.

And what was the reaction of the media to my efforts?

One element wanted to know why I had delayed so long in doing something. Pelé, they said, had never bothered to help others either in his profession or in his race, and any attempt now could only be a gesture aimed at making him look good to the public. This was therefore basically dishonest; it may even have been done, they added, with the connivance of the clubs, since the concessions we gained were insignificant and cost the clubs little.

Other elements of the press said that on the contrary Pelé was trying to destroy the clubs and disrupt the game of football, making the clubs into little football factories instead of the social gathering places they had always been. They claimed that now that Pelé was looking forward to ending his years at the game, he didn't want the upcoming young players to have the advantages of freedom of choice he had always enjoyed.

That's why I like football—at least sometimes you can win!

In 1973 Giora Breil, who at that time was involved with creative development for the Pepsi-Cola Company, had a genuinely brilliant idea. It was his thought that a movie based on the training methods and football skills Professor Mazzei and I were trying to impart to children around the world would be extremely helpful. It would be the easiest way to reach a truly mass audience; after all, even with sixty clinics a year, I could see and teach only a fraction of the number who could be taught with a film.

To that end he started to put together a team to produce the picture, eventually called *Pelé: The Master and His Method.* Poor Giora! He had never attempted anything on this scale, had never before been involved in filmmaking, yet he accepted the full responsibility for the project. As usual, when there is someone willing to do all the work, a great deal more fell on Giora's shoulders than would normally fall on one man's. The result of his extraordinary effort was a breakdown that demanded complete rest—but even this Giora managed to delay until the film was completed. The film he delivered is today considered the finest of its kind in the history of sports, and is therefore a monument to Giora Breil and his sacrifice.

For the producer and director, Giora chose Sal Lanza, an experienced moviemaker, which Giora was not. The script had been written in ten hectic days by Professor Mazzei and Steve Richards, practically locked in a hotel room, using an ashtray as a ball to demonstrate the various moves, after which Steve would tackle the typewriter until they had the general idea on paper. To adapt the script to the screen, Giora picked Paul Gardner, an excellent writer and one with much experience in reporting the game of football for publications on both sides of the Atlantic. Professor Mazzei was made the technical assistant on the film, and the picture was finally in progress.

We filmed the action in Brazil, many of the scenes being shot at the Vila Belmiro Stadium at the Santos Club, others taken with children in one of the poorer neighborhoods, where the kids were as anxious to be given instruction as they were anywhere else. All the things I had learned from watching my early idols in action, from Dondinho and Valdemar de Brito, or Lula, or Zizinho of the 1950 World Cup team who I had seen often in pictures, or from Jair or Vasconcelos or Del Vecchio—everything I had ever learned about the art and skill of the game of football, we attempted to put into this film. It is one of the things I believe everyone connected with should be extremely proud of.

The film was an instant success, and today, four years later, it is still being shown around the world. It had the effect Giora Breil had foreseen when he first conceived of the project: It enabled millions to be reached who could never have been reached in any other manner. The film won eleven international awards, for the excellence of its writing, for its production, its direction, and for everything else a film can excel in. Professor Mazzei was given the assignment to see to the proper distribution of the film in the Americas, while Steve Richards was given the same responsibility in Europe, Africa, and the Middle East.

The film was—and still is—available for any school or organization who wishes to show it. It is free for such performance. The film was never shown commercially, nor will it ever be. The purpose of the film was not to make money, but to promote the game of football, and this it does excellently.

Chapter 18

When the World Cup games of 1974 were about to begin, I was quite anxious to attend. Getting the time from the Santos Club was no problem; during the World Cup everything stops in Brazil, including football. However, the problem was that if I were to attend as a mere spectator, those newspapers who insisted I should be there in uniform were sure to raise the issue in their columns. To avoid this, I accepted an offer from the Bandeirantes Television network to be a commentator for them. Rather than prevent controversy, however, I discovered I had started it. There was an immediate outcry from the media that I was not a member of the proper syndicate, that I was inexperienced as a commentator, and that I was taking bread from the mouth of some more deserving and better-prepared member of the union. So that was that.

I did, however, receive an invitation to take part in the opening ceremonies together with Uwe Seeler, the former West German captain and an old friend as well as opponent. We were to exchange cups; he handing me the Jules Rimet Trophy Brazil had retired, while I handed him the new FIFA Cup that was now the target of the competing teams. A rare thing now occurred, an attack on me in the foreign press.

Someone started the rumor that I had demanded $20,000 for my appearance there. This was, of course, a pure fabrication; I accepted the honor without any fee, obviously, nor could I ever have considered accepting a fee, any more than Uwe Seeler would have. It was a misunderstanding that was quickly cleared up as soon as the proper facts were put before the press.

Together with Professor Mazzei, I watched the games and gave my opinions of them to Steve Richards, who wrote them up for the British press. The first night we were in Frankfort, the night prior to the opening game which was scheduled to be played between Brazil and Yugoslavia, the professor and I went to visit the Brazilian concentration at their hotel. I wanted to wish each one of them luck, and also to see how their morale was. The Brazilian press was sure Brazil would repeat its win of 1970; after all, Zagalo was coach again, the technical commission was the same as in 1970, so how could we lose?

I was not so sure; the players weren't the same. This year's team had only three members of our strong 1970 team: Rivelino, Jairzinho, and Paulo Cesar. Tostão had dropped football after his doctor had advised him that another accident to his eye could result in permanent blindness, a blow to the Selection as well as to the game of football in general. Clodoaldo had been injured, an injury that prevented him from playing, and the others of that 1970 team had either not been selected or had been unable to play for one reason or another. Besides, since this was a relatively new team, I was sure they would never disagree with an experienced coach like Zagalo on tactics. I also knew that Zagalo had come to prefer defensive play rather than offensive play. In 1970 there were enough experienced players on the team to convince him to let us play our style, but I was afraid this team would never argue. They would play defensively and would probably lose.

Nor was the morale as high as it should have been. One thing stands out in my mind from that night. When I went to say hello to Paulo Cesar, I expected him to talk about strategy or training or the strengths of the opponents—but instead, he asked my opinion on something he obviously considered more important.

"Pelé," he said, "I've been offered a fantastic job with a French club once the World Cup is over. It would pay far more than what I'm getting now. I'm pretty sure I'm going to accept the offer, but I don't know if I should ask even more. It's a real problem! What do you think?"

I couldn't believe it!

"What I think, Paulo Cesar," I said, "is that you are out of your mind! You've got a World Cup game tomorrow, and all you're thinking about is this job offer? Forget the offer for now! Concentrate on the games you have to play, starting with the one against Yugoslavia tomorrow. When you've won the cup, then you can think about the offer. It might be bigger, then. But if all you have on your mind is the offer, I doubt you'll see the final!"

Prophetic words, but I meant them. The morale was far from as good as the newspapers at home would have you believe; the players were tense and nervous. Still, there was no doubt that any Brazilian Selection was far from beaten until someone better came along. They were, after all, the world champions. But I was disturbed by the visit, as was the professor.

The following day we watched the opening game, and I knew as soon as the play started that Zagalo had decided to play defensively—as if in Rivelino and Jairzinho he didn't have proven capable attackers, and a strong mid-fielder who could also attack in Paulo Cesar. But Zagalo played his careful game, keeping his men back, and the result was a scoreless tie, a great disappointment to the fans, of course, as well as the Brazilians present.

The next game was much the same. Against a valiant Scottish team, Brazil again tied, and this time it was an extremely rough game, with most of the violence seemingly coming from Brazil, a team that normally avoided such tactics. The fans were bitter, as were the newspapers; they accused Rivelino in particular of violent, unfair play. In defense of Brazil, it must be said that any violence on their part was bound to be less subtle than violence on the part of a European team, where they were much more practiced in fouling an opponent without being caught.

Yet, despite the two ties, Brazil was still not eliminated, and I thought for a moment that possibly Zagalo was right, and I was wrong. But after the game with Zaire—which Brazil won, 3–1—I knew I was right and Zagalo was wrong. Against a team like Zaire, Brazil should have won 10–0! But again Brazil fell back on defense as if they were playing England in 1970, and the scoring was limited. But they had won, and I could not deny that.

Their next game, the game that would bring them to the quarter-finals if they won, was against East Germany, and again they managed to eke out a small victory, 1–0. Although Brazil was now in the quarter-finals, it was obvious that the radio and newspaper reports of the game were disturbing many Brazilians at home as much as they were disturbing me. Protests over Zagalo's defensive style of play continued to roll in from all corners of Brazil, but Zagalo was coach and refused to be influenced by anyone's ideas other than his own. And, after all, he was winning, so why should he change? In Brazil the protests even took the form of people stoning Zagalo's home—an act far more reprehensible, in my opinion, than the style of play Zagalo insisted upon playing.

The quarter-final was played against Argentina, and I wondered what would happen between the newly defensive team of Brazil and the Argentinians, who played attacking football combined with an extensive use of physical violence. I hoped Zagalo would let the team attack and win by a decent margin. But in that game, if anything, Brazil played even more defensively than ever, while Argentina failed to take advantage. Brazil still won, 2–1, but that game convinced me that Brazil was playing a bad style of play and that they would probably not reach the finals. Both Jairzinho and Rivelino scored goals, but they lacked acceleration when the situation demanded it. The same was true of Paulo Cesar. Rivelino was playing back, almost in mid-field most of the time; he had done a good job there and as an anchor man in general, but he was only half as effective as he should have been, staying that far back of the front line. It was significant to me that the only time he moved into the firing line he scored. And Jairzinho actually looked weary when he came into the area. I began to wonder if possibly it was lack of proper physical training that led Zagalo to style his tactics to the lack of energy of his top players. If so, it spoke very poorly of the training program of the team.

Besides, I had watched Holland, Brazil's next opponent in the semifinals, when they had played against Uruguay. It was like watching a Brazilian team of 1958 or 1962. They played the same imaginative, ball-controlling game that was so popular in South America for so many years, and I knew that against that team, with its spectacular attacking forward, Johann Cruyff, the defensive tactics of Zagalo simply would not work. The newspapers referred to Cruyff as the "white" Pelé, but I never thought of him in those terms. He was Johann Cruyff, a genius at the game of football in his own right. I was sure that if Zagalo played his defensive game against Holland and Cruyff, he was in trouble.

Before the World Cup games had started I had predicted that the final four teams in the semifinals would be Brazil, West Germany, Holland, and Italy. Now Italy had been eliminated by Poland, but three of my four final selections remained. The game with Holland was crucial. I felt that if Brazil could get by Holland, they might have a decent chance against the winner of the other semifinal.

Well, Brazil did not get by Holland. The Dutch were fast and tough—and also as physical as any Uruguayan or Argentinian team in history. Once again the Brazilians demonstrated a lack of subtlety in playing a physically violent game, and the crowd booed them constantly. A Brazilian player was sent from the game and Holland won easily by a score of 2–0. The newspapers in Europe took Brazil to task for the roughness of their play; what they failed to report was that Holland was just as rough, only they were far more cunning, more astute, in using their tactics. After the game I visited the Brazilian dressing room. It looked like a hospital. There was not a single player who did not have an injury of some sort. Cuts, bruises, and—in the case of Marinho—a gash on one leg from knee to ankle.

This is a side of football that the public does not see. The Dutch, for all I admit and admire their skills, know how to be rough, but they also know how to be clever about it. The Brazilians were naïve in allowing themselves to be provoked into tactics they did not know how to use.

The reaction in Brazil to the defeat was deep bitterness. As usual, I came in for my share of the blame for not having participated, but it would have made little difference had I played or not. The coach of a team is the boss, as he should be, and it was in the style of play selected, not the individual talent of the players, that cost Brazil that tournament. We can only hope that Brazil will learn from the defeat and play differently in 1978.

Why do I find fault with defensive football, when it obviously is the style preferred by many coaches throughout the world? For one main reason: The only way—or certainly the most possible way—to score goals is if your team is in possession of the ball. Ball control, to me, is the most important tactic in the game, and defensive football trades ball control for apparent safety in the goal area, a trade that seldom gives the expected result. In defensive football generally, the goalkeeper will often kick the ball as far downfield as he can, simply to get the ball out of what he considers a danger zone. I agree that at times, under great pressure, or against a team that is unusually strong on attack in the area, such a move is sometimes necessary, but as a standard tactic, is it good one?

In my opinion it seldom is. It loses possession of the ball. Of course it is always possible that one of your players will take possession of the ball after such a kick, but a defensive team normally has fewer forwards downfield than an attacking team, so the chances of this recontrol are reduced.

I also believe that violence increases when a team plays defensively, rather than the opposite, as the uninformed might think. When a team plays defensively, there are far more long kicks downfield, leaving the ball in nobody's possession, and therefore up for grabs—or for kicks—by all the players on both sides. The clashes between players under such circumstances are always more fierce than in the one-to-one tackling as a player takes the ball down the field under his own control.

Another point, and one I think very important, is that the full beauty of the game is best seen in the inventiveness, the ingenuity, and the skill of the players both individually and in team combination, and this is only seen in an attacking style of football, where the ball is constantly under control. Kicking it the length of the field and hoping that with God's help one of your own players might be there to head the ball into the net can scarcely be called artistic. Besides, football is a game that is supported by the fans, the spectators, and the game will not continue to dominate the world of sports if it becomes dull—and scoreless ties are dull, in any game. Anyone who has witnessed a game between two strong attacking teams as opposed to two strong defensive teams will know what I mean. There is no comparison. The only defensive star who ever gets mention is the goalkeeper, and he has to be defensive. When the forwards are defensive, you have a dull game. Defensive forwards are almost the definition of an antifootball tactic!

The time was coming for me to complete my contract with Santos and play my final game. As usual, the Santos management permitted the press and the public to believe that every game I played that final month would be the last, thus ensuring a full house for game after game, since most of the fans wanted to be able to say they had been at Pelé's "final" game. I recall this day we played at Pacaembú Stadium to a jammed-in crowd, all sure they were seeing Pelé for the last time, only to learn later that Santos, and Pelê, would be playing in Rio in Maracanã Stadium for the "last" game.

This one was. It was October 2, 1974, and we played Ponte Preta. I was not in 100 per cent physical shape to play that game, but I made up my mind I would go out onto the field and end my playing career in proper style, before the fans I always loved and who had more than once demonstrated their love for me. The game was only twenty minutes old when the ball was kicked to me, and I knew it was the time. I caught the ball in my hands—the ultimate in football movements to startle a crowd—and I could hear a sharp gasp of astonishment from the packed stadium. I ran with the ball to the center of the field, placed it on the center spot, and knelt, my knees on either side of the ball, and raised my arms in a cross to face the fans, turning from side to side so that all could see me—and so that I could see all of them, the fans who had supported me all those years. The tears were running down my cheeks without control. The crowd realized what I was doing; they realized I was honoring them for the years they had honored me. They came to their feet with a roar. I stood up and tried to wipe my face with my shirt; then I ran around the field, my arms up, trying my best to thank them for the help and support they had given me since my first day as a professional. But it was too emotionally devastating; I took one last look at the standing crowd, their cheers echoing in my ears, and then I ran into the tunnel and into the dressing room.

I slowly changed my clothes while the crowd outside cheered and then allowed the game to continue. Then I bent my head in tears. One man, other than the dressing-room attendant, was there, hiding in the shower—a photographer named Domicio Pinheiro, from *O Estado,* a São Paulo newspaper. He got a picture of me, head bent, crying. Then I was out of there, into my car and away, while I could hear the crowd in the stadium.

It was hard to believe, but it was true: I was no longer Pelé! Now I was Edson Arantes do Nascimento once again, and now for all times. And I honestly thought at the time I was telling the truth. ...

Now, at last, my dream had come to pass—to go to the office at nine in the morning, and come home at five, and live with my family like any other person. During these years my business had progressed, becoming more and more complicated as well as more and more lucrative, to a point where I realized I needed professional guidance. Finally in 1973 I hired an economist with experience in business management, José Roberto Ribeiro Xisto, to take over the management of the enterprise and advise me on new projects. When I look back, I am amazed that Xisto didn't throw up his hands and walk out after taking one look at the various interests I had gotten myself involved with through the years. Many people had come to me—as Ramundini had so accurately predicted—and in order to satisfy old friends, or former teammates with problems, I had invested a little here, a little more there, in more businesses and schemes than I can recall, or that I could possibly keep track of. I had properties in Santos, in São Paulo, in Rio, in Baurú, in Três Corações. I had stores and apartments and lands and houses. I had a dairy farm, my own farm, a trucking company, an export-import business, an interest in a radio station, and parts of a dozen more enterprises. Heaven may have known what I was involved in; I didn't.

The first thing Xisto did, after listing everything and studying the list, was to divest us of many small and losing investments as well as properties with poor returns. Then he began to concentrate on the major investments, getting the company properly organized and running on a day-to-day basis. There was, however, one small investment he could not relieve me of, although he would have been glad to. That was my participation in a company called Fiolax.

Fiolax was a company that manufactured components of rubber for use in the automotive industry, in which I was involved with Zito and several other partners. Although I was a very minor stockholder—holding only 6 per cent of the shares—through poor legal advice prior to hiring Xisto, I had signed a note guaranteeing a bank loan for the company. When the loan fell due and the company could not pay, the bank came to me. In addition, at the same time there had been a rather serious breach of the government regulations covering the import of some raw material—a breach I am sure was due more to ignorance on the part of the factory management than to cupidity—and the government imposed a tremendous fine on the company. It was then I discovered that among the other papers I had signed were ones making me responsible for all liabilities of the company, so there was the fine as well as the bank loan.

I remember very well my feeling when the news was given me! Together, the loan and the fine came to more than a million dollars! I felt as I had when I learned that Sanitaria Santista had gone broke—not only taken, but stupid! Once again, after all the warnings and all the bad experience, I had signed something I should not have signed. I had been foolish for not getting the best legal talent available, rather than hiring the first lawyer, just to get the matter over with quickly. As with Sanitaria Santista, I could have let the company go bankrupt, but although I only had 6 per cent of the shares, the public would be sure to say that Pelé was being cute, to save taxes.

I had enough resources by that time to pay both the fine and the loan, but it would have meant selling off very valuable properties to raise the money, taking a large loss because of the forced sale, and it would have meant more than doubling the loss I would take for not having sought competent legal counsel. The final bill would be about two million dollars, between what I paid and what I lost.

Still, there was little I could do about it. I refused to let the company go bankrupt as long as my name was connected with it, and there was no way to disconnect my name at this point.

Then, one evening, a delegation came to the house. I remember there was Xisto, Professor Mazzei, Zoca, and Edevar, a former Santos goalkeeper who was now a member of our office staff. Xisto had telephoned earlier to make sure Rosemeri and I were home and were free. Xisto began the discussion.

"Pelé," he said flatly, "I'm strongly opposed to selling properties at a substantial loss, in order to make up this debt of Fiolax. It's just poor business practice!"

"Do you see anything else that can be done?"

"Yes," Xisto said. "The Cosmos still want you to play with them." He held up his hand. "Before you say anything, I suggest we listen to the professor."

Mazzei had a sheet of paper in his hand. He glanced at it and then looked up.

"What I have done," he said, "is make a list of the pros and cons of your signing with the Cosmos. Let me read them to you, and then we can discuss them in detail, if there are any questions. Or any additions or subtractions on either side."

I nodded. The professor began.

"In order to be completely impartial," he said, "let us look at the negative side first. One, the reaction of the people in Brazil. Here you refuse to play in the World Cup, and yet right afterward you sign to play with a foreign team. Two, the reaction of the Brazilian government. They once opposed your playing abroad, declaring you a national monument. How are they going to react now? Three, you stated to the people through the press and the radio that you were stopping all football. Now it will seem that you are going against your word. Four, you are black, and you have to recognize that being black in the United States is not the same thing as being black in Brazil. Five, there is the matter of language; you will have to learn English, but seriously, this time. Six, it is very possible that going to New York to live will set Kelly Cristina back in school. Seven—"

He went on and on, listing twelve negative points, as I recall. I sat silent. At that point I was sure the professor was opposed to my going, but neither Xisto nor Zoca had said a word. I waited. The professor turned the sheet of paper over.

"There are, however, eighteen points in favor of your going. Let me start. One, and the obvious one: If you go to play with the Cosmos, you can undoubtedly arrange a contract that will enable you to pay off the debt to the bank, and the fine to the government, and still have plenty left over, even after taxes. You wouldn't have to touch those properties. You worked hard for them, and you worked hard to build an equity for your family; you could even increase that equity.

"Two, you have to remember that the Cosmos are not just another football club, like Santos—or most of the other American teams, as far as that goes. The Cosmos are owned by Warner Communications, who also own Warner Brothers movies, Licensing Corporation of America, a record division, and many other things. You would not be signing with a small club, where you might wonder if you'd get paid. You would be signing with one of the major companies in the United States. They are a power.

"Three, if you were to accept an offer, even of the same size, from a club in Mexico or Spain or Italy, it would not be the same thing. Those countries have developed their football to a point where you could contribute very little to football there, other than to play. But in the United States you could make a major contribution to the development of the game.

"Four, now that you've stopped playing football, the truth is the name Pelé will begin to decline in value for endorsements. You're in business now, you must consider things in a businesslike manner. In five years after you retire, the upcoming generation won't know who Pelé is, and the endorsements will slow down and eventually disappear. And except for your real estate—much of which you would have to sell to settle the Fiolax thing—the endorsements represent a major part of your income.

"Five, the United States is the largest market in the world, and Warner's licensing corporation is in the best position there to exploit the name Pelé. The name has to become better known there, of course, but playing with the Cosmos would do that.

"Six, playing in the United States would not be like playing for Santos, where you played twelve months a year, and almost a hundred games a year. Playing in the United States, the season begins in April or May, and ends in August or September. You would still have half of the year to yourself, to come back to Brazil and see to your business, or anything else.

"Seven, while it is true that Kelly Cristina might lose a year in school by the move, the fact is the educational system there is excellent. There is a United Nations school which is considered one of the best in the world, and I'm sure both she and Edinho would have no trouble entering.

"Eight, I—and Zoca and the rest of us—think you miss football. This would give you a chance to get back into harness. We're convinced you'll never be fully happy without it.

"Nine—"

He went through the list of eighteen points, trying to be as impartial in both tone and emphasis as he had been when presenting arguments against my going. It was obvious from the presentation that both Zoca, now a lawyer in my company, and Xisto had worked with the professor on his presentation for many long and thoughtful hours.

When at last the professor was done, I looked at Rose. She looked back steadily.

"Well?" I said.

"It's your decision," she said. "It's a lot of money to lose, this Fiolax matter, but if we have to lose it to keep your name clean, we will. We won't starve without it. If you go to New York, the children and I will go with you, happily. If you decide to stay here in Santos, we'll stay with you here, happily."

It was the answer I was sure she would give.

I sighed and stared at the wall, and thought of all the work and years I had put into building my equity, not once, but twice. Paying the loan and the fine would not reduce me to poverty, but there was no doubt it would hurt me to part with that much money. Even if the lawyers and Xisto managed to reduce the fine through appeals, it was still going to be a lot of money, especially if I had to sell valuable properties to make the payment. It was money I intended for Kelly and Edinho, and money I had sweated for.

One thing the professor had said was very true; whether Kelly lost a year at school or not, the education opportunities for my two children, not only by going to school in the United States, but the education they would gain through the experience, would be invaluable. And they would become fluent in English far faster than I would, and I judged fluency in languages to be important.

And I could help the game of football there; Toye had said so and meant it, and I agreed.

And it would also be nice to be back in uniform again, feeling the wind of an open field on my face, the springy sod underfoot, matching my wits against a tricky opponent, feinting him out of position, dribbling around him, passing off to a knowledgeable teammate who would know the exact moment to return the pass so I could feel the leather of my shoe strike the leather of the ball and see it curve past a startled goalkeeper into the net. I could almost feel the scream of *Goooooaaaaalllllll*!!!!! in my throat again, and know the exuberant sensation of leaping into the air and striking it with my fist, while the crowds in the stands chanted "*Pelé*! *Pelé*!" I took a deep breath and turned to Professor Mazzei.

"Professor," I said, "would you telephone Clive Toye and tell him I'm interested? And if necessary, would you be able to go to the United States for me to discuss this with him?"

To go into detail on the negotiations that followed the professor's trip, between Warner Communications and my organization, would take another book—and if it were ever made into a movie, it would look like an old Keystone Kops chase. There were meetings in Rome, in Belgium, in the United States, in Brazil; there were international telephone calls to the extent that one of the big winners had to be the stockholders of the telephone company. There were calls to airplanes in flight; having the police wake up one recipient of a call who had taken the telephone off the hook to ensure a decent night's rest. There were mysterious methods worthy of a spy novel to keep the matter a secret from the press until the last moment. There was even a formal statement by a representative of the United States government saying that having Pelé come to the United States to play with the Cosmos could only help cement relations between our two great nations—something thought up by Warner Communications to ease any possible difficulty with the Brazilian government over my taking the job.

It is true that lawyers often tend to complicate negotiations between two agreeable parties, but they also see to it that their client's interests are properly represented, by not allowing him to be victimized by his own impatience or ignorance. This time I got the best legal aid available, being represented by Dr. Sergio Chermont de Brito, from the law firm of Dr. Nabuco in Rio, one of the most prestigious legal firms in the country. After seeing Dr. de Brito at work, I wished I had had his services in the past on many occasions, and particularly when signing the papers relating to Fiolax! Still, if I had not signed those papers relating to Fiolax, it is very possible I would never have come to New York and the Cosmos, and that was a decision I have never regretted.

The negotiations went on for weeks, months, with lawyers, executives, tax consultants, and other interested parties traveling back and forth between Brazil and the United States—all terminating in an all-night conference where the final details were hammered out at last. I must say here that while the discussions were often heated between the attorneys representing the two sides, from the moment agreement was reached, there has never been the slightest disagreement between myself and the people of Warner Communications on any point, no matter how slight. They have treated me, in every way, perfectly.

The final session required the services of three secretaries beyond my own personal secretary, all of them constantly typing the various changes that evolved from the meeting. But at last, at three o'clock in the afternoon of a meeting that had begun the previous morning, all the details had been worked out.

I was to be employed by Warner Communications to play football with the New York Cosmos for a period of three years; during those three years I was also to be available to Licensing Corporation of America (LCA), a Warner subsidiary, for any endorsements they could arrange within the limits imposed by my feelings about certain products, as well as any other promotions they could arrange using the name "Pelé." This relationship with LCA would continue for an additional three years after my football-playing contract terminated, making the Warner contract extend for a total of six years. For these efforts I would receive a sum of money that was more than I had received for all the years I had played for Santos! And in addition, I would also receive one half of whatever the Pelé endorsements and promotions produced in revenue.

It was a very satisfactory contract. So Rosemeri and I, together with Kelly Cristina and Edinho, came to the United States.

Chapter 19

The city of New York has its critics, I understand, but the Arantes do Nascimento family are not numbered among them. I had found the city fascinating years before, on my many trips here with the Santos team, and Rosemeri had joined me on more than one trip and had fallen in love with the city. To all of us, including the children, New York is a place of endless allurement and much beauty, one of the truly great cities of the world, and we were very happy to be moving there, even temporarily. Rose liked the many advantages of New York: the wonderful sanitary conditions, the ease of shopping, the theater, the museums—even the fact that the telephones worked, which was not always the case in South America.

To make things better, the Cosmos and Clive Toye had persuaded Professor Mazzei to take on the job of physically preparing the Cosmos team and acting as assistant coach, and the professor had accepted, so both our families were in New York. It not only gave me a bilingual companion to translate for me in restaurants and taxis, but it gave Rosemeri an old friend in the person of Maria Helena, Mrs. Mazzei.

On June 11, 1975, in an overcrowded room built for far fewer diners in the famous 21 Club, the Cosmos held their news conference to announce my signing with the club. The place was jammed with reporters, television crews including one from Brazil, radio commentators, and private and syndicated photographers. Rosemeri, who usually avoided events of this nature, tried to make herself as inconspicuous as possible until, under the pressure of photographers, she dutifully kissed me for the cameras. These amenities observed, the press got down to its primary job—asking questions.

Why were the Cosmos willing to pay such an exorbitant sum of money for a player when the sport itself, in all fairness, didn't really attract that many fans at the gate? Why had I felt compelled to accept the Cosmos offer after saying repeatedly that when I left Santos I was through playing for all time? Did I think, at the advanced age of thirty-four, that I could still perform the magic on the field that had brought me my fame? And the always present question—how did I rate American soccer and what did I think of its future? And what of my own future when my contract with the Cosmos was finished?

With Professor Mazzei translating, I managed to field most questions. After being interviewed by newspapermen in all parts of the world, not always as politely as the American press, it was not too difficult a task. But there was one thing it was important to me to try to get across to the media:

"Association football—soccer," I said, "is the most widely played game in the world—except in the United States. It is my hope that I can help to make this game, which I love so much, as important a sport here as it is in the rest of the world." I smiled at them. "After all, in Brazil we have been importing know-how from the United States for a long time. Now we're exporting a little bit. ..."

And on that note the conference ended and Rosemeri and I could escape.

Before starting to train with the Cosmos, Professor Mazzei and I had watched the team play in two games, one in New York and the other in Philadelphia. At Randall's Island in

New York we had seen Vancouver beat the Cosmos, 1–0; and in Philadelphia we had seen the team beaten by the same score in overtime. There was a much larger crowd in Philadelphia, largely because I made an appearance there, I believe, even though I did not play. But my attention wasn't on the crowd in either of these games; I was intent upon watching and studying the Cosmos.

Their coach was Gordon Bradley, who had come to the game of soccer with Sunderland in the English First Division at the age of sixteen, and who was still with the game twenty-three years later. Gordon had come to the Cosmos in 1971 as a player-coach, playing mid-field, and in 1975 he turned to full-time coaching. I remembered Gordon when he covered me on defense in 1968, when Santos had come to New York to play the New York Generals, a game the New Yorkers won, 5–3. Gordon managed to hold me scoreless that day, and my respect for his ability was born there and has never died.

There were those who claimed that if Gordon had a fault, it was that he was too nice a guy, which is possible in coaching sports even if it isn't in everyday life. They felt Gordon was not enough of a disciplinarian to whip the team into winning. It may be so, but I felt at the time that the team lacked a good deal of individual talent. It takes years of training together to make a team into the equivalent of the great Brazilian teams, and the Cosmos roster was changed too often for a strong team to emerge. Besides, when a team only plays six months of the year, it is very difficult for them to maintain the degree of physical fitness needed for top play. My first reaction at seeing the Cosmos play for the first time was to shake my head sadly.

"Edson," I said to myself, "your new team isn't the greatest in the world, I'm afraid! I have a sinking feeling you're going to suffer a little, playing here!"

But then I thought that the other teams in the North American Soccer League—at least based on the two games I had witnessed—probably were no better. If all the teams in the league are that weak, I thought, then with a little work and proper physical preparation, we should be able to make the Cosmos shine like a jewel in a cabbage patch. And I had come here to work, as had Professor Mazzei; between us and Gordon Bradley, and the individual talent they did have, we should quickly bring the Cosmos out of the doldrums.

There was only one thing wrong with the theory: When we came to play the other teams in the league, I discovered that they were *not* on a par with the teams I had seen the Cosmos play. They were much better. Teams like Dallas, Seattle, Los Angeles, Portland, Toronto, Tampa Bay—they were clubs with teams that demanded and received respect on the field.

"Edson," I said to myself, even more sadly, "I'm afraid you really *are* going to suffer!"

But all that could be done was to do the best we could, and this we did, working as hard as we could. We struggled through that season. Before I had joined the Cosmos they had lost six games and won three; after I joined them we won seven and lost six in regular season play. In exhibition games during the regular season we did not do as well, winning one, losing three, and tying two. Still, we were improving with age, even though our improvement could hardly be called spectacular. But far more important to me was the fact that before my arrival, the Cosmos averaged 8,000 spectators per game, while after I came we played before an average attendance of better than 20,000 per game during the regular season and over 27,000 in our foreign and exhibition games.

When I was injured in our game against San Jose and did not play in later games during our regular season, attendance once more dropped precipitously. We had played Boston on July 9 in Randall's Stadium before a crowd of over 18,000 spectators; on August 6 while I was benched, playing the same opponent in the same stadium, attendance dropped to 6,000. This is not a question of modesty or immodesty. I had come to the United States to arouse interest in the game, and there seemed little doubt that in this regard, at least, I was being successful. I hope the interest will remain after I leave the game, and I am sure it will. There will be new heroes to bring the new crop of fans to their feet; it is the history of all sports.

After our regular season ended, we were scheduled to play ten exhibition games, five in Europe and five in the Caribbean. My heart sank at the thought. After all, I had played with Santos in Europe and in the Caribbean many times, and we had seldom lost. What would the Cosmos do against competition that was international in caliber? It would be embarrassing to be beaten by some lopsided score, even though the opponent was a top team. We discussed this in detail and both Gordon Bradley and Clive Toye asked me for the names of some South American players who might be obtained to strengthen our squad. I recommended Nelsi Morais, a Brazilian, and Ramon Mifflin, the Peruvian who had played on their Selection during the games in Mexico. Both men were now playing for Santos and both were excellent attacking mid-fields, capable of strong support for the forward line. They both were able to join us in time to travel with us on our European trip.

We lost our first game against Malmö, 5–1, but the team did not look nearly as bad as the score seemed to indicate. After all, we had played together as a team with our new members in only a very few training sessions; it took time for us to mold them into our squad. We came back by beating Göteborg, 3–1, in our next game, but Nelsi Morais suffered a severely broken leg in the game, a serious loss to the team. But when I arrived in Göteborg I did get a surprise; as we came into the airport I was met by an old friend—Lena, whom I hadn't seen since I left Göteborg in 1958! She was married, with two blond children of her own, both looking much as their mother had when we first met at the age of seventeen. It made me realize how quickly time flew; it seemed like only weeks before when we had beaten Russia and Wales in the Nya Ullevi Stadium there!

From Göteborg we traveled to Stockholm, and here we lost again, but only by a score of 3–2, which was not bad against that strong team. Then to Oslo, Norway where we brought our record back to even with a victory there, 4–2. By the time we left for Rome and our final game in Europe against Roma, Italy, I felt the Cosmos had done very well by any standard. And even when we lost to Roma, 3–1, our spirits were not dampened. We had won two and lost three, but we were an untried team playing against first-rate competition. We had nothing to be ashamed of.

In the Caribbean we maintained our average, with two wins, two losses, and one tie, and our next to last game of the exhibition tour gave everyone on the team a chance to star in a 12–1 win over the Puerto Rican Selection. The entire team looked like an international squad that day. There was only one game left on the tour—the game the Cosmos tied with Violette in Haiti—but I had to miss it. It was time for a trip to give football clinics for Pepsi-Cola, so Professor Mazzei and I left the team and set off on our travels.

I had played in twenty-three games for the Cosmos that year, far less than the eighty or ninety I usually played with Santos and the Brazilian Selection; I had scored only fifteen goals, far less than my usual average for a year. But the twenty-three games had given me a lot of satisfaction. I looked forward to the following season with greater hopes for the Cosmos, and for the future of soccer in general in the United States.

My trips for Pepsi-Cola were really the most pleasurable travel that I ever made. It put me in direct contact with children of all races and colors in all countries and in all languages. It constantly reminded me of a truth I had always known—there are no differences between children. On a football field, eager to learn and to practice their new-found knowledge, all children are alike in every sense. It is only when adults teach them hate or bigotry that they begin to change.

With the professor showing them proper exercises and training methods, and with me demonstrating the techniques of dribbling, tackling, passing, kicking, trapping the ball, and other moves, it was our hope that the children would learn to understand the only difference between football players was in their skills, not in the color of their skin or the slope of their eyes. Those were happy days working with children, having them listen intently to their instructions and then try their best to duplicate the proper moves, or the proper exercises.

We spent three weeks on that particular trip, giving football clinics to children in Mexico and Colombia. Our first stop was in Guadalajara, a city with wonderful memories for me of our Brazilian victories there in 1970. Then we traveled to Puebla, a very interesting old city, and finally to Mexico City. In addition to the children on the field participating in the clinic, the stands were always full of other children and adults, watching the demonstrations and applauding the efforts of the youngsters. From Mexico we went to Bogotá in Colombia, and then to Bucaramanga, high in the Colombian Andes. Everywhere it was the same—the rapt attention of the children, then the exuberant effort of each youngster attempting to copy my motions or the professor's calisthenics.

Then it was a quick trip back to Brazil for me, for a brief meeting with Xisto and a rapid review of the business, and then a far more leisurely and welcome visit with my in-laws and my family. It had been a very long time since I had seen Dona Celeste, Dondinho, or Dona Ambrosina, or Zoca and Maria Lúcia. Maria Lúcia had married a professional football player named Davi Magalhaes whom she had known since Baurú. Davi was an excellent player, who had started at Noroeste in Baurú, but who quickly went on to play at Corinthians in São Paulo, then Cruzeiro in Belo Horizonte, and was now playing for Portuguesa Santista in Santos. I was an uncle now, and as I raised my little nieces in my arms—Danielle and her younger sister, Deborah—I realized I was getting old. Somehow my nieces made me feel much more ancient than my own children. If my baby sister, Maria Lúcia, was a mother twice, then her older brother, Dico, was getting on, indeed!

Rosemeri, the children, and I spent the Christmas holidays in Brazil with our families, and then it was time to rush back to the United States to put the children back in school.

Rosemeri had found us a lovely apartment on the east side of the city and was busy decorating it; the children in addition to regular school, were studying guitar and karate. Edinho had not been too happy about entering school when we first arrived, and it had taken some of Rosemeri's most persuasive methods to get him to go. Now, however, he could hardly wait for classes to begin. So, with the children and Rosemeri all occupied, I could go off on another trip for Pepsi-Cola without feeling I was abandoning my family in a strange land. They all spoke English perfectly, which is more than could be said for their father and husband, and they now felt as much at home in the United States as they did in Santos.

This time we were off on a trip that would take us around the world. Accompanied by Steve Richards, of the Pepsi-Cola Company, as well as Professor Mazzei, we planned football clinics in many new places. But first I had to stop in Japan on business and I took the opportunity to spend a few extra days there. I have always liked Japan and the Japanese people. I admire their fortitude, their self-discipline, their hard work, and their philosophy of calm self-appraisal. In Brazil we have the greatest number of Japanese outside of Japan; São Paulo has more Japanese than most Japanese cities, and many have been in Brazil for many generations. Most of the vegetables we now consider common in Brazil did not exist until the Japanese introduced them and cultivated them; their farming and fishing co-operatives are the most successful in Brazil and have contributed greatly to the Brazilian economy. I have always had many Japanese friends ever since Baurú, and I suppose I will always remember a Japanese girl named Neuza Sakai, whom I worshiped from afar. So visiting Japan is always a pleasure.

From Japan we flew to India for a visit to Bombay on our way to Africa. There our first stop was in Mauritius, an island in the Indian Ocean, where the children were exactly as enthusiastic and energetic as in every other place we stopped.

Take away the language difference, or the clothing differences, and one would be hard put to tell where he was, from the children. Then on to Kenya, where, in addition to our work with the youngsters, we were able to visit the famous game preserve there, and see the wild animals free and protected—which is more than can be said for many people in other parts of Africa.

Our next stop was Uganda, and once again we were invited to visit the country's game preserve. This time we flew to the preserve; the President of the country arranged a private plane for us, and I thought it would surely be at least a Lear Jet. Instead, it was a DC-3, a plane I thought gone from the airways many years before. This one was apparently used by the army for parachute training, since there were two rows of bucket seats facing each other on either side of the narrow fuselage. I would have felt better with a parachute myself, in that plane. When we took off amid all the vibration and noise I had forgotten since the advent of the jet, I kept trying to tell myself that the DC-3 was the safest and most successful aircraft ever built, but it was hard to convince myself when every instinct kept telling me we were about to come apart in the air. To add to my general conviction of impending disaster, before landing the pilot buzzed the airfield at about thirty feet altitude, waggling the wings violently; I was sure he had suddenly gone mad but then I saw he was merely trying to frighten the herds of elephant, zebra, and impala from the runway. He frightened me much more. I closed my eyes and started a short prayer but before I could finish he had landed and bumped his way to a stop on a landing strip filled with potholes. It made me think of Rua Rubens Arruda, my first football field.

From Uganda we flew to Nigeria to hold our final clinic for children before returning to the United States, and once more ran into trouble!

We had finished our work in Lagos, the capital, and were planning on leaving the following day. We were in the hotel, taking it easy, when someone came in and announced that there had been a revolutionary attempt to take over the government and that the President of the country had been assassinated! We started at each other, wondering what the situation would mean for us. We soon found out. The coup had failed, but the killers were still at large, and as a result the airport was closed indefinitely, a rigid 6 P.M. to 6 A.M. curfew was instituted, and all foreigners were advised to stay in their hotels. So we stayed in the hotel, having meals in shifts and trying to find out what was happening from the radio.

The federal government was reportedly reinstated within hours, but a week of mourning for the dead leader was announced, the airport remained closed, and the curfew remained in effect. There were reportedly demonstrations outside the American Embassy as well as the British High Commission, and all visitors were again reminded to remain in their hotels. There was a WCT Tennis team in Nigeria at the same time, with such stars as Arthur Ashe, Stan Smith, Bob Lutz, and Tom Ocker; they were also staying at the hotel but as soon as the trouble started they moved to the American Embassy. We had agreed with the tennis players that whoever got permission to leave first would take along the others, and a few days later we were informed that the tennis group had received that permission and was flying out. However, we were told not to move until we received the word from a Dr. Soraqui, the appointed contact man. The good doctor never showed up, of course, and we were still in the hotel when the plane with the tennis players took off.

On the sixth day the city was calm again and we received our permission to depart for home. A brief red-carpet stop in Ghana, long enough to politely decline an invitation to play football the next Saturday there, and then we were on our way to Zurich to change planes for New York. It had been a long trip and we were happy at the thought of getting home. And just in time, it appears. The rumor had started that we had been imprisoned in our hotel and were in real danger, and Rosemeri was about to make an international incident out of it. She had telephoned the Cosmos, Pepsi-Cola headquarters, the U.S. State Department, the Brazilian Embassy, trying to get information and suggesting subtly that they all drop whatever else they were doing and get me out of Nigeria, if they knew what was good for them!

It seemed a pity to tell her the greatest danger I faced in Nigeria that week was losing money to Steve Richards playing gin rummy—so I didn't.

The 1976 season for the Cosmos began with some major changes in our line-up, occasioned principally by the hiring of a new coach. Gordon Bradley had been promoted to vice-president of Player Personnel and Development, and in his place the Cosmos brought in Ken Furphy to handle the coaching assignment.

Furphy's credentials were certainly impressive enough. He had played in over seven hundred games as a mid-fielder for Everton, Darlington, and Watford in his native England, before becoming first a player-coach and then a coach for fourteen years for many prestigious teams, including Sheffield United. He further aided the Cosmos by bringing with him, or hiring soon after his arrival, such talent as Keith Eddy in defense, Tony Garbett at mid-field, and Tony Field at forward, all from Sheffield United and all excellent players. Later he added Brian Tinnian at forward and Charlie Aitken, a fine lateral defender. With Furphy's credentials and the talent he now had at his disposal, many of them his personal choice for the position, the Cosmos looked forward to an extremely successful season.

But Furphy's credentials were not enough; in my estimation he did not know how to motivate men. He was stubborn, for one thing. Where some claimed that Gordon Bradley had not been sufficiently a disciplinarian, Furphy was simply rigid. He would listen to no idea contrary to his own on tactics, training, or any other phase of the game. In addition, I had the feeling that Furphy had long felt the Brazilian and other

South American players had always been overrated, and he refused to be impressed, or influenced, by having players like Mifflin or Siega or Pelé on his team. Still, if Furphy's methods had brought the team success, I would have been the first to give him credit. Unfortunately, they did not.

Among other things, Furphy liked the defensive style of game, a style he was thoroughly familiar with, having played it all his life. Even though I was not in agreement with this tactic, I play as I am told and I play as well as I can. Still, when I was placed at mid-field rather than forward, I was scarcely as effective as I could be. And Ramon Mifflin often sat on the bench during games when his style of attacking mid-field was exactly what the team needed.

In our first five games we won three and lost two—both in overtime and both low-scoring games typical of defensive-style play. With the talent at our disposal and against the teams we played to that point in our schedule, we should have won all five games. Had we done so, we would have won our division title at the end of the season, and possibly have gone on to win the league title.

After our fifth game we were joined by Giorgio Chinaglia, an old friend of mine from Italy against whom I had played many times, and whom I both like and respect as an excellent forward. With Chinaglia joining us, I could see nothing but victory ahead. We had to have one of the strongest forward walls in the North American Soccer League: Chinaglia, Tony Field, Brian Tinnian, and Pelé, with men like Jorge Siega in reserve. In mid-field we had men like Tony Garbett, Ramon Mifflin, Dave Clements, Nelsi Morais, whose leg was now healed. Our defense was also strong: men like Charlie Aitken, Bob Smith, Charlie Mitchell, Werner Roth, and Mike Dillon. And Bob Rigby was our goalie, with one of the best records in the league, and Kurt Kuykendall to back him up. I was sure that with this team, getting more and more used to playing together as time went on, we could hardly lose.

But I was wrong. Furphy kept Mifflin on the bench much of the time and had me play mid-field. As a result we often had a situation where Giorgio Chinaglia or Tony Field would take the ball through the opponent's defense only to find himself all alone at the moment he needed another forward there to pass the ball to, facing the defenders with the choice of trying an impossible kick, or giving up the ball. The result of such tactics could be forecast. Before Chinaglia came to the Cosmos, we had won three and lost two of our games. In the first game after Giorgio appeared, we won, 6–0: Giorgio and I each scored two goals and Keith Eddy added two more on penalty kicks. We were sure we were on the right track—but then we went back to defensive play, and in the next eight games we won four and lost four. It was certainly no way to win the title.

The final loss in that particular series of games was to Washington on June 27. The game was played on a high school field in rather poor condition, and the refereeing, to give it a true critique, was awful. It was a game we should have won, except we all played the defensive game we were instructed to play; I played mid-field, and our forwards played almost as far back as I did. It was also the game in which Bob Rigby, our goalkeeper, broke his collarbone and was out for the rest of the season. But it was also the game that led to Ken Furphy leaving the Cosmos, bringing back Gordon Bradley for the balance of the season.

The difference in morale as well as in tactics was noted instantly. Of the following eight games, the Cosmos won seven, and ended the season only a few points back of Tampa Bay in the Eastern Division. Giorgio Chinaglia, despite playing in fewer games than most other players in the league, led them all in goals scored and in total points.

When our regular season ended with an 8–2 win over Miami—a game in which Giorgio Chinaglia scored five goals, I scored two, and Mike Dillon one—we found we had made the play-offs. Tampa Bay, the leader in our division, drew a bye in the first round, while we faced Washington in Shea Stadium in New York. It was not our finest game, but we did win by a score of 2–1, one goal by me and another by Tony Garbett, and we were then set to face Tampa Bay in the second round of the play-offs.

We played the game in Tampa, where Tampa had never lost a game. The Tampa team is probably the strongest in our league, and has played together with fewer changes the longest time. They also play an extremely aggressive style of attacking football, the best style in my estimation, and I knew we were in for a battle. If we could get by Tampa, we would be the heavy favorite to take the title. All newspapermen and commentators agreed that this game was, to all intents and purposes, for the championship, since it had the two strongest teams in the league facing each other. Most were sorry that the pairings had not been such that the two of us would meet in the Superbowl in Seattle on August 28. And had the Cosmos won even one of the games they needlessly lost early in the season, they would have won a by in the finals and would have played Tampa, if at all, either in Shea Stadium before our own fans, an advantage that every football player is aware of, or in Seattle.

But the Cosmos lost and Tampa won. We lost, 3–1, in a hard-fought and physical game where refereeing, once again, played a major part in the final decision. I had tied the score at 1–1 when I was fouled. The foul was so evident that the play almost stopped, the players expecting the referee to whistle down the infraction—but while the play was almost stopped an enterprising Tampa player proceeded to pass the ball downfield, where Stewart Scullion, of Tampa, kicked it past Shep Messing for the goal. And four minutes later mid-fielder Rodney Marsh completed the scoring against a momentarily demoralized Cosmos team by making their third goal. To me, the outstanding player was Arnold Mausser, the Tampa goalkeeper, whose magnificent saves brought the crowd to their feet time and again and won the game for his team.

And so my second season with the Cosmos ended. We had won sixteen games and lost eight, a far better record than in 1975, and we could look forward to an even better season in 1977, with a team that was beginning to properly mesh, to play together as a team. And even more important was the fact that our attendance both at home and away had doubled over the previous year. Including the two play-off games, we had performed before over half a million spectators; there were almost 40,000 in the stands when Tampa Bay defeated us, plus a television audience that grew with each game telecast. And there is every indication that as the 1977 season gets under way, the number will be even higher.

In 1976, again at the famous 21 Club, the Pony Sporting Goods Company awarded me a twenty-four-carat gold-encrusted football shoe in commemoration of my 1,250th goal. It is an award I shall be proud to add to my other awards; there is no doubt that the Pony Company has made many contributions to the game of football, as they have to so many other sports. In like fashion, 1976 also saw established the Pelé Award, inaugurated by the Pepsi-Cola Company, and an award I feel will do much to help speed the day when the United States and Canada can field teams of international caliber. The Pelé Award will give annually the sum of $10,000 to the outstanding player of either United States or Canadian citizenship, and I am extremely proud to have my name given to the award, as well as being allowed to chair the committee making the selection. The United States Selection for the 1978 World Cup games to be held in Argentina has already been made, and among the American players on it are three from the Cosmos, Bob Smith, Werner Roth, and Shep Messing. A good showing by the American team in the games will carry forward the work we have all been so busily engaged in since my arrival in the United States in 1975—that is, to bring the game of association football, soccer, to its rightful place among the other great sports of America.

Chapter 20

In the two years since I joined the Cosmos, I have traveled with the team across America many times; I have played in cities I had not had an opportunity to know before, playing against teams whose ability I could see constantly improving. In addition, since coming to America I had begun to hold clinics for Pepsi-Cola in American cities, something that I had not done before. Often there would be news conferences, and the two questions I was always asked were: What did I think of the future of soccer in the United States? and, What was the future of Pelé? Through the services of Professor Mazzei as my translator, I usually managed to gloss over both questions, because in regard to the first one, I had not completely made up my mind; and as to the second question, I also hadn't completely made up my mind.

Now, after two years, I think I can safely answer both questions.

I believe the success of soccer in the United States is inevitable. Nor do I think it will come about at the expense of some other sport, such as baseball or American football, or hockey or any other sport; in fact, I feel it would be a major mistake to attempt to take fans from any other sport to support soccer. Soccer will be successful on its own, for many reasons.

For one, it is a game that is demonstrating itself to be more and more attractive to growing numbers of children; and these children will be both the players and the spectators of the future. Its reasons for appealing to children as it does are many: It is a far safer game than either football or hockey, with injuries at the juvenile level almost unknown; it requires a minimum of equipment, and is therefore a game that is within the reach of every class of child in the country. In addition there are no physical limitations for a person to play the game; he need not be excessively tall, as in basketball, nor large and heavy, as in football. It gives a child the maximum of exercise and permits him to participate with no particular skill, as is often necessary or at least desirable in Little League baseball. As a result, Little League soccer is growing rapidly in popularity, and involving more and more children and their parents.

These facts are also becoming apparent to high schools and colleges, where soccer is also becoming a major sport. A college or high school can equip two complete soccer teams for the cost of equipping one football player, and this fact is bound to become influential as school costs increase. And from these schools and colleges will come the American soccer stars of the future.

At present there are many foreign players on American teams—I am one example. I do not believe this is a bad thing, and even when the United States develops its soccer abilities to equal those of Europe or South America, I think there will still be room for foreign players, to bring to the United States new talents, new ideas, new methods, and to help maintain the high quality of club play. After all, Brazil still imports players from other countries, as does Real Madrid of Spain, clubs like Internazionale of Italy, and many others. But the true future of American soccer lies in the development of American players. To truly give impetus to the growth of soccer in the United States, it will be necessary for the United States to field a team in World Cup competition within a reasonable number of years that will give a decent account of themselves. This will not necessarily be easy, but it is essential. The limited season of college soccer does not give enough time to properly develop the talents necessary for top competition. The American boy of high school or college age has been trained from childhood to respond to an eye-hand co-ordination; throw him a ball and he will catch it and throw it back. The Brazilian boy of equal age would be unable to catch the ball, or to throw it; he has been trained to an eye-foot co-ordination, and he would trap the ball with his foot and kick it back. To train for eye-foot co-ordination at high school or college age requires more time than the short season allows. To think of World Cup soccer for an American team, one must think of longer training periods and longer playing seasons, all under proper guidance.

In this sphere, the importation of coaches will be essential for many years to come, since the best coaches come from the playing field, and have had successful World Cup experience behind them. Even more important will be the importation of trained referees. The weakest factor in American soccer today is the poor quality of the field judging; unless a player is trained where he must not only know the rules of the game, but must know he must follow them through proper and strict field judging, the American game will never develop to World Cup dimensions.

In my opinion, the game will develop in the United States at a faster rate in cities where there is no major-league baseball or major football to compete for the attention and support of the fan. This is evident when one sees the success of the game in cities such as Seattle, Portland, San Jose, and Tampa. A city such as New York, of course, is large enough to accommodate interest in all sports, but there is only one New York. It is also interesting to note that the cities where the game is most successful are also the cities with the best fields on which to play. There are no stadiums in the United States specifically built for soccer, as most stadiums in other countries are. A soccer field is larger than a football field, and in most cases in the United States it is cramped into a stadium built for another sport. In addition, all soccer fields built in South America, as an example, have means of preventing the fans from storming the field; this may not be required in the United States, but proper dimensions and proper grass are. In the United States most fields are also used for baseball, and they have an infield where the ball reacts much differently than it does on grass, making the play uneven. In the future, I hope that consideration for the game of soccer is taken into account in the design and construction of stadiums.

But what will hasten the development of the game above all else, undoubtedly, is television. One need only look at professional American football forty years ago and today, or to look at tennis five years ago and today, to recognize the fact. And as the game continues to grow in popularity with the young, and hundreds of thousands of children and their parents and teachers and coaches get involved, the commercial possibilities of the game will not be long overlooked. And when all games are televised commercially, the economics, alone, will make the game successful.

Still, the game will always depend, basically, on the player himself. Clubs must be willing to invest enough money in their players, their coaches, trainers, and other personnel necessary to a total organization, to attract the finest talent from the college or other level. A player must earn a decent salary; he should not be forced to drop a game he loves because he cannot make a living at it, or choose another sports career because it pays more. And clubs must be willing to develop farm clubs, as in baseball, where younger players can be trained properly and where they can play in leagues appropriate to their skills, and where the period of their training and playing extends beyond the short seasons now existent. Clubs must aid juvenile soccer and infantile soccer, as they do in Brazil. Clubs must be willing to invest in these expenses knowing that the future of the game in the United States is worth it.

Then, at last, the game will come up to the expectations of all who worked so hard and so long to make the game a success in the United States. And I hope that my being here and playing in this country has helped to bring that day a bit closer.

And what of the future of Pelé?

The year 1977 shall be my last year as an active club player. After that my football will be limited to a few invitational games each year, ten or so, as well as my continued clinics for children. I hope to renew my contract with Pepsi-Cola, but on a reduced basis. And for the next few years Rosemeri and I expect to share our time between the United States and Brazil, so that we and our children can continue to enjoy the benefits of both great countries as Kelly Cristina and Edinho grow up.

And then? When football is finally and definitely behind me? When Pelé at long last finally disappears to be replaced forever by Edson Arantes do Nascimento?

Then I hope to return to Santos with my family. There I hope to see to my business, go fishing off the rocks near Santos, spend some time on my small farm, pick up my guitar again. When I first came to Santos, everyone on the team played guitar to some extent or other and I picked it up a bit in those long, lonely evenings at Vila Belmiro, and even wrote love songs to Rosemeri, some of which have been published. I should like to do more with my music, in those wonderful future days. And I have made several movies; I should like to learn the trade of acting and producing pictures, whether I act or produce or not, because I think acting and producing are exciting professions. And I should like to spend as much time with my family as I can; children grow up so fast!

And above all I want to find some small juvenile team, some group of youngsters like we were in Baurú, who only live for the beautiful game of football. I want to work with them, to help them get shoes and uniforms, to find them a flat field with decent grass, and then to teach them everything I ever learned about this game in a lifetime dedicated to football, a game that gave me everything in this world that I have today. And then, one fine day, I hope to be able to take some fourteen- or fifteen-year-old boy to a major club and say to the directors and the coach of that club:

"Here is a boy you need. Take him and work with him and bring him along in your club. He is another Pelé."

And when I listen to the radio when that boy plays, or when I watch him on television, improving, getting ahead in the world through his talent and his work, then and then alone will I feel I have at least partially paid my debt to Dondinho, to Dona Celeste, to Valdemar de Brito, to all those who helped me through the years—and, mainly, to God.

Appendix I

THE BEAUTIFUL GAME

The origins of the game we call association football, which is also known in parts of the world as soccer, are obscure. Encyclopedias claim it came from an old Roman game called *harpastum*—from the Greek meaning "handball"—in which players were divided into two groups, each of which tried to force a ball across a line drawn behind their opponents. These early games employed a ball which was usually made from an inflated animal bladder, and the use of the hands, feet, or any portion of the body was permitted in the attempt to get the ball across the opponent's line. This game was undoubtedly the forerunner not only of present day Rugby and American football, but of association football as well. (The name "soccer," incidentally, is generally considered to have come from the shortening of the word "association" into "assoc" by those early enthusiasts who introduced the game to America.)

It can logically be assumed that the Romans introduced their shoving game to Britain during their occupation of the islands, and it is known that some form of the game has been played in Britain ever since. The village green was the usual scene of the contest, with each village establishing its own rules, and with the rivalry between villages often leading to feuds. It is claimed that the rulers of England felt the popularity of the game distracted the youth of the country from the study of archery, a sport more in keeping with the training for war, and that at some point in history these rulers attempted to ban the games, but the prohibition—much as the prohibition of the game of golf in Scotland, or the prohibition of liquor in twentieth-century America—was unsuccessful. Actually, the early games were not all that different from war; historians claim that the violence employed often resulted in serious injury, and present-day association football has had its victims as well.

As the game grew in popularity, it was taken up by the British public schools, and the need for some universal rules became evident. In 1823 there was a final break between those who felt the game should be played with the use of the hands and body, and those who felt the game should be restricted to the use of the feet, and the result was the division into Rugby and association football.

The present-day game can be traced to 1863, when an actual football association was formed. The spread of the game throughout the world followed naturally, carried by British sailors and British settlers in other countries. In each country, as the game increased in popularity, football associations were formed, and it was then only a matter of time before a world organization would be formed. In 1904, under the leadership of the French, The Fédération Internationale des Football Associations—FIFA—was founded, and with a world group organized, a world competition eventually became inevitable. In 1930 the FIFA organized its first competition for the Jules Rimet Cup, named for its president and now more commonly known as the World Cup, specifying that a country had to win it three times to retire it and keep it.

One major reason for the swift acceptance of the sport was and is that it requires the minimum of equipment, and is therefore ideally suited to countries where complex and special equipment is not easily available, or where expensive equipment games cannot be afforded. All one basically needs to play the game is a ball, a reasonable amount of space in which to kick it, and sufficient people to oppose each other in trying to put the ball through the opponent's goal. If a regulation ball is not available for a pick-up game, a tin can has served, or a rolled-up bunch of old clothes, or a grapefruit, or a taped-up wad of crumpled newspapers; legend has it that the first ball ever used was the skull of a Danish brigand. If a regulation field is not available the beach will do fine, or a street with minimal traffic—and preferably few potholes—or even somebody's back yard. If the standard number of eleven players per side is either oversubscribed or undersubscribed, the more (or less) the merrier. The important thing to the player is to be in competition, trying to use his particular skill to outwit and outplay his opponent in getting the ball down the field and into whatever passes for a goal.

Even uniform equipment is neither complicated nor expensive. The standard official uniform consists of a shirt, shorts, socks, and either football shoes or sneakers; and although some players use shin guards under their socks, and some goalkeepers wear gloves, there is none of the heavy-duty expensive protective equipment necessary in many other sports. And many a game has been played and will be played by players both barefoot and shirtless.

The rules of association football are extremely simple, and for this reason the game is easily followed and enjoyed even by someone completely unfamiliar with the sport. Primarily, each team has eleven players who try to get the ball into the opponent's net. This they may do by propelling the ball in any manner except through the intentional use of the hands or arms. One player on each team, designated the goalkeeper, is permitted the use of his hands, but only within his own penalty area.

As in baseball, where the dimensions of the infield are fixed while the dimensions of the outfield vary from stadium to stadium, so the outer limits of a football field may vary within certain limits while all other dimensions remain fixed. These variations, as in baseball, undoubtedly had their origin in the different-sized fields available to the various teams:

The length must not be more than 130 yards nor less than 100 yards.

The width must not be more than 100 yards nor less than 50 yards.

(The length, however, must always be greater than the width.) All other dimensions remain the same, regardless of the size of the field:

The *goal area* is 20 yards wide by 6 yards deep.

The *penalty area* is 44 yards wide by 18 yards deep, the goal area being part of the penalty area.

The *penalty spot* is 12 yards from the goal line.

The *penalty arc* has a radius of 10 yards from the penalty spot.

The *goal* is 8 yards wide by 8 feet high.

The *center circle* has a radius of 10 yards from the center spot.

The *corner area* is 1 yard in radius.

Flags must be placed at the corners of the field but are optional at the halfway line positions.

The game of football is usually played in two forty-five-minute halves with an interval of ten or fifteen minutes between halves. Shorter games are often played with younger players. Play is controlled by a referee on the field and two linesmen, one on either side of the field. In professional football there are no time-outs, and substitutions are limited to two per game. The referee may call a time-out in case of injury to a player, but such time-outs are fairly rare, and are limited to the minimum time necessary to replace the player or to revive him. (Time-outs have been called, however, when fans have rioted and come onto the field, usually to try to kill the referee, and in certain parts of the world these time-outs are far from rare.)

The players move the ball using their feet, body, or head, but only the goalkeeper is allowed the use of his hands, and then only within the limits of his own penalty area. Dribbling is not to be confused with the dribble in basketball, but means running while keeping the ball always within the player's constant control. Tackling, again not to be confused with the tackling in American football, means legally taking the ball from an opponent using only the feet. Heading means propelling the ball by striking it with the head.

If, during the play, the ball goes over the sideline, it is thrown back by a member of the opposing team, as in basketball; here the hands may be used but the player is outside the field of play at the time. If the ball goes over the goal line (other than into the goal) and was last touched by the attacking team, it is put back into play by a *goal kick:* The ball is placed within the goal area and is kicked up-field by a member of the defending team, usually, but not always, the goalkeeper. If the ball was last touched by a member of the team defending the goal, the ball is put back into play with a *corner kick,* taken by a member of the attacking team from the corner area.

There are nine major fouls in football. Four of them involve the use of the hands or arms, the principal one being, of course, the intentional touching of the ball, and the others being holding, pushing, or striking an opponent. Two of the fouls involve the use of the body: charging an opponent in a violent or dangerous manner, or charging him from behind. Three involve the use of the feet: tripping, kicking, or jumping at an opponent. After any one of these nine major fouls the referee will award a *direct free kick,* to be taken at the point where the foul occurred against the opposing team, whose members must back off at least ten yards from the ball. The kicker can score a goal from such a kick.

If one of the major fouls is committed by the defending team inside its own penalty area, the attacking team is awarded a *penalty kick*. The ball is placed on the penalty spot and a player from the attacking team is permitted to kick it toward the goal. All the other players of both teams, other than the defending goalkeeper, must remain outside the penalty area and the penalty arc. The defending goalkeeper is not permitted to move his feet until after the ball has been kicked. In present-day professional football it is extremely rare when a penalty kick fails to score a goal, often a decisive one.

There are other minor infractions of the rules, such as obstructing an opponent, or arguing with the referee, which are penalized with an *indirect free kick*. Here the kicker cannot score a goal directly but must kick the ball to another player first. The most common offense for which an indirect free kick is awarded is called *offside*. The main purpose of the offside rule is to prevent players from congregating around the opponent's goal looking for easy shots. The rule states that when the ball is played the player must have at least two opposing players (one of whom is usually the goalkeeper) nearer the goal than he is. However, a player cannot be offside if the ball is nearer the goal than he is when he approaches it to kick it, or if he is in his own half of the field. He also cannot be offside if he receives the ball from an opponent, or directly from a goal kick, a corner kick, or a throw-in.

Arguing with the referee can also result in a penalty far more serious than an indirect free kick. Referees, like umpires in baseball—or like most of us—have feelings that are easily hurt, and if the discussion reaches a point where family background or eyesight or sanity is questioned by a player, the referee has the authority to send the player to the showers. In a game where substitutions are extremely limited, and are often needed to replace injured players, being sent from the field can result in a team playing with fewer men than its opponent, and in professional football this is a tremendous disadvantage.

These, briefly, then, are the rules of the game. Compared to almost every other organized sport, the rules are simple and easily grasped. There are no restrictions in which a player may or may not kick the ball, nor to whom he can kick it. If a goalkeeper chooses to leave his position and attempt to take the ball down the field to try for the opponent's goal, there is nothing in the rules to prevent him from doing so. (He may, of course, find himself on the bench the next game and fined by an irate coach, but it will not be because he had breeched the rules.) But the rules are basic and the idea is a simple one: Put the ball into your opponent's net—nothing more nor less.

Because of the no-time-out rule and the limited-substitution rule, football is the most physically demanding of all sports. And since the standard uniform provides little protection, injuries are far from uncommon. Yet, despite this, association football is, without a doubt, the most popular sport in the world today. Millions of men and boys play it in hundreds of countries (more countries belong to FIFA than belong to the United Nations), and an estimate of the number of spectators watching this game each week is beyond calculation, but the game outdraws any other single sport in attendance, and very likely all other sports combined.

And the man that this book is about was one of these who most helped to popularize the sport, and became famous in doing so:

Edson Arantes do Nascimento.

Appendix II

A BRIEF WORD ON PORTUGUESE PRONUNCIATION

It is well known that the British look with disdain upon foreigners who fail to pronounce place names such as Leicester properly, as Lester; or who call Worcester, place or sauce, anything but Wooster. (I can imagine them calling Niagara Falls, Niffles—but I digress.)

In similar fashion, the Brazilian cavils a bit at having his language mispronounced, although—but to a much lesser extent than in English—the proper pronunciation does not come readily to the foreign eye.

The diminutive ending *-inho* is a good example. Pelé's father, Dondinho, frequently mentioned in this book, is *not* pronounced *don din ho*, like one of Don Ho's forefathers. The digraph *nh* corresponds roughly to the *ni* in the English word *onion*, but is exactly the same as the French *gn* (*oignon*), the Italian *gn* (*ogni*), or the Spanish *ñ* (*niño*). Dondinho therefore becomes *dondee'nyo*.

Another overly mispronounced word, especially by American newscasters, is the name of the largest city in Brazil, São Paulo—Saint Paul, for the interested. It is *not*—newscasters please note—pronounced *say-oh paulo*. The diphthong *ão* is pronounced like the *oun* in the word *ounce*, nasalized, with the *n* unarticulated. Thus São Paulo becomes *soun paulo*. In like manner the great football forward Tostão becomes *tostoun* (a nickname, of course—the *tostão* was the smallest coin ever minted in Brazil).

Since the letter ç is pronounced like the letter *s, ção* is also pronounced *soun;* this is the augmentative, meaning "large."

As the *nh* in Portuguese is similar to the *ñ* in Spanish, so the *lh* is similar to the Spanish *ll*, or like the English *li* in *filial*, and exactly like the *gl* in the Italian *egli*. Thus, *filho de mãe* is pronounced *filyo de ma-een* and means "son of mother!" which is what the polite Brazilian says when he would prefer to say son of something else!

There are a few other idiosyncrasies in Portuguese pronunciation. For example, no word can be pronounced to end in the sound of the letter *m;* it must be pronounced as if it ended in the letter *n*. Thus the city of Belém is pronounced Belé*n*, and Dom Helder Camara is called, in Brazil, Do*n* Helder Camara.

There are, of course, many other rules to the pronunciation of the Portuguese language, and even a few to differentiate between the language as spoken in Portugal and Brazil, but fortunately few of these appear in this book. Still, when one considers that English pronunciation is far more complicated—with letter combinations such as *ough* being pronounced differently in words such as *rough* and *through* and *though* and *slough*—one must face the fact that Portuguese pronunciation is not difficult at all. At least once they make a rule, they stand by it.

Appendix III

THE GAMES OF PELÉ

NO.	DATE	TEAM		OPPONENT	SCORE	GOALS
1.	9/7/56	Santos	vs	Corinthians— Santo André	7–1	1
2.	11/15/56	Santos	vs	Espanha Football Club	4–2	1
3.	1/12/57	Santos	vs	AIK—Sweden	1–0	-
4.	2/9/57	Santos	vs	Portuguesa Desportos	2–4	-
5.	2/17/57	Santos	vs	América—Joinville	5–0	-
6.	2/19/57	Santos	vs	América—Joinville	3–1	-
7.	3/12/57	Santos	vs	Gremio—Pôrto Alegre	2–3	-
8.	3/14/57	Santos	vs	Gremio—Pôrto Alegre	5–0	-
9.	3/17/57	Santos	vs	Rio Grandense	5–3	-
10.	3/19/57	Santos	vs	Pelotas	3–2	-
11.	3/22/57	Santos	vs	E. Clube Brasil	2–2	-
12.	3/24/57	Santos	vs	Selection Guarani/Bajé	1–1	1
13.	3/27/57	Santos	vs	Renner—Pôrto Alegre	3–5	-
14.	3/31/57	Santos	vs	Selection Framengo Juventude	4–1	1
15.	4/7/57	Santos	vs	Vasco da Gama—Rio	4–2	-
16.	4/11/57	Santos	vs	Corinthians—São Paulo	5–3	1
17.	4/14/57	Santos	vs	Guarani—Campinas	6–1	2
18.	4/26/57	Santos	vs	São Paulo Football Club	3–1	1
19.	5/1/57	Santos	vs	Corinthians—São Paulo	1–1	-
20.	5/5/57	Santos	vs	Flamengo—Rio	0–4	-
21.	5/9/57	Santos	vs	Portuguesa Desportos	2–4	-
22.	5/11/57	Santos	vs	Botafogo—Rio	5–1	-
23.	5/13/57	Santos	vs	Botafogo—Ribeirão Preto	1–3	-
24.	5/15/57	Santos	vs	Palmeiras—São Paulo	3–0	2
25.	5/19/57	Santos	vs	Londrina—Paraná	7–1	2
26.	5/26/57	Santos	vs	Fluminense—Rio	2–2	-
27.	5/29/57	Santos	vs	América—Rio	4–0	1
28.	6/1/57	Santos	vs	Vasco da Gama—Rio	2–3	1
29.	6/9/57	Santos	vs	Lavras—Minas	7–2	4
30.	6/19/57	Santos/ Vasco	vs	Belenenses—Portugal	6–1	3
31.	6/20/57	Santos	vs	Rio Branco	3–2	-

NO.	DATE	TEAM	OPPONENT	SCORE	GOALS
32.	6/22/57	Santos/ Vasco	vs Dinamo—Zagreb	1–1	1
33.	6/26/57	Santos/ Vasco	vs Flamengo—Rio	1–1	1
34.	6/29/57	Santos/ Vasco	vs São Paulo Football Club	1–1	1
35.	7/7/57	Selection Brazil	vs Selection Argentina	1–2	1
36.	7/10/57	Selection Brazil	vs Selection Argentina	2–0	1
37.	7/14/57	Santos	vs Nov. XV—Piracicaba	5–3	1
38.	7/21/57	Santos	vs Corinthians—São Paulo	1–2	-
39.	7/23/57	Santos	vs Benfica—Portugal	3–2	1
40.	7/25/57	Santos	vs Ponte Preta—Campinas	7–2	3
41.	7/28/57	Santos	vs Arapongas—Paraná	3–1	-
42.	7/31/57	Santos	vs Jabaquara	4–6	-
43.	8/4/57	Santos	vs Ferroviaria—Araraquara	2–3	-
44.	8/11/57	Santos	vs Botafogo—Ribeirão Preto	4–2	-
45.	8/15/57	Santos	vs Guarani—Campinas	8–1	4
46.	8/18/57	Santos	vs Portuguesa Desportos	5–2	-
47.	8/20/57	Santos	vs Selection Salvador (Bahia)	2–2	-
48.	9/8/57	Santos	vs Palmeiras—São Paulo	1–2	1
49.	9/11/57	Santos	vs Nacional—São Paulo	7–1	4
50.	9/15/57	Santos	vs São Paulo Football Club	2–3	1
51.	9/22/57	Santos	vs A.A. Portuguesa	1–1	1
52.	9/25/57	Santos	vs Ipiranga	9–1	3
53.	9/29/57	Santos	vs Juventus—São Paulo	6–1	1
54.	10/2/57	Santos	vs Esporte—Recife	1–1	-
55.	10/4/57	Santos	vs Nautico—Recife	0–0	-
56.	10/6/57	Santos	vs Sampaio Correia—São Luís	2–1	2
57.	10/8/57	Santos	vs Esporte—Recife	2–1	1
58.	10/10/57	Santos	vs Canto do Rio—Rio	1–0	-
59.	10/20/57	Santos	vs Botafogo—Ribeirão Preto	2–4	-
60.	10/23/57	Santos	vs A.A. Portuguesa	2–2	-
61.	10/26/57	Santos	vs Palmeiras—São Paulo	4–3	1
62.	11/3/57	Santos	vs Corinthians—São Paulo	3–3	3
63.	11/4/57	Santos	vs Bandeirantes—São Carlos	0–3	-
64.	11/6/57	Santos	vs Portuguesa Desportos	3–1	-
65.	11/10/57	Santos	vs Nov. XV—Piracicaba	3–0	1
66.	11/17/57	Santos	vs São Paulo Football Club	2–6	-
67.	11/24/57	Santos	vs Jabaquara	5–1	3
68.	11/27/57	Santos	vs Nov. XV—Piracicaba	6–2	2
69.	12/1/57	Santos	vs. A.A. Portuguesa	6–2	4
70.	12/3/57	Santos	vs São Paulo Football Club	2–2	-
71.	12/8/57	Santos	vs Ponte Preta—Campinas	2–1	1
72.	12/15/57	Santos	vs Portuguesa Desportos	6–0	2
73.	12/22/57	Santos	vs Corinthians—São Paulo	1–0	-
74.	12/28/57	Santos	vs Palmeiras—São Paulo	4–1	-
75.	12/29/57	Santos	vs Nitro Química—São Miguel	10–3	1
76.	1/19/58	Santos	vs Bragantino	4–1	1
77.	1/26/58	Santos	vs Prudentina	4–0	1
78.	1/30/58	Santos	vs Atlético—Minas	2–5	1

NO.	DATE	TEAM	OPPONENT	SCORE	GOALS
79.	2/2/58	Santos	vs Atlético–Minas	2–0	1
80.	2/5/58	Santos	vs Atlético–Minas	2–2	-
81.	2/7/58	Santos	vs Botafogo–Ribeirão Preto	4–2	2
82.	2/26/58	Santos	vs América–Rio	5–3	4
83.	3/2/58	Santos	vs Botafogo–Rio	2–2	-
84.	3/6/58	Santos	vs Palmeiras–São Paulo	7–6	1
85.	3/9/58	Santos	vs Flamengo–Rio	2–3	1
86.	3/13/58	Santos	vs Portuguesa Desportos	2–3	1
87.	3/16/58	Santos	vs São Paulo Football Club	2–4	-
88.	3/22/58	Santos	vs Vasco da Gama–Rio	0–1	-
89.	3/23/58	Santos	vs Noroeste–Baurú	2–3	-
90.	3/27/58	Santos	vs Corinthians–São Paulo	1–2	1
91.	5/4/58	Selection Brazil	vs Selection Paraguay	5–1	2
92.	5/14/58	Selection Brazil	vs Selection Bulgaria	4–0	-
93.	5/18/58	Selection Brazil	vs Selection Bulgaria	3–1	2
94.	6/15/58	Selection Brazilvs	Selection Russia	2–0	-
95.	6/19/58	Selection Brazil	vs Selection Wales	1–0	1
96.	6/24/58	Selection Brazil	vs Selection France	5–2	3
97.	6/29/58	Santos	vs Selection Sweden	5–2	2
98.	7/16/58	Santos	vs Jabaquara	7–3	2
99.	7/20/58	Santos	vs Juventus–São Paulo	2–0	1
100.	7/23/58	Santos	vs Nov. XV–Piracicaba	6–0	4
101.	7/27/58	Santos	vs Botafogo–Ribeirão Preto	2–2	2
102.	7/31/58	Santos	vs Comercial–São Paulo	1–1	1
103.	8/3/58	Santos	vs América–Rio Preto	0–0	-
104.	8/6/58	Santos	vs Portuguesa Desportos	4–3	1
105.	8/10/58	Santos	vs Noroeste–Baurú	0–1	-
106.	8/13/58	Santos	vs Ferroviaria–Araraquara	4–3	1
107.	8/17/58	Santos	vs São Paulo Football Club	1–0	1
108.	8/20/58	Santos	vs Ponte Preta–Campinas	4–0	1
109.	8/24/58	Santos	vs Palmeiras–São Paulo	1–0	-
110.	8/28/58	Santos	vs Nov. XV–Jaú	5–2	1
111.	8/31/58	Santos	vs A.A. Portuguesa	2–1	-
112.	9/4/58	Santos	vs E. Clube Taubaté	3–0	1
113.	9/7/58	Santos	vs Ipiranga–São Paulo	4–1	-
114.	9/11/58	Santos	vs Nacional–São Paulo	10–0	4
115.	9/14/58	Santos	vs Corinthians–São Paulo	1–0	1
116.	9/17/58	Santos	vs Guarani–Campinas	8–1	1
117.	9/21/58	Santos	vs Prudentina	2–2	1
118.	9/25/58	Santos	vs Internacional–Pôrto Alegre	1–5	-
119.	9/28/58	Santos	vs Gremio–Pôrto Alegre	0–4	-
120.	10/1/58	Santos	vs Ipiranga–São Paulo	8–1	5
121.	10/5/58	Santos	vs E. Clube Taubaté	2–3	-
122.	10/11/58	Santos	vs Noroeste–Baurú	3–0	-
123.	10/15/58	Santos	vs. A.A. Portuguesa	6–1	3

NO.	DATE	TEAM		OPPONENT	SCORE	GOALS
124.	10/19/58	Santos	vs	Nov. XV—Piracicaba	5–0	2
125.	10/22/58	Santos	vs	Jabaquara	6–2	3
126.	10/26/58	Santos	vs	Botafogo—Ribeirão Preto	4–0	3
127.	10/29/58	Santos	vs	Portuguesa Desportos	1–1	-
128.	11/1/58	Santos	vs	Nov. XV—Jaú	0–0	-
129.	11/5/58	Santos	vs	América—Rio Preto	3–1	1
130.	11/9/58	Santos	vs	Ferroviaria—Araraquara	1–2	-
131.	11/16/58	Santos	vs	Palmeiras—São Paulo	2–1	1
132.	11/19/58	Santos	vs	Comercial—São Paulo	9–1	4
133.	11/23/58	Santos	vs	Ponte Preta—Campinas	2–1	-
134.	11/27/58	Santos	vs	A.A. Portuguesa	4–3	1
135.	11/30/58	Santos	vs	Nacional—São Paulo	4–3	1
136.	12/7/58	Santos	vs	Corinthians—São Paulo	6–1	4
137.	12/10/58	Santos	vs	Juventus—São Paulo	7–1	3
138.	12/14/58	Santos	vs	Guarani—Campinas	7–1	4
139.	12/18/58	Santos	vs	São Paulo Football Club	2–2	2
140.	12/21/58	Santos	vs	Coritiba	1–1	1
141.	12/23/58	Santos	vs	Cruzeiro—Minas	4–2	3
142.	12/30/58	Santos	vs	Soccer Union Players—São Paulo	3–0	2
143.	1/4/59	Santos	vs	Sports Boys—Lima	3–0	2
144.	1/6/59	Santos	vs	Sporting Cristal—Lima	4–0	2
145.	1/9/59	Santos	vs	Dep. Municipal—Lima	5–1	-
146.	1/11/59	Santos	vs	Emelec—Equador	3–1	2
147.	1/15/59	Santos	vs	Saprissa—Costa Rica	3–1	2
148.	1/18/59	Santos	vs	Comunicaciones—Guatemala	2–1	1
149.	1/21/59	Santos	vs	Selection—Costa Rica	2–1	-
150.	1/29/59	Santos	vs	Guadalajara—Mexico	4–2	3
151.	2/5/59	Santos	vs	León—Mexico	2–0	-
152.	2/8/59	Santos	vs	Atlas—Mexico	4–1	1
153.	2/12/59	Santos	vs	América—Mexico	5–0	2
154.	2/15/59	Santos	vs	Uda Duklas—Czechoslovakia	3–4	-
155.	2/17/59	Santos	vs	Selection Curaçao	3–2	-
156.	2/19/59	Santos	vs	Dep. Espanhol—Caracas	4–0	-
157.	2/22/59	Selection São Paulo	vs	Selection Rio	1–5	1
158.	2/25/59	Selection São Paulo	vs	Selection Rio	0–1	-
159.	3/10/59	Selection Brazil	vs	Selection Peru	2–2	1
160.	3/15/59	Selection Brazil	vs	Selection Chile	3–0	2
161.	3/21/59	Selection Brazil	vs	Selection Bolivia	4–2	1
162.	3/26/59	Selection Brazil	vs	Selection Uruguay	3–1	-
163.	3/29/59	Selection Brazil	vs	Selection Paraguay	4–1	3
164.	4/4/59	Selection Brazil	vs	Selection Argentina	1–1	1

NO.	DATE	TEAM	OPPONENT	SCORE	GOALS
165.	4/9/59	Santos	vs Botafogo—Rio	4–2	1
166.	4/12/59	Santos	vs Flamengo—Rie	3–2	1
167.	4/15/59	Santos	vs Colo-Colo—Chile	2–6	-
168.	4/18/59	Santos	vs Fluminense—Rio	1–1	-
169.	4/21/59	Santos	vs Portuguesa Desportos	2–0	-
170.	4/23/59	Santos	vs E. Clube Bahia	2–1	-
171.	4/26/59	Santos	vs São Paulo Football Club	4–3	2
172.	4/30/59	Santos	vs Cerinthians—São Paulo	3–2	1
173.	5/13/59	Selection Brazil	vs Selection England	2–0	-
174.	5/17/59	Santos	vs Vasco da Gama—Rio	3–0	1
175.	5/19/59	Santos	vs Santa Cruz—Recife	5–1	3
176.	5/23/59	Santos	vs B. Selection Bulgaria	3–3	2
177.	5/24/59	Santos	vs A. Selection Bulgaria	2–0	1
178.	5/26/59	Santos	vs Royal Standard—Belgium	1–0	-
179.	5/27/59	Santos	vs Anderlecht—Belgium	4–2	2
180.	5/30/59	Santos	vs Gantoise—Ghent-Belgium	1–2	-
181.	6/3/59	Santos	vs Feyenoord—Groningen	3–0	1
182.	6/5/59	Santos	vs Internazionale—Italy	2–3	2
183.	6/6/59	Santos	vs Fortuna—Düsseldorf	6–4	1
184.	6/7/59	Santos	vs Nuremberg—Germany	3–3	-
185.	6/9/59	Santos	vs Servette—Geneva	4–1	1
186.	6/11/59	Santos	vs Selection Hamburg	6–0	1
187.	6/13/59	Santos	vs Selection Niedersachsen—Germany	7–1	3
188.	6/15/59	Santos	vs Selection Enschede—Holland	5–0	3
189.	6/17/59	Santos	vs Real Madrid—Spain	3–5	1
190.	6/19/59	Santos	vs Sporting—Lisbon	2–2	1
191.	6/21/59	Santos	vs Botafogo—Rio	4–1	1
192.	6/24/59	Santos	vs Valencia—Spain	4–4	1
193.	6/26/59	Santos	vs Internazionale—Italy	7–1	4
194.	6/28/59	Santos	vs Barcelona—Spain	5–1	2
195.	6/30/59	Santos	vs Genoa—Italy	4–2	-
196.	7/2/59	Santos	vs Vienna—Austria	0–3	-
197.	7/5/59	Santos	vs Betis—Seville	2–2	1
198.	7/18/59	Santos	vs Fortaleza—Ceará	2–2	2
199.	7/19/59	Santos	vs Selection Pernambuco	0–0	-
200.	7/23/59	Santos	vs Jabaquara	7–0	1
201.	7/26/59	Santos	vs Nov. XV—Jaú	8–2	3
202.	8/2/59	Santos	vs Juventus—São Paulo	4–0	3
203.	8/16/59	Santos	vs E. Clube Taubaté	1–1	1
204.	8/19/59	Santos	vs Ferroviaria—Araraquara	0–0	-
205.	8/21/59	6th Coast Guard (Army)	vs Guards of the Docas Co.	9–0	3
206.	8/23/59	Santos	vs Noroeste—Baurú	4–3	3
207.	8/26/59	Santos	vs Corinthians—São Paulo	3–2	1
208.	8/27/59	6th Coast Guard (Army)	vs CIA Q.G.2A R.M.	7–0	3

NO.	DATE	TEAM	OPPONENT	SCORE	GOALS
209.	8/30/59	Santos	vs América—Rio Preto	3–2	1
210.	9/5/59	6th Coast Guard (Army)	vs A.A. Portuguesa (amateurs)	0–0	-
211.	9/7/59	Santos	vs Portuguesa Desportos	5–0	3
212.	9/10/59	Santos	vs Guarani—Campinas	4–1	2
213.	9/11/59	6th Coast Guard (Army)	vs Santos (mixed team)	8–4	3
214.	9/13/59	Santos	vs Botafogo—Ribeirão Preto	3–1	1
215.	9/17/59	Selection Brazil	vs Selection Chile	7–0	3
216.	9/20/59	Selection Brazil	vs Selection Chile	1–0	-
217.	9/27/59	Santos	vs São Paulo Football Club	1–2	-
218.	9/28/59	6th Coast Guard (Army)	vs Selection Armed Forces	4–2	1
219.	10/1/59	Santos	vs Comercial—São Paulo	3–1	-
220.	10/3/59	Santos	vs Palmeiras—São Paulo	7–3	3
221.	10/6/59	6th Coast Guard (Army)	vs Selection 2nd Army	3–2	1
222.	10/11/59	Santos	vs Coritiba	1–0	-
223.	10/12/59	1st Army	vs 2nd Army	4–3	-
224.	10/14/59	Santos	vs América—Rio Preto	8–0	4
225.	10/25/59	Santos	vs Nov. XV—Piracicaba	5–2	2
226.	10/27/59	Selection Brazilian Army	vs Selection Brazilian Navy	6–1	3
227.	10/29/59	Santos	vs Noroeste—Baurú	6–1	-
228.	11/1/59	Santos	vs Comercial—Ribeirão Preto	6–2	1
229.	11/4/59	Santos	vs Comercial—São Paulo	4–2	1
230.	11/5/59	Selection Brazilian Army	vs Selection Uruguayan Army	4–3	-
231.	11/8/59	Santos	vs Nov. XV—Jaú	0–1	-
232.	11/11/59	Santos	vs Juventus—São Paulo	5–1	2
233.	11/15/59	Santos	vs Nacional—São Paulo	4–0	2
234.	11/17/59	Santos	vs Gremio—Pôrto Alegre	4–1	-
235.	11/22/59	Santos	vs Portuguesa Desportos	5–1	3
236.	11/24/59	Selection Brazilian Army	vs Selection Argentinian Army	2–1	-
237.	11/25/59	Santos	vs Gremio—Pôrto Alegre	0–0	-
238.	11/29/59	Santos	vs Palmeiras—São Paulo	1–5	1
239.	12/6/59	Santos	vs Ferroviaria—Araraquara	5–2	2
240.	12/10/59	Santos	vs E. Clube Bahia	2–3	1
241.	12/13/59	Santos	vs São Paulo Football Club	4–3	2
242.	12/20/59	Santos	vs Guarani—Campinas	2–3	-

NO.	DATE	TEAM		OPPONENT	SCORE	GOALS
243.	12/23/59	Santos	vs	E. Clube Taubaté	2–0	-
244.	12/27/59	Santos	vs	Corinthians—São Paulo	4–1	2
245.	12/30/59	Santos	vs	E. Clube Bahia	2–0	1
246.	1/5/60	Santos	vs	Palmeiras—São Paulo	1–1	1
247.	1/7/60	Santos	vs	Palmeiras—São Paulo	2–2	-
248.	1/10/60	Santos	vs	Palmeiras—São Paulo	1–2	1
249.	1/19/60	Selection São Paulo	vs	Selection Bahia	2–0	-
250.	1/24/60	Selection São Paulo	vs	Selection Bahia	7–1	3
251.	1/27/60	Selection São Paulo	vs	Selection Minas Gerais	4–3	1
252.	1/31/60	Selection São Paulo	vs	Selection Pernambuco	2–4	-
253.	2/3/60	Selection São Paulo	vs	Selection Rio	4–1	-
254.	2/10/60	Selection São Paulo	vs	Selection Pernambuco	3–1	2
255.	2/14/60	Selection São Paulo	vs	Selection Rio	2–1	-
256.	2/16/60	Santos	vs	University—Lima	2–2	-
257.	2/18/60	Santos	vs	Sporting Cristal—Lima	3–3	-
258.	2/24/60	Santos	vs	Alianza—Lima	2–1	-
259.	2/26/60	Santos	vs	University—Lima	2–3	-
260.	3/6/60	Santos	vs	Dep. Medelin—Colombia	2–1	1
261.	3/9/60	Santos	vs	América—Cali	1–0	-
262.	3/12/60	Santos	vs	Milionários—Bogotá	1–2	-
263.	3/13/60	Santos	vs	Deportivo—Cali	4–0	1
264.	3/16/60	Santos	vs	América—Cali	1–0	-
265.	3/20/60	Santos	vs	Liga Universitaria—Equador	6–2	-
266.	4/19/60	Santos	vs	Portuguesa Desportos	2–2	-
267.	4/21/60	Santos	vs	São Paulo Football Club	1–1	-
268.	4/24/60	Santos	vs	Vasco da Gama—Rio	0–0	-
269.	4/29/60	Selection Brazil	vs	Selection UAR	5–0	-
270.	5/1/60	Selection Brazil	vs	Selection UAR	3–1	3
271.	5/6/60	Selection Brazil	vs	Selection UAR	3–0	-
272.	5/8/60	Selection Brazil	vs	Malmö Fotbolförening—Sweden	7–1	2
273.	5/10/60	Selection Brazil	vs	Selection—Denmark	4–3	-
274.	5/12/60	Selection Brazil	vs	Internazionale—Italy	2–2	2
275.	5/16/60	Selection Brazil	vs	Sporting—Portugal	4–0	-
276.	5/19/60	Santos	vs	Royal Standard—Belgium	4–3	1
277.	5/25/60	Santos	vs	Selection Poland	5–2	2
278.	5/27/60	Santos	vs	T.S.V. 1860—Germany	9–1	3
279.	5/28/60	Santos	vs	Anderlecht—Belgium	6–0	2

NO.	DATE	TEAM	OPPONENT	SCORE	GOALS
280.	5/31/60	Santos	vs Royal Beerschot–Belgium	10–1	4
281.	6/1/60	Santos	vs A.S. Roma–Italy	3–2	1
282.	6/3/60	Santos	vs Fiorentina–Italy	0–3	-
283.	6/7/60	Santos	vs Stade Reims–France	5–3	1
284.	6/9/60	Santos	vs Racing–Paris	4–1	1
285.	6/11/60	Santos	vs Gantoise–Belgium	5–2	2
286.	6/12/60	Santos	vs Selection–Antwerp	3–1	-
287.	6/14/60	Santos	vs Eintracht–Germany	4–2	2
288.	6/15/60	Santos	vs Selection Berlin	4–2	1
289.	6/17/60	Santos	vs Stade Reims–France	3–1	1
290.	6/19/60	Santos	vs Dep. Español–Barcelona	2–2	-
291.	6/23/60	Santos	vs Toulouse–France	3–0	2
292.	6/25/60	Santos	vs Valencia–Spain	1–0	-
293.	7/2/60	Santos	vs Barcelona–Spain	3–4	1
294.	7/9/60	Selection Brazil	vs Selection Uruguay	0–1	-
295.	7/12/60	Selection Brazil	vs Selection Argentina	5–1	1
296.	7/17/60	Santos	vs Ponte Preta–Campinas	6–3	1
297.	7/21/60	Santos	vs Portuguesa Desportos	1–1	-
298.	7/24/60	Santos	vs Guarani–Campinas	2–2	-
299.	7/27/60	Santos	vs Jabaquara	8–3	3
300.	7/31/60	Santos	vs Corinthians–São Paulo	1–1	1
301.	8/3/60	Santos	vs Botafogo–Ribeirão Preto	5–1	1
302.	8/7/60	Santos	vs Comercial–Ribeirão Preto	0–2	-
303.	8/10/60	Santos	vs Noroeste–Baurú	4–1	3
304.	8/14/60	Santos	vs Corinthians–Presidente Prudente	1–0	1
305.	8/15/60	Santos	vs Itau Sport Club	3–2	1
306.	8/21/60	Santos	vs Palmeiras–São Paulo	3–1	1
307.	8/31/60	Santos	vs São Paulo Football Club	1–1	-
308.	9/4/60	Santos	vs Ferroviaria–Araraquara	0–4	-
309.	9/8/60	Santos	vs A.A. Portuguesa	0–0	-
310.	9/11/60	Santos	vs Nov. XV–Piracicaba	0–0	-
311.	9/15/60	Santos	vs Juventus–São Paulo	5–2	3
312.	9/17/60	Santos	vs América–Rio Preto	0–1	-
313.	9/21/60	Santos	vs Jabaquara	3–2	-
314.	9/24/60	Santos	vs Juventus–São Paulo	3–1	2
315.	9/28/60	Santos	vs Portuguesa Desportos	3–4	1
316.	10/23/60	Santos	vs Ponte Preta–Campinas	4–1	1
317.	11/6/60	Santos	vs Nov. XV–Piracicaba	2–0	2
318.	11/9/60	Santos	vs A.A. Portuguesa	1–0	1
319.	11/23/60	Santos	vs Noroeste–Baurú	3–1	2
320.	11/30/60	Santos	vs Goiania	6–1	-
321.	11/20/60	Santos	vs Botafogo–Ribeirão Preto	4–2	1
322.	11/23/60	Santos	vs Corinthians–Presidente Prudente	5–0	1
323.	11/30/60	Santos	vs Corinthians–São Paulo	6–1	1
324.	12/4/60	Santos	vs E. Clube Taubaté	6–1	2
325.	12/7/60	Santos	vs Ferroviaria–Araraquara	5–0	3
326.	12/11/60	Santos	vs São Paulo Football Club	1–2	-

NO.	DATE	TEAM		OPPONENT	SCORE	GOALS
327.	12/16/60	Santos	vs	Palmeiras—São Paulo	2–1	1
328.	1/8/61	Santos	vs	Uberlandia E. Clube	6–1	1
329.	1/10/61	Santos	vs	Guarani—Campinas	10–2	2
330.	1/14/61	Santos	vs	Colo-Colo—Chile	3–1	2
331.	1/18/61	Santos	vs	Selection Colombia	2–1	2
332.	1/22/61	Santos	vs	Saprissa—Costa Rica	7–3	1
333.	1/25/61	Santos	vs	Herediano—Costa Rica	3–0	1
334.	1/29/61	Santos	vs	Selection Guatemala	4–1	2
335.	2/2/61	Santos	vs	Necaxa—Mexico	3–4	-
336.	2/19/61	Santos	vs	Guadalajara—Mexico	6–2	-
337.	2/22/61	Santos	vs	América—Mexico	6–2	2
338.	2/24/61	Santos	vs	Atlas—Guadalajara	2–0	-
339.	2/26/61	Santos	vs	América—Rio	3–3	-
340.	3/2/61	Santos	vs	Vasco da Gama—Rio	5–1	-
341.	3/5/61	Santos	vs	Fluminense—Rio	3–1	2
342.	3/11/61	Santos	vs	Flamengo—Rio	7–1	3
343.	3/15/61	Santos	vs	São Paulo Football Club	1–0	-
344.	4/1/61	Santos	vs	Botafogo—Rio	4–2	2
345.	4/5/61	Santos	vs	Alético—Minas	3–1	2
346.	4/10/61	Santos	vs	América—Rio	6–1	1
347.	4/13/61	Santos	vs	Vasco da Gama—Rio	1–2	-
348.	6/1/61	Santos	vs	F.C. Basel—Switzerland	8–2	3
349.	6/3/61	Santos	vs	Wolfsburg—Germany	6–3	2
350.	6/4/61	Santos	vs	Selection Antwerp	4–4	-
351.	6/7/61	Santos	vs	Racing—Paris	6–1	1
352.	6/9/61	Santos	vs	Olympic Lyonnaise	6–2	2
353.	6/11/61	Santos	vs	Selection Israel	3–1	1
354.	6/13/61	Santos	vs	Racing—Paris	5–4	1
355.	6/15/61	Santos	vs	Benfica—Portugal	6–3	2
356.	6/18/61	Santos	vs	Juventus—Turin	2–0	1
357.	6/21/61	Santos	vs	A.S. Roma—Italy	5–0	2
358.	6/24/61	Santos	vs	Internazionale—Italy	4–1	1
359.	6/26/61	Santos	vs	Karlsruher—Germany	8–6	3
360.	6/28/61	Santos	vs	AEK—Greece	3–0	1
361.	6/30/61	Santos	vs	Panathinaikos—Greece	3–2	2
362.	7/4/61	Santos	vs	Olimpiakos—Greece	1–2	-
363.	7/23/61	Santos	vs	E. Clube Taubaté	0–0	-
364.	7/30/61	Santos	vs	Palmeiras—São Paulo	2–1	-
365.	8/6/61	Santos	vs	Jabaquara	4–0	1
366.	8/9/61	Santos	vs	Guarani—Campinas	3–1	1
367.	8/13/61	Santos	vs	Noroeste—Baurú	7–1	3
368.	8/16/61	Santos	vs	Corinthians—São Paulo	5–1	1
369.	8/19/61	Santos	vs	Nov. XV—Piracicaba	6–1	3
370.	8/25/61	Santos	vs	Nacional—Uruguay	0–1	-
371.	8/30/61	Santos	vs	Olympico—Blumenau	8–0	5
372.	9/3/61	Santos	vs	São Paulo Football Club	6–3	4
373.	9/6/61	Santos	vs	Juventus—São Paulo	10–1	5
374.	9/10/61	Santos	vs	Botafogo—Ribeirão Preto	3–0	1
375.	9/13/61	Santos	vs	Esportiva—Guaratinguetá	5–1	4
376.	9/17/61	Santos	vs	Portuguesa Desportos	6–1	4
377.	9/20/61	Santos	vs	Londrina—Paraná	2–1	-
378.	9/28/61	Santos	vs	Racing Club—Argentina	4–2	2

NO.	DATE	TEAM		OPPONENT	SCORE	GOALS
379.	10/1/61	Santos	vs	Newells Old Boys—Argentina	1–1	1
380.	10/4/61	Santos	vs	Colo-Colo—Chile	3–2	1
381.	10/8/61	Santos	vs	Colo-Colo—Chile	3–1	1
382.	10/15/61	Santos	vs	Botafogo—Ribeirão Preto	4–1	1
383.	10/18/61	Santos	vs	A.A. Portuguesa	5–2	2
384.	10/22/61	Santos	vs	Guarani—Campinas	2–1	-
385.	10/28/61	Santos	vs	Portuguesa Desportos	3–1	2
386.	11/1/61	Santos	vs	Juventus—São Paulo	3–1	1
387.	11/4/61	Santos	vs	E. Clube Taubaté	4–2	1
388.	11/8/61	Santos	vs	Esportiva—Guaratinguetá	4–0	3
389.	11/11/61	Santos	vs	América—Rio	6–2	2
390.	11/15/61	Santos	vs	Flamengo—Rio	1–1	1
391.	11/19/61	Santos	vs	América—Rio	0–1	-
392.	11/21/61	Santos	vs	América—Rio	6–1	2
393.	11/26/61	Santos	vs	Comercial—Ribeirão Preto	4–1	1
394.	11/29/61	Santos	vs	Palmeiras—São Paulo	2–3	1
395.	12/3/61	Santos	vs	Corinthians—São Paulo	1–1	-
396.	12/6/61	Santos	vs	Noroeste—Baurú	4–2	2
397.	12/10/61	Santos	vs	Nov. XV—Piracicaba	7–2	3
398.	12/13/61	Santos	vs	Ferroviaria—Araraquara	6–2	2
399.	12/16/61	Santos	vs	São Paulo Football Club	4–1	1
400.	12/19/61	Soccer Union Players—São Paulo	vs	Soccer Union Players—Rio	4–1	1
401.	12/22/61	Santos	vs	E. Clube Bahia	1–1	-
402.	12/27/61	Santos	vs	E. Clube Bahia	5–1	3
403.	1/3/62	Santos	vs	Botafogo—Rio	0–3	-
404.	1/7/62	Santos	vs	Barcelona—Guaiaquil (Ecuador)	6–2	-
405.	1/14/62	Santos	vs	University League—Ecuador	6–3	3
406.	1/17/62	Santos	vs	Alianza—Lima	5–1	-
407.	1/20/62	Santos	vs	Universitario—Lima	5–2	1
408.	1/24/62	Santos	vs	Sporting Cristal—Lima	5–1	1
409.	1/27/62	Santos	vs	Dep. Municipal—Lima	3–2	1
410.	1/31/62	Santos	vs	National—Uruguay	3–2	1
411.	2/3/62	Santos	vs	Racing—Argentina	8–3	1
412.	2/6/62	Santos	vs	River Plate—Argentina	1–2	-
413.	2/9/62	Santos	vs	Ginazia Y Esgrima—Argentina	2–2	-
414.	2/14/62	Santos	vs	Selection Brazil	3–1	1
415.	2/18/62	Santos	vs	Dep. Municipal—Bolivia	4–3	-
416.	2/21/62	Santos	vs	Dep. Municipal—Bolivia	6–1	-
417.	2/28/62	Santos	vs	Cerro Portenho—Paraguay	9–1	2
418.	3/18/62	Santos	vs	Palmeiras—São Paulo	5–3	2
419.	4/21/62	Selection Brazil	vs	Selection Paraguay	6–0	1

NO.	DATE	TEAM		OPPONENT	SCORE	GOALS
420.	4/24/62	Selection Brazil	vs	Selection Paraguay	4–0	2
421.	5/6/62	Selection Brazil	vs	Selection Portugal	2–1	-
422.	5/9/62	Selection Brazil	vs	Selection Portugal	1–0	1
423.	5/12/62	Selection Brazil	vs	Selection Wales	3–1	1
424.	5/16/62	Selection Brazil	vs	Selection Wales	3–1	2
425.	5/30/62	Selection Brazil	vs	Selection Mexico	2–0	1
426.	6/2/62	Selection Brazil	vs	Selection Czechoslovakia	0–0	-
427.	7/25/62	Santos	vs	Wolkswagem—São Bernardo do Campo	2–0	-
428.	8/5/62	Santos	vs	Prudentina	2–0	1
429.	8/8/62	Santos	vs	Juventus—São Paulo	2–0	-
430.	8/12/62	Santos	vs	Palmeiras—São Paulo	4–2	1
431.	8/19/62	Santos	vs	Jabaquara	5–1	3
432.	8/26/62	Santos	vs	Guarani—Campinas	1–1	1
433.	8/30/62	Santos	vs	Penarol—Uruguay	3–0	2
434.	9/2/62	Santos	vs	São Paulo Football Club	3–3	2
435.	9/5/62	Santos	vs	Botafogo—Ribeirão Preto	5–2	2
436.	9/15/62	Santos	vs	Ferroviaria—Araraquara	7–2	4
437.	9/19/62	Santos	vs	Benfica—Portugal	3–2	2
438.	9/23/62	Santos	vs	Corinthians—São Paulo	5–2	1
439.	9/26/62	Santos	vs	Noroeste—Baurú	4–0	2
440.	9/30/62	Santos	vs	Comercial—Ribeirão Preto	3–1	1
441.	10/6/62	Santos	vs	Portuguesa Desportos	2–3	1
442.	10/11/62	Santos	vs	Benfica—Portugal	5–2	3
443.	10/17/62	Santos	vs	Racing—Paris	5–2	2
444.	10/20/62	Santos	vs	F.C. Hamburger—Germany	3–3	2
445.	10/22/62	Santos	vs	Sheffield Wednesday—England	4–2	1
446.	10/27/62	Santos	vs	E. Clube Taubaté	3–0	1
447.	10/31/62	Santos	vs	Guarani—Campinas	5–0	3
448.	11/4/62	Santos	vs	Corinthians—São Paulo	2–1	1
449.	11/7/62	Santos	vs	Juventus—São Paulo	3–0	1
450.	11/11/62	Santos	vs	Noroeste—Baurú	1–1	-
451.	11/14/62	Santos	vs	Palmeiras—São Paulo	3–0	1
452.	11/18/62	Santos	vs	Nov. XV—Piracicaba	1–1	-
453.	11/21/62	Santos	vs	Portuguesa Desportos	4–1	2
454.	11/25/62	Santos	vs	Ferroviaria—Araraquara	1–1	-
455.	11/28/62	Santos	vs	Comercial—Ribeirão Preto	6–2	2
456.	12/2/62	Santos	vs	Jabaquara	8–2	4
457.	12/5/62	Santos	vs	São Paulo Football Club	5–2	1
458.	12/10/62	Santos	vs	Selection Russia	2–1	1
459.	12/12/62	Santos	vs	Botafogo—Ribeirão Preto	1–0	-

NO.	DATE	TEAM		OPPONENT	SCORE	GOALS
460.	12/15/62	Santos	vs	Prudentina	4–0	2
461.	12/19/62	Soccer Uni-on Players —São Paulo	vs	Soccer Union Players—Rio	4–6	2
462.	1/9/63	Santos	vs	Selection Sergipe	3–2	2
463.	1/12/63	Santos	vs	Esporte—Recife	1–1	-
464.	1/16/63	Santos	vs	Esporte—Recife	4–0	-
465.	1/23/63	Santos	vs	Colo-Colo—Chile	2–1	2
466.	1/30/63	Santos	vs	Dep. Municipal—Lima	8–3	3
467.	2/2/63	Santos	vs	Alianza—Lima	2–1	1
468.	2/6/63	Santos	vs	Universidad—Chile	3–4	2
469.	2/10/63	Santos	vs	Naval Club—Talcahuano	5–0	2
470.	2/16/63	Santos	vs	Vasco da Gama—Rio	2–2	2
471.	2/20/63	Santos	vs	Portuguesa Desportos	6–3	2
472.	3/3/63	Santos	vs	Corinthians—São Paulo	2–0	2
473.	3/7/63	Santos	vs	São Paulo Football Club	6–2	3
474.	3/13/63	Santos	vs	Palmeiras—São Paulo	3–0	-
475.	3/16/63	Santos	vs	Olaria—Rio	5–1	3
476.	3/19/63	Santos	vs	Botafogo—Rio	4–3	-
477.	3/23/63	Santos	vs	Fluminense—Rio	2–4	1
478.	3/27/63	Santos	vs	Flamengo—Rio	3–0	1
479.	3/31/63	Santos	vs	Botafogo—Rio	1–3	-
480.	4/2/63	Santos	vs	Botafogo—Rio	5–0	2
481.	4/13/63	Selection Brazil	vs	Selection Argentina	2–3	-
482.	4/16/63	Selection Brazil	vs	Selection Argentina	4–1	3
483.	4/21/63	Selection Brazil	vs	Selection Portugal	0–1	-
484.	4/28/63	Selection Brazil	vs	Selection France	3–2	3
485.	5/2/63	Selection Brazil	vs	Selection Holland	0–1	-
486.	5/5/63	Selection Brazil	vs	Selection West Germany	2–1	1
487.	5/12/63	Selection Brazil	vs	Selection Italy	0–3	-
488.	5/29/63	Santos	vs	Selection Niedersachsen —Germany	3–2	1
489.	6/2/63	Santos	vs	Schalke 04—Germany	2–1	1
490.	6/5/63	Santos	vs	Eintracht—Germany	5–2	4
491.	6/8/63	Santos	vs	Stuttgart—Germany	3–1	1
492.	6/12/63	Santos	vs	Barcelona—Spain	0–2	-
493.	6/15/63	Santos	vs	A.S. Roma—Italy	4–3	2
494.	6/19/63	Santos	vs	Internazionale—Italy	0–2	-
495.	6/22/63	Santos	vs	Milan—Italy	0–4	-
496.	6/26/63	Santos	vs	Juventus—Italy	3–5	1
497.	7/21/63	Santos	vs	Noroeste—Baurú	4–3	4
498.	7/24/63	Santos	vs	Portuguesa Desportos	1–1	-
499.	7/28/63	Santos	vs	Jabaquara	5–2	1

NO.	DATE	TEAM	OPPONENT	SCORE	GOALS
500.	7/31/63	Santos	vs Esportiva—Guaratinguetá	2–2	1
501.	8/4/63	Santos	vs Guarani—Campinas	2–1	1
502.	8/7/63	Santos	vs Palmeiras—São Paulo	1–1	-
503.	8/15/63	Santos	vs São Paulo Football Club	1–4	1
504.	8/18/63	Santos	vs Nov. XV—Piracicaba	0–0	-
505.	8/22/63	Santos	vs Botafogo—Rio	1–1	1
506.	8/28/63	Santos	vs Botafogo—Rio	4–0	3
507.	9/1/63	Santos	vs Ferroviaria—Araraquara	1–4	1
508.	9/4/63	Santos	vs Boca Juniors—Argentina	3–2	-
509.	9/11/63	Santos	vs Boca Juniors—Argentina	2–1	1
510.	9/18/63	Santos	vs Prudentina	2–2	1
511.	9/22/63	Santos	vs Corinthians—São Paulo	3–1	3
512.	9/25/63	Santos	vs Juventus—São Paulo	2–1	-
513.	9/29/63	Santos	vs Botafogo—Ribeirão Preto	3–1	1
514.	10/2/63	Santos	vs Noroeste—Baurú	4–2	1
515.	10/5/63	Santos	vs Prudentina	4–0	3
516.	10/16/63	Santos	vs Milan—Italy	2–4	2
517.	10/24/63	Santos	vs Portuguesa Desportos	2–3	1
518.	10/27/63	Santos	vs Comercial—Ribeirão Preto	3–0	2
519.	10/30/63	Santos	vs São Bento—Sorocaba	2–3	1
520.	11/2/63	Santos	vs Juventus—São Paulo	0–0	-
521.	1/16/64	Santos	vs Gremio—Pôrto Alegre	3–1	1
522.	1/19/64	Santos	vs Gremio—Pôrto Alegre	4–3	3
523.	1/25/64	Santos	vs E. Clube Bahia	6–0	2
524.	1/28/64	Santos	vs E. Clube Bahia	2–0	2
525.	2/1/64	Santos	vs Independiente—Argentina	1–5	-
526.	2/6/64	Santos	vs Penarol—Uruguay	0–5	-
527.	2/22/64	Santos	vs Sport Boys—Lima	3–2	2
528.	2/25/64	Santos	vs Alianza—Lima	3–2	-
529.	2/28/64	Santos	vs Colo-Colo—Chile	2–3	-
530.	3/1/64	Santos	vs Godoy Cruz—Mendoza	3–2	-
531.	3/6/64	Santos	vs Colo-Colo—Chile	4–2	-
532.	3/8/64	Santos	vs Talleres—Córdoba	2–1	-
533.	3/18/64	Santos	vs Corinthians—São Paulo	3–0	1
534.	3/22/64	Santos	vs Fluminense—Rio	1–0	-
535.	4/25/64	Santos	vs Botafogo—Rio	3–1	1
536.	5/1/64	Santos	vs Flamengo—Rio	2–3	1
537.	5/5/64	Santos	vs Boca Juniors—Argentina	4–3	1
538.	5/7/64	Santos	vs Racing—Argentina	2–1	1
539.	5/10/64	Santos	vs Colon—Santa Fé (Argentina)	1–2	1
540.	5/30/64	Selection Brazil	vs Selection England	5–1	1
541.	7/3/64	Selection Brazil	vs Selection Argentina	0–3	-
542.	7/5/64	Santos	vs América—Rio Preto	1–2	1
543.	7/7/64	Selection Brazil	vs Selection Portugal	4–1	1
544.	8/19/64	Santos	vs Guarani—Campinas	6–1	1
545.	8/23/64	Santos	vs Palmeiras—São Paulo	2–1	1

NO.	DATE	TEAM	OPPONENT	SCORE	GOALS
546.	9/23/64	Santos	vs São Bento–Sorocaba	1–1	1
547.	9/27/64	Santos	vs Portuguesa Desportos	3–4	2
548.	9/30/64	Santos	vs Corinthians–São Paulo	1–1	1
549.	10/4/64	Santos	vs América–Rio Preto	3–1	1
550.	10/7/64	Santos	vs Colo-Colo–Chile	1–3	1
551.	10/11/64	Santos	vs São Paulo Football Club	3–2	-
552.	10/14/64	Santos	vs Comercial–Ribeirão Preto	3–2	1
553.	10/18/64	Santos	vs Atlético–Minas	4–1	1
554.	10/21/64	Santos	vs Esportiva–Guaratinguetá	0–2	-
555.	10/25/64	Santos	vs Atlético–Minas	5–1	2
556.	10/28/64	Santos	vs Prudentina	8–1	4
557.	11/1/64	Santos	vs Nov. XV–Piracicaba	6–3	3
558.	11/4/64	Santos	vs Palmeiras–São Paulo	3–2	1
559.	11/7/64	Santos	vs Palmeiras–São Paulo	2–3	-
560.	11/10/64	Santos	vs Palmeiras–São Paulo	4–0	-
561.	11/15/64	Santos	vs Ferroviaria–Araraquara	0–0	-
562.	11/18/64	Santos	vs Guarani–Campinas	1–5	-
563.	11/21/64	Santos	vs Botafogo–Ribeirão Preto	11–0	8
564.	11/29/64	Santos	vs Noroeste–Baurú	3–0	1
565.	12/2/64	Santos	vs Juventus–São Paulo	5–2	2
566.	12/6/64	Santos	vs Corinthians–São Paulo	7–4	4
567.	12/9/64	Santos	vs São Bento–Sorocaba	6–0	3
568.	12/13/64	Santos	vs Portuguesa Desportos	3–2	-
569.	12/16/64	Santos	vs Flamengo–Rio	4–1	3
570.	12/19/64	Santos	vs Flamengo–Rio	0–0	-
571.	1/10/65	Santos	vs Botafogo–Rio	2–3	-
572.	1/13/65	Santos	vs Universidad Católica–Chile	2–1	1
573.	1/16/65	Santos	vs Selection Czechoslovakia	6–4	3
574.	1/22/65	Santos	vs River Plate–Argentina	2–3	1
575.	1/29/65	Santos	vs Colo-Colo–Chile	3–2	1
576.	2/2/65	Santos	vs Universidad–Chile	3–0	1
577.	2/4/65	Santos	vs River Plate–Argentina	1–0	-
578.	2/9/65	Santos	vs River Plate–Argentina	4–3	2
579.	2/13/65	Santos	vs Universidad–Chile	5–1	3
580.	2/19/65	Santos	vs Universitario–Lima	2–1	-
581.	2/21/65	Santos	vs Dep. Galicia–Caracas	3–2	3
582.	2/23/65	Santos	vs Independiente–Argentina	4–0	2
583.	2/26/65	Santos	vs Universidad–Chile	1–0	1
584.	3/6/65	Santos	vs Universitario–Lima	2–1	1
585.	3/6/65	Santos	vs Portuguesa Desportos	4–1	-
586.	3/25/65	Santos	vs Penarol–Uruguay	5–4	1
587.	3/28/65	Santos	vs Penarol–Uruguay	2–3	-
588.	3/31/65	Santos	vs Penarol–Uruguay	1–2	1
589.	4/4/65	Santos	vs Vasco da Gama–Rio	0–3	-
590.	4/11/65	Santos	vs Botafogo–Rio	2–3	-
591.	4/15/65	Santos	vs Corinthians–São Paulo	4–4	4
592.	4/18/65	Santos	vs Fluminense–Rio	5–2	1
593.	4/21/65	Santos	vs América–Rio	2–0	-
594.	4/29/65	Santos	vs Clube do Remo–Pará	9–4	5
595.	5/2/65	Santos	vs E. Clube Bahia	6–1	1
596.	5/5/65	Santos	vs E. Clube Bahia	3–1	-

NO.	DATE	TEAM		OPPONENT	SCORE	GOALS
597.	5/8/65	Santos	vs	Dom Bosco—Cuiabá	6–2	3
598.	5/11/65	Santos	vs	Comercial—Campo Grande	4–1	3
599.	5/14/65	Santos	vs	Olimpia—Paraguay	2–2	1
600.	5/16/65	Santos	vs	Maringa—Paraná	11–1	2
601.	6/2/65	Selection Brazil	vs	Selection Belgium	5–0	3
602.	6/6/65	Selection Brazil	vs	Selection West Germany	2–0	1
603.	6/9/65	Selection Brazil	vs	Selection Argentina	0–0	-
604.	6/17/65	Selection Brazil	vs	Selection Algeria	3–0	1
605.	6/24/65	Selection Brazil	vs	Selection Portugal	0–0	-
606.	6/30/65	Selection Brazil	vs	Selection Sweden	2–1	1
607.	7/14/65	Selection Brazil	vs	Selection Russia	3–0	2
608.	7/14/65	Santos	vs	Noroeste—Baurú	6–2	5
609.	7/18/65	Santos	vs	Ferroviaria—Araraquara	3–1	2
610.	7/21/65	Santos	vs	Comercial—Ribeirão Preto	5–3	3
611.	7/25/65	Santos	vs	C.R. Brazil—Alagoas	6–0	2
612.	7/28/65	Santos	vs	Santo Antonio—Vitória	3–1	1
613.	8/1/65	Santos	vs	São Paulo Football Club	1–1	-
614.	8/4/65	Santos	vs	A.A. Portuguesa	2–0	1
615.	8/8/65	Santos	vs	Boca Juniors—Argentina	4–1	2
616.	8/12/65	Santos	vs	River Plate—Argentina	2–1	-
617.	8/15/65	Santos	vs	Prudentina	3–1	3
618.	8/22/65	Santos	vs	Portuguesa Desportos	4–0	3
619.	8/28/65	Santos	vs	Corinthians—São Paulo	4–3	2
620.	9/4/65	Santos	vs	Botafogo—Ribeirão Preto	7–1	3
621.	9/8/65	Santos	vs	Juventus—São Paulo	3–1	2
622.	9/11/65	Santos	vs	Guarani—Campinas	7–0	4
623.	9/15/65	Santos	vs	Selection Minas	1–2	-
624.	9/19/65	Santos	vs	Palmeiras—São Paulo	0–1	-
625.	9/22/65	Santos	vs	Ferroviaria—Araraquara	4–2	-
626.	10/3/65	Santos	vs	Noroeste—Baurú	3–0	1
627.	10/7/65	Santos	vs	São Bento—Sorocaba	4–2	1
628.	10/10/65	Santos	vs	Comercial—Ribeirão Preto	2–0	1
629.	10/13/65	Santos	vs	A.A. Portuguesa	3–0	1
630.	10/16/65	Santos	vs	São Paulo Football Club	0–0	-
631.	10/24/65	Santos	vs	América—Rio Preto	4–0	3
632.	10/27/65	Santos	vs	Portuguesa Desportos	1–0	-
633.	10/31/65	Santos	vs	Prudentina	5–2	5
634.	11/3/65	Santos	vs	Palmeiras—São Paulo	4–2	-
635.	11/7/65	Santos	vs	Nov. XV—Piracicaba	2–0	-
636.	11/10/65	Santos	vs	Palmeiras—São Paulo	1–1	1
637.	11/14/65	Santos	vs	Corinthians—São Paulo	4–2	1
638.	11/21/65	Selection Brazil	vs	Selection Russia	2–2	1
639.	11/25/65	Santos	vs	Botafogo—Ribeirão Preto	5–0	4
640.	11/27/65	Santos	vs	Juventus—São Paulo	4–0	3

NO.	DATE	TEAM	OPPONENT	SCORE	GOALS
641.	12/1/65	Santos	vs Vasco da Gama—Rio	5–1	-
642.	12/4/65	Santos	vs Guarani—Campinas	1–0	1
643.	12/8/65	Santos	vs Vasco da Gama—Rio	1–0	1
644.	12/12/65	Santos	vs Palmeiras—São Paulo	0–5	-
645.	1/9/66	Santos	vs Stad Club—Abidjan	7–1	2
646.	1/13/66	Santos	vs Selection San Martin/ Atlético—Argentina	2–0	1
647.	1/16/66	Santos	vs Alianza—El Salvador	1–2	1
648.	1/19/66	Santos	vs Botafogo—Rio	1–2	1
649.	1/22/66	Santos	vs Botafogo—Rio	0–3	-
650.	1/26/66	Santos	vs Universitario—Lima	2–2	1
651.	1/29/66	Santos	vs Alianza—Lima	4–1	1
652.	2/6/66	Santos	vs Melgar—Arequipa	1–1	-
653.	2/9/66	Santos	vs Universidad—Chile	6–1	3
654.	2/11/66	Santos	vs Rosario Central—Argentina	1–0	-
655.	2/13/66	Santos	vs Sarmiento—Argentina	1–1	-
656.	2/17/66	Santos	vs Colo-Colo—Chile	2–2	1
657.	3/29/66	Santos	vs Cruzeiro—Minas	3–4	1
658.	3/31/66	Santos	vs Atlético—Minas	1–0	1
659.	5/19/66	Selection Brazil	vs Selection Chile	1–0	-
660.	6/4/66	Selection Brazil	vs Selection Peru	4–0	1
661.	6/8/66	Selection Brazil	vs Selection Poland	2–1	-
662.	6/12/66	Selection Brazil	vs Selection Czechoslovakia	2–1	2
663.	6/15/66	Selection Brazil	vs Selection Czechoslovakia	2–2	1
664.	6/21/66	Selection Brazil	vs Atlético—Madrid	5–3	3
665.	6/25/66	Selection Brazil	vs Selection Scotland	1–1	-
666.	6/30/66	Selection Brazil	vs Selection Scotland	3–2	-
667.	7/4/66	Selection Brazil	vs AIK—Sweden	4–2	2
668.	7/6/66	Selection Brazil	vs Malmö Fotbolförening—Sweden	3–1	2
669.	7/12/66	Selection Brazil	vs Selection Bulgaria	2–0	1
670.	7/19/66	Selection Brazil	vs Selection Portugal	1–3	-
671.	8/17/66	Santos	vs Juventus—São Paulo	1–1	-
672.	8/21/66	Santos	vs Benfica—Portugal	4–0	1
673.	8/24/66	Santos	vs AEK—Grecia	1–0	-
674.	8/28/66	Santos	vs Toluca—Mexico	1–1	-
675.	8/30/66	Santos	vs Atlante—Mexico	2–2	1
676.	9/5/66	Santos	vs Internazionale—Italy	4–1	1
677.	9/11/66	Santos	vs Prudentina	3–1	2
678.	9/14/66	Santos	vs Portuguesa Desportos	0–2	-

NO.	DATE	TEAM		OPPONENT	SCORE	GOALS
679.	10/8/66	Santos	vs	Corinthians—São Paulo	3–0	-
680.	10/13/66	Santos	vs	Comercial—Ribeirão Preto	7–5	-
681.	10/16/66	Santos	vs	São Bento—Sorocaba	2–2	1
682.	10/23/66	Santos	vs	A.A. Portuguesa	3–0	1
683.	10/26/66	Santos	vs	Noroeste—Baurú	4–1	2
684.	10/30/66	Santos	vs	São Paulo Football Club	1–2	1
685.	11/5/66	Santos	vs	Juventus—São Paulo	3–0	1
686.	11/9/66	Santos	vs	Nautico—Recife	2–0	1
687.	11/13/66	Santos	vs	Bragantino	3–2	3
688.	11/17/66	Santos	vs	Nautico—Recife	3–5	-
689.	11/19/66	Santos	vs	Nautico—Recife	4–1	-
690.	11/23/66	Santos	vs	Palmeiras—São Paulo	2–0	1
691.	11/26/66	Santos	vs	Guarani—Campinas	2–1	-
692.	11/30/66	Santos	vs	Cruzeiro—Minas	2–6	-
693.	12/4/66	Santos	vs	Botafogo—Ribeirão Preto	3–1	1
694.	12/7/66	Santos	vs	Cruzeiro—Minas	2–3	1
695.	1/15/67	Santos	vs	Selection Mar Del Plata	4–1	-
696.	1/19/67	Santos	vs	River Plate—Argentina	4–0	1
697.	1/22/67	Santos	vs	Milionários—Bogotá	1–2	-
698.	1/25/67	Santos	vs	Atlético Juniors—Colombia	3–3	-
699.	1/29/67	Santos	vs	River Plate—Argentina	2–4	2
700.	2/1/67	Santos	vs	River Plate—Argentina	2–1	1
701.	2/7/67	Santos	vs	Universidad—Chile	1–1	-
702.	2/10/67	Santos	vs	Vazas—Hungary	2–2	1
703.	2/17/67	Santos	vs	Penarol—Uruguay	2–0	-
704.	2/21/67	Santos	vs	Universidad Católica—Chile	6–2	4
705.	2/25/67	Santos	vs	Alianza—Lima	4–1	1
706.	2/28/67	Santos	vs	Colo-Colo—Chile	2–1	-
707.	3/8/67	Santos	vs	Atlético—Minas	1–0	-
708.	3/12/67	Santos	vs	Gremio—Pôrto Alegre	1–1	1
709.	3/15/67	Santos	vs	Internacional—Pôrto Alegre	5–1	1
710.	3/19/67	Santos	vs	Flamengo—Rio	1–0	-
711.	3/22/67	Santos	vs	Botafogo—Rio	0–0	-
712.	3/26/67	Santos	vs	Vasco da Gama—Rio	1–2	1
713.	4/1/67	Santos	vs	São Paulo Football Club	1–1	1
714.	4/8/67	Santos	vs	Palmeiras—São Paulo	1–2	-
715.	4/15/67	Santos	vs	Portuguesa Desportos	2–2	2
716.	4/19/67	Santos	vs	Cruzeiro—Minas	1–3	-
717.	4/23/67	Santos	vs	Bangú—Rio	3–0	1
718.	4/30/67	Santos	vs	Fluminense—Rio	0–3	-
719.	5/3/67	Santos	vs	Ferroviario—Curitiba	3–0	1
720.	5/7/67	Santos	vs	Selection Ilhéus	3–1	1
721.	5/10/67	Santos	vs	Santa Cruz—Recife	5–0	1
722.	5/13/67	Santos	vs	Corinthians—São Paulo	1–1	1
723.	5/15/67	Santos	vs	Olimpia—Paraguay	0–0	-
724.	5/23/67	Santos	vs	Portuguesa Desportos	3–2	1
725.	5/25/67	Santos	vs	Selection Brasilia	5–1	1
726.	5/28/67	Santos	vs	Selection Senegal	4–1	3
727.	5/31/67	Santos	vs	Selection Gabon	4–0	1
728.	6/2/67	Santos	vs	Leopards (Selection Dem. Congo)	2–1	1

NO.	DATE	TEAM		OPPONENT	SCORE	GOALS
729.	6/4/67	Santos	vs	Selection Ivory Coast	2–1	1
730.	6/7/67	Santos	vs	Selection Congo	3–2	3
731.	6/13/67	Santos	vs	T.S.V. München 1860–Germany	5–4	2
732.	6/17/67	Santos	vs	Mantova–Italy	2–1	1
733.	6/20/67	Santos	vs	Venice–Italy	1–0	-
734.	6/24/67	Santos	vs	U.S. Lecce–Italy	5–1	3
735.	6/27/67	Santos	vs	Fiorentina–Italy	1–1	-
736.	6/29/67	Santos	vs	A.S. Roma–Italy	3–1	1
737.	7/9/67	Santos	vs	São Bento–Sorocaba	4–3	1
738.	7/15/67	Santos	vs	Juventus–São Paulo	4–0	1
739.	7/23/67	Santos	vs	Guarani–Campinas	2–1	-
740.	8/6/67	Santos	vs	Palmeiras–São Paulo	1–1	1
741.	8/19/67	Santos	vs	Comercial–Ribeirão Preto	4–1	1
742.	8/22/67	Santos	vs	A.A. Portuguesa	3–1	-
743.	8/26/67	Santos	vs	Internazionale–Italy	0–1	-
744.	8/28/67	Santos	vs	Dep. Español–Málaga	1–4	-
745.	8/29/67	Santos	vs	Málaga–Spain	2–1	-
746.	10/8/67	Santos	vs	América–Rio Preto	3–2	1
747.	10/15/67	Santos	vs	São Paulo Football Club	2–2	1
748.	10/22/67	Santos	vs	Prudentina	3–1	2
749.	10/29/67	Santos	vs	Palmeiras–São Paulo	4–1	1
750.	11/1/67	Santos	vs	Juventus–São Paulo	4–1	2
751.	11/4/67	Santos	vs	Selection Maranhão	1–0	-
752.	11/7/67	Santos	vs	Selection Fortaleza	5–0	1
753.	11/11/67	Santos	vs	Comercial–Ribeirão Preto	1–1	1
754.	11/19/67	Santos	vs	São Bento–Sorocaba	1–1	1
755.	11/26/67	Santos	vs	Portuguesa Desportos	0–0	-
756.	12/3/67	Santos	vs	Guarani–Campinas	1–1	1
757.	12/10/67	Santos	vs	Corinthians–São Paulo	2–1	1
758.	12/17/67	Santos	vs	A.A. Portuguesa	3–1	1
759.	12/21/67	Santos	vs	São Paulo Football Club	2–1	-
760.	1/13/68	Santos	vs	Selection Czechoslovakia	4–1	-
761.	1/23/68	Santos	vs	Vazas–Hungary	4–0	1
762.	2/2/68	Santos	vs	Colo-Colo–Chile	4–1	-
763.	3/3/68	Santos	vs	Ferroviaria–Araraquara	4–1	2
764.	3/6/68	Santos	vs	Corinthians–São Paulo	0–2	-
765.	3/9/68	Santos	vs	Botafogo–Ribeirão Preto	5–1	1
766.	3/16/68	Santos	vs	Portuguesa Desportos	3–0	1
767.	3/19/68	Santos	vs	Goiaz E. Clube	3–3	1
768.	3/23/68	Santos	vs	Juventus–São Paulo	4–0	2
769.	3/27/68	Santos	vs	São Paulo Football Club	5–2	2
770.	3/31/68	Santos	vs	América–Rio Preto	4–3	2
771.	4/7/68	Santos	vs	Comercial–Ribeirão Preto	8–2	2
772.	4/10/68	Santos	vs	Guarani–Campinas	2–0	-
773.	4/13/68	Santos	vs	Palmeiras–São Paulo	1–0	-
774.	4/18/68	Santos	vs	São Bento–Sorocaba	1–0	-
775.	4/21/68	Santos	vs	Corinthians–São Paulo	2–0	1
776.	4/24/68	Santos	vs	Juventus–São Paulo	3–2	2
777.	4/28/68	Santos	vs	Nov. XV–Piracicaba	1–0	-
778.	5/1/68	Santos	vs	Ferroviaria–Araraquara	0–0	-
779.	5/4/68	Santos	vs	Portuguesa Desportos	1–0	-

NO.	DATE	TEAM		OPPONENT	SCORE	GOALS
780.	5/8/68	Santos	vs	Flamengo—Rio	0–0	-
781.	5/12/68	Santos	vs	Botafogo—Ribeirão Preto	3–1	-
782.	5/15/68	Santos	vs	A.A. Portuguesa	1–2	-
783.	5/19/68	Santos	vs	Palmeiras—São Paulo	3–1	1
784.	5/23/68	Santos	vs	Boca Juniors—Argentina	0–1	-
785.	5/29/68	Santos	vs	Comercial—Ribeirão Preto	5–0	1
786.	6/1/68	Santos	vs	São Paulo Football Club	3–1	-
787.	6/9/68	Santos	vs	Cagliari—Italy	2–1	-
788.	6/12/68	Santos	vs	Alexandria—Italy	2–0	1
789.	6/15/68	Santos	vs	F.C. Zurique—Switzerland	4–5	1
790.	6/17/68	Santos	vs	Selection Saar—Germany	3–0	1
791.	6/21/68	Santos	vs	Naples—Italy	4–2	1
792.	6/26/68	Santos	vs	Naples—Italy	6–2	2
793.	6/28/68	Santos	vs	Naples—Italy	5–2	2
794.	6/30/68	Santos	vs	St. Louis Stars—USA	3–2	1
795.	7/4/68	Santos	vs	Kansas City Spurs—USA	4–1	1
796.	7/6/68	Santos	vs	Necaxa—Mexico	4–3	1
797.	7/8/68	Santos	vs	Boston Beacons—USA	7–1	1
798.	7/10/68	Santos	vs	Cleveland Stokers—USA	1–2	-
799.	7/12/68	Santos	vs	New York Generals—USA	3–5	-
800.	7/14/68	Santos	vs	Washington Whips—USA	3–1	-
801.	7/17/68	Santos	vs	Olympic Selection—Colombia	4–2	1
802.	7/25/68	Santos	vs	Selection Paraguay	4–0	2
803.	7/28/68	Selection Brazil	vs	Selection Paraguay	0–1	-
804.	8/4/68	Santos	vs	Ferroviaria—Ceará	0–0	-
805.	8/6/68	Santos	vs	Paissandu—Pará	3–1	1
806.	8/9/68	Santos	vs	Nacional Fast Clube—Manaus	3–0	1
807.	8/11/68	Santos	vs	Nacional Fast Clube—Manaus	2–1	1
808.	8/15/68	Santos	vs	River Plate—Argentina	2–1	-
809.	8/18/68	Santos	vs	Benfica—Portugal	4–2	-
810.	8/20/68	Santos	vs	Nacional—Uruguay	2–2	1
811.	8/25/68	Santos	vs	Boca Juniors—Argentina	1–1	-
812.	8/28/68	Santos	vs	Atlanta Chiefs—USA	6–2	3
813.	8/30/68	Santos	vs	Oakland Clippers—USA	3–1	2
814.	9/1/68	Santos	vs	Benfica—Portugal	3–3	-
815.	9/15/68	Santos	vs	Flamengo—Rio	2–0	-
816.	9/18/68	Santos	vs	Palmeiras—São Paulo	0–0	-
817.	9/21/68	Santos	vs	Fluminense—Rio	2–1	1
818.	9/25/68	Santos	vs	Bangú—Rio	1–1	-
819.	10/6/68	Santos	vs	Vasco da Gama—Rio	2–3	-
820.	10/6/68	Santos	vs	Corinthians—São Paulo	2–1	1
821.	10/10/68	Santos	vs	E. Clube Bahia	9–2	3
822.	10/13/68	Santos	vs	Cruzeiro—Minas	2–0	1
823.	10/16/68	Santos	vs	Portuguesa Desportos	2–0	-
824.	10/20/68	Santos	vs	São Paulo Football Club	0–0	-
825.	10/23/68	Santos	vs	International—Pôrto Alegre	3–1	1
826.	10/27/68	Santos	vs	Nautico—Recife	3–0	1

NO.	DATE	TEAM		OPPONENT	SCORE	GOALS
827.	10/31/68	Selection Brazil	vs	Selection Mexico	1–2	-
828.	11/3/68	Selection Brazil	vs	Selection Mexico	2–1	1
829.	11/6/68	Selection Brazil	vs	Selection FIFA	2–1	-
830.	11/10/68	Selection São Paulo	vs	Selection Rio	3–2	1
831.	11/13/68	Selection Brazil	vs	Selection Paraná	2–1	-
832.	11/19/68	Santos	vs	Racing—Argentina	2–0	1
833.	11/21/68	Santos	vs	Penarol—Uruguay	1–0	-
834.	11/24/68	Santos	vs	Atlético—Minas	2–2	1
835.	11/27/68	Santos	vs	Gremio—Pôrto Alegre	3–1	1
836.	12/1/68	Santos	vs	Botafogo—Rio	2–3	-
837.	12/4/68	Santos	vs	Internacional—Pôrto Alegre	2–1	1
838.	12/8/68	Santos	vs	Palmeiras—São Paulo	3–0	-
839.	12/10/68	Santos	vs	Vasco da Gama—Rio	2–1	1
840.	12/10/68	Selection Brazil	vs	Selection West Germany	2–2	-
841.	12/17/68	Selection Brazil	vs	Selection Yugoslavia	3–3	1
842.	1/17/69	Santos	vs	Selection Point Noire	3–0	1
843.	1/19/69	Santos	vs	Selection Congo	3–2	2
844.	1/21/69	Santos	vs	Selection (B) Congo	2–0	-
845.	1/23/69	Santos	vs	Selection (A) Congo	2–3	2
846.	1/26/69	Santos	vs	Nigerian Football Association	2–2	2
847.	2/1/69	Santos	vs	Austria S. Club	2–0	-
848.	2/4/69	Santos	vs	Selection Middle West (Africa)	2–1	-
849.	2/6/69	Santos	vs	Hearts of Oak—Africa	2–2	1
850.	2/9/69	Santos	vs	Selection Algeria	1–1	-
851.	2/14/69	Santos	vs	Nov. XV—Piracicaba	6–2	2
852.	2/22/69	Santos	vs	Portuguesa Desportos	4–1	1
853.	2/26/69	Santos	vs	Ferroviaria—Araraquara	3–0	2
854.	3/2/69	Santos	vs	Paulista—Jundiaí	2–1	-
855.	3/5/69	Santos	vs	Guarani—Campinas	0–1	-
856.	3/9/69	Santos	vs	São Paulo Football Club	3–0	1
857.	3/12/69	Santos	vs	São Bento—Sorocaba	4–2	2
858.	3/15/69	Santos	vs	Juventus—São Paulo	2–1	1
859.	3/19/69	Santos	vs	América—Rio Preto	2–1	-
860.	3/22/69	Santos	vs	Palmeiras—São Paulo	2–3	2
861.	3/26/69	Santos	vs	Botafogo—Ribeirão Preto	4–1	1
862.	3/29/69	Santos	vs	A.A. Portuguesa	3–1	3
863.	4/7/69	Selection Brazil	vs	Selection Peru	2–1	-
864.	4/9/69	Selection Brazil	vs	Selection Peru	3–2	1
865.	4/13/69	Santos	vs	Corinthians—São Paulo	0–2	-
866.	4/23/69	Santos	vs	Portuguesa Desportos	3–2	-

NO.	DATE	TEAM	OPPONENT	SCORE	GOALS
867.	4/27/69	Santos	vs América—Rio Preto	1–1	1
868.	4/30/69	Santos	vs A.A. Portuguesa	1–2	1
869.	5/3/69	Santos	vs Palmeiras—São Paulo	0–1	-
870.	5/1/69	Santos	vs Ferroviaria—Araraquara	1–2	1
871.	5/21/69	Santos	vs São Paulo Football Club	1–0	-
872.	5/25/69	Santos	vs Corinthians—São Paulo	1–1	-
873.	5/28/69	Santos	vs Paulista—Jundiaí	3–2	1
874.	5/31/69	Santos	vs Botafogo—Ribeirão Preto	5–1	4
875.	6/8/69	Santos	vs Corinthians—São Paulo	3–1	2
876.	6/12/69	Selection Brazil	vs Selection England	2–1	-
877.	6/18/69	Santos	vs Palmeiras—São Paulo	3–0	1
878.	6/21/69	Santos	vs São Paulo Football Club	0–0	-
879.	6/24/69	Santos	vs Internazionale—Italy	1–0	-
880.	7/6/69	Selection Brazil	vs E. Clube Bahia	4–0	1
881.	7/9/69	Selection Brazil	vs Selection Sergipe	8–2	-
882.	7/13/69	Selection Brazil	vs Selection Pernambuco	6–1	1
883.	8/1/69	Selection Brazil	vs Milionários—Bogotá	2–0	-
884.	8/6/69	Selection Brazil	vs Selection Colombia	2–0	-
885.	8/10/69	Selection Brazil	vs Selection Venezuela	5–0	2
886.	8/17/69	Selection Brazil	vs Selection Paraguay	3–0	-
887.	8/21/69	Selection Brazil	vs Selection Colombia	6–2	1
888.	8/24/69	Selection Brazil	vs Selection Venezuela	6–0	2
889.	8/31/69	Selection Brazil	vs Selection Paraguay	1–0	1
890.	9/3/69	Selection Brazil	vs Selection Minas Gerais	1–2	1
891.	9/10/69	Santos	vs Red Star—Yugoslavia	3–3	1
892.	9/12/69	Santos	vs Dinamo—Yugoslavia	1–1	-
893.	9/15/69	Santos	vs Danick—Kragujevac	4–4	1
894.	9/17/69	Santos	vs Atlético—Madrid	3–1	-
895.	9/19/69	Santos	vs Zeljesnicar—Yugoslavia	1–1	1
896.	9/22/69	Santos	vs Stoke City—England	3–2	2
897.	9/24/69	Santos	vs Combination Geneva/ Sampdoria—Italy	7–1	2
898.	9/28/69	Santos	vs Gremio—Pôrto Alegre	1–2	1
899.	10/12/69	Santos	vs Palmeiras—São Paulo	1–2	1
900.	10/15/69	Santos	vs Portuguesa Desportos	6–2	4
901.	10/22/69	Santos	vs Coritiba	3–1	2
902.	10/26/69	Santos	vs Fluminense—Rio	0–0	-
903.	11/1/69	Santos	vs Flamengo—Rio	4–1	1
904.	11/4/69	Santos	vs Corinthians—São Paulo	1–4	-
905.	11/9/69	Santos	vs São Paulo Football Club	1–1	-

NO.	DATE	TEAM		OPPONENT	SCORE	GOALS
906.	11/12/69	Santos	vs	Santa Cruz—Recife	4–0	2
907.	11/14/69	Santos	vs	Botafogo—Paraíba	3–0	1
908.	11/16/69	Santos	vs	E. Clube Bahia	1–1	-
				PELÉ SCORES 1,000 GOALS		
909.	11/19/69	Santos	vs	Vasco da Gama—Rio	2–1	1
910.	11/23/69	Santos	vs	Atlético—Minas	0–2	-
911.	11/29/69	Santos	vs	Racing—Argentina	1–2	-
912.	12/2/69	Santos	vs	Penarol—Uruguay	1–2	1
913.	12/4/69	Santos	vs	Estudientes of La Plata—Argentina	1–3	-
914.	12/6/69	Santos	vs	Velez Sarsfield—Argentina	1–1	1
915.	12/9/69	Santos	vs	Racing—Argentina	0–2	-
916.	12/11/69	Santos	vs	Penarol—Uruguay	2–0	1
917.	12/14/69	Selection	vs	Selection Bahia São Paulo	2–1	-
918.	12/17/69	Selection São Paulo	vs	Selection Minas	2–1	1
919.	12/21/69	Selection São Paulo	vs	Selection Rio	0–0	-
920.	1/10/70	Santos	vs	Coritiba	3–1	1
921.	1/16/70	Santos	vs	Boca juniors—Argentina	2–2	1
922.	1/18/70	Santos	vs	Talleres—Argentina	2–0	-
923.	1/21/70	Santos	vs	Colo-Colo—Chile	3–4	1
924.	1/24/70	Santos	vs	Universitario—Lima	4–1	2
925.	1/28/70	Santos	vs	Dinamo—Zagreb	2–2	-
926.	1/30/70	Santos	vs	Universidad—Chile	2–0	2
927.	2/4/70	Santos	vs	América—Mexico	7–0	3
928.	2/7/70	Santos	vs	Universidad Católica—Chile	3–2	2
929.	3/4/70	Selection Brazil	vs	Selection Argentina	0–2	-
930.	3/8/70	Selection Brazil	vs	Selection Argentina	2–1	1
931.	3/14/70	Selection Brazil	vs	Bangú—Rio	1–1	-
932.	3/22/70	Selection Brazil	vs	Selection Chile	5–0	2
933.	3/26/70	Selection Brazil	vs	Selection Chile	2–1	-
934.	4/5/70	Selection Brazil	vs	Selection Amazon	4–1	1
935.	4/12/70	Selection Brazil	vs	Selection Paraguay	0–0	-
936.	4/19/70	Selection Brazil	vs	Selection Minas	3–1	-
937.	4/26/70	Selection Brazil	vs	Selection Bulgaria	0–0	-
938.	4/29/70	Selection Brazil	vs	Selection Austria	1–0	-
939.	5/6/70	Selection Brazil	vs	Guadalajara—Mexico	3–0	1

NO.	DATE	TEAM		OPPONENT	SCORE	GOALS
940.	5/17/70	Selection Brazil	vs	León—Mexico	5–2	2
941.	5/24/70	Selection Brazil	vs	Irapuato—Mexico	3–0	-
942.	6/3/70	Selection Brazil	vs	Selection Czechoslovakia	4–1	1
943.	6/7/70	Selection Brazil	vs	Selection England	1–0	-
944.	6/10/70	Selection Brazil	vs	Selection Rumania	3–2	2
945.	6/14/70	Selection Brazil	vs	Selection Peru	4–2	-
946.	6/17/70	Selection Brazil	vs	Selection Uruguay	3–1	-
947.	6/21/70	Selection Brazil	vs	Selection Italy	4–1	1
948.	7/5/70	Santos	vs	Palmeiras—São Paulo	2–0	-
949.	7/8/70	Santos	vs	Ferroviaria—Araraquara	0–1	-
950.	7/12/70	Santos	vs	São Paulo Football Club	2–3	-
951.	7/15/70	Santos	vs	São Bento—Sorocaba	2–1	-
952.	7/19/70	Santos	vs	Guarani—Campinas	5–2	2
953.	7/22/70	Santos	vs	Goiaz E. Clube	3–1	1
954.	7/25/70	Santos	vs	Portuguesa Desportos	2–1	1
955.	7/29/70	Santos	vs	S.C. Sergipe—Brazil	9–1	4
956.	8/2/70	Santos	vs	Corinthians—São Paulo	2–2	1
957.	8/5/70	Santos	vs	Guarani—Campinas	5–1	1
958.	8/9/70	Santos	vs	São Paulo Football Club	2–3	-
959.	8/12/70	Santos	vs	Ferroviaria—Araraquara	5–0	1
960.	8/16/70	Santos	vs	Ponte Preta—Campinas	1–0	-
961.	8/19/70	Santos	vs	Botafogo—Ribeirão Preto	0–0	-
962.	8/22/70	Santos	vs	Portuguesa Desportos	0–1	-
963.	8/26/70	Santos	vs	São Bento—Sorocaba	2–2	1
964.	8/30/70	Santos	vs	Corinthians—São Paulo	1–1	-
965.	9/2/70	Santos	vs	Gremio—Pôrto Alegre	2–0	1
966.	9/6/70	Santos	vs	Palmeiras—São Paulo	1–1	-
967.	9/9/70	Santos	vs	Cruzeiro—Minas	0–0	-
968.	9/12/70	Santos	vs	Deportivo Galicia—Caracas	5–1	1
969.	9/15/70	Santos	vs	All-Stars—USA	4–3	-
970.	9/18/70	Santos	vs	Washington Darts—USA	7–4	4
971.	9/20/70	Santos	vs	Guadalajara—Mexico	2–1	1
972.	9/22/70	Santos	vs	West Ham United—England	2–2	2
973.	9/24/70	Santos	vs	Santa Fé—Bogotá	2–1	-
974.	9/30/70	Selection Brazil	vs	Selection Mexico	2–1	-
975.	10/4/70	Selection Brazil	vs	Selection Chile	5–1	1
976.	10/14/70	Santos	vs	Atlético Minas	1–1	1
977.	10/17/70	Santos	vs	Vasco da Gama—Rio	1–5	-
978.	10/22/70	Santos	vs	Ponte Preta—Campinas	1–1	1
979.	10/25/70	Santos	vs	Selection Alagoas	5–0	2

NO.	DATE	TEAM	OPPONENT	SCORE	GOALS
980.	10/28/70	Santos	vs Atlético Paranaense	0–1	-
981.	11/1/70	Santos	vs Corinthians—São Paulo	0–2	-
982.	8/11/70	Santos	vs Botafogo—Rio	2–2	-
983.	11/11/70	Santos	vs Palmeiras—São Paulo	1–1	-
984.	11/14/70	Santos	vs Flamengo—Rio	0–2	-
985.	11/18/70	Santos	vs Fluminense—Rio	1–0	-
986.	11/21/70	Santos	vs América—Rio	0–0	-
987.	11/25/70	Santos	vs Universitario—Lima	2–3	-
988.	11/29/70	Santos	vs São Paulo Football Club	3–2	1
989.	12/2/70	Santos	vs E. Clube Bahia	5–1	1
990.	12/6/70	Santos	vs Santa Cruz—Recife	0–1	-
991.	12/10/70	Santos	vs Selection Hong Kong	4–1	2
992.	12/11/70	Santos	vs Selection Hong Kong	4–0	3
993.	12/13/70	Santos	vs Selection Hong Kong	5–2	1
994.	12/17/70	Santos	vs Selection Hong Kong	4–0	2
995.	1/13/71	Santos	vs Selection Cochambamba	3–2	1
996.	1/16/71	Santos	vs Bolívar—La Paz	4–0	2
997.	1/19/71	Santos	vs Atlético Marte—El Salvador	1–1	-
998.	1/23/71	Santos	vs Selection Martinique	4–1	1
999.	1/26/71	Santos	vs Selection Guadeloupe	2–1	1
1,000.	1/28/71	Santos	vs Transvaal—Paramaribo	4–1	1
1,001.	1/31/71	Santos	vs Selection Jamaica	1–1	-
1,002.	2/2/71	Santos	vs Chelsea—England	1–0	-
1,003.	2/2/71	Santos	vs Milionários—Bogotá	3–2	2
1,004.	2/7/71	Santos	vs Atlético Nacional—Medellín	3–1	1
1,005.	2/10/71	Santos	vs Deportivo—Cali	1–2	1
1,006.	2/14/71	Santos	vs Alianza—El Salvador	2–1	-
1,007.	2/17/71	Santos	vs Selection Haiti	2–0	-
1,008.	3/3/71	Santos	vs Botafogo—Ribeirão Preto	4–0	1
1,009.	3/7/71	Santos	vs Ferroviaria—Araraquara	1–4	-
1,010.	3/28/71	Santos	vs Palmeiras—São Paulo	0–2	-
1,011.	3/31/71	Santos	vs Selection O. Marseilles—St.-Étienne	0–0	-
1,012.	4/4/71	Santos	vs E. Clube Bahia	2–3	1
1,013.	4/7/71	Santos	vs Galicia—Bahia	2–0	1
1,014.	4/11/71	Santos	vs Corinthians—São Paulo	2–4	1
1,015.	4/18/71	Santos	vs Paulista—Jundiaí	0–0	-
1,016.	4/21/71	Santos	vs São Paulo Football Club	1–0	-
1,017.	4/25/71	Santos	vs Ponte Preta—Campinas	0–0	-
1,018.	4/28/71	Santos	vs Juventus—São Paulo	1–1	-
1,019.	5/2/71	Santos	vs Botafogo—Ribeirão Preto	2–1	1
1,020.	5/9/71	Santos	vs Paulista—Jundiaí	1–0	-
1,021.	5/12/71	Santos	vs São Bento—Sorocaba	1–0	-
1,022.	5/16/71	Santos	vs São Paulo Football Club	0–0	-
1,023.	5/20/71	Santos	vs Juventus—São Paulo	1–1	-
1,024.	5/23/71	Santos	vs Oriente Petrolero—Bolivia	4–3	1
1,025.	5/26/71	Santos	vs The Strongest—Bolivia	2–0	1
1,026.	5/30/71	Santos	vs Palmeiras—São Paulo	1–2	-
1,027.	6/2/71	Santos	vs Guarani—Campinas	1–0	-
1,028.	6/6/71	Santos	vs Ferroviaria—Araraquara	1–0	-

NO.	DATE	TEAM		OPPONENT	SCORE	GOALS
1,029.	6/10/71	Santos	vs	Portuguesa Desportos	1–1	1
1,030.	6/13/71	Santos	vs	Ponte Preta—Campinas	2–1	1
1,031.	6/20/71	Santos	vs	Corinthians—São Paulo	3–3	1
1,032.	6/23/71	Santos	vs	Bologna—Italy	2–1	1
1,033.	6/27/71	Santos	vs	Bologna—Italy	1–1	-
1,034.	6/30/71	Santos	vs	Bologna—Italy	1–0	1
1,035.	7/11/71	Selection Brazil	vs	Selection Austria	1–1	1
1,036.	7/18/71	Selection Brazil	vs	Selection Yugoslavia	2–2	-
1,037.	7/24/71	Santos	vs	Monterrey—Mexico	1–1	-
1,038.	7/28/71	Santos	vs	Jalisco—Mexico	2–1	-
1,039.	7/30/71	Santos	vs	Hanover—Germany	3–1	-
1,040.	8/2/71	Santos	vs	Desportivo—Cali	2–2	1
1,041.	8/4/71	Santos	vs	All-Stars—USA	5–1	2
1,042.	8/8/71	Santos	vs	E. Clube Bahia	0–0	-
1,043.	8/11/71	Santos	vs	Esporte—Recife	2–0	-
1,044.	8/14/71	Santos	vs	São Paulo Football Club	3–1	-
1,045.	8/18/71	Santos	vs	Botafogo—Rio	0–0	-
1,046.	8/22/71	Santos	vs	América—Rio	0–0	-
1,047.	8/25/71	Santos	vs	Boca Juniors—Argentina	3–0	1
1,048.	8/29/71	Santos	vs	Milionários—Bogotá	0–1	-
1,049.	9/1/71	Santos	vs	Gremio—Pôrto Alegre	0–1	-
1,050.	9/5/71	Santos	vs	Atlético—Minas	1–2	-
1,051.	9/18/71	Santos	vs	Portuguesa Desportos	0–0	-
1,052.	9/23/71	Santos	vs	Atlético—Três Corações	1–2	-
1,053.	9/26/71	Santos	vs	Internacional—Pôrto Alegre	1–1	-
1,054.	10/3/71	Santos	vs	Cruzeiro—Minas	1–0	-
1,055.	10/7/71	Santos	vs	Nacional—Manaus	5–1	1
1,056.	10/10/71	Santos	vs	Ceará	0–0	-
1,057.	10/16/71	Santos	vs	Palmeiras—São Paulo	1–0	-
1,058.	10/24/71	Santos	vs	Vasco da Gama—Rio	2–0	-
1,059.	10/27/71	Santos	vs	Coritiba	0–1	-
1,060.	10/30/71	Santos	vs	Corinthians—São Paulo	1–1	-
1,061.	10/30/71	Santos	vs	Internacional—Pôrto Alegre	1–1	-
1,062.	11/25/71	Santos	vs	Atlético—Minas	2–1	-
1,063.	11/28/71	Santos	vs	Vasco da Gama—Rio	0–0	-
1,064.	12/1/71	Santos	vs	Atlético—Minas	0–2	-
1,065.	12/5/71	Santos	vs	Internacional—Pôrto Alegre	0–1	-
1,066.	12/9/71	Santos	vs	Vasco da Gama—Rio	4–0	-
1,067.	12/12/71	Santos	vs	América—Natal	3–1	1
1,068.	12/15/71	Santos	vs	Botafogo—Paraíba	2–0	-
1,069.	1/8/72	Santos	vs	América—Rio	2–1	-
1,070.	1/12/72	Santos	vs	Flamengo—Rio	0–1	-
1,071.	1/15/72	Santos	vs	Palmeiras—São Paulo	0–4	-
1,072.	1/30/72	Santos	vs	Dep. Español—Honduras	3–1	-
1,073.	2/2/72	Santos	vs	Dep. Saprissa—Costa Rica	1–1	-
1,074.	2/6/72	Santos	vs	C.A. Medellín—Colombia	2–2	-

NO.	DATE	TEAM	OPPONENT	SCORE	GOALS
1,075.	2/13/72	Santos	vs Comunicaciones—Guatemala	1–1	1
1,076.	2/15/72	Santos	vs Olympia Club—Honduras	0–0	-
1,077.	2/18/72	Santos	vs Dep. Saprissa—Costa Rica	5–3	1
1,078.	2/21/72	Santos	vs Aston Villa—England	1–2	-
1,079.	2/23/72	Santos	vs Sheffield Wednesday—England	2–0	0
1,080.	2/26/72	Santos	vs Bohemians/Druncondra—Ireland	3–2	-
1,081.	3/1/72	Santos	vs Anderlech—Belgium	0–0	-
1,082.	3/3/72	Santos	vs A.S. Roma—Italy	2–0	-
1,083.	3/5/72	Santos	vs Naples—Italy	3–2	2
1,084.	3/8/72	Santos	vs América—Rio Preto	1–0	-
1,085.	3/12/72	Santos	vs Portuguesa Desportos	1–0	-
1,086.	3/18/72	Santos	vs Juventus—São Paulo	3–2	-
1,087.	3/26/72	Santos	vs Palmeiras—São Paulo	1–2	-
1,088.	3/30/72	Santos	vs São Bento—Sorocaba	2–1	-
1,089.	4/16/72	Santos	vs São Paulo Football Club	1–3	-
1,090.	4/23/72	Santos	vs Guarani—Campinas	0–1	-
1,091.	4/25/72	Santos	vs Ferroviaria—Araraquara	2–0	1
1,092.	4/29/72	Santos	vs Naples—Italy	1–0	-
1,093.	5/1/72	Santos	vs Cagliari—Italy	3–2	2
1,094.	5/3/72	Santos	vs Fenerbache—Turkey	6–1	1
1,095.	5/5/72	Santos	vs Taj Sports Organization	5–1	3
1,096.	5/14/72	Santos	vs Corinthians—São Paulo	1–1	-
1,097.	5/17/72	Santos	vs Nov. XV—Piracicaba	1–0	-
1,098.	5/21/72	Santos	vs Ponte Preta—Campinas	3–2	1
1,099.	5/26/72	Santos	vs Selection Japan	3–0	2
1,100.	5/28/72	Santos	vs South China—Hong Kong	4–2	-
1,101.	5/31/72	Santos	vs Syu Fong—Hong Kong	3–1	-
1,102.	6/2/72	Santos	vs Selection Korea	3–2	1
1,103.	6/4/72	Santos	vs Newcastle United—England	4–2	3
1,104.	6/7/72	Santos	vs Caroline Hill Hong Kong	4–0	3
1,105.	6/10/72	Santos	vs Selection Bangkok	6–1	2
1,106.	6/13/72	Santos	vs Conventry City—England	2–2	1
1,107.	6/17/72	Santos	vs Selection Australia	2–2	-
1,108.	6/21/72	Santos	vs Selection Indonesia	3–2	1
1,109.	6/25/72	Santos	vs Catanzaro—Italy	7–1	2
1,110.	6/30/72	Santos	vs Boston Astros—USA	6–1	3
1,111.	7/2/72	Santos	vs Universidad—Mexico	2–0	2
1,112.	7/5/72	Santos	vs Toronto Metros—Canada	4–2	1
1,113.	7/7/72	Santos	vs Selection Vancouver	5–0	-
1,114.	7/9/72	Santos	vs Universidad—Mexico	5–1	2
1,115.	7/11/72	Santos	vs América—Mexico	4–2	2
1,116.	7/23/72	Santos	vs São Paulo Football Club	0–2	-
1,117.	7/30/72	Santos	vs América—Rio Preto	1–0	-
1,118.	8/2/72	Santos	vs Guarani—Campinas	4–2	3
1,119.	8/6/72	Santos	vs Ferroviaria—Araraquara	3–0	1
1,120.	8/9/72	Santos	vs Juventus—São Paulo	2–1	2
1,121.	8/13/72	Santos	vs Palmeiras—São Paulo	0–1	-
1,122.	8/15/72	Santos	vs Avai E.C.—Paraná	2–1	-

NO.	DATE	TEAM	OPPONENT	SCORE	GOALS
1,123.	8/20/72	Santos	vs Portuguesa Desportos	3–1	1
1,124.	8/27/72	Santos	vs Nov. XV—Piracicaba	0–1	-
1,125.	8/30/72	Santos	vs Corinthians—São Paulo	0–1	-
1,126.	9/5/72	Santos	vs Selection Trinidad	1–0	1
1,127.	9/9/72	Santos	vs Botafogo Rio	1–1	-
1,128.	9/13/72	Santos	vs C.S. Sergipe—Brazil	1–0	1
1,129.	9/17/72	Santos	vs Vitoria—Bahia	0–1	-
1,130.	9/24/72	Santos	vs Fluminense—Rio	1–2	-
1,131.	10/25/72	Santos	vs Palmeiras—São Paulo	1–0	1
1,132.	10/29/72	Santos	vs E. Clube Bahia	2–0	-
1,133.	11/12/72	Santos	vs Portuguesa Desportos	0–2	-
1,134.	11/16/72	Santos	vs Atlético—Minas	1–0	-
1,135.	11/19/72	Santos	vs Santa Cruz—Recife	4–2	1
1,136.	11/23/72	Santos	vs Flamengo—Rio	0–0	-
1,137.	11/26/72	Santos	vs Corinthians—São Paulo	4–0	-
1,138.	11/29/72	Santos	vs ABC—Natal	2–0	1
1,139.	12/3/72	Santos	vs Ceará	1–2	1
1,140.	12/9/72	Santos	vs Santa Cruz—Recife	2–0	-
1,141.	12/14/72	Santos	vs Gremio—Pôrto Alegre	0–1	-
1,142.	12/17/72	Santos	vs Botofogo—Rio	1–2	-
1,143.	2/2/73	Santos	vs Vitoria—Australia	2–0	-
1,144.	2/9/73	Santos	vs Selection Ryad	3–0	2
1,145.	2/12/73	Santos	vs Selection Kuwait	1–1	1
1,146.	2/14/73	Santos	vs National Club—Doha	3–0	1
1,147.	2/16/73	Santos	vs Selection Bahrain	7–1	2
1,148.	2/18/73	Santos	vs National Club—Cairo	5–0	2
1,149.	2/20/73	Santos	vs Hilal Club—Sudan	1–0	-
1,150.	2/22/73	Santos	vs Club All Nasser	4–1	1
1,151.	2/27/73	Santos	vs Comb. Bavaro—Germany	0–3	-
1,152.	3/4/73	Santos	vs Girondins—Bordeaux	2–2	1
1,153.	3/6/73	Santos	vs Royal Standard—Belgium	1–0	-
1,154.	3/12/73	Santos	vs Fulham—England	1–2	1
1,155.	3/14/73	Santos	vs Plymouth—England	2–3	1
1,156.	3/25/73	Santos	vs São Paulo Football Club	2–2	1
1,157.	4/4/73	Santos	vs Juventus—São Paulo	6–0	2
1,158.	4/8/73	Santos	vs Portuguesa Desportos	1–0	-
1,159.	4/18/73	Santos	vs América—Rio Preto	1–0	-
1,160.	4/22/73	Santos	vs Guarani—Campinas	1–0	-
1,161.	4/29/73	Santos	vs Corinthians—São Paulo	3–0	2
1,162.	5/6/73	Santos	vs Palmeiras—São Paulo	1–1	1
1,163.	5/13/73	Santos	vs Botafogo—Ribeirão Preto	2–1	-
1,164.	5/20/73	Santos	vs Ponte Preta—Campinas	5–1	2
1,165.	5/25/73	Santos	vs Lazio—Italy	3–0	1
1,166.	5/28/73	Santos	vs Lazio—Italy	4–2	2
1,167.	5/30/73	Santos	vs Baltimore Bays—USA	6–4	3
1,168.	6/1/73	Santos	vs Deportivo—Guadalajara	1–0	1
1,169.	6/3/73	Santos	vs Deportivo—Guadalajara	2–1	1
1,170.	6/6/73	Santos	vs Miami Toros—USA	6–1	1
1,171.	6/10/73	Santos	vs Arminia Bielefeld—Germany	5–0	1
1,172.	6/15/73	Santos	vs Baltimore Bays—USA	7–1	1
1,173.	6/17/73	Santos	vs Rochester Lancers—USA	2–1	1

NO.	DATE	TEAM	OPPONENT	SCORE	GOALS
1,174.	6/19/73	Santos	vs Baltimore Bays—USA	4–0	2
1,175.	7/1/73	Santos	vs União Tijucana—Rio	1–0	-
1,176.	7/4/73	Santos	vs Goiaz E. Clube	1–2	-
1,177.	7/8/73	Santos	vs Botafogo—Ribeirão Preto	2–0	1
1,178.	7/15/73	Santos	vs São Bento—Sorocaba	1–0	-
1,179.	7/22/73	Santos	vs Corinthians—São Paulo	1–1	1
1,180.	7/26/73	Santos	vs Juventus—São Paulo	0–0	-
1,181.	7/29/73	Santos	vs São Paulo Football Club	0–0	-
1,182.	8/5/73	Santos	vs América—Rio Preto	1–0	-
1,183.	8/8/73	Santos	vs Portuguesa Desportos	0–1	-
1,184.	8/12/73	Santos	vs Palmeiras—São Paulo	0–1	-
1,185.	8/15/73	Santos	vs Guarani—Campinas	1–0	1
1,186.	8/26/73	Santos	vs Portuguesa Desportos	0–0	-
1,187.	8/29/73	Santos	vs Vitoria—Bahia	0–2	-
1,188.	9/2/73	Santos	vs Palmeiras—São Paulo	0–0	-
1,189.	9/9/73	Santos	vs Flamengo—Rio	1–0	-
1,190.	9/12/73	Santos	vs Comercial—Mato Grosso	0–1	-
1,191.	9/16/73	Santos	vs Atlético—Paranaense	2–0	-
1,192.	9/19/73	Santos	vs Atlético—Minas	0–0	-
1,193.	9/23/73	Santos	vs Ceará	0–2	-
1,194.	9/26/73	Santos	vs América—Natal	6–1	3
1,195.	9/30/73	Santos	vs Nautico—Recife	3–0	-
1,196.	10/3/73	Santos	vs C.S. Sergipe—Brazil	3–0	1
1,197.	10/7/73	Santos	vs Santa Cruz—Recife	2–3	1
1,198.	10/14/73	Santos	vs Vasco da Gama—Rio	1–1	-
1,199.	10/17/73	Santos	vs Goiaz E. Clube	0–0	-
1,200.	11/11/73	Santos	vs Portuguesa Desportos	3–2	2
1,201.	11/11/73	Santos	vs Atlético—Paranaense	1–0	1
1,202.	11/14/73	Santos	vs Guarani—Campinas	1–1	1
1,203.	11/18/73	Santos	vs Coritiba	2–1	1
1,204.	11/28/73	Santos	vs Internacional—Pôrto Alegre	2–0	1
1,205.	12/5/73	Santos	vs Huracan—Argentina	4–0	1
1,206.	12/9/73	Santos	vs Palmeiras—São Paulo	1–1	-
1,207.	12/12/73	Santos	vs Gremio—Pôrto Alegre	4–0	2
1,208.	12/17/73	Santos	vs São Paulo Football Club	1–0	1
1,209.	12/19/73	Selection Brazil	vs Selection of Foreigners	2–1	1
1,210.	1/9/74	Santos	vs Palestra—São Bernardo do Campo	4–0	1
1,211.	1/13/74	Santos	vs Santa Cruz—Recife	1–1	-
1,212.	1/20/74	Santos	vs Botafogo—Rio	3–0	1
1,213.	1/23/74	Santos	vs Fortaleza—Ceará	5–1	2
1,214.	1/27/74	Santos	vs Gremio—Pôrto Alegre	0–1	-
1,215.	1/29/74	Santos	vs São Paulo Football Club	1–2	1
1,216.	1/31/74	Santos	vs Vitoria—Bahia	1–0	-
1,217.	2/3/74	Santos	vs Guarani—Campinas	2–0	1
1,218.	2/6/74	Santos	vs Goiaz E. Clube	4–4	-
1,219.	2/10/74	Santos	vs Cruzeiro—Minas	0–0	-
1,220.	2/22/74	Santos	vs Vila Nova—Goiaz	2–1	-
1,221.	3/3/74	Santos	vs Uberaba—Minas	2–0	-
1,222.	3/6/74	Santos	vs A.A. Caldense	1–0	-

NO.	DATE	TEAM		OPPONENT	SCORE	GOALS
1,223.	3/10/74	Santos	vs	Portuguesa Desportos	1–2	-
1,224.	3/17/74	Santos	vs	América—Minas	2–0	-
1,225.	3/20/74	Santos	vs	CEUB—Brasilia	3–1	1
1,226.	3/24/74	Santos	vs	Guarani—Campinas	2–2	2
1,227.	3/30/74	Santos	vs	Nautico—Recife	1–1	1
1,228.	4/3/74	Santos	vs	Guarani—Juazeiro (Ceará)	2–0	-
1,229.	4/6/74	Santos	vs	Esporte—Recife	1–1	1
1,230.	4/13/74	Santos	vs	Cruzeiro—Minas	1–0	-
1,231.	4/20/74	Santos	vs	Palmeiras—São Paulo	4–0	1
1,232.	4/24/74	Santos	vs	A.A. Francana	0–0	-
1,233.	4/28/74	Santos	vs	Nacional—Manaus	1–0	1
1,234.	5/2/74	Santos	vs	Atlético Rio Negro—Manaus	3–0	1
1,235.	5/19/74	Santos	vs	Corinthians—São Paulo	1–1	-
1,236.	6/2/74	Santos	vs	São Paulo Football Club	1–1	-
1,237.	6/9/74	Santos	vs	Atlético—Minas	1–2	-
1,238.	7/18/74	Santos	vs	Fortaleza—Ceará	1–1	-
1,239.	7/21/74	Santos	vs	Vasco da Gama—Rio	1–2	1
1,240.	7/24/74	Santos	vs	Internacional—Pôrto Alegre	2–1	-
1,241.	7/28/74	Santos	vs	Cruzeiro—Minas	1–3	-
1,242.	8/3/74	Santos	vs	Noroeste—Baurú	2–1	-
1,243.	8/11/74	Santos	vs	Portuguesa Desportos	0–1	-
1,244.	8/14/74	Santos	vs	Botafogo—Ribeirão Preto	2–1	-
1,245.	8/24/74	Santos	vs	Saad E. Club	1–3	-
1,246.	8/31/74	Santos	vs	Dep. Español—Barcelona	0–2	-
1,247.	9/1/74	Santos	vs	El F.C.—Barcelona	1–4	1
1,248.	9/3/74	Santos	vs	Real Saragoça—Spain	3–2	2
1,249.	9/9/74	Santos	vs	Palmeiras—São Paulo	0–0	-
1,250.	9/15/74	Santos	vs	São Paulo Football Club	1–1	-
1,251.	9/18/74	Santos	vs	Comercial—Ribeirão Preto	1–0	-
1,252.	9/22/74	Santos	vs	Guarani—Campinas	2–2	1
1,253.	9/29/74	Santos	vs	Corinthians—São Paulo	0–1	-
1,254.	10/2/74	Santos	vs	Ponte Preta—Campinas	2–0	-
				PELÉ WITH COSMOS		
1,255.	6/15/75	New York Cosmos	vs	Dallas Tornado—USA	2–2	1
1,256.	6/18/75	New York Cosmos	vs	Toronto Metros—Canada	2–0	-
1,257.	6/27/75	New York Cosmos	vs	Rochester Lancers—USA	3–0	1
1,258.	6/29/75	New York Cosmos	vs	Washington Diplomats—USA	9–2	2
1,259.	7/3/75	New York Cosmos	vs	Los Angeles Aztecs—USA	1–5	-
1,260.	7/5/75	New York Cosmos	vs	Seattle Sounders—USA	0–2	-
1,261.	7/7/75	New York Cosmos	vs	Vancouver Whitecaps—Canada	2–1	-
1,262.	7/9/75	New York Cosmos	vs	Boston Minutemen—USA	3–1	-

NO.	DATE	TEAM		OPPONENT	SCORE	GOALS
1,263.	7/16/75	New York Cosmos	vs	Portland Timbers—USA	1–2	1
1,264.	7/23/75	New York Cosmos	vs	Toronto Metros—Canada	0–3	-
1,265.	7/23/75	New York Cosmos	vs	San Jose Earthquakes—USA	2–1	1
1,266.	7/27/75	New York Cosmos	vs	Dallas Tornados—USA	2–3	-
1,267.	8/10/75	New York Cosmos	vs	St. Louis Stars—USA	1–2	-
1,268.	8/27/75	New York Cosmos	vs	San Jose Earthquakes—USA	2–3	-
1,269.	8/31/75	New York Cosmos	vs	Malmö—Sweden	1–5	1
1,270.	9/2/75	New York Cosmos	vs	Alliansen—Göteborg	3–1	2
1,271.	9/4/75	New York Cosmos	vs	Stockholm All-Stars—Sweden	2–3	2
1,272.	9/11/75	New York Cosmos	vs	Valarengen—Norway	4–2	2
1,273.	9/13/75	New York Cosmos	vs	A.C. Rome—Italy	1–3	-
1,274.	9/18/75	New York Cosmos	vs	Victory—Haiti	2–1	-
1,275.	9/19/75	New York Cosmos	vs	Viollete—Haiti	1–2	-
1,276.	9/21/75	New York Cosmos	vs	Santos—Jamaica	0–1	-
1,277.	9/26/75	New York Cosmos	vs	Selection Puerto Rico	12–1	1
1,278.	3/24/76	New York Cosmos	vs	San Diego Jaws—USA	1–1	-
1,279.	3/28/76	New York Cosmos	vs	Dallas Tornado—USA	1–0	1
1,280.	3/31/76	New York Cosmos	vs	San Antonio Thunder—USA	0–1 0–1	- -
1,281.	4/5/76	New York Cosmos	vs	Los Angeles Aztecs—USA	0–0	-
1,282.	4/8/76	New York Cosmos	vs	Honda—Japan (in Hawaii)	5–0	4
1,283.	4/10/76	New York Cosmos	vs	Seattle Sounders—USA	3–1	2
1,284.	4/11/76	New York Cosmos	vs	Los Angeles Aztecs—USA	1–0	1
1,285.	4/18/76	New York Cosmos	vs	Miami Toros—USA	1–0	-
1,286.	5/2/76	New York Cosmos	vs	Chicago Sting—USA	1–2	1
1,287.	5/5/76	New York Cosmos	vs	Hartford Bicentennials—USA	3–1	1
1,288.	5/8/76	New York Cosmos	vs	Philadelphia Atoms—USA	1–2	1

NO.	DATE	TEAM		OPPONENT	SCORE	GOALS
1,289.	5/15/76	New York Cosmos	vs	Hartford Bicentennials—USA	3–0	-
1,290.	5/17/76	New York Cosmos	vs	Los Angeles Aztecs—USA	6–0	2
1,291.	5/19/76	New York Cosmos	vs	Boston Minutemen—USA	2–1	-
1,292.	5/23/76	American All-Stars	vs	Selection Italy	0–4	-
1,293.	5/31/76	American All-Stars	vs	Selection England	1–3	-
1,294.	6/3/76	New York Cosmos	vs	Violette—Haiti (in Santo Domingo)	2–1	1
1,295.	6/6/76	New York Cosmos	vs	Tampa Bay Rowdies—USA	1–5	-
1,296.	6/9/76	New York Cosmos	vs	Minnesota Kicks—USA	2–1	-
1,297.	6/12/76	New York Cosmos	vs	Portland Timbers—USA	3–0	-
1,298.	6/16/76	New York Cosmos	vs	Boston Minutemen—USA	2–3	1
1,299.	6/18/76	New York Cosmos	vs	Toronto Metros—Canada	3–0	-
1,300.	6/23/76	New York Cosmos	vs	Chicago Sting—USA	1–4	-
1,301.	6/27/76	New York Cosmos	vs	Washington Diplomats—USA	2–3	1
1,302.	6/30/76	New York Cosmos	vs	Rochester Lancers—USA	2–0	-
1,303.	7/2/76	New York Cosmos	vs	St. Louis Stars—USA	3–1	-
1,304.	7/10/76	New York Cosmos	vs	Philadelphia Atoms—USA	2–1	1
1,305.	7/14/76	New York Cosmos	vs	Tampa Bay Rowdies—USA	5–4	2
1,306.	7/18/76	New York Cosmos	vs	Washington Diplomats—USA	5–0	1
1,307.	7/28/76	New York Cosmos	vs	Dallas Tornado—USA	4–0	-
1,308.	8/7/76	New York Cosmos	vs	San Jose Earthquakes—USA	1–2	-
1,309.	8/10/76	New York Cosmos	vs	Miami Toros—USA	8–2	2
1,310.	8/17/76	New York Cosmos	vs	Washington Diplomats—USA	2–0	1
1,311.	8/20/76	New York Cosmos	vs	Tampa Bay Rowdies—USA	1–3	1
1,312.	9/1/76	New York Cosmos	vs	Dallas Tornado—USA (in Cleveland)	2–2	-
1,313.	9/5/76	New York Cosmos	vs	Dallas Tornado—USA (in New Orleans)	2–1	-
1,314.	9/6/76	New York Cosmos	vs	Dallas Tornado—USA (in Detroit)	3–2	1

NO.	DATE	TEAM		OPPONENT	SCORE	GOALS
1,315.	9/8/76	New York Cosmos	vs	Selection Canada (in Edmonton)	1–1	-
1,316.	9/10/76	New York Cosmos	vs	Selection Canada (in Vancouver)	1–3	-
1,317.	9/14/76	New York Cosmos	vs	Paris St. Germain—France	1–3	-
1,318.	9/16/76	New York Cosmos	vs	Royal Antwerp—Belgium	1–3	1
1,319.	9/23/76	New York Cosmos	vs	West Japan All Stars—Japan (in Kobe)	0–0	-
1,320.	9/25/76	New York Cosmos	vs	Selection Japan (in Tokyo)	2–2	-
1,321.	10/6/76	Selection Brazil	vs	Flamengo—Rio	0–2	-